ALWAYS
REFORMING

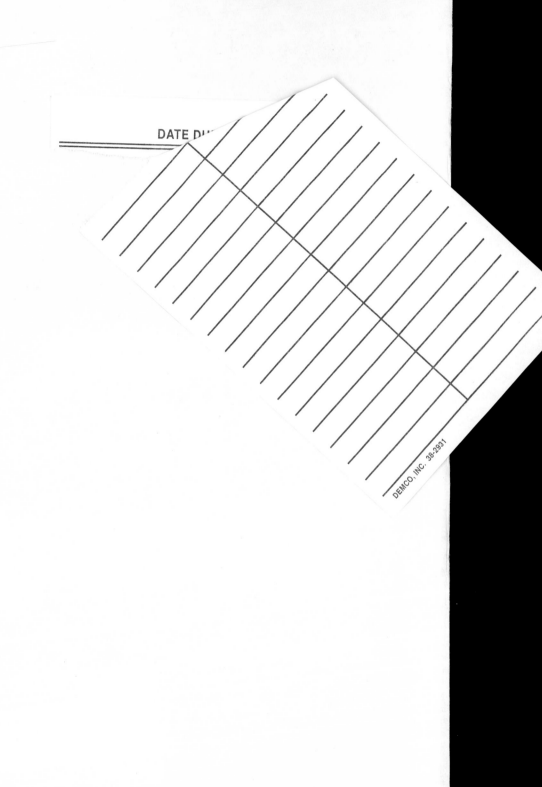

DATE DUE

DEMCO, INC. 38-2931

CRAIG D. ATWOOD

ALWAYS REFORMING

A History of Christianity Since 1300

MERCER UNIVERSITY PRESS
2001

ISBN 0-86554-679-7
MUP/P205

First Edition.

∞The paper used in this publication
meets the minimum requirements of
American National Standard for
Information Sciences—Permanence of
Paper for Printed Library Materials,
ANSI Z39.48-1992.

Library of Congress Cataloging-in-Publication Data

Atwood, Craig D.
Always Reforming : a history of Christianity since 1300 / Craig
Atwood.—1st ed. p. cm.
Includes bibliographical references and index.
ISBN 0-86554-679-7
1. Church History—Middle Ages, 600-1500. 2. Church
History—Modern Period, 1500–
I. Title.

BR252.A89 2001
270—dc21

2001030243

Contents

Preface   vii
Introduction   1

Part 1 Renaissance and Reform: 1300-1500   5

Chapter 1 The Character of the Medieval Church   7
Chapter 2 The Fourteenth Century Papacy   16
Chapter 3 The Modern Way in Theology   27
Chapter 4 Mysticism and Piety in the Late Middle Ages   32
Chapter 5 Radical Reformers   42
Chapter 6 Christianity in the East   56
Chapter 7 The Spanish Reformation   62
Chapter 8 Renaissance Humanism   68

Part 2 The Protestant Reformation   79

Chapter 9 The Reformation in Germany   81
Chapter 10 The Swiss Reformation   92
Chapter 11 The Radical Reformation   104
Chapter 12 The Spread of the Reformation and the Wars of Religion   113
Chapter 13 The Reformation in England   124
Chapter 14 The Catholic and Counter-Reformations   143
Chapter 15 The Final Wars of Religion   153

Part 3 Religion of the Heart in the Age of Reason   159

Chapter 16 Creating a Christian Society in the Old World and the New   161
Chapter 17 The Enlightenment   175
Chapter 18 Religion of the Heart   197
Chapter 19 Methodism and the Great Awakening   215

Part 4 The Nineteenth Century   229

Chapter 20 Catholicism, Eastern Orthodoxy, and Nationalism   231
Chapter 21 Nineteenth-Century American Evangelicalism   242
Chapter 22 Liberalism   254
Chapter 23 Radical Changes: New Sects and Secularism   269
Chapter 24 Missions to the World   280

Part 5 The Twentieth Century   299

Chapter 25 Christianity and Two World Wars   301
Chapter 26 Modernism, Ecumenism, and Fundamentalism   315
Chapter 27 Vatican II and the Modern Catholic Church   338
Conclusion A New World Order?   350

Suggested Readings   355
Index   363

To Allyson Hope, Emily Elizabeth, Sarah Faith, and Madeleine Grace, who was born after this book was written, and to my wife, Julie, who said, "why not?"

Preface

IN THE SPRING of 1995 I picked up Glenn Hinson's book *The Church Triumphant: A History of Christianity up to 1300* at the Southeastern Regional meeting of the American Academy of Religion in Columbia, South Carolina. I innocently asked Marc Jolley, of Mercer University Press, when volume two would appear. He responded that they were looking for someone to write it. At the time, I was teaching a course on Modern Western Religious Traditions at Salem College and had not found a textbook that effectively covered the history of Christianity from the Reformation to the present. I wanted a work that would integrate Protestant and Catholic histories, demonstrate the connection between the medieval church and post-Reformation Christianity, and discuss American Christianity in its broader context. I also had found that most textbooks on the history of Christianity focused so much on Christianity's institutional forms that the broader historical and social issues were ignored. After pondering Marc's response, I decided that I should simply write the textbook I was looking for. Ironically, now that this book has appeared, I no longer teach the course for which it was designed.

I have tried in this volume to deal with the history of ordinary believers as well as the church elites during this period, or at least to relate the official actions of the church to the lives of the laity. Thus I discuss spirituality, worship, and popular devotion as well as theology and doctrine. Included in this discussion are churches that other Christian churches would not consider churches, such as the Church of Jesus Christ of Latter Day Saints and the Shakers. At the risk of sounding glib, this volume highlights the fact that in the modern era the notion of heresy has fallen apart. Every church has been declared heretical at some time or other by another church, and it is not the role of the historian to decide who is right or wrong on doctrinal issues. I have tried instead to show how Christians have adapted to sweeping social changes, including scientific discoveries and changing world-views.

This is not intended to be a volume on winners and losers, but an exploration of the rich diversity of Christianity in the modern era. It attempts to uncover some of the hidden dynamics of faith within the institutions of Christianity and to help show each of us the many ways in which other Christians have tried to live out the gospel in an uncertain world. It also demonstrates that all human institutions, including churches, change over time.

This is a story of conflict, controversy, and even violence that at times seems quite divorced from the peaceful teachings of Jesus; however, I have tried to make sense of the conflict in its own setting. Certainly in these conflicts we see power struggles, greed, hatred and even cruelty manifesting itself. It is important that Christians not be naive about their own history, particularly in the light of the Holocaust. However, in most of the conflicts in this book we also see Christians striving to put the gospel into action. It is not a black and white story of saints being persecuted by sinners, but a complex story of real humans trying to be faithful amidst the confusion and ambiguity of human life.

Much of this book was written after midnight and during vacations, therefore I wish to thank my wife, Julie, and my daughters, Allyson, Emily, and Sarah for their patience and encouragement. It was Julie who had to read the early, painful, drafts of the book. It was also Julie who helped me through two major surgeries and allowed me to write during my recuperation.

This book arose out of my teaching at Salem College, a women's liberal arts college in North Carolina. I would like to express my appreciation for the many students who listened to these materials in class, asked difficult questions, and even read drafts of the book. In particular, I wish to single out Melissa Hall who proof-read the manuscript, Pauline Loggins, Helen Mitchell Dupuis, Rebecca Bushey, Lara Owensby, Katherine Rowe, Jo Bjorling, Sally Mauney, and Bronwyn Shiffer. A special word of thanks to my colleagues in the Religion and Philosophy Department at Salem: Tasha Rushing, Sid Kelly, and Marlin Adrian.

Much of this volume is based on years of study at the University of North Carolina, Moravian Theological Seminary, and Princeton Theological Seminary. I wish to thank these professors in particular for their role in my education and indirect contributions to this text: John Headley, William Peck, David Schattschneider, Arthur Freeman, Richard Fenn, Jane Dempsey Douglass, Karlfried and Ricarda Froehlich, Richard Fenn, Anthony Grafton, Ed Gaustad, Kathleen McVey, and especially James Moorhead.

I would also like to thank friends who have been a support through the past few difficult years: Paul Kemeny, Robert McGee, Ulrike Wiethaus, Tim Auman, Gerry Harris, and the members of Parkway United Church of Christ and Home Moravian Church who are too numerous to name but to whom I am very grateful.

Introduction

IN THE FIRST volume, Professor Hinson described "the triumph of Christianity." He showed how Christianity grew from an obscure Jewish sect centered around the charismatic figure of Jesus of Nazareth to become a major world religion that profoundly shaped European culture. By the thirteenth century, the Catholic and Orthodox Churches dominated all institutions in both halves of Europe. The church had enormous political, legal, and economic power displayed beautifully in Gothic and Byzantine architecture. Christianity also exerted great influence on intellectual, aesthetic, and cultural life of Europe, helping to shape individual and corporate mores and morality. While there was quite a bit of religious diversity within Europe, some of which was more or less accepted and some which was the object of official and unofficial persecution, it is reasonable to use the word Christendom to describe Europe in the high middle ages and to equate the words Christianity and Church. That would no longer be true after the fourteenth century.

The dominant themes for Christianity after 1300 are change and division. Throughout the next 700 years there would be repeated efforts at reforming the church, and many of those reformations would divide Christians and even lead to war. The idea of reforming the church has a two-fold thrust. On the one hand, it means rectifying perceived abuses or errors in the institutional church; to bring the church back into line with its proper purpose. There would, of course, be conflict over the need for and proposals for reforming the church. Some reformers simply gave up on the institution they knew and attempted to recreate the church according to their understanding of the original church of the apostles. We see this already in the fifteenth century when the first permanent break with the Roman Catholic Church was accomplished in Bohemia. Each century brought more splintering of the institutional church and more diversity within most denominations.

On the other hand, reforming the church means reshaping or remolding the church or even the Christian religion itself to meet the demands and challenges of a new day. As human society changed with the introduction of new technologies, discoveries of new worlds (on the earth and in the skies above), and new insights about humans themselves, Christianity had to adapt or become a relic of a bygone era. Adaptation could take many forms: from a complete rethinking of Christian teaching to merely adopting new methods of presenting the Christian message. Again, conflict ensued as reformers confronted changed historical realities. At times, the two types of reformation coincided, as in the sixteenth century Protestant Reformation; at other times they clashed. If we look carefully, though, we see that even conservatives who vigorously argued that Christ "is the same yesterday, today, and tomorrow" also tried to reform the church according to their vision of what Christianity should be. As the English novelist and Christian convert G. K. Chesterton once noted, the only way to keep a fence post white is by the revolutionary act of repainting it every year.

For the modern period in particular, Christianity has been continually reforming and adapting to new social situations. In the process, thousands of different Christian churches have developed, and it is no longer possible simply to equate the words Church and Christianity. The dynamism of Christianity has produced a bewildering array of churches which have resisted repeated efforts at full reintegration. In the pages that follow, we will see the origins and development of many of these churches or families of churches, but it should be noted that some of these churches do not accept others as truly Christian. Unlike Islam in which the four great branches of Sunnism each accept the other as orthodox, Christianity is marked by repeat-ed mutual denunciations that force the historian of Christianity to make a choice of whom to include in the history of Christianity. I have chosen to use the broadest terms possible in order to be the most inclusive. For the purposes of this history, those who claim to make the person and teaching of Jesus Christ the center of their religion are considered Christian.

I have also tried to bring into this story Christian voices that have often been silenced in the long history of the church, particularly women. We must remember that from its beginnings in Palestine, the majority of Christians have been women. Denied ordination for most of Christian history and thus excluded from official positions of leadership, the written record of Christianity does not equally represent women and men. Thus, as with the laity in general, the vast majority of women who made up the active life of the church, those who prayed, worked, and believed, have been lost to history. Contemporary scholarship is diligently working to uncover the lost world of women's history, but the sources remain scanty. I have tried to integrate women into this history more than in previous studies of Christianity, but that story is not complete.

Time and space limit all things, and I deeply regret that I had to make the choice to exclude certain figures and movements. This volume could have been greatly expanded and still not have exhausted all of the rich resources of the past 700 years. There is no doubt some arbitrariness in my decisions, which I regret, but I hope I have presented representative as well as influential thinkers, leaders, and believers. I hope that this volume, which I intend to be an introduction for the general reader, will open new avenues for future exploration. The past cannot tell us how to live in the future, but the past is really all that we can know. By the time we become aware of the present, it has become the past, and decisions once made affect those yet to be made. This history is not complete, of course. Much has been omitted, and even more has been forgotten through the ages. We stitch history together from the tattered fragments of our past in a way that helps us make sense of our present. If we learn nothing else from our history than the fact that institutions and teachings continually change as time flows inexorably on, then that alone will give us greater wisdom as we play our part in creating what is to come.

This book arose out of my teaching modern Western religious history at Salem College, and I am grateful to the students who participated in those classes. Readers may question my decisions and speculate on my own Christian convictions and theology. Probably the greatest intellectual influence on this work has been the theologian, philosopher, and historian Ernst Troeltsch who encouraged his students to look for the inner dynamic of faith in history, not simply at the creeds and pronouncements of officials and hierarchies. This is intended to be the story of men and women of faith who have tried to make sense of the Christian gospel in a complex and ever changing world. I hope that their struggles can assist us today.

Part 1

Renaissance and Reform: 1300-1500

THE WESTERN CHURCH reached a great summit of creativity and influence in the thirteenth century. Professor Hinson correctly calls it the Great Century of the church. The gothic style matured and flourished in the thirteenth century; the great masterpieces of medieval intellect, the *summae*, were produced; the institution of the university was firmly established; and the papacy could successfully influence international politics. St. Augustine's vision of the City of God holding sway over the City of Man appeared close to a realization in the thirteenth century. Many in Europe expected that the fourteenth century would reap the fruits of the church's successes, and the century opened with great pomp as people celebrated the Year of Jubilee in the holy city of Rome.

During the year 1300, pilgrims to Rome who visited St. Peter's cathedral were promised full forgiveness of their sins. Tens of thousands of persons from all walks of European society made the arduous trip across the Alps to Italy, spending freely as they traveled. The Jubilee was a colorful and success-ful attempt to highlight the importance of the pontiff as the vicar of Christ who could forgive the penitent and command the faithful. The Year of Jubilee also brought in much needed revenues to the papal coffers and led to a brief economic surge in central Italy.

However, the jubilation orchestrated in 1300 masked the beginning of dire straits in which the Western church found itself in the fourteenth and fif-teenth centuries. Contrary to expectations, the church in the fourteenth century would not be a shining light uniting all of Christendom. Instead this would be a century of turmoil, scandal, and varied attempts at reformation that failed to achieve the goal of reforming the church "in head and mem-bers."

Chapter 1

The Character of the Medieval Church

THE MIDDLE AGES has often been called "the age of faith." Indeed it was an age when the church had greater power in the world than it had in the days of the apostles or in our day, but the great era of Christendom was as much a blending of faith and doubt, trust and despair, obedience and violence as every age in the history of Christianity. It is not helpful to judge which age was truly an age of faith, either to praise or condemn it. Instead we must ask what was the nature of the faith in that age. Or, to put it another way, how did the Christian faith conform and reform to meet the needs of that period? It is important to have some understanding of the medieval church in order to make sense of the story of reformation that follows.

The Social Order

Medieval society was based on land, honor, and personal obligation. Those with lands were lords. Government was a personal matter of loyalty or rebellion towards one's lord. Offices were supported through rents from land. The church played an integral part in medieval society. Nobles endowed monasteries with lands so that the monks could devote themselves to prayer and study. The monastery then became a landlord with jurisdiction over those who lived on and worked the land. In times of war or invasion, the secular ruler pledged to defend the monks who prayed for the welfare of those engaged in battle. As the centuries passed, the church accumulated much land in Europe. Celibacy meant that there would be no disputes over inheritance. Moreover, since church officials were better educated than most people in society and had no children, medieval rulers used them to help govern their realm. Certain major bishoprics became more important as secular offices rather than religious ones. Bishops, archbishops, and abbots of monasteries thus had secular authority as landlords and officers of the realm in addition to their role as spiritual leaders.

The blending of governmental and sacred affairs was a distinguishing feature of the Middle Ages. The ideal of a unified Christian society, Christendom, was the basis for political and ecclesiastical theory up to the modern age. Although church and state remained frequently at odds in the Middle Ages, particularly over the issue of papal supremacy, the modern idea of a strict separation between the secular and religious was unthinkable in AD 1200 or 1600. Thus church reforms equaled social reforms.

As the period advanced, society accepted the idea that heresy was a crime against the government as well as against God. In the thirteenth century, the Inquisition was established to root out heresies that were believed to threaten the church and the state.The church would convict a heretic and hand him or her over to the state for punishment. Furthermore, social changes led to changes in theology and church practice. For instance, since medieval society was primarily a warrior society, it is hardly surprising that the church actively participated in the violence of the period. The church sanctioned military religious orders, such as the Knights Templar, as well as crusades.

Popular Religion

There is a lively debate among scholars over just how religious medieval Europe was. The majority of people during this time were illiterate and left few clues as to their beliefs and practices. Existing evidence suggests that popular piety was a creative blend of official Christian theology and pagan folk beliefs and practices. Christian holy days were often joined with ancient religious festivals; such as in Ireland when All Saints Day was joined to the pagan festival of Samhain, the night of the dead. All Hallow's Eve, or Halloween, resulted from this syncretism as popular religion and official teaching existed in a strained relationship. Much of popular religion was focused on the adoration of the saints who listened to the prayers of believers. The church used statues of saints as a means to educate people and to inspire devotion. Many reformers viewed the adoration of the statues of the saints as a thinly veiled pagan idolatry. Known as iconoclasts (image breakers), such reformers viewed themselves as followers of the Hebrew prophets who smashed the idols of Baal and Ashterah in biblical times.

Medieval religion was very concrete and tangible. Since the days of the early church, many Christians believed that holy men and women could use their spiritual power to perform miracles on earth. The saints, like the apostles in the Bible, could heal with their touch or answer prayers. By the fifth century, people accepted that this miraculous power of the saints could continue even after the saint's soul had journeyed to God. Pious persons (and some that took advantage of this popular piety) collected relics of the saints. These relics were tangible reminders of the saint. Often the relic consisted of a piece of the saint's own body: an arm, vertebra, knuckle, or some other bone. Sometimes it was an object associated with the saint, such as John the Baptist's leather girdle or a splinter from the true cross. Possession of a relic by an individual, a congregation, or even a kingdom brought people into a close relationship with that saint.

In the early church some priests celebrated the Eucharist on the tomb of a famous local saint at particular times during the year. Gradually the practice was brought inside the building and altars were made into tombs for the relics of revered saints. Churches would be named for the saint whose relics were housed within. Certain relic sites of great power became sites for pilgrimages. Believers from all over Europe visited important places, such as the city of Rome where Peter and Paul had died or the shrine of St. Joseph of Campostello. Chaucer's *Canterbury Tales*, tells the story of a group of pilgrims on their way to Canterbury to visit the relics of Thomas a'Becket. When the relics of St. Andrew were brought to Scotland, he became the patron saint of that entire nation, and eventually his X-shaped cross would be joined to the British flag.

The increasing number of relics and treasures around the altar forced priests in the West to move to the front of the altar when performing the Mass. With his back to the congregation, the priest conducted the sacred ritual in the holy language of Latin, saying certain portions of the rite under his breath. This gave a great air of mystery to the celebration of the Mass. The high point of the service, for the common person, came when the priest lifted the Host high so all could see it. The evidence indicates that few of the laity actually partook of the sacrament itself. Most stayed content with seeing the elevation and offering their own prayers and gifts to God. In the East, priests conducted the consecration of the Eucharist behind a scene filled with beautiful images of the saints. This iconostasis emphasized the holiness of the action being performed and kept the Eucharist from being profaned while educating the illiterate in the faith through images.

Clergy and Laity

In the Middle Ages, the word "religious" applied to those who had a calling to the monastic life. The monastery became the home of religious men and women who focused their attention on their salvation. Monasteries abounded in medieval Europe. Those who entered a religious house took vows of poverty, celibacy, and obedience that were irrevocable. Only by special dispensation could a monk or nun put aside the habit and reenter the secular world. Monasticism was first developed in the early church as the Roman Empire collapsed, but it reached its height in the Middle Ages, especially in Western Europe. During those years, the health of monasticism signaled health in the church. Monasteries provided most of the church's missionaries and many of its most effective church leaders. Monasteries also offered hospitality to strangers and frequently operated hospitals for the sick and infirm. Diligent monastic scribes preserved much of the learning of the ancient and medieval world. The monastery played an integral part in medieval society and was the heart of the medieval church, but after 1500, the institution came under attack and virtually disappeared in large parts of Christendom.

The distinction between clergy and laity was clear in the medieval church and in society. Those ordained as priests were no longer the same as other persons. Such men, and it was only men who were ordained to the priesthood, could offer up Christ in the sacrifice of the Mass. They had the spiritual power, given by God through the church, to make the wine and bread into the body and blood of Christ. They also had the authority to pronounce forgiveness for sins and could impose a penance on sinners to help them avoid future sins. Priests were under the direct authority of the church and had to be obedient to the law of the church, known as canon law. Secular courts could neither try nor punish the servants of the church without the permission of the bishop. This Canon law was based on old Roman law and the doctrine of the church. It covered the rules and regulations of the priesthood, such as the proper means of choosing a bishop or abbot, and the rules governing lay persons, such as what constitutes a legal Christian marriage.

Two types of priests existed in the Roman Catholic Church. Regular priests were those who took monastic vows to live according to a rule (*regula*). Secular priests were those who ministered in the world, caring for a flock of lay persons. They might be humble village pastors who could barely read or write or they could be powerful bishops who were the head of the church in major cities or territories known as bishoprics or diocese. The resident church for a bishop was called a cathedral, and the great Gothic cathedrals of the late Middle Ages stand as enduring testimonies to the faith of the age. Bishops had assistants known as deacons who were entrusted with the material needs of the church and the poor. Deacons administered the gifts to the church and distributed alms to the poor on a regular basis. Deacons could grow very wealthy and powerful in their position and were not bound by as many rules of conduct as priests were.

In the thirteenth century, a new type of ministry emerged. The Friars were men who took monastic vows, but who lived in the world as preachers. Both of the great orders of Friars, the Franciscans and Dominicans, were mendicant orders, that is they were supposed to live off of begging without possessing property. By 1300, though, both orders had accepted endowments and large gifts for the sake of the order. They also established permanent dwellings, known as friaries, in urban areas. In many instances, the church allowed the friars to serve the spiritual needs of the neighboring people, much as a parish church would do. While they continued their efforts to preach to the common person and inspire people to follow the teachings of Christ more devoutly, the mendicant orders also became integral parts of the major universities of Europe. The Franciscans and Dominicans produced some of the greatest scholars of the late Middle Ages.

The medieval ideal was a universal ideal where church and society were joined in an interlocking harmony and hierarchy. In theory it was to be a stable society in which everyone knew his or her place and obeyed those in authority. In truth, both church and society remained divided among countless loyalties, duties, and self-interests. Religious orders competed with one another for prestige, privileges, and power. Nobles fought with one another over land and authority. Often the princes of the church (bishops) fought with secular princes. Peasants rioted and rebelled when their lords grew oppressive and ignored their rights and privileges. Towns and cities granted their citizens freedoms not available in the countryside and at times fought for greater independence. Guilds of artisans fought for their rights and restricted others from entering their trade. Some merchants grew wealthy and brought impoverished nobles under their control.

The church did try to bring some stability to a world threatening to dissolve into chaos. The regular rhythm of holy days, feast days, and fast days sanctified the calendar. Religious festivals became social festivals that helped bring a sense of community to a village or town. Priests and prophets at times used their spiritual authority to intervene in secular affairs and help mediate peace and mercy.

The Seven Sacraments

The most important area in which the church impacted the lives of ordinary persons was through the sacraments. The sacraments, or mysteries as they were known in the East, were physical things that communicated a spiritual grace or blessing. The Eastern church never officially declared a definite number of sacraments. Almost anything could be invested with spiritual blessing and serve as a mystery of the grace of God. In the West, theologians decided that there were a total of seven sacraments, seven being a number of perfection. The number of sacraments was written into canon law in 1214 but was in effect long before.

There were two major sacraments necessary for salvation in both East and West: baptism and Holy Communion, also known as the Eucharist (from the Greek word for thanksgiving). According to the traditional teaching of the Church, the Holy Spirit uses the waters of baptism to wash an infant from the stain of original sin. Throughout the Middle Ages, the washing of sin was considered necessary for salvation; therefore a lay person, even a woman, could perform a baptism in an emergency. The Eucharist, on the other hand, could only be given by a priest who had the power to transform the bread and wine into the body and blood of Christ. The Western church defined the transformation of the elements of communion as a transubstantiation, meaning that the substance had completely changed. The Eastern church refused to be so precise in describing the mysterious action of God, but also taught that Christ was physically present in the communion elements. The major point to remember is that through *Eucharist* worshipers could partake of God directly. Much of medieval piety was directed toward the Eucharist. Reports show that some nuns even attempted to live only on Eucharist wafers and water.

The other sacraments in the West were confirmation, confession, marriage, ordination, and extreme unction. The Eastern Church kept to the practice of the early church where confirmation was a part of the baptism ceremony when the priest anointed the baptized person with oil and prayed that the Holy Spirit would strengthen the child in faith. In the West, only the bishop could administer confirmation, and over time the ritual of confirmation was separated from baptism. Normally given in early adolescence, confirmation thus became a rite of passage into adulthood. Only confirmed persons could partake of Eucharist. It appears, though, that in many parts of Western Europe in the Middle Ages, bishops went years, sometimes generations without confirming the youth. Reports show that some bishops confirmed entire villages from their carriage as they traveled through the region.

The church did not invent marriage, obviously, but it became an important point of contact between the laity and the church. Marriage was a sacrament, a sacred moment invested with great meaning and dignity by the church, but it was also filled with secular traditions associated with paganism and folk religion. Canon law tried to bring marriage under the influence of Christianity in part by sanctifying folk traditions, such as the wedding ring, and by requiring specifically Christian rituals. Some traditions, such as the rather bawdy and boisterous wedding feasts, the church simply overlooked. The church also determined who could and could not be married, and forbade divorce except with special dispensation. The church could educate the average person in the duties of Christian living through the avenue of marriage.

The church could also influence individuals in a very personal and intimate manner through confession. Confession was a time for the religious, clergy, and laity alike to examine their souls and lives in light of the church's teaching. There was some latitude given in the choice of a confessor, but according to canon law, every Christian should confess at least once per year. Confessors were trained in how to help persons uncover secret or forgotten sins. Unforgiven sin, particularly if it was a mortal sin, could lead to damnation; therefore confession was a very serious affair. Confessors were also instructed to determine if the person confessing appeared truly repentant or if he or she remained secretly pleased with the sin. Those who were unrepentant remained unforgiven and in danger of hell. If the sincerity of the confession and the desire to change one's way convinced the priest, he pronounced absolution, washing the penitent's soul clean. However, along with absolution, the priest gave the person some type of penance to do. The action of penance helped rectify the harm that the sin had caused in the world and trained the person not to do the sin again. Penance could be private or public, depending on the nature of the sin. It generally involved some type of sacrifice, often a gift of money to the church or to the poor. At times, penance could be going on a pilgrimage or a crusade. Failure to complete the promised penance endangered one's soul.

Extreme unction was related to confession, but it was given near the time of death. Ideally, it would be given in the final moments of a person's life so that she or he could face the Final Judgment absolved of sin. Extreme unction involved a final confession, the partaking of Eucharist, and an anointing on the forehead with blessed oil. Death was a constant reality in the Middle Ages, particularly during times of plague, such as the Black Death that decimated Europe in 1349. Preachers and religious artwork in churches and cathedrals reminded people of all walks of life that death comes for all. With death comes judgment and damnation for those unprepared. Extreme unction served as the final opportunity to save one's soul from the demons that lurked by the bedside ready to snatch the soul as it departed to the other world.

The seven sacraments did not exhaust the ways in which the church touched the lives of medieval people. They wanted visible and tangible ways to communicate with the divine, and Christianity provided such means. Believers could kiss relics, statues and icons, offer gifts at the shrines of the saints, gaze at intricate stained glass windows that powerfully portrayed the history of Christianity, the horrors of hell, and the wonders of heaven. People believed in the power of holy water, salt, incense and other things to ward off evil. Priests blessed fields, homes, cattle, and marriage beds. Beautifully decorated vestments clearly displayed the authority and hierarchy of the church offices. Sacred rituals were used to knit together feudal and Byzantine society.

Yet, at the same time, the church proclaimed that this world is little more than a shadow or a symbol of the heavenly realm. Theologically, at least, the importance of physical signs was that they pointed to what is invisible and eternal. It was an age of allegory and symbol where the spiritual was more real than the physical. As such, much of the piety of the age was ascetic in nature. Those who would be religious and insure the salvation of their souls must be celibate. Fasts and vigils disciplined the flesh so the soul could flourish. Conversion to God meant a turning away from the vanity of worldly pleasure. Much of the charity of the age was not given for the sake of the poor, but for the salvation of the giver. Pomp and visible splendor coexisted with fasting and flagellation in the church. As the great historian Johan Huizinga described the late Middle Ages, Europe was filled with "the smell of blood and roses."[1]

Perhaps no one gave a better view of the complex nature of medieval society and medieval Christianity than the Italian poet Dante Alighieri (1265-1321) in his classic *The Divine Comedy*. Heavily influenced by the theology of Thomas Aquinas, *The Divine Comedy* takes the reader on a pilgrimage through twenty-four circles of Hell, up seven layers of Mount Purgatory, beyond the heavenly spheres and stars to the realm of heaven where the blessed can see God. The three realms of the afterlife, Hell, Purgatory, and Heaven in

---

[1] J. Huizinga, *The Waning of the Middle Ages* (Garden City NY: Doubleday, 1954) 27.

Dante's vision are peopled with real individuals from Dante's time. In cataloging the sins of the damned and those in purgatory, Dante gives a critique of medieval Italian society. Dante reminds the reader that though the church produces saints, and teaches the virtues of voluntary poverty and self-sacrifice, even bishops may fall short of the saintliness of ordinary men and women.

Chapter 2

The Fourteenth Century Papacy

AT LEAST SINCE the time of Leo the Great in the fifth century, the Bishop of Rome had been accepted as the supreme head of the Christian church in Western Europe. Attempts to assert control over the church in the East had largely failed, but people in the West universally acknowledged the Pope as the head of the church and the Vicar of Christ. He was the living successor of St. Peter and bishop of the city where Peter and Paul were both executed. Through the centuries, the papal office had created an effective legal system and bureaucracy by which the pope could administer his vast spiritual realm. Early in the thirteenth century, the greatest of the medieval popes, Innocent III was not only the one who defined the church's doctrine and discipline, he was also arguably the most powerful monarch in Europe. He humbled the kings of England and France, mediated disputes among princes, launched crusades, and vigorously contended with the Holy Roman emperor over who was the supreme ruler in Christendom. For Innocent, the papacy was the sun and the emperor was the moon reflecting the splendor of the priesthood.

The struggle over papal supremacy in secular affairs continued throughout the thirteenth century. In 1245 Pope Innocent IV went so far as to depose emperor Frederick II and release his subjects from their oaths of loyalty to him; however, the century-long struggle between papacy and empire exhausted both institutions and their leaders. The papacy had become so involved in the expensive game of international politics and intrigue that it was losing its ability to govern the spiritual life of the church. By the end of the century, the office had become prey to the rivalry of powerful Italian families. For nearly two years (1292-1294) the office sat vacant as the cardinals disputed about a successor. Finally, they were persuaded to choose a man of great integrity who could restore the office to its pastoral and spiritual role. A hermit named Peter de Murrone accepted the miter and staff as Celestine V. Many hailed him as the "angelic pope" whom the prophecies of Joachim of Fiore proclaimed would usher in the millennial age of the Holy Spirit, but Celestine quickly discovered that the papal office was no place for an uneducated hermit unfamiliar with the intrigues of politics and the intricacies of finance. After only five months, upon the advice of canon lawyer Benedetto Gaetani, Celestine took the unprecedented step of abdicating his office. He claimed that he had heard the voice of God, but many suspected he had really heard the influential voice of Gaetani who would succeed him as the next pope.

Boniface VIII and Philip the Fair

The cardinals now felt eager to elect a candidate better versed in the ways of the world. Benedetto Gaetani was such a priest. He was a canon lawyer who had served for nearly twenty years in the curia. As a papal ambassador he knew the realities of European politics. When he assumed office as Boniface VIII (1294-1303) on Christmas Eve 1294, Gaetani was prepared to restore the papacy to the heights of power and prestige it had enjoyed in the days of Innocent III. For one of his first acts he imprisoned his predecessor, Celestine V, in case he had a change of heart. When the former pontiff died in 1296, many believed that Boniface had had him poisoned. Although there is no truth to the rumor, it is indicative of the reputation of Boniface that many would believe that he had murdered the pope.

No pope pushed the claim of papal supremacy more vigorously than Boniface; few suffered a more humiliating defeat. The source of Boniface's conflict came from France, not the Empire. During the thirteenth century, the kings of France and England had been building a new thing, the nation state under a single sovereign. They were mastering new methods of finance and taxation, creating their own bureaucracies and systems of law, and developing new nationalist sentiments. In the process, both nations threw off notions of feudal loyalty to the emperor and pope alike. They were also bitter rivals, and as the century was ending, Edward III and Philip the Fair were preparing to go to war over English possessions in France. War requires money, and the church possessed vast material resources in both England and France; therefore the two monarchs demanded that the church contribute to the expected war just as they required the nobility to contribute. Boniface saw their demand as an egregious violation of the ancient rights of the church. In 1296 he issued the bull Clericis Laicos which threatened princes with excommunication if they attempted to tax the clergy without the prior approval of the pontiff. Gone were the days of Gregory VII when the threat of excommunication could lead a prince or even an emperor to repentance. Edward declared the clerics who refused to pay the tax, and most of the clergy relented to royal pressure. Philip used a different tactic. He used his preroga-tives to forbid anyone to export gold and other precious metals out of the country without royal permission, thus effectively cutting off a major source of revenues for the Holy See and its bankers. Shortly after, Boniface retracted his earlier statements and allowed kings to tax the church in times of national crisis.

Edward and Philip signed a truce rather than waged a war. Philip, however, was not finished with Boniface. He arrested a bishop in Paris on charges of treason, violating the ancient principle that clerics stood immune from secular judgment. The arrest goaded Boniface into action. In late 1301, he revoked his earlier concessions and reasserted the rights of the church against the state. This time, Philip whipped up popular support in France against the pope. Forged documents purporting to be papal bulls were distributed to the nobility and bourgeoisie who met in Paris in April 1302. Even some of the clergy were persuaded that the pope had become a spiritual tyrant, a foreign ruler meddling in the affairs of France. Medieval universal-ism was being replaced by modern nationalism.

When Boniface learned that Philip's proud armies had been completely humiliated by Flemish artisans and craftsmen at Courtrai on June 11, 1302, he took advantage of the moment and issued the famous bull Unam Sanctum. This was the boldest statement of medieval claims of papal supremacy ever made. Throwing away all of the tact of Innocent III, Boniface declared that the secular power was completely subordinate to the spiritual power of the church. Each wields a sword for God, but the Vicar of Christ has the superior sword. In addition, Boniface declared "that it is necessary to salvation for every human creature to be subject to the pontiff of Rome."

Philip's response did not rely on words or legal arguments. In September 1303, his advisor, Guillaume de Nogaret and a number of Florentine, Tuscan, and Roman enemies of the pope broke into the papal residence at Anagni and captured Boniface. They intended to take him to France and force him to stand trial for heresy, simony, sorcery, and the murder of Celestine V, but they were thwarted by Boniface's supporters who took the aged pope to Rome. He died there on October 11, probably from the beating he received from Nogaret's soldiers. The new pope, Benedict XI (1303-1304), protested the humiliation of the pontiff and demanded that Nogaret and his conspirators be tried in Rome on charges of sacrilege. Benedict died of dysentery shortly after issuing that command, and rumors widely spread that Philip's supporters had poisoned him.

The Avignon Papacy

Philip exerted his growing influence in Italy to get a French archbishop elected as pope, Clement V (1305-1314), who was crowned at Lyons in Philip's realm. The new pope soon appointed nine new French cardinals. In 1309 he took up residence at Avignon, just to the south of Philip's realm. The move to Avignon brought the papacy directly under the influence of the powerful French monarch, and Clement acceded to most of Philip's demands. The demands included absolution for Nogaret and his men, annulment of many of Boniface's acts against French interests, and the canonization of Celestine V as a confessor (not a martyr). He even publicly praised Philip for his persecution of the dead Boniface. Clement V gave the greatest indication of his submission to Philip through his participation in the destruction of the order of the Knights Templar.

The Templars had been founded in 1118 as a military religious order dedicated to the protection of pilgrims visiting the Holy Land. It was originally an efficient and disciplined crusading body, but it had accumulated much property over the years through pious gifts. By the time that Acre fell in 1291 and the Templars lost their original mission, the order had grown wealthy enough to serve as a banking house for the princes of Europe. Philip greedily eyed the vast ready capital of the Templars. Already in 1306 he had expelled all of the Jews from France on charges of deicide (killing God) in order to appropriate their resources and collect all debts owed to them. He found his persecution of the Jews so successful that the following year he boldly moved to extinguish the Knights Templar and confiscate their resources.

All of the knights of the order in France were arrested on October 13. Under extreme torture they confessed to a variety of extraordinary crimes including sodomy, heresy, treason, and sorcery. It appears that Pope Clement believed that the confessions to be genuine, and he supported Philip's destruction of the most powerful chivalric order. About 100 of the knights were eventually burned at the stake. In the clash between early modern absolutism and medieval religious chivalry, the state won.

Clement intended Avignon to be a temporary residence, but his successor, John XXII (1316-1334) established the episcopal palace as his permanent abode. The papacy would not return to Rome until 1378. In many ways, the move to Avignon was itself an attempt at church reform. Avignon was close to France, one of the major financial resources for the church as well as a powerful military ally against the Empire. Moreover, Avignon was safer than Rome and was free from the riotous crowds, feuding noble families, and military threats from Naples and the expanding city-states of Florence and Milan that had plagued the papacy for years. The papal palace in Avignon was strengthened into a formidable fortress. Last, Avignon was more comfortable with a healthier climate than Rome. As a result, the papal court at Avignon became one of the most impressive and luxurious courts in Europe, housing the largest centralized government of the time.

The Avignon popes are not remembered for their sanctity or the brilliance of their pastoral leadership, but they were among the most effective administrators in fourteenth-century Europe. John XXII set out to make the church financially independent of secular rulers in order for the church to be able to compete with princes and kings on equal terms. He effectively reorganized the papal bureaucracy and increased revenues dramatically. He systematized and increased the fees charged by the papal chancery, the official law court, and aggressively encouraged people to refer their disputes to the Holy See for judgment. In every country, new appointees to endowed church offices (known as benefices) had to pay their first years' income (the Annate) directly to the Holy Office. Minor benefices were held open for three years so that the papacy could receive the income directly. John also took the selection of bishops out of the hands of the local chapter and reserved it for the Holy See. This would make possible the later practice of selling episcopal offices to the highest bidder. As the glory of the Renaissance took hold in Italy and France, John's financial policies allowed the papacy to compete with secular rulers as art patrons. Such attention to glamour, luxury, and the amassing of wealth drew increasing condemnation from religious reformers and patriots over the next 200 years.

Controversies

The Avignon papacy was splendid, but very controversial for a number of reasons. One, the pope is first and foremost the Bishop of Rome. Residence outside of one's diocese (or see), though common, was routinely regarded as an abuse. Two, the pope acted as the secular ruler of Rome and the Papal

States. These areas suffered during the long papal vacancy. Three, the king of France exerted great influence over the church while the papacy was in Avignon. Petrarch, the great Renaissance poet, dubbed this seventy-year period the Babylonian Captivity of the Church, echoing the captivity of the Jews in Babylon (587-538 BC). For him, and many Italians, the king of France held captive the Holy Office. The close connection with powerful France also offended the national sentiments of many in Europe and undermined the credibility of the papacy in mediating European disputes. As the years passed, intellectuals, princes, and even the common people called for the pope to return to Rome. The mystics Bridget in Sweden and Catherine of Sienna, related that they had received divine summons for the pope to return to Rome.

The struggles between the pope and emperor did not end with the removal to Avignon. John became embroiled in a controversy with Emperor Louis the Bavarian in 1322 when Pope John insisted that Louis receive his crown as a papal gift. During the struggle, Louis proclaimed John deposed as a heretic and had an antipope elected. The most significant thing about this conflict between pope and emperor was the participation of two of the age's leading intellectuals, William of Occam (1285-1349) and Marsilius of Padua (1280-1343), both of whom supported the state against the church.

Occam was a leading nominalist philosopher who attacked the very basic claims of the papal authority. Popes can err. For that matter, so can councils and even the church fathers. The only infallible guide, for Occam, was sacred scripture. Marsilius was more concerned with politics than with sacred theology, but his ideas also cut to the heart of medieval society and would eventually find new life during the Protestant Reformation. In *Defender of the Peace*, Marsilius rejected half-a-millennium of church teaching on the relationship of church and state. The secular prince has the duty of maintaining public order and defending the peace, but sovereignty itself rests with the people. Government is a purely secular matter and the church should be divested of all its secular affairs. It has a spiritual role, to be sure, but it should not have an existence separate from the *res publica*. Moreover, no legal distinction between the clergy and the laity should exist; all should be subject to the same laws and the same sovereign. Later kings and princes would use Marsilius' ideas on the church's subordination to the state, but few embraced Marsilius' radical vision of a conciliar form of secular government deriving its authority from the people. That would have to wait until the eighteenth century.

The Return to Rome

The papacy successfully weathered the storm caused by Occam and Marsilius. Europe was not ready to abandon the idea of a universal Christendom under a single pontiff. Moreover, the next pope, Innocent VI (1352-1362), instituted a number of reforms to reduce the opulence of the curia. He vigorously pursued suspected heretics, so much so that St. Bridget (1303-1373) of Sweden accused him of being a persecutor of his own sheep.

When Guillaume de Grimoard became Pope Urban V (1362-1370), he remained loyal to his Benedictine vows even in the midst of papal luxury. He wore his black habit, spent much time each day in prayer and study, and shared the desire of Petrarch and Catherine of Sienna that the Bishop of Rome should reside in Rome. He made plans to move his court there as soon as the city became safe from insurrections.

Many of its churches and palaces, including the Lateran, lay in ruins. When Urban arrived in the city in 1367 he moved into the Vatican palace and set about rebuilding the Holy City. His plans came to naught, however. He had to flee the city during a rebellion in 1370 and his cardinals convinced him to return to Avignon where he might be able to intervene in the Hundred Years War between France and England. Ignoring St. Bridget's prophecy that if he left Rome he would meet an early death, Urban returned to Avignon in September 1370. He died in December. His successor Gregory XI (1370-1378) made careful plans to return to Rome when the time was right. The mystic Catherine of Sienna (d. 1380) convinced him during her visit to Avignon in 1376 that the time had come to return the Holy Office to the Holy City. He arrived in 1377 and found that his presence alone could not bring peace to tumultuous Italy. He died soon after coming to Rome.

The Great Schism and the Reforming Councils

Gregory's early death precipitated the worst crisis faced by the church before the rise of Protestantism. Throughout the history of the papacy there had been times when emperors tried to depose the elected pontiff and install an antipope, but the events following Gregory's death were unique in the history of the church. In spring 1378 the cardinals gathered in the Vatican to choose a successor to Gregory. By this time, most of the cardinals were French and attached to Avignon; however, the crowds in Rome agitated for a Roman Pope. The conclave of Cardinals was warned by city leaders that there would be trouble if another Frenchman were elected pope. During deliberations, a mob broke into the proceedings and threatened the assembled cardinals who soon chose an Italian, Bartolomeo Prigano, as Pope Urban VI (1378-1389).

Although the cardinals appeared to have had no reservations when they selected Urban VI, they soon regretted their choice. Urban combined a desire for reform with paranoia and a tyrannical disposition. He insulted and abused his cardinals and powerful lay rulers, and proposed drastic reductions in the lifestyle of the upper clergy. The cardinals became convinced that Urban was insane and unfit to rule, particularly after he refused to compromise with them. From the safety of Anagni, the cardinals declared the earlier election invalid because the threat of violence from the Roman crowds influenced their choice. On August 9, 1378 they declared Urban deposed, and the following month they elected Robert of Geneva, infamous for his brutal suppression of a popular insurrection at Cesena, as Clement VII. Urban refused to acknowledge the cardinals' actions. In fact, he had already deposed them and appointed twenty-nine new cardinals to head his curia. After a series of military maneuvers by the two popes, Clement made Avignon the seat of his government while Urban remained in Rome.

This period is known to history as the Great Schism (1378-1417). Two popes, both of whom had been duly elected by the same college of cardinals, vied for control of the one catholic church. The monarchs of Christendom had to choose to whom to give allegiance. Every king and prince claimed obedience to the holy mother church, but in practical terms each ruler chose which pope he liked the best. The opposing sides in the Hundred Years War chose different popes. France, Scotland, and parts of Italy went with Clement. Eventually Aragon and Castile joined Clement. England, Germany, and most of Italy went with Urban.

The division of the church doubled expenses and divided revenues. Each pope had to take extraordinary measures to raise revenues. Dispensations were sold readily with more concern for income than morality. Church offices were openly sold to the highest bidder. Clerics were transferred to new sees merely in order to extract new fees from them. Such abuses had begun before the schism but were worsened by it. Opposition to such crass money-grubbing grew throughout Western Christendom, particu-larly in Germany where angry mobs occasionally killed church tax collectors.

The death of one pope did not end the schism because each pontiff had established his cardinals and curia that viewed him as the legitimate successor of St. Peter. When one pope died another was elected to replace him; thus the schism continued into the fifteenth century. Neither claimant would abdicate, nor would any accept an arbiter. Eventually some of the monarchs applied pressure on the rival popes by withdrawing obedience. In parts of Europe the secular authority took charge over church affairs, much to the displeasure of the clerics who found their situation worse under secular authority. As the situation worsened, some of the cardinals of both popes opened negotiations to solve the crisis. They decided to call a general council of the church to resolve the schism. It was to meet at Pisa in March 1409.

The Council of Pisa based its actions on a new theory developed by theologians such as Jean Gerson (1363-1429) and Pierre d'Ailley (1350-1420) at the University of Paris. They argued that while the pope is indeed the vicar of Christ, the body of Christ is the universal church. Therefore a council of the universal church represents Christ in his fullness and is superior to the pope. The representatives of the Christian people could assert authority over the pope himself.

This conciliar idea was radical for its time and did not meet with universal acceptance. Neither of the popes accepted the legitimacy of the Council of Pisa and ignored its decrees of deposition and excommunication, but the officials gathered in Pisa went on to elect a new pope who took the title of Alexander V. Alexander promptly established his own curia and excommunicated his rivals. Rather than ending the schism, Pisa merely increased it. After 1409 there were three popes, each with his own government.

Again, the death of one of the popes did not end the schism. In 1410 Baldassare Cossa, a Neapolitan nobleman who had served as a pirate and adventurer before becoming a lawyer and church financier, replaced Alexander. Rumor had it that he had seduced more than 200 women just while he was a cardinal, a rumor he did not dispel. Despite his ill-concealed greed and lust, he was elected John XXIII (1410-1415) (not to be confused with John XXIII who called the Second Vatican Council) and soon had the widest support of the three rival popes. John's position in the papal states remained insecure, however, and in 1413 his war with a rival state went so badly that he was forced to turn to the recently elected emperor Sigismund for help. Sigismund demanded that John call a general council of the church to meet on a neutral site in order to settle the schism. The Council of Constance met from 1415 to 1418. More will be said about the council below. For now our focus remains on the ending of the schism.

On April 6, 1415 the council, under the leadership of Jean Gerson, issued the decree *Sacrosanct* which declared in definite terms that a general council was the highest authority in the church. The council "has its power immediately from Christ; and that all men, of every rank and condition, including the Pope himself, is bound to obey it in matters concerning the faith, the abolition of the schism, and the reformation of the Church of God in its head and its members."[2] John was shocked to see how quickly the council he called turned against him as the council placed him on trial for a great variety of abuses and misdeeds. Much to his displeasure, he found himself deposed along with Benedict and Gregory; however, the council declared Gregory's pontifical actions legal. Gregory accepted the decision of the Council. Benedict did not, but his few supporters deserted him and joined the council. Eventually the council selected a new pope, Martin V, and most of the rulers of Europe gladly acknowledged him as legitimate. The schism was ended, but the damage to the church was not so easily repaired. The forty years of schism and the actions of two councils raised profoundly disturbing questions about the proper authority in the church. Reformers would offer a variety of answers to that question, some of which would lead to the permanent division of Western Christendom in the sixteenth century.

The conciliarists vigorously proposed a parliamentary-style of government for the church. The pope would be the administrative head and executive of the bureaucracy, but regular church councils would be the final authority. Before the Council of Constance ended, the decree *Frequens* was issued. The document attempted to put into effect the theories of the conciliarists, namely that regular councils were the best way to reform the church. "The frequent holding of general councils is one of the chief means of cultivating the Lord's field. It serves to uproot the briars, thorns, and thistles of heresies, errors, and schisms, to correct excesses, to restore what is marred, and to cause the Lord's vine to bring forth fruit of the richest fertility."[3] The next council was to meet in five years. After that councils should be called by the pope every ten years. Martin did call a council to meet in Pavia in 1423, but an outbreak of the plague kept many representatives away. It dissolved the following year without accomplishing anything of substance.

The next great council occurred at Basle in 1431. Pope Martin V called it in order to deal with the Hussite conflict (see below), but he died shortly after the council convened. His successor, Eugenius IV (1431-1447), tried to disband the council and reassemble it at Bologna. The council refused and revived the notion that the authority of councils remained superior to that of popes. In 1433 Eugenius was forced to acknowledge the actions of the council,

---

[2] Henry Bettenson, ed. *Documents of the Christian Church* (New York: Oxford University Press, 1980) 135.f

[3] G. R. Elton, *Renaissance and Reformation, 1300-1648*, 3rd ed. (New York: MacMillan, 1976) 19.

including its compromise with the moderate Hussites, but the council continued to meet and legislate. It pressed for substantive reforms of the church's administration, such as increasing the authority of bishops and diocesan synods at the expense of papal authority. In short, the council attempted to make the church into a constitutional monarchy with a regularly meeting parliament.

At this point, the Byzantine Emperor John VIII Palaeolgus contacted the Roman church in the hopes of healing the centuries-old schism between East and West in order to join forces against the Turkish threat in the Balkans. The Byzantine representatives chose to meet with the pope rather than the council at Basle. In March 1438 the emperor and some of the leading bishops and theologians of Byzantium met with the papal party at Ferrara in Italy.

A minority of the Council of Basle left Basle for Ferrara, leaving the council of Basle in more radical hands. In 1439 the council deposed Eugenius and elected a new pope. The council's action alienated many of the rulers of Europe because it seemed to revive the old schism that Constance had healed. Moreover in 1439, the papal council, now meeting at Florence, negotiated a reunion with the Greek Orthodox Church. The Greek delegation made a number of concessions, including acknowledging papal primacy and the *filioque* clause (the addition of the phrase "and the son" in the Nicene Creed), and in return were allowed to continue ordaining married men as priests and using Greek in worship. The reunion lived only a short time, though, because when monks and lay persons back home in Greece heard about the concessions, they responded violently against the compromise made with Rome. Much to the emperor's displeasure, his new allies in Europe sent no soldiers to protect Constantinople, which fell in 1453. However, news of the reunion enhanced the pope's prestige in the West just as the Council of Basle fell into disrepute and dissension. The era of the reforming councils ended with a new statement of papal supremacy affirmed by the Council of Florence.

Chapter 3

The Modern Way in Theology

DURING THE POLITICAL and religious struggles of the late Middle Ages, new ideas were affecting the intellectual life of the church. Many assert that scholasticism reached its summit with Thomas Aquinas in the middle of the thirteenth century, but scholasticism did not end with Thomas. The magnificent *Summa Theologiae* of Thomas is indeed a masterpiece that offers a vision of reason, revelation, inquiry, and faith brought together into a seamless whole so that the philosophy of Aristotle becomes an agent of Christian theology. Physics leads to metaphysics, which confirms the rationality of Christian doctrine. God's revelation in nature and human reason confirms God's revelation in scripture. However, scholars continued debating the issues of faith and reason long after the death of Thomas in 1274. Some, like Giles of Rome (d. 1316), defended Thomas' great system, but the foundation of Thomism was vigorously attacked by Duns Scotus (1265-1308), one of the greatest minds of the day.

Scotus was born in Scotland and joined the Franciscans in 1281. He studied and taught at both Oxford and Paris, and his order sent him to Cologne in 1307. He died there the following year. Scotus was a brilliant interpreter of Aristotle and the Islamic philosopher Avicenna, and he rejected the Augustinian-Platonic idea that God can directly illuminate the mind. In other words, Scotus was an empiricist—all knowledge comes through the senses. For him, one cannot go from physical effects to metaphysical causes. Something finite cannot prove the existence of something infinite. In short, Scotus rejected Thomas' famous five proofs for the existence of God because the human mind cannot go beyond the physical world to the spiritual world. Aquinas' proofs, therefore, do not prove the existence of a transcendent God, only a physical cause, the unseen mover of the universe. Scotus offered his own proofs of God's existence, similar to Anselm's arguments, but he asserted that even his proofs do nothing more than prove the existence of an infinite being. They say nothing about this infinite being's attributes. Reason cannot demonstrate that this infinite being is the same as the Christian (or for that matter Jewish and Muslim) understanding of God as all-powerful, just, and merciful. That is a matter of revelation and faith.

Scotus also objected to Thomas' and the other scholastics' view of human beings. They agreed with most ancient philosophers that reason is the highest human faculty, but Scotus argued that the will is higher because it directs the intellect. The mind may agree with a proposition, but the will acts. Moreover, love occurs as an act of the will, and it is better to love God than to know God. The exaltation of the freedom of the will to act, love, and direct the intellect is known as "voluntarism." Voluntarism would be the foundation for a new philosophy in the fourteenth century, the *via moderna* (modern way) opposed to the *via antiqua* of the Thomists who emphasized intellect. Scotus' high valuation of the will led him to assert that unconditional freedom is a necessary attribute of God. God can freely choose to do anything that is not self-contradictory. God is not bound by human law or our sense of morality. In fact, what is good is only good because of the free choice of God. Thomas asserted that God wills what is good. Scotus argued that whatever God wills is good. Creation, natural law, the history of salvation, and the church are all good because of the will of God, not in their essence. God could have saved humankind by any means God chose, but God chose to do so through the death of Jesus.

Scotus made a distinction in the powers of God between absolute power (*potentia absoluta*) and God's ordained power (*potentia ordinata*). God is infinitely free in absolute power, but remains limited by God's own decision to act and is bound by that decision. Thus when God chose to create the cosmos God limited God's self to a predictable set of natural laws. Likewise, in salvation God has set up a system for salvation, a covenant (*pactum*) so that those who follow the order of salvation will be saved. Thus, those who follow the church's divinely-ordained sacramental system will be saved according to the free choice of God. Variations on this understanding of salvation dominated Christian theology before 1500.

Nominalism

William of Occam built on Duns Scotus' work while giving theoretical support for the emperor against the pope. Occam was excommunicated along with Marsilius of Padua for arguing that the pope was not the supreme authority in Christendom. While his political ideas had little immediate fruit, Occam's approach to philosophy had a profound impact on the history of West-ern thought. Occam's understanding of human knowledge (*episte-mology*) broke entirely with the tradition of the church since the patrisitic period. The older idea held that universals really exist and that the mind can grasp them. According to this epistemology, we know an individual person because our minds understand the universal human. For Platonists, such as Augustine, universals have an existence that is more real than the particular expressions of the universals. Some philosophers and theologians argued that these universals do exist in the mind of God. For Aristotelians, such as Thom-as, the senses perceive universals or ideals by a process of abstraction by the mind. The universal does not exist separately from the individual; the individual contains the universal.

Theologians might debate the nature of the universals and the relationship of linguistics, mind, and matter, but few challenged the idea of universals themselves until Occam. His famous "razor" was his rule of economy. "Plurality is not to be postulated without necessity." In other words, the simplest explanation is the best, and for him, the simplest explanation of knowledge is that only individual things can be directly perceived. We do not know if there is a universal or ideal tree. We only know that a particular tree exists. Thus the individual is the true basis of our knowledge while the mind merely constructs the universal. Humans invented the universal as a sign to signify similar things. Universals such as human, tree, and so forth are mere names that humans agree on. Occam and his followers are thus be known as "nominalists" from the Latin word for name.

Contrary to older assumptions, nominalism did not destroy medieval theology or the authority of the church, but it did raise serious questions. In Christian theology, the concept of the universal had been used to help explain how the three persons of the Trinity could share in the divine essence. It could also justify the doctrine that Christ is physically present on every altar during the Mass, but Occam rejected this epistemology. He did not reject the doctrines themselves, but he removed the philosophical support for them. They were again seen as unfathomable mysteries.

Furthermore, nominalism undermined the whole medieval tradition of natural theology whereby the created world proved the existence of the uncreated God. Nominalists rejected the notion that the world is a shadow of the eternal world, or even that one can argue from natural cause to divine effect. All that can be known by the unaided reason are existent things accessible to the senses. What about metaphysics, then? Humans know the divine world only through revelation. We know the existence and attributes of God, heaven, hell, angels, and demons through God's free revelation of God's self in scripture and in the church, not by abstract reasoning. Reason was free to search for understanding within God's revelation, but the power of reason was limited. Outside of revelation, no one could ever know God or the way to salvation.

Nominalism encouraged the study of nature and the questioning of Aristotle's authority. The empirical study of nature came out of the same Franciscan tradition that produced Duns Scotus and Occam. Robert Grosseteste (1168-1253) was the chancellor of the University of Oxford, and was one of the first Europeans to use controlled experiments rather than relying on ancient authorities. Grosseteste's student Roger Bacon (d. 1292) strongly advocated experimentation and innovation. Such clerics viewed the world as God's creation and reason as God's gift to humans for the improvement of the world. They were part of an under appreciated technological and scientific revival centered in monasteries in the thirteenth and fourteenth centuries. Much of this scientific endeavor focused on optics and astronomy. Christianity directed people to seek the light and long for heaven; Grosseteste and Bacon took these commands literally. Instruments to study the stars, such as the astrolabe, were improved and new ones developed. Experiments with a mysterious stone that was attracted to iron led to the development of the compass that always points north. Nicholas d'Oresme (d. 1382), the bishop of Lisieux, criticized Aristotle's science and even suggested that the earth rather than the stars move. Such research declined in the latter fourteenth century, in part because of the Black Death, but the work of scientific theologians like Oresme and Bacon prepared the way for the great discoveries of the seventeenth century.

Salvation

Occam also promoted the essential features of Scotus' voluntarism although he rejected the idea that predestination is based on God's choice. He argued instead that predestination comes from God's foreknowledge of those who are worthy of salvation. Salvation thus becomes largely a matter of individual choice. Individuals must do what they have within themselves to do, namely to love God and use the church's sacraments. Sinners who choose to love God and turn from sin earn merit while in a natural state, and when they make use of the sacraments, they receive God's supernatural grace that allows them to achieve true merit worthy of salvation. Grace is still necessary for salvation, but salvation is based on one's merits. God, though, has promised to give grace to those who do their best and make use of the divinely ordained sacraments. This new approach to salvation and theology, the *via moderna*, dominated the theology schools of the late Middle Ages, particularly that of the University of Paris where Gerson the chancellor in 1395.

The modern way had its opponents as well. Many Dominicans defended Thomism, but the major opposition to the *via moderna* came from a circle of theologians who were reviving the theology of St. Augustine. These new Augustinians, known as the *schola augustiniana moderna*, objected to Occam's order of salvation which they considered little more than Pelagianism revived. Thomas Bradwardine (d. 1349), in *The Cause of God Against Pelagianism*, reaffirmed Augustine's idea that without divine grace the will stays in bondage to sin and self-love. He rejected the idea that humans in a natural state can choose to love God or achieve any merit without God's grace. Moreover, Bradwardine asserted that the grace of God is irresistible since God is all-powerful. The human will cannot refuse to accept God's salvation. Therefore those who are saved are saved by predestination alone.

Gregory of Rimini (d. 1358) echoed the Augustinian themes of Bradwardine, but he laid even more emphasis on the fall of humankind. Human nature is hopelessly corrupt without the unmerited grace of God (prevenient grace). Moreover, Rimini boldly asserted the idea that some are predestined to damnation, contrary to the church's official doctrine. The Augustinian challenge to the *via moderna* was met most vigorously by Gabriel Biel (d. 1495), sometimes called the last of the scholastics. Biel argued that God placed God's self under obligation to humans so that if humans do their part for salvation, God will save them. It is a covenant arrangement that God cannot ignore. Biel's works would be among the most widely read theology works of the late fifteenth century. Among his readers was Martin Luther who would eventually embrace both Augustinianism and nominalism.

Chapter 4

Mysticism and Piety in the Late Middle Ages

CHURCH REFORM WAS not divorced from concerns with spirituality and piety. In fact, the fourteenth and fifteenth centuries were a creative period for spirituality and devotion in Western Christianity. This period offered more latitude to those who experienced a sense of direct encounter with God than would be the case in later periods. It was also a particularly strong period for women mystics and spiritual guides, some of whom left their cloisters and engaged in church reform. The religious conflicts and turmoil of the fifteenth century, though soon, led to a repression of mystical expression. The church sometimes responded with violence to those who claimed to have mystical revelations and supernatural gifts, particularly women.

Mystical Stages

Mysticism has always been a feature of the Christian life, but it is subject to many definitions. In general terms, mysticism is the experience of a direct personal encounter with the divine. We may interpret mysticism in terms of the soul's complete union with God, or more as an intellectual experience. Augustine described his own mystical experience, saying that he momentary left the sensory world behind and then "in a flash of mental energy attained the eternal wisdom which abides beyond all things."[4] Christian mysticism has usually been connected with renunciation of the world; thus the great mystics have tended to be monastics or hermits. Even hermits, though, did not renounce all contact with the world. In fact, they frequently served as

---

[4] Augustine, *Confessions*, trans. Henry Chadwick (New York: Oxford University Press, 1992) 172.

spiritual guides, leaving voluminous records of their own spiritual journey and directions for others to follow.

Most Christian mystics have pointed to three main stages of the spiritual journey. The first is purgation, or the cleansing of the soul from sin, sensuality, and the world. For some mystics, purgation involves a renunciation of the will, knowledge, and even the self. Purging of the soul usually comes after some type of awakening or from feeling a call from God. Following the difficult process of purgation comes illumination, occasionally accompanied by visions or voices. Often the illumination is intellectual; a deeper insight into the divine mysteries as taught by the church. The final stage of union or consummation occurs when the soul becomes one with absolute reality. Mystics record that the last stage may be fleeting, but is nevertheless life-changing. Although mysticism is rightly associated with long hours of quiet contemplation and reflection, most of the medieval mystics connected spiritual growth with active love expressed in service to the world.

Types of Christian Mysticism

The late Middle Ages had representatives of each of the four main types of mysticism. The rationalistic mystics stressed the aspect of illumination whereby the experience of the divine brings new insight and enlightens the mind. This school is very much indebted to neo-platonic philosophy. For the rationalist mystics, the life of the mind and the life of the soul are one. The affective mystics, on the other hand, stress the aspect of love in spiritual devotion. Affective mysticism is more emotional and frequently makes use of marriage imagery to describe the soul's union with God. Spiritual experience and erotic desire entwine as the soul becomes the bride of Christ and unites with him in blissful love. The third type is volative mysticism or mysticism of the will. The distinctive feature of this school is that the human will joins to the divine will so that the person united with God acts only according to the desire of God. Some volative mystics go so far as to teach that the divine will annihilates the mystic's will, but the church rejected this idea of the anni- hilation of the will as heretical. The fourth major school of mystical devotion is essential mysticism or mysticism of being that teaches that the soul's own self unites directly with the absolute being of God. Some essential mystics taught that the soul is completely absorbed into the divine being. It should be noted that these schools of thought do not completely separate, and a single mystic may describe more than one type of experience of illumination or union.

Late Medieval Women Mystics

Women actively participated in the spiritual movements of the late Middle Ages, and most of the literature written by women in this period are mystical works. One such woman was Mechthild of Magdeburg (1207-1294) who felt a special calling by God at twelve years old. She left her family and joined the Beguines, a semi-monastic religious order popular in the Netherlands. The Beguines lived in a community, but could keep personal property and did not take irrevocable vows. They drew most of their members from the artisan classes in the increasingly prosperous Low Countries, especially from the weavers and fullers. The Beguines and their male counterparts, the Beghards, dedicated themselves to acts of charity and operated many hospitals and schools for the poor. The church viewed them with suspicion because they did not have a rule approved by the church, nor did they have a mother superior. Many inquisitors believed that Beguines and Beghards were prone to heresy, particularly the heresy of the Free Spirit that taught that human law does not bind true believers, including the laws of marriage.

In 1250, Mechthild wrote *The Flowing Light of the Godhead*, which included dialogues between God and the Soul. It is filled with allegorical visions and symbols, but is essentially a love song to God in which she describes God as pure fire. She examines the shame the soul feels when naked in the world of sense, and she expresses her burning desire to embrace the nothingness; the abyss of God. Unlike spiritual writers who talk of the soul's rest with God, Mechthild wrote of the anguish of desire for God and the anguish within God who seeks for lost souls. The pain of divine love equals the descent to Hell before the resurrection.

Mechthild mercilessly criticized the clergy of her day who preached without having experienced a passionate union with God. They were preaching about things they did not know. She also called for the government to repent of its mistreatment of the poor, whom God especially loved. She eventually had to retire to a safe Cistercian monastery where she could escape her critics. Her last years, though, were bittersweet as she felt her spiritual energy and gifts fading. Her last writings speak poignantly of the absence of God.

Similar to Mechthild was the thirteenth-century mystic Hadewijch of Antwerp (dates uncertain) of whom we know little other than that she acted as a spiritual guide to a group of Beguines. Her writings demonstrate that she was schooled in the rich culture of the court of Burgundy. She cites a number of great medieval mystics, such as Richard of St. Victor and William of St. Thierry, and she knew Latin and French scholarly works as well as the music of troubadours. Hadewijch was a master of rhetoric and she can be credited with being one of the creators of Dutch lyrical poetry. Her mystical poetry personifies love and explores the conflict felt by the lover who knows her inadequacy before God. She also tells us that she had once been guided by a male scholar who was unable to accompany her to the summit of mystical experience because he valued his intellect more than love, but she promises that those who persist and achieve detachment will receive the gift of being filled and perfected in God.

Marguerite Porete (d. 1310), another Beguine mystic, was convinced of a divine call to bring others to the complete love of God, but unlike her sisters, the church condemned Marguerite's works. She was forced to watch her book *Mirror of Simple Souls* be publicly burned in Valenciennes some time between 1296-1306. The book, however, continued to circulate for years under different names. In 1310 Marguerite suffered the same fate as her book when she was burned at the stake as an unrepentant heretic. She was blamed for starting the heresy of the Free Spirits, those who believed that their spirituality included release from all church authority and even common morality. In *Mirror*, Marguerite urges her reader "to save oneself by faith with no works." Even acts of charity and the sacraments do not help because the soul must be naked before God in order to be transformed. Even the will must be annihilated so that the true lover of God can accept whatever happens, whether heaven or hell, so long as she unites with God.

According to the *Mirror*, the spiritual life consists of seven stages. The virtuous life is merely the first stage. The true mystic must learn to be virtuous only out of love for God. True to Beguine teachings, Marguerite proclaimed that there was no need to withdraw from the world in order to be united with God; rather the believer can learn to keep hold of God in everything until she reaches the final stage of complete devotion when the soul is completely absorbed in the divine nature without asking why. The soul who is enthralled with the love of God is truly free, even from the demands and dogmas of the church and its hierarchy. Most church officials found her last idea too radical, but Marguerite did not renounce her beliefs. She remained convinced that Christ had died for her personally, and would have even if she alone had sinned.

Rhineland Mystics

Very similar to Marguerite, but more at ease with the institutional church, was the Dominican scholar and mystic Meister Eckhart (1260-1327) who taught at Paris, Cologne, and Strasbourg. Influenced by medieval Platonism and writings of pseudo-Dionysius, Eckhart taught that every soul was pre-existent in God and longs to return to God through contemplation. He urged his listeners to retreat into the interior away from the changing world of sensation. Flee from the troubles of the world and seek consolation within. Find what is unchanging and of enduring value. He referred to the innermost part of the human soul as the spark of the divine where one may find God. To find peace, a person must be detached from all that is not God and contemplate only what is truly divine.

Like many medieval preachers and theologians, Eckhart taught that true poverty is necessary for salvation, but for him poverty was more than a turning from material goods. True poverty of the soul renounces everything, even the self, on the journey to God. The final goal is complete absorption in the divine and a total passivity before God. Eckhart's views would get him into trouble with the church, and he has often been accused of being pantheistic. He did say that the true essence of God goes beyond the symbol of the Trinity. Ultimate unity exists within God and between God and all creation. It transcends all thought.

In 1329 a number of his writings were condemned, but one of his disciples in Cologne, Johannes Tauler (1300-1361), tried to preserve the essence of Eckhart's teaching while moving away from the condemned views. For instance, Tauler taught that as an act of grace God gives the spark of divinity in each soul. The spark is not intrinsic to the soul. Moreover, the return to God is an act of grace and is a union of wills, not of essences. Tauler carefully stated that the divine union does not annihilate the self; rather, the self is completed in God.

Another defender of Eckhart was Henry Suso (1295-1366) whose conversion at the age of eighteen led him into the Dominican Order. He found no final peace in the cloister, however. A spiritual crisis in the late 1330s drove him out of the monastery and into the world as an itinerant preacher. He became a spiritual guide to a group of laymen known as the Friends of God, and he also advised several Beguines and nuns. Like Mechthild and Hadewijch, Suso drew upon the songs of the troubadours who sang of human love, but he sang only of the soul's love of God. He described his visions and revelations, but stressed that the mystical experience transcends all images and symbols. The mystical experience consists of the human being poured out and God being poured in. Since Christ is the true image of God, the true mystic must become more Christlike, which includes sharing in the suffering of Christ because his suffering was a necessary part of his divinity. Suso eloquently advocated the contemplation of the passion of Christ that figured so prominently in late medieval literature and art.

The influence of Tauler and Suso is evident in the so-called *Theologia Germanica*, an anonymous work written in the latter half of the fourteenth century. The *Theologia Germanica* would have a profound impact on the young Martin Luther, and through him, later German hymnody and devotion. It focuses on the theme of following and imitating Christ. Following Christ involves contemplation, but rather than banishing all the concerns of active life, it overshadows them. True union with God means that the will desires nothing but the good. Following Christ is higher than the law but is not lawless; rather self-will which opposes the will of God is abolished as the will of God is internalized. The will that originates with God is truly free to lead a life of sacrificial love for one's neighbors.

English Mysticism

Mystics in England promoted similar ideas, among whom the most popular was Richard Rolle (d. 1349) whose works *Fire of Love, Mending of Life*, and *Form of Perfect Living* emphasize the practical rather than speculative aspects of the spiritual life. Rolle lived as a rigorous ascetic and hermit, but his devotion was very sensual. The contemplative should feel the experience of love, especially its heat, music, and sweetness. Prayer can lead to ecstatic rapture. The anonymous work *Cloud of Unknowing* (c. 1380), on the other hand, warns against such emotional and sensual experiences. The path to full union leads down the path of not-knowing, not feeling, and not trying. The soul should reach the point of perfect rest in God which is its goal.

In an age of great spiritual guides, Julian of Norwich (1342?-1416) stands out as unique. She tells us that as a young woman she had prayed to be ill to the point of death so that she would know if she could survive the final testing. This was a period just after the devastation of the Black Death in which popular piety focused on the Danse Macabre (Dance of Death) that stressed that death comes for all. Manuals, such as the often reproduced *Art of Dying*, helped people prepare for their own death before the end came. Julian wanted to see if she was prepared for the final assaults of Satan. Her illness was so severe that the priest gave her last rites and prepared her soul for the final judgment. She records that during this five-hour ordeal on May 8, 1373 as her eyes began to fix into their death-stare and her extremities grew cold, she received a total of sixteen visions or showings. In one of them she saw Christ on the crucifix held by the priest pouring forth blood, washing everything with his blood. The blood of Christ drove back the legions of devils that she saw surrounding her deathbed ready to drag her into hell. In another vision she became aware of the insignificance of the entire universe in comparison with the creator who suffered to redeem it.

After Julian regained her health, she took the vows of an anchoress and was locked in a cell attached to her local church. There she lived in seclusion until her death. During her seclusion, Julian continued to meditate on the meaning of her sixteen revelations. She wrote her experience down in *Showings of Divine Love,* one of the earliest works written in the English language. She did more than just record the visions, however, she presented a profound theological commentary on her experience. Unlike many mystics, Julian's writing is not about how one becomes a mystic; rather it is a sophisticated theological work on the unfathomable love of God for all creation. She presents Christ as the final end of all creation. Christ is in all things, and all things are in him. She also records that she became aware of the motherhood of Christ who "can feed us with himself" and who continually labors until "all his beloved children are born and brought to birth."[5]

Italian Mysticism

No account of fourteenth-century spirituality would be complete without mention of the Italian mystic and political agitator Catherine of Sienna (1347-1380) who began experiencing visions and physical phenomena as a young child. She made a vow of virginity and strict austerity, but her family never allowed her to enter a convent. A vision of St. Dominic led her to join the Dominican tertiary. For Catherine, sin comes from a blindness of the soul which separates us from God, but through faith we can see the soul for what it is and conceive a hatred for the sensual. More concerned for dogma and orthodox teaching than the northern mystics, Catherine drew heavily on the theology of Aquinas. She did not reject reason in preference to love, but saw reason as the distinctive property of humankind that leads the soul to God's own truth. Even more important than reason, though, are the sacraments, which are the soul's path to light and virtue.

---

[5] Julian of Norwich, *Showings,* trans. Edmund Colledge, *The Classics of Western Spirituality* series, ed. Richard Payne (New York: Paulist Press, 1978) 298, 304.

During her short life, Catherine claimed to hold conversations with Christ that were accompanied by raptures and eventually the stigmata, the wounds of Christ in her own body. She reported that she experienced true mystical marriage with Christ just before Lent in 1367. Accounts of her visions and miracles led to her widespread reputation as a saint during her life, and she was allowed to preach in public in order to urge people to partake of the sacraments and cleave to God. Her sense of apostolic mission eventually led her to admonish Pope Gregory XI himself and remind him of his sacred task to reform the church and return the papacy to Rome. In Catherine we see just how far a woman of spirit could go in the late Middle Ages if the people and the church accepted her as an authentic spokesperson for God.

The "Modern Devotion"

Mysticism was not the only expression of spirituality in the later Middle Ages. People continued to attend the Mass, even though it had become largely a drama one watched rather than a participatory ritual. Pilgrimage sites and saints' relics proliferated as Christians of all degrees of faith sought supernatural help in their daily struggle for life and happiness. New forms of piety, though, emerged along with the development of the new bourgeois culture of northern Europe. New piety, such as the famous Devotio Moderna, would help pave the way for early Protestant spirituality in the Netherlands, Germany, and England as well as the devotion of post-Tridentine Catholicism.

The instigator of this new devotion was Gerard Groote (1340-1384) who was born into property and who had studied at the University of Paris. Groote experienced a religious conversion in 1370. A few years later, he gave his house in Deventer to a group of poor devout women and went into an intense retreat at a Carthusian monastery where he studied various mystical works. He left the monastery in 1380 convinced of the need to reform the church morally and spiritually. His license to preach was revoked by the bishop because of his vigorous attacks on the clergy, but many responded to his call for a more serious spiritual life. He organized the women in his home as the Sisters of the Common Life. Similar informal home communities cropped up around the Netherlands as his followers continued to spread his call for reform. Florentinus Radewijns (1350-1400) organized the Brothers of the Common Life in Deventer and established the very influential Windesheim congregation of Augustinian canons.

The Brothers and Sisters of the Common Life defended their movement against charges that they were Beguines, Beghards, Pickarts, or other groups suspected of heresy. They were theologically orthodox; in fact, the Brothers and Sisters generally avoided theological and speculative issues. What distinguished their new devotion was its attitude toward their life in community. The Brothers and Sisters did not beg for alms and support like the mendicant orders, nor did they live in endowed monastic houses in the countryside like the Benedictines and Cistercians. Instead, they lived in private homes in cities and supported their common life by their own labor. They resolved neither to beg, nor live off of rents. The brothers specialized in copying books and the sisters worked in the thriving textile industries of Burgundy. They lived in simplicity, not apostolic poverty and took no irrevocable vows. In fact, they remained part of their local parishes and participated in normal parish worship, but they dedicated themselves to prayer and the mutual correction of faults. They also devoted themselves to acts of charity, particularly to setting up hospitals and schools for the poor.

Even their enemies acknowledged that the Brothers and Sisters were virtuous and devout, but some in the church found their lack of vows bothersome. They were not religious in the medieval sense of the word; that is they were not part of a religious order. Rather they were religious in what would become the modern sense; someone personally devoted to a moral and pious life. Many of the Sisters of the Common Life would eventually join the Franciscan tertiaries, in part for self-protection. Some of the Brothers' houses, such as the one at Windesheim, would become part of the Augustinian Canons Regular while maintaining many of the features of the *Devotio Moderna*.

The Brothers and Sisters wrote and distributed many devotional works in the vernacular for the edification of common persons. These included translations of portions of the liturgy and scripture. Devotional reading of scripture and contemplation on the life of Christ was the centerpiece of the new devotion. Turning away from the eroticism of marriage mysticism and the intellectualism of scholasticism, the Brothers and Sisters focused on following in the footsteps of Christ. They sought to "relive" Christ's life and his suffering for humankind and to keep his example ever present in their minds. The contemplation of Christ should then change the life of the believers who in turn revealed Christ in their own lives through their treatment of other people. The discipline of the community and development of one's spiritual life was expected to bear the fruit of love for all of God's children. The *Devotio Moderna* produced one of the greatest classics of

Western spirituality in the *Imitatio Christi* (*Imitation of Christ*), commonly attributed to Thomas á Kempis (d. 1471). *Imitatio Christi* is one of the most republished spiritual works in history, and it continues to inspire serious-minded Christians who try to live spiritual lives in a materialistic world.

Chapter 5

Radical Reformers

DID JESUS AND the apostles own property? That was the burning question of the early fourteenth century. Theologians, bishops, preachers, lawyers, and popes debated whether Jesus owned his own clothing or only made use of them. What did it mean that Jesus had to ask someone for a coin in order to see the image on it? It was not a question of idle curiosity or biblical interest; it was a debate on the wealth and power of the medieval church and the papacy itself. If Christ was indeed poor, then should the church not follow his example instead of the example of the Roman emperors who had put the martyrs to death? If Peter devoted himself to absolute poverty and had no earthly authority, should his successors not do likewise? Seen from this perspective, one can understand why Pope John XXII in 1323 declared it a heresy to teach that Christ did not own anything.

The Spiritual Franciscans

The debate began within the Franciscan Order. Francis, as you may recall from volume one, had given away all his possessions and dedicated himself to Dame Poverty. His original rule commanded his followers to do likewise. They lived on whatever people would give them. That is, they were to be mendicants or beggars. Francis stood in a long church tradition of voluntary poverty and sacrificial activity in the world, and his first rule for his followers, the so-called Primitive Rule, in 1209 commanded strict poverty. Even before his death, though, his successor, Elias of Cortona, formulated a less austere rule in 1221 that acknowledged that some Christians could not renounce all possessions. The Franciscan Order was growing rapidly and wealthy patrons had started giving land and endowments to support it. The new rule accepted such gifts.

Officially, after 1245, the pope held the property of the order and permitted the order to use it. Thus the order enjoyed the use of endowments without violating the rule against ownership of property. Moreover, permanent houses were soon established for the Franciscans where brothers or sisters could live in common rather than wandering homeless as Francis had encouraged. Despite the founder's suspicion of scholarly work, the order quickly became established in the universities of Europe. By the time of Pope John XXII about 1400 Franciscan houses existed, one fifth of which housed women (the Poor Clares). Some of the leading minds of the century, Roger Bacon, Duns Scotus, and William of Occam were Franciscans.

The drift away from poverty and sacrificial service alarmed Francis himself, and shortly before his death he wrote the *Testament* which again endorsed complete poverty. The document caused a rift in the movement. Those who accepted the *Testament's* demand for absolute poverty called themselves the Observants and were led by Francis' own confessor, Brother Leo (d. 1271). Those who lived by the more lenient rule approved by the papacy were called the Conventuals. Observants and Conventuals lived in an uneasy relationship until the end of the century. John of Parma, one of the Observants, led the order for ten years, but when the mystical scholar Bonaventure replaced John, he reorganized the order along Conventual lines. Bonaventure resorted to imprisoning those Observants who opposed his loosening of Franciscan discipline.

The controversy became more intense when the Observants appropriated the prophecies of Joachim of Fiore (d. 1202) to support their cause. Joachim had been a Cistercian monk in Calabria who prophesied that there were three ages of the world. The age of the Father covered the period of the Old Testament (from Adam to Christ). The age of the Son is the period of the New Testament and the church down to Joachim's own time. The age of the Spirit would be the millennial age. For Joachim it would be the "monastic age" when communal values of peace and harmony would reign rather than values of competition and acquisition. The Age of the Spirit was already breaking into the church, as evidenced by the Cistercian order. Soon the monastic age would replace the corruption of the medieval church with its wealth and hierarchies, and Christendom would be ruled directly by the Holy Spirit, but the transformation would not come without conflict. An "angelic pope" would inaugurate the coming age, but he would die and be succeeded by Pope

Antichrist who would try to crush the reformation of the Holy Spirit and persecute the true believers.

Such ideas gave fuel for the Franciscan fire. The most rigorous of the Observants, including John of Parma, used Joachite prophecy against Bonaventure and the papacy. These "Spiritualists" placed Francis himself in the story of the Apocalypse as the angel of the sixth seal, the one who announces the final stages of the struggle against the Antichrist. The election of a pious hermit as Pope Celestine V in 1294 was greeted by many of the Spiritual Franciscans as the fulfillment of the Joachite prophecy of the angelic pope. Needless to say, the abdication and imprisonment of Celestine was viewed as an ominous sign of the rise of the Antichrist. Peter John Olivi (1248-1298) published his *Commentary on the Apocalypse* in 1297. Contemporary events were shown to be the signs of the end times as predicted in Revelation, but it was the Roman Church rather than the Roman Emperor who played the role of the Antichrist.

The pontificate of John XXII, 1316-1334, brought the controversy over poverty to a head. John was a brilliant administrator and financial wizard who reorganized the curia and the entire tax system of the church. He, like most of the popes of the Renaissance, sought to reform the church by increasing its secular and financial power. Franciscan views on poverty would undermine his efforts to increase the power of the papacy and Joachite prophecies about the Age of the Spirit would destroy the church as an institution. Shortly after taking office, John, with the acquiescence of the Franciscan General Michael of Cesena (d. 1329), moved against the Spirituals. Michael insisted that obedience is superior to poverty and that the storing of goods for future use was necessary. Four Spiritual Franciscans were burned at the stake in 1318; many more suffered at the hands of the Roman Inquisition. Four years later, however, at their general meeting at Perugia, the Franciscans declared officially that Christ and his apostles had owned no property. Pope John perceived their declaration as a threat to his own authority, and he declared the teaching heretical on November 12, 1323. He also returned the ownership of Franciscan property back to the order, removing the fiction that the order was poor.

Michael led a large minority of the Spirituals out of the Order and declared John to be a heretic. Emperor Louis gave support to the Spiritual cause because it aided his own power struggle against the papacy. However, the call for renunciation of papal allegiance and the proclamation of the millennial age produced movements more radical than the secular authorities could tolerate. Among them were the Fraticelli and the followers of the apocalyptic warrior Fra Dolcino who waged war on all those who held property without using it for the good of the poor. After being convicted of heresy by the Inquisition secular authorities publicly tortured and executed Dolcino and his consort. Many followers of Dame Poverty shared their fate. In the fourteenth century, theological arguments could have radical social consequences as the poor looked for salvation in the words of prophets and visionaries.

Wyclif

The struggle between church and state over the issue of property took a slightly different turn in England where the most popular teacher at Oxford planted ideas that would bear fruit during the reign of Henry VIII. John Wyclif (1325?-1384) was a scholastic philosopher and theologian whose *Summa de ente* of 1369 defended the *via antiqua* from the attacks of Occam and the nominalists, an indication that we should avoid the simplistic notion that the nominalists were all progressive and revolutionary while the antinominalists were traditionalists and reactionaries. Wyclif was philosophically a realist; that is, he held strongly to the belief that universals actually exist. Universals are not mental constructs; they are more real than the visible world. Such views alone would not have earned him a prominent place in the history of Western Christianity; however, King Edward III noticed his talents as a thinker, writer, and preacher and he hoped to use Wyclif in his ongoing struggle with the church. In 1374 Wyclif entered into royal service while continuing to teach at Oxford.

In 1375 and 1376 Wyclif produced two seminal works, *On Divine Lordship* and *On Civil Lordship* which attacked the foundation of the medieval church and its relationship to society. In short, Wyclif argued that all property and rule belongs to God alone. God allows certain humans to manage property as lords, but they have the right to lordship only as long as they remain faithful to their sacred tasks. Thus, the church has a right to property only so long as its agents fulfill their sacred duties. If the lords of the church (bishops, abbots, popes) are guilty of mortal sin and fail to perform their holy duties, then the secular authority has been empowered by God to punish them by taking away their property and rule. The spiritual lords have less right to temporal property and power than do the temporal lords. God has appointed the church to instruct and admonish the king, but God has appointed the king to punish the church if it fails in its spiritual mission.

In effect, Wyclif endorsed what Henry II had tried to do in the days of Thomas a'Becket, and he found strong support from John of Gaunt, the ambitious son of King Edward. John and his band of nobles were eager to confiscate wealthy abbeys from clerics guilty of sins real and imagined. Many of the commoners were also eager to be relieved from the increasingly onerous church taxes and fees. Thanks to the strong support from secular powers, Wyclif avoided conviction when he appeared before the bishops in London in 1377. Pope Gregory XI ordered Wyclif to defend his views before him in Rome, but the Great Schism intervened.

The Schism helped radicalize Wyclif's view of the church. In 1378 he produced two works that would have a profound effect on the history of Christianity. In the first, *On the Truth of the Holy Scriptures*, Wyclif argued that the pope has only a limited authority and even church councils have erred; therefore the only reliable guide is the Bible, interpreted according to the doctrine of the Church Fathers. Scripture is "the highest authority for every Christian and the standard of faith and of all human perfection." His idea helped inspire the Protestant Reformation's rejection of the authority of the papacy and canon law, leading to the idea of "Scripture alone" as the basis of the church's life. Wyclif did not abandon the church's tradition and creeds, but he did argue that the church's practice must be examined and reformed in the light of scripture.

The other work, *On the Church*, addresses the meaning of the Christian church itself. Is the church the same as the institutional, sacramental church one sees throughout Christendom? Is the church the visible body of monks, nuns, bishops, clerics, and the baptized that give allegiance to the Bishop of Rome and live according to canon law? Wyclif rejected this view and drew on the renewed interest in Augustine's theology to argue for a different definition of the church. The Body of Christ is the "totality of the predestined" or simply all of the elect. The true church is universal and invisible; it is a spiritual reality that is more real than its visible expression (remember, Wyclif is a philosophical realist). Only God knows the members of the invisible church, but they may be recognized by their fruits. Clerics who live in luxury wrung from the sweat of the poor do not belong to the elect. The pope acts as head of the church only when his lifestyle matches that of the apostles. Eventually Wyclif would call for the abolition of the papacy as a human institution inconsistent with the teaching of Christ and for the confiscation of most of the church's endowments. His disciples at Oxford called themselves the "poor priests" and lived like Waldensians. They also translated the Vulgate Bible into English so that commoners could understand the teaching of scripture better. Wyclif provided the poor priests with a large body of sermons to use as they went into the countryside preaching their gospel of simple faith.

English Peasants' Revolt

As stated earlier, at first Wyclif had the support of many in the king's court. His ideas supported their claims on church property, but soon it became evident that the same notions about property could be applied to the secular authority as well. In 1381, a priest by the name of John Ball led the largest and most successful peasants' rebellion of the Middle Ages. The Peasants' Revolt, like the *Jacquerie* uprisings in France, was caused primarily by changing social and economic conditions as feudalism slowly collapsed in the years following the Black Death of 1349. Wealth had become concentrated in the hands of the few; artisan guilds became more restrictive and worker's wages depressed; landlord's rescinded traditional peasant rights as they tried to maximize their profits. Poverty increased as bishops, princes, and merchants spent lavishly in displays of conspicuous consumption. The restless and disenfranchised lower classes transformed Wyclif's cry for the disendowment of the church by the restless and disenfranchised lower classes into a call for a radical redistribution of God's property for all of God's people. John Ball managed to focus the inchoate rage of the unpropertied into a successful assault on the city of London itself. His mob killed the Archbishop of Canterbury and the royal treasurer, making clear to all that they understood that both church and state abused their power. Eventually, though, the secular authority reasserted control and butchered the followers of Ball.

Church and state joined forces in the effort to crush the threat to their power and property. The new Archbishop of Canterbury condemned twenty-four propositions from Wyclif's works at a synod in London in 1382, blaming Wyclif's ideas for the rebellion. Wyclif's disciples at Oxford were forced to recant on the threat of death; many lost their posts. "Poor priests," derisively called Lollards, were hunted down and imprisoned. In 1401 King Henry IV issued *De haeretico comburendo*, a royal decree that called for the burning of heretics. It would be first used on the Lollards, later on suspected witches, Protestants, and other heretics. In 1428, the bishop of London went so far as to have Wyclif's body exhumed and the remains burned. The ashes were then thrown into the River Swift in order to deny his followers any relics. No doubt one reason for this drastic measure was the surprising reform occurring at that time in distant Bohemia.

Hus and the Czech Reformation

The kingdom of Bohemia was in many ways the center of Europe in the mid-fourteenth century. The Holy Roman Emperor Charles IV(1346-1378) made Prague his capital city and spent great sums in building a city worthy to be his capital. He also made Prague an archbishopric and began the famous St. Vitus cathedral that overlooks the city. One of his most important acts was the establishment of the University of Prague, the first university in central Europe, in 1348. The university attracted scholars from all over Christendom and became a center of a reformation in central Europe that led to the establishment of two non-Roman Catholic churches decades before Luther nailed his theses to the door of the castle church in Wittenberg. The Bohemian, or Czech, reformation is closely associated with its most eloquent and courageous advocate, Jan Hus (1372-1415).

While Hus attended the university he became acquainted with the ideas of church reform circulating in Bohemia at that time. Milic of Kromeriz (d. 1374) had recently gained a large audience in his call for an intense reformation in preparation for the return of Christ. Milic had created a sensation by preaching in Czech rather than German or Latin in order to reach the common people of Bohemia, and he harshly criticized the moral life of the clergy. Milic warned his listeners that the Antichrist was about to be revealed, and vigorously promoted frequent and ferverent communion as the best defense. Contrary to common practice, Milic's followers began having weekly communion.

Though less apocalyptic and popular than Milic, Matthew of Janov (d. 1394), was instrumental in bringing Milic's reform effort into the scholarly community of the university. Matthew turned away from his more worldly ambitions in the church during the Great Schism. He offered scripture as the best way to heal the divisions in the church. Since none of the three papal claimants could be the final authority; scripture itself must be. Followers of Matthew established a home for redeemed prostitutes (called the Magdalene House) in Prague as well as Bethlehem Chapel dedicated to the preaching of edifying sermons in the Czech language for the common people. Although the Magdalene House soon closed, the chapel became very popular. After 1402, the most popular preacher at the Bethlehem Chapel was Hus.

Hus' direct and impassioned sermons attracted large crowds from Prague and the countryside. Anticlericalism was high at that time and many in the crowds came to hear Hus expose and attack the immorality of the priests and other clerics. Others came because of the practice of singing hymns in Czech using popular tunes. Verses painted on the walls of the chapel taught people the new religious music. Many came because of their concern about salvation, and they were unsure whether they could trust the church as it then existed.

Hus, like Wyclif, taught that the best way to judge the worthiness of a priest was by the worthiness of his life. He painted a grim picture of the priesthood of his own time; a priesthood corrupted by drunkeness, concubinage, and simony. He warned people not to trust their souls to priests who were servants of Satan rather than Christ. Although church doctrine stated that the merit of the sacraments do not depend on the holiness of the priest, Hus urged concerned Christians not to risk their souls with an unworthy priest. They should reject him and only go to worthy priests for baptisms, communions, weddings, and confessions.

Hus directly challenged the medieval parish system and soon earned the enmity of more traditional priests. Hus crusaded tirelessly against the practice of selling church offices to the highest bidder, a practice called simony. Simony had been a problem in the church for centuries, and in every age reformers, including some popes, had tried to stop it. Despite the general opposition to the idea of selling spiritual offices, simony had become rampant during the Great Schism as rival popes tried to raise revenues and political support. Hus, like Luther a century later, demanded that the church authorities obey their own canon law and the commandments of scripture. His stance against a lucrative enterprise eventually cost him the support of the king and other powerful figures in Bohemia.

Hus was more than a popular preacher and moral reformer; he was also a theologian and philosopher. Wyclif's ideas and books appeared at the University of Prague, just as Hus was preparing to become a doctor of theology. When Anne of Bohemia married King Richard II of England in 1382, close ties were established between Wyclif's Oxford and Hus' Prague. When Hus was preparing to receive his doctor of theology degree in 1409, his main resource for his thesis was Wyclif's *On the Church*. The use of Wyclif's book led to a great conflict at the university between the Czech masters who advocated Wyclif and the masters from Germany who viewed the English theologian as a heretic. Eventually the Germans were forced out of the university and the remaining masters united behind Hus and reform.

Opposition outside of the university increased, however, and Pope John XXIII condemned Hus' works. The Pope placed the city of Prague under an interdict in 1412 for harboring a heretic. Hus went into hiding, and during that time, he critically examined the concept of the papacy and the church in light of the Great Schism. In 1412 he published his greatest work, *De ecclesia*, (*On the Church*), in which he promoted the Wyclifite idea that the church is the body of the predestined. The true church is the invisible body of the elect, not the institution controlled by the pope. True believers, the elect, are bound by the law of Christ rather than to human authorities. The pope as the head of the visible, institutional church should be respected, but not confused with Christ, the true head, whom scripture revealed. Moreover, Hus advocated Wyclif's idea that the only law of the visible church should be the Bible. Although Hus remained orthodox in his theology and accepted traditional dogmas, his view on the primacy of the Bible seriously challenged canon law.

In many ways, Hus repeated some of the arguments of the conciliarists, like Peter d'Ailley, but his final position was too radical even for those who wanted to bring the papacy under the control of a council. In a world built on clear lines of status, authority, and obedience, Hus' plan for reformation sounded like a call for the overturn of society. Moreover, as Hus grew more popular with the students and the common people, he gained more and more bitter enemies. The rich and powerful feared that Bohemia might erupt in a Peasants' War such as England had seen.

The Holy Roman Emperor and future king of Bohemia was the same Sigismund who decided to end the Schism by calling a great council to meet in Constance. He also figured it would be a good time to settle the controversy swirling in his capital city of Prague. Therefore Hus was invited to appear before the council of Constance by the same John XXIII who had already condemned his works and excommunicated him. The emperor promised Hus safe passage to Constance, and so Hus left for the Council planning to debate his thoughts as if it were a university exercise.

When he arrived in Constance he found that his enemies were prepared. The emperor withdrew his support and Hus was imprisoned in a local monastery. When he was brought before the great Council he was presented with a list of errors gleaned from the works of Wyclif and told to recant. Hus tried to point out that he had never held some of the views attributed to him, and he refused to recant any position unless convinced by Scripture. Finally the Council decided that Hus was a stubborn heretic and perverter of the faith, and so they condemned him to die. On July 6, 1415 he went to the stake and as the flames rose around, observers reported, he could be heard singing one of his hymns. The authorities then ground his remains and scattered them in the river so that his followers would have no relics.

The Hussite Revolution

Jean Gerson and Pierre d'Ailley, the leading judges at Constance, hoped to end all schisms through the authority of a church council. They succeeded in restoring the unity of the papacy, but failed to solve the Bohemian question. Hus' death became the symbol of faithful resistance to a corrupt church and the Hussite reform movement became more determined. Jakoubek of Stribo (d. 1429) led the reform movement in Prague centered at the university, and he became convinced that the Scripture requires all believers to take the wine as well as the bread in the Eucharist. The Fourth Lateran Council in 1214 had officially prohibited the laity from partaking of the wine, asserting that the bread contained both the body and the blood of Christ. The Hussite practice of giving communion "in both kinds," known as *utraquism*, soon became the symbolic centerpiece of the Czech reformation. Jakoubek also simplified the rituals of worship and rewrote portions of the service in Czech so that the common people could more fully participate.

Initially, King Vaclav allowed these innovations as a way to keep peace, but at his brother Sigismund's urging, in the summer of 1419, he replaced the Hussite town councilors of Prague with men opposed to the reform. Hussite priests lost their positions and anti-reform priests replaced them. One of the priests replaced was Zelivsky (d. 1421) who condemned the Roman mass as idolatry. He urged his followers to purify the church and nation from the abuses of the Antichrist. On June 30, 1419 he and his followers forcibly took over his old pulpit, throwing the priest into the streets. After celebrating communion in Hussite fashion, he led the crowd through the streets of Prague to the town square where they threw the councilors from the window of the town hall. This first defenestration of Prague placed the kingdom in open revolt. King Vaclav died shortly after, and Sigismund took over the throne. In 1420, imperial forces laid siege to the capital city. The rebellious Hussite forces were led by the military genius Jan Zizka (1360-1424), a one-eyed knight who had embraced the radical side of the reform. They defeated imperial forces, and the Hussites set about organizing their church.

The reformers were divided, however. The university masters in Prague remained closest to Hus' conservative reformation of church doctrine and practice. Since they focused primarily on the issue of giving communion to the laity, they were known as the Utraquists. More radical were the reformers in the countryside and in the slums of the New Town section of Prague. Zelivsky and others proclaimed that the millennium age of equality and peace was approaching. Feudal laws would be abolished and all believers would live in the simplicity of the early church. The signs of the end were at hand. Hus and fellow martyr Jerome of Prague were seen as the two faithful witnesses that the book of Revelation predicted would be killed by the Antichrist. Millennial prophets, such as Mikulas of Hus, convinced as many as 40,000 common people to sell their belongings and establish communal living on a mountain they called Tabor. There they celebrated the sacraments in Czech, without vestments or ceremony.

However, when Christ did not come to establish his kingdom on earth, the priests of Tabor decided that idolatry and corruption delayed the eschaton. In February of 1420, the Taborites captured the town of Utsi, located on a hill overlooking the Luznica River, and rebuilt its abandoned fortress. The military stronghold became the new Mt. Tabor, the most important of the five Taborite military communes, and in the same year the Independent Taborite Church was officially established.

Unlike the Utraquists who wanted to keep ties with the Catholic Church, the Taborites were inspired by the apocalyptic zeal of Zelivsky who preached that all who cooperated with the Roman Church served the Antichrist. All evil must be destroyed before the final consummation and renewal of the world. God was about to destroy Prague, just as God had destroyed Sodom. John Capek wrote that the faithful were to show no mercy to the enemies of God because God's servants must slay the servants of the Antichrist. "Accursed is the man who withholds his sword from shedding the blood of the enemies of Christ."[6] The nobility, the merchants, the magistrates, the bishops, and all who supported the oppressive feudal order were the sinners the Taborites resolved to kill. Zizka came to Tabor in 1420 and was given charge of the army, which he commanded until his death in 1424. He never lost a battle, and when some of the Taborites grew too radical for him, he exterminated them as well.

Although Zizka felt that the university masters in Prague were too attached to Catholic theology and ritual, he was instrumental in getting the Utraquists and Taborites to agree to the famous Four Articles of Prague which were the basis for the Hussites' common defense against the Catholic forces. The articles declared that 1) the Word of God should be preached everywhere freely; 2) Christians should receive both the body and the blood (wine and bread) every Sunday reverently from baptism until death; 3) clerical abuses such as simony and indulgences should be abolished; and 4) all

---

[6] Quoted in Norman Cohn, *The Pursuit of the Millannium* (New York: Oxford University Press, 1970) 212.

sins in the kingdom, whether that of laity, clergy or nobility should be destroyed. The Taborites pursued the last goal with a violence that frightened the Utraquists into eventually joining forces with the Roman Church.

In 1433, at the Council of Basle, representatives of the Utraquists made an agreement with the church that they intended to pave the way for reunification and would allow Sigismund to regain his throne. The Compacta gave some concessions to the church in Bohemia. In return the Utraquists joined the battle against the Taborites. In 1434 at the battle of Lipany, the Utraquists and Catholics decisively slaughtered the Taborite army that had struck terror throughout central Europe. Fire and sword consumed the Taborite vision of a millennial kingdom.

The Unitas Fratrum

During this period of religious warfare and bloodshed, one strong voice opposed both the conservatism of the Prague masters and the militancy of the priests of Tabor. Peter Chelcicky (d. 1460) was from a small town in southern Bohemia where he lived most of his life. Chelcicky was in Prague during that crucial year of 1419 when the citizens defenestrated thetown's councilors and the Taborites proclaimed the inbreaking of the eschaton. He engaged in theological discussions with the Utraquists theologians at the university, but his sympathies lay with the Taborites. The simplicity of their worship, their communalism in Tabor, and the biblicism of the priests impressed him. He also admired their willingness to suffer persecution for the gospel, but he rejected apocalypticism. Christ will return some day, but humans can do nothing to hasten that return, he argued.

Chelcicky promoted the Waldensian idea that the Catholic Church had fallen into apostasy when the Roman emperor Constantine became a Christian. The Waldensians shared many of the ideas on poverty advocated by the Franciscans, but they had been declared heretical in the twelfth century. By Chelcicky's time they believed that their founder Peter Waldo (or Valdes) had been a Catholic bishop at the time of Constantine's conversion. He preserved the true church that avoided being corrupted by secular power and remained true to the original teachings of Jesus. In his writings Chelcicky presents a literal reading of Jesus' Sermon on the Mount to show that the medieval church feudal society contradicted the law of Christ. The state and its lust for power was destroying the Church, and true Christians must separate completely from the state and the world. Most important, Chelcicky was appalled by the militarism of Tabor and the enthusiasm of its priests for war.

Christ, Chelcicky argued, commanded his followers to love their enemies. You do not love the person you kill. For Chelcicky, no violence is holy.

Although Chelcicky never organized a religious community, his writings did lead to the formation of one of the most important pre-Reformation Protestant churches, the Unity of the Brethren. In 1457, Brother Gregor, the nephew of Utraquist archbishop Jan Rokycana, gathered a small following of university students and former Taborites who dedicated themselves to living according to Chelcicky's teachings and the New Testament. They renounced violence and service to the state, began to share their labor and goods, and called themselves the Unity of Brethren or Unitas Fratrum. In 1467 the Brethren took the decisive step of establishing their own priesthood and episcopacy, breaking completely with the Utraquists and the Roman Catholics. The Unity suffered severe persecution until 1609 when the emperor Rudolph granted limited toleration. Unfortunately, the period of toleration lasted only a dozen years, and the church was virtually destroyed during the Thirty Years War.

Savonarola

The Hussites were not the only reformers more radical than the conciliarists or even Wyclif. One such figure was Girolamo Savonarola (1452-1498), a Dominican who lived in Italy during the exciting and troubled years of the late Renaissance. Unlike Spain, England, or France which were rapidly developing into nation states with strong central governments, Italy was a patchwork of several small territories, the most important of which were the city states. In the fourteenth century, wealthy cities such as Venice, Florence, Milan, and Genoa managed to consolidate their authority over surrounding territories, but incessant fighting occurred between the powerful city-states. The popes of the fifteenth century competed with princes of the rival Italian states for prestige and power. The competition among the wealthy cities fueled the creativity of the Renaissance as princes spent lavishly on art and literature, but it also generated corruption and increased the poverty of the lowest classes.

Florence, under the control of the Medici family, was perhaps the greatest of the Renaissance cities. It was a center of art, music, and learning. Even the courtesans of Florence were respected in society for their learning and culture. Savonarola rejected the luxury and loose morals of the Renaissance court, such as he witnessed in his own family. In 1474 he fled to a Dominican monastery at Bologna and in 1481 he was transferred to Florence. At first

people rejected his preaching as coarse and unappealing in such a sophisticated city. He withdrew from Florence but continued preaching in the area.
More and more he became a new Jeremiah, a prophet of impending doom
who urged the people to forsake their frivolous way of life.

Surprisingly, the great neoplatonic scholar Pico della Mirandola viewed
him as a prophet of the Lord and convinced his patron Lorenzo de' Medici to
appoint Savonarola as the prior of the Florentine convent of San Marco in
1490. Over the next four years the prophet's sermons grew increasingly
popular as they grew more apocalyptic and violent in their condemnation of
Italian corruption. When the armies of the French king Charles VIII invaded
Italy in 1494, it seemed that the prophet's warnings of divine punishment had
come true. During the ensuing chaos there was a popular revolt against the
Medici in Florence. The apocalyptic prophet Savonarola emerged as the new
dictator of the city.

The kingdom of God had arrived in Italy, according to Savonarola, and he
set about purifying Florence of all "vanities." Instruments of gambling, irreligious books and pictures, jewelry, fine clothing, and other things of the flesh
were burned in the public square. He enacted laws to close theaters, brothels,
and similar forms of entertainment. Savonarola remained personally determined to reform the church in "head and members," and he called upon
Charles VIII to execute God's wrath on Pope Alexander VI who refused to
heed his commands. While the nature of Savonarola's reform was consistent
with other medieval reform efforts, his success in taking over Florence from
the powerful Medici family frightened many in Italy, especially the pope. In
1497 Savonarola was excommunicated. When he failed to produce an expected miracle before the Florentine public in 1498, the crowds turned against
him. The local court arrested and tortured him. Like many would be
reformers of the fifteenth century, Savonarola was then burned at the stake as
a heretic and rebel.

Chapter 6

Christianity in the East

FROM THE FOURTH and fifth centuries, Christianity in what had been the eastern half of the Roman Empire had been divided into three major branches: Nestorian, Monophysite, and the Orthodox Church with its patriarch in Constantinople. The Nestorians, who originated in Syria, believed that the human and divine natures of Christ were clearly distinguished. Despite intermittent persecution, Nestorianism flourished as a minority religion in the Persian Empire. The Muslim rulers of Persia granted a limited toleration to the Christians so long as they paid a special tax and did not interfere with Islamic law. Nestorians were prominent among the intelligentsia, government officials, and financial classes. Nestorian scholars helped translate Greek philosophical works into Arabic, stimulating the golden age of Islamic philosophy and science.

Before 950, Nestorian missionaries established churches, monasteries, and bishoprics throughout central Asia, particularly along the trading routes. Sixteenth-century travelers encountered Christians in South India using Syriac liturgies and scriptures. Nestorians even brought Christianity to China in 635, but by 980 no trace of the church remained in that country. Enjoying the favor of the Mongol rulers of central Asia, the Nestorian Patriarch in Baghdad could report in the fourteenth century that he was the head of a church that had twenty-five metropolitans and over 200 bishops. However, with the rise of the aggressive Ottoman Turks as the new rulers of an Islamic Empire, Nestorians and other Christians suffered greatly. The Turks destroyed churches, forced Christians to convert, and drove the Patriarch from Baghdad. Although the church would maintain a tenuous existence through the centuries and preserve its ancient liturgy and ritual, it never recovered from the losses of the fifteenth century.

A number of Monophysite churches existed in Africa and central Asia during the Middle Ages. These churches rejected the Chalcedonian formula of the fifth century and held to the belief that the human and divine natures found unity in Christ. They also opposed the centralizing tendencies of the Patriarch in Constantinople and allowed their churches to develop along national lines. Thus the Monophysites encouraged the translation of the scripture and liturgy into a variety of local languages.

The Armenians broke decisively with the Orthodox Church in 491 and developed a strongly nationalistic faith. The Arabs could not completely subjugate Armenia despite 200 years of warfare, and eventually they granted the Armenians a great measure of autonomy and toleration for their religion. The Patriarch of Constantinople made efforts on several occasions to bring the Armenians back in the Orthodox community, but differences over theology, liturgy, language, and the nature of the priesthood (the Armenian priesthood tended to be hereditary) prevented reunion. The Armenian kingdom, which had been closely allied with the crusaders, finally dissolved in 1375. The territory was divided up into ethnic Armenian, Turkoman, and Kurdish principalities until it was taken over by Persia in the sixteenth century.

During this time, the Roman Catholic Church welcomed some of the Armenian Christians as Uniates. This meant that they could keep many local customs so long as their creeds agreed with Rome and they acknowledged the supremacy of the pope. Most Armenian Christians, though, remained attached to their church as a separate institution. Despite corruption in the hierarchy, the church persisted under Turkish rule, and the Turkish emperor named the Armenian bishop in Constantinople as the head of the Armenian peoples in the empire.

The Egyptian Monophysites used the Coptic language of the peasants and had close ties with the Ethiopian churches before the rise of Islam. The Arab rulers of northern Africa placed restrictions on Christianity, but did not outlaw the religion. From the tenth century on, however, the state actively encouraged Islam against Christianity. They forbade intermarriage; crosses could not be publicly displayed; and Christians could not drink wine in public or even ride thoroughbred horses. In Cairo in 1389 a group of Christians who had renounced their faith in favor of Islam publicly repented of their apostasy. All of them, men and women alike, were publicly beheaded, the first act of a major persecution. Through the years the Coptic Church diminished, in part because of persecution and in part also because of corruption in the hierarchy, but it has maintained an existence to the present day.

The situation appeared quite different in Ethiopia and Nubia during this period. Although there has been little research on the history of African Christianity, we know that Monophysite Christianity remained strong throughout the Middle Ages. Most of Nubia was Christian in the tenth century and Christian princes resisted Islamic advances. Slowly Islam grew dominant, however. In the twelfth century, Christian princes who promoted the expansion of the church southward ruled Ethiopia. The expansion continued in the next century, with Coptic manuscripts being translated into other vernacular languages. The expansion of Ottoman rule in the sixteenth century, though, hindered such efforts.

Constantinople, on the other hand, was the capital of the most important Christian empire during the Middle Ages. The fortunes of the Byzantine Empire waxed and waned during this period, but unlike the Christian kingdoms of the West, it maintained an unbroken cultural and administrative history throughout the Middle Ages. Byzantine culture creatively blended Christianity and Hellenism, and its administration was an effective blending of Roman law and skillful diplomacy. The Patriarch of Constantinople served at the discretion of the Emperor who used the church as an important part of his international diplomacy. Foreign powers who wished to make alliances with Byzantium were required to accept Christianity and receive bishops under the authority of the Patriarch. In this way, Christianity was brought to the Bulgars, Russians, Moravians, Serbians and other Slavic peoples before the year 1000. The liturgy and scriptures were provided in Slavonic, and some of these peoples were eventually granted their own patriachates.

The Fourth Crusade dealt a mortal wound to the Byzantine Empire in 1204 when the crusaders attacked Constantinople on their way to the Holy Land. The city that had withstood countless attacks by barbarian hordes and the armies of the crescent fell to Christians who claimed to be allies in the defense of the cross. Pope Innocent III protested the perversion of crusading ideals, but was pleased that the church was thus united under his authority, if only in name. The Latin rulers of Byzantium stripped the empire of many of its spiritual and material treasures. During the half-century of Western rule, the Orthodox Church became an important symbol of nationalism and resistance, and supported the emperor Michael Paleologus in 1261 when he led a successful rebellion against the unpopular Catholic rulers. However, neither the city nor the empire fully recovered from the experience of subjugation, and the Paleologi Dynasty never restored the empire to its former strength. The Second Council of Lyons in 1274 achieved a formal reunion between the Eastern and Western churches, but the Byzantine rulers, both secular and spiritual, soon repudiated it.

As in the medieval West, monasticism was the heart of the Orthodox Church before 1500. Orthodox monasteries tended to be self-governing without the large orders, such as the Cistercians and Benedictines, that defined Western monasticism. Moreover, no mendicant movement existed, such as the Franciscans, where monks also served as preachers, teachers, and pastors of parishes. Monasteries tended to be in isolated and austere locations, far away from human habitation, such as the famous monasteries on Mt. Athos in Greece; however, many monasteries did engage in philanthropic activities, such as operating hospitals. Eastern monasteries suffered from many of the abuses that plagued Western monasticism, primarily the fact that some monks chose the monastery as an easier life than working in the world. Limited reforms often attempted to correct such abuses.

Simeon Neotheologus (the New Theologian) started the most interesting revival movement in the Eastern, the Hesychast movement, focused on meditative techniques and spiritual practices that could lead to the beatific vision of God. The goal was for the believer to be transfigured by the light of God the way Christ was on Mt. Tabor. Archbishop Palamas defended the Hesychasts against those who accused them of heresy. When the Roman church opposed the movement as heretical, the Orthodox rallied to their defense. In 1341, a synod in Constantinople officially endorsed Hesychastism as a legitimate form of spirituality. It would experience a revival in nineteenth-century Russia, years after its initial enthusiasm waned in Greece.

In the fourteenth century, though, a new secular power rose in the East. The Ottoman Turks emerged as the dominant force in the Middle East, and in the 1350s they began to settle in the Balkans. The Serbians, Bulgarians, and Croatians could not stop the Turkish advance and lost decisively at the battle of Kosovo Polye in 1389. As a result, the formerly independent Bulgarian Church came directly under the control of the patriarch of Constantinople. In contrast, this period of conflict with the Turks led to the formation of an independent Serbian Orthodox Church, which became a major force in Serbian nationalism and anti-Muslim sentiment.

May 30, 1453 was the darkest day in the long history of the Greek Orthodox Church. Constantinople, the city built by the first Roman emperor to embrace the faith, and the capital of the Byzantine Empire, fell to the forces of Mohammed II, ruler of the Ottoman Turks. Constantinople had been the second Rome, a holy city to the Orthodox. Its beautiful basilica, Hagia Sophia, was one of the wonders of the Christian world, a touch of heaven on earth, but the weakened Byzantine Empire could not resist the Turkish armies.

Despite the concessions made by the Orthodox at the Council of Florence, the Western Christian kingdoms did not come to the rescue of Constantinople. The emperor died defending the walls of the city, but others lived to see Hagia Sophia turned into a mosque. The fall of Constantinople was a blow to the Eastern church, far greater than the loss of Jerusalem or the sacking of Rome in 410 had been to the Western church. Constantinople was now the capital of a great Islamic Empire which, under Suleiman the Magnificent in the sixteenth century, embraced the Black Sea, Asia Minor, northern Africa, Mesopotamia, and threatened Budapest in Hungary.

After the fall of Constantinople, some compulsory conversions to Islam occurred, and many Christians parents were forced to give their children to serve in the imperial army, but Christianity survived in the East, particularly in Greece. Synods continued to elects patriarchs who also became the administrative rulers of all Christian peoples under Turkish rule. The church had the responsibility for keeping law and order among the Christians. The patriarch, however, could be removed without cause by the emperor, who also demanded a high payment from the holder of the office. Corruption in the highest levels of the church hierarchy became as common in the Greek Church as it had in the late medieval Roman Church, but the church itself survived.

Orthodoxy was threatened on all fronts in the fifteenth and sixteenth centuries, but it flourished in Russia, a nation just emerging as a great power in Europe and Asia. The church supported the efforts of the Muscovite princes to establish a realm independent of the Mongols. After the fall of Constantinople, some of the Russian church leaders put forth the claim that Moscow was to be the Third Rome.

Ivan III, who had married a descendent of the last Byzantine Emperor, adopted much of the ceremony and power of the old empire. As in Constantinople, the church in Moscow remained closely tied to the imperial authority and benefited as the Tsar extended his domain. Thus, the sixteenth century was a period of growth for the Russian Church. As earlier in the West, the monasteries led the spread of Christian faith in Russia, often by individual monks who set off into the wilderness to live as hermits. A reputation for personal holiness attracted converts and followers. As the monasteries grew they became centers for learning and art, particularly the distinctive Russian iconography that became the center of popular piety.

In the late fifteenth century, Joseph of Vaolokolamsk set about reforming the lax discipline of Russian monastic life. He insisted that his Josephite monasteries devote themselves to learning, fasting, and public service rather than mystical contemplation. Josephite monks trained generations of public officials, but the type of monasticism popular north of the Volga River stood in marked contrast to the Josephite monasteries.

Inspired by the irenic and austere monk Nilus Sorsky(1433-1508), the Transvolgians rejected accumulation of wealth and withdrew from the affairs of the world. They preferred prayer and manual labor to the reading and writing of books. It appears that the Hesychast movement in Greece influenced Nilus, and he organized his monasteries as small groups of twelve with an elder. Although the Transvolgians remained Orthodox in faith, they rejected elaborate ritual, beautiful churches and liturgies, and the punishment of heretics. Like many Christian reform movements, they attempted to recapture the teachings of Jesus in a new situation. Nilus, for example, preferred to be called friend rather than teacher, and he was surprisingly tolerant in an intolerant age. He was in the center of a conflict over what the church should do to the so-called Judaizers, Christians who secretly converted partly or wholly to Judaism. Nilus argued for leniency and toleration, but he lost. Those convicted of Judaizing were burned or imprisoned for life.

Chapter 7

The Spanish Reformation

WESTERNERS ARE ACCUSTOMED to speaking of *the* Reformation, which we will discuss in part two of this book, making it easy to forget that many different efforts at reforming the church took place throughout Europe before 1517. Some of the reform efforts successfully addressed many of the abuses of clerical power and made the church an effective institution in national life without separating from Rome.

This was the case in the Iberian Peninsula where a Catholic reformation was so successful by 1517 that Protestantism never achieved a foothold. There the Spanish reformation was largely the work of Spanish monarchs who managed to assert their will over the church in much the same way that Philip the Fair had done in France in the 1300s and Henry VIII would attempt to do in England in the 1530s. King Henry would have to break with the pope in order to assert control over the Church of England, but in Spain, the story was different. As a result, Spain became the bulwark of Catholicism during the tumultuous sixteenth century.

Christians and Muslims in Spain

Spain has a unique history in Western Europe because it was the only country that had a significant Islamic presence. Islam was introduced to the Iberian Peninsula in 711 when invaders crossing the strait of Gibraltar quickly overcame the divided and corrupt Christian kingdoms. During the Middle Ages, the region was divided into several petty kingdoms, some of which were Moorish and some Christian. Frequent fighting took place among the kingdoms, but the Muslims and Christians did not always fight each other. The legendary El Cid, for instance, offered his service to Moor and Christian alike. As the crusades in the Holy Land captured the imagination of Christian nobles, though, the conflicts in Spain slowly took on the character of a crusade. Christian warriors took on the cause of the *reconquista*, or reconquest of Spain from the "infidel invaders" who had lived there for six centuries. Four of the Christian kingdoms, Portugal, Navarre, Aragon and Castile, grew in power and prominence as Muslim power waned. By the fifteenth century, the Moors were confined to Granada.

Isabella, who would become queen of Castile in 1474, and Ferdinand, the future king of Aragon, married in 1469, uniting the major regions of modern Spain. In 1492, the year Columbus made his discoveries, the Alhambra, the last Muslim fortress, fell to the crusaders and Granada became part of Castile. The monarchs consolidated their power by curtailing the autonomy of the cities, reducing the nobility to civil servants, and imposing royal law and bureaucracy across their realm. Already in 1482, the monarchs had forced the papacy to sign a concordat that granted them nearly complete administrative control of the church in Spain. The government made all major church appointments and had to approve all papal bulls and taxes within their realm. The Catholic Church in Spain thus became largely a national church. In return for such concessions, Spain promised to protect the papacy in Rome.

Inquisition

The militant zeal of the reconquista helped shape the Spanish church and heavily influenced European and American history for the next century and a half. Queen Isabella was extremely devout, surprisingly so for a monarch, and was determined to reform the religious life of all of her subjects and unify her realm under a single religion. In 1478, she asked for papal permission to establish the Inquisition in Castile.

The Inquisition had been used in France and Italy since the Middle Ages to root out suspected heresy; however, the Spanish Inquisition was set up differently than its predecessors. First, this Inquisition was designed to deal with Muslims and Jews who professed Christianity but still remained faithful to their old religion. As Moorish power waned in Spain, thousands converted to Christianity in order to avoid persecution. Baptized Jews were known as *Marranos* and baptized Muslims were called *Moriscos*. Isabella worried that these converts would pervert Christianity and undermine her rule. What was the use of fighting for the Christian faith all those years, she reasoned, and then allow infidels to corrupt the church from within? The Inquisition was empowered to aggressively seek out secret Jews and Muslims, arrest them, and burn them at the stake.

Second, the papacy did not have authority over this Inquisition. Instead, the monarchs themselves directed it. For the first time in the church's history, the Inquisition became an arm of the state itself, prefiguring the secret police of modern states. The arrangement, which Pope Sixtus IV granted in 1480, gave the Spanish monarchs unprecedented powers over the religious lives of their subjects. Thomas de Torquemada (d. 1498), prior of Dominican houses in Segovia and Seville, inspired Isabella's request, and he was appointed to the task of organizing the Inquisition. Although the Spanish Inquisition would become infamous for cruelty and arbitrariness, it should be remembered that the intention of the Inquisition was church reform. The Spanish Inquisition attempted to use the full power of the state to enforce religious conformity on all of the subjects of a realm. It stands as a reminder that church and social reform can lead to great injustices.

The scope of the Inquisition's activities increased after the fall of Granada in 1492 when the crown decreed that all Jews who refused baptism were banished from Castile and Aragon. The Inquisition mercilessly hounded those who stayed. The year 1492, which marks such a significant date in American history, represents one of the lowest points in the history of the Jews in Europe. For centuries Spain had been a model of inter-religious toleration and mutual learning, but Ferdinand and Isabella followed the lead of England and France who had expelled the Jews in 1290 and 1306, respectively. Many Jews converted; others fled to the Netherlands, the New World, and Arab countries. Thousands became unnamed martyrs to their faith, executed by men who believed stories that Jews sacrificed Christian babies in Satanic rituals.

In 1502, the Moors suffered the same fate. Under threat of arrest and execution Muslims left their homes. After 1517, the Inquisition focused on suspected Protestants. The Inquisition even suspected some saints of the church, such as Theresa of Avila and Ignatius Loyola.

Reform of the Clergy

Isabella pursued an austere and ascetic form of devotion to the suffering Christ, and she appointed Ximenes de Cisneros (1436-1517) as her personal confessor in 1492. Ximenes would be the true architect of the Spanish reformation, and he pursued his goal of a purified church with prophetic zeal. Although he came from an impoverished noble family, Ximenes rose rapidly in the church hierarchy through his enormous natural talents and drive. He studied law at the University of Salamanca, one of the leading universities of Europe, and in 1459, received a post in the papal curia. When he returned to his homeland six years later, Pedro Gonzalez de Mendoza, who would later become Archbishop of Toledo, noticed his talents. In 1480, Mendoza appointed Ximenes vicar general of one of the leading dioceses in Spain, but just four years later he renounced his high office to live as a strict Franciscan. Isabella called him out of his hermitage in 1492 when she could not find a personal confessor she respected.

Ximenes' sacrificial devotion impressed the queen so much that she assisted him in his rise to great power. When he became the Vicar General of Franciscan Observants in Castile in 1494, he insisted that all Franciscans be as rigorous as he was. The following year he succeeded his old patron Mendoza as the archbishop of Toledo, thus becoming the head of the church in Spain. In 1507 he became a cardinal and the Inquisitor General a year later. Throughout his tenure as the head of the Spanish church, he vigorously supported the effort to force Jews and Muslims to convert, and he also enforced clerical discipline to a degree unknown in Spain before. His decision to force priests to give up their common-law wives led to a mass exodus of parish priests to Muslim lands, but he replaced them with men dedicated to the ideals of poverty, chastity, and above all, obedience.

Ximenes did not rely only on force, though, in order to purify and reform his church. He believed in the ideal of an educated clergy, making use of the new technology of printing to provide resources for priests and confessors. In 1498 he used his personal revenues to found the University of Alcal de Henares. The University did not open until 1508, but it quickly became one of the premier universities in Europe, and a center for humanism. The university had a number of small colleges, one dedicated to theology, another to law, and a third to the study of biblical languages (Greek, Hebrew, and Latin).

The next generation of Spanish bishops was educated at Alcal. They used what they learned at Alcal to establish diocesan seminaries to train priests throughout Spain. The greatest achievement of the humanist scholars at Alcal was the Complutensian Polyglot Bible, so named because Complutum was the ancient Roman name for Alcal. The Polyglot Bible represents one of the great landmarks in biblical scholarship since it produced in parallel columns the text of the Old Testament in Hebrew, Greek, Latin, along with Aramaic Targums. The New Testament, ready for the press in 1514, included Greek and Latin texts, but papal permission for publication was not given until 1520. Thus Ximenes lost the honor of publishing the first Greek version of the

New Testament to Erasmus. Ximenes' educational reforms also led to a revival of Thomistic theology, particularly at Salamanca. This Thomism would be an important tool in the later struggle against Protestantism.

The New World

The Spanish reformation of Ximenes and Isabella strengthened Catholicism in Spain at the same time that Spain struggled to establish a world empire in the Western hemisphere. It should go without saying that Christopher Columbus (1451-1506) did not really discover the New World since it had been inhabited for some 20,000 years; however, Columbus' landing in America did open up a New World for Europeans, and greatly expanded the geographical scope of Christianity. More will be said about Christianity in the New World in later sections, but it is important to note that the conquest of the native peoples of America was carried out in the spirit of the Spanish reformation. The very ambitious Columbus believed that the millennial age was dawning and that he had been given the task of bringing the Gospel to the Indies. His quest was both financial and spiritual. Wealth would flow from the Indies while a benighted land received the Gospel, preparing the world for the coming of the Savior. Europe knew something of the Indies from the recent, and very profitable, explorations of the Portuguese.

Notice that Columbus did not set sail to prove that the world was round. The educated classes of Europe commonly accepted this fact, particularly since the revival of ancient cartography and astronomy. Globes based on Ptolemy's cartography could be found in many universities, academies, and even private homes. Columbus, however, argued that the distance from Europe to Asia across the western sea was short enough for a crew to reach it before running out of food. Of course, his argument was wrong. If his ships had not run into the Caribbean islands, the crew would have perished.

Still, Columbus' reports of the "Indies" inspired the missionary zeal of the monarchs and bishops of Spain. At the turn of the century, Amerigo Vespucci proved that Columbus had come upon an entirely new continent, a world unknown to the ancient authorities where the Gospel had not been heard and where ambitious nobles could create new estates. By 1520 Cortes had subjugated the great Aztec Empire in Mexico and a decade later Pizarro overthrew the Inca Empire. Under an agreement with the papacy, most of the New World was awarded to Spain, but Portugal received Brazil and the true Indies.

Men steeled in battle against the Moors, and priests schooled in the strict orthodoxy of Ximenes' church saw little good in the native culture of America and worked to replace it with a Christian culture. More important for the Spanish state, silver poured out of American mines and into the royal treasury. Natives were enslaved, against the initial objections of Isabella, to work the mines and plantations. Untold tens of thousands died in the labor camps, were slaughtered by the conquering lords, or were decimated by new diseases, such as smallpox.

Under Emperor Charles V, Africans were also enslaved and brought to Latin America to work and die in the mines and plantations. Spanish and Portuguese priests, such as Bartolome de las Casas (1474-1566), worked to convert the natives and tried to protect their flocks from the violence of the conquistadors, with some success. The Franciscans labored in Brazil, Venezuela, Mexico, Peru, and Argentina, while the Jesuits worked extensively in Brazil, Colombia, Mexico, Ecuador, Bolivia, Paraguay, and Chile. Most of the priests shared the asceticism of Spanish piety and the longing to suffer with Christ in the cause of Christ. Their efforts in the wilderness can only be described as heroic even if one criticizes their methods.

Gradually a distinctive Latin American Catholicism emerged which was patriarchally organized and dependent on Europe, but which also found creative ways to blend local practices with Spanish piety. Moreover, the Catholic monarch of Spain in 1551 founded the first universities in America (at Lima and Mexico City), paving the way for an indigenous and educated priesthood, although the majority of the priests would be of Spanish, not Indian, descent.

Chapter 8

Renaissance Humanism

ONE OF THE most important movements to emerge during the Renaissance was humanism. As with all things dealing with our past, humanism has been subject to widely varied interpretations. The Enlightenment latched on to the renaissance humanists as the forerunners of secularism. The *philosophes* portrayed the humanists as bold thinkers who defied the power of the church and replaced faith with reason. Their interpretation continues to color our view of the humanists as secularists and individualists who helped inaugurate a modern age they did not fully understand. However, reasons to doubt the popular appraisal of the renaissance writers exist. As a group, the humanists were very religious. Their writings are filled with discussions of Christian virtue, the nature of the soul, and how to worship God. Dante's greatest work is the *Divine Comedy*, a presentation of the afterlife based on the theology of Thomas Aquinas. Dante's work shows that Catholic doctrine could be combined with humanist literary concerns and a fervent desire for social reform.

Francesco Petrarch (1304-1374) opposed scholasticism early on in part because he saw it as an oppressive force contrary to the spirit of true Christianity. He called for a return to Christian virtue and eloquence exemplified by Augustine. Far from reviving paganism, Petrarch tried to free Augustine's eloquence and insight from centuries of dogmatic interpretation and seemingly pointless debate. As we will see below, in northern Europe, humanism would be primarily a movement of religious reform.

Characteristics of Humanism

Humanism cannot be easily defined, but we can generally describe the movement as a return to the ancient classics and a revival of eloquence. Humanism was connected to the great recovery of ancient literature and the rebirth of the study of the Greek language in the fifteenth century. As the Byzantine Empire crumbled, many scholars found refuge in Italy. Among them was Manuel Chrysoloras (1355?-1415). He became the chair of Greek language and literature at the University of Florence in 1397. Florence thus became the leading light of humanist scholarship for over a century and played a major role in preserving Byzantine manuscripts before the final capture of Constantinople.

Humanism was a movement well suited for the city-state culture of renaissance Italy since many of the texts they preserved and studied had originated in the city-state culture of ancient Greece. Therefore many of the humanists promoted the ideals of republican-ism and civic virtue enshrined in the classics and reinterpreted them for their own republican age. The focus on human society and personal responsibility has led to the claim that humanism was essentially pagan and opposed to the life of faith. That is an overstatement at best. The humanists promoted an understanding of faith that stressed one's responsibility in the world and that saw the individual human as a special divine creation. It is little wonder that the religious art of the Renaissance often focused intensely on the humanity of Jesus and his followers. Unlike the mystics and ascetics who urged the lovers of Christ to separate themselves from emotion and the cares of the world, the humanists praised noble motives and advocated engagement in human affairs. However, they also promoted the classical ideals of balance and harmony. Passion should not rule the mind; neither should the head be divorced from the heart.

The humanists rejected the scholastic method that had dominated medieval education in favor of a literary education. Rather than studying the authoritative interpretation of traditional texts, the humanists embraced a fresh reading of the original sources; a direct encounter with the ancient authors. Humanism, not surprisingly, stressed the study of grammar and rhetoric and developed sophisticated philological tools in an effort to establish the original texts.

The Middle Ages was a great period of forgery and pseudopigrapha, and the humanists labored in their studies to separate the authentic from the forged; the text from the interpretation. The greatest of the humanist detectives was Lorenzo Valla (1406-1457) who proved that the so-called Donation of Constantine was actually an eighth-century forgery written to buttress papal claims against the claims of secular rulers. Valla also demonstrated that the mystical writings attributed to Dionysius the Aereopagite were written hundreds of years after the New Testament; therefore the author could not be the Dionysius converted by St. Paul.

While such investigations into the authenticity of authoritative texts disturbed many in the church, particularly when Valla argued that the apostles did not write the Apostle's Creed, he did not intend to undermine Christianity. To the contrary, Valla tried to purify Christianity by removing forged documents and spurious writings so that the true words of the apostles and church fathers could be better understood and appreciated. We err when we judge the humanists by the use that later thinkers made of their work.

The New Platonism

Aristotle was the philosopher for the scholastics; in many ways Plato was the philosopher for the humanists. Platonism had been very influential in the development of Christian theology in the early church, particularly in the writings of Origen, the Cappadocians, and Augustine, but most of Plato's own works were lost to the West for a thousand years. The revival of Greek studies led to a recovery of Plato, and in 1462 Cosimo de' Medici founded the Platonic Academy in Florence, an informal collection of scholars led by the brilliant Marsilio Ficino (1433-1499).

Ficino revived neoplatonism and the concept of the hierarchy of being. All things flow from the divine and share in the divine nature, but humans have a special position in the middle of the hierarchy. Humans have a soul and body, thus they bridge the gap between the world of spirit and the material world. The divine *logos,* Christ, illumines the soul so that it can return to the divine. While the church and sacraments may help in the ascent of the soul, philosophy and virtue are more important than outward observance. Pico della Mirandola (1463-1494) who gave a stirring account of human worth in his *Oration on the Dignity of Man,* expounded similar ideas. In his quest for knowledge and religious truth, Pico della Mirandola also promoted the study of Hebrew texts, particularly the mystical Kabbala.

The brilliance of Italian scholarship attracted the attention of northern scholars, many of whom traveled to Italy to study Greek and Latin. Nicholas of Cusa (1401-1464) studied canon law at Padua in preparation for a career in the church. While in Italy he learned classical Latin and Greek and was influenced by the new Platonism, although he never fully took part in the humanist circles. Cusa brought together neoplatonism with medieval mysticism in a creative synthesis that would influence German philosophy four centuries after his death. For Cusa, God is the unity of opposites, the transcendent that embraces all reality. We can never know God fully, but can only reason through symbols and analogy. Ultimately, God's reality must be grasped by intuition rather than reason. Cusa argued that worship and religion point us to the greater reality of God; therefore ultimately no conflict exits between Judaism, Islam, and Christianity. All three are different expressions of the one divine unity. Interestingly, Cusa's concern for unity and harmony led him to reject conciliarism in favor of papalism. He believed that only a single, authoritative pope could guarantee the unity of Christendom.

As a cardinal of the church, Cusa was the most prominent supporter of the new learning, but Rudolf Agricola (1444-1485), a professor at Heidleberg who studied in Italy in the 1470s, did the most to promote humanist educational reform in German schools. Rhetoric and classics slowly gained a larger place in school curricula, particularly in the secondary schools. The introduction of the printing press by Johann Gutenberg in Mainz around 1450 aided reform efforts immensely. The humanists made extensive use of the new technology to publish rediscovered classics, new grammars and dictionaries, and their own literary creations. For the first time in human history, scholars could work independently on identical texts confident in the purity of the source. The printing press also lessened the costs of books, which assisted the humanist goal of bringing education to a greater number of common persons. The effect of the printing press on the history of Christianity, the study of the Bible, and modern culture itself can hardly be overestimated.

Hebrew Studies

Johannes Reuchlin (1455-1522), followed the lead of Pico della Mirandola and in 1485 began studying with Jewish scholars to learn Hebrew and the Kabbala. In 1506, he published *De rudimentis Hebraicis*, the first printed Hebrew grammar and lexicon. This volume allowed contemporary and later scholars to make new translations of the Old Testament from Hebrew, but Reuchlin also pointed out disturbing differences between the Latin Vulgate and the Hebrew scriptures, such as the fact that the Vulgate included a number of books not found in the Jewish scriptures. Even the books common to both scriptures differed in significant details, an observation that gave impetus to the modern critical study of the Old Testament.

Reuchlin's love of Hebrew led to one of the most bitter intellectual battles of the late Renaissance when, in 1509, a converted Jew named Pfefferkorn turned against his people and sought to outlaw all Jewish books and writings in Hebrew. Reuchlin was appalled at the news of a public burning of Jewish books in Cologne, and he defended both the rights of Jews to their own literature and the need for Christian scholars to learn Hebrew. The Inquisition brought him to trial and eventually ordered him to surrender his Hebrew works. Humanists all over Europe defended Reuchlin and the right to free inquiry, sometimes resorting to satire and ridicule to make their point.

English Humanism

Humanism was promoted in England by John Colet (1467-1519) who had studied with the early Greek scholars Grocyn and Linacre. Inspired by their example, Colet left for Italy in 1493 and for three years associated with the Platonic Academy in Florence. Colet, though appreciative of Plato, was less interested in philosophy than in scripture, and when he returned to England he began lecturing on the Pauline epistles at Oxford University. Colet rejected the scholastic approach of presenting the authoritative and traditional commentaries of Paul. His only text was the letters of Paul themselves. Moreover, he applied humanist methods to the scripture, presenting Paul's writings in their historical and literary context. He examined Paul's rhetoric, for instance, in order to uncover what Paul intended to communicate rather than using isolated verses from Paul to support a certain theological system. He wanted to help students discern the "pure doctrine" of Paul for themselves. He offered a radically new approach to the study of scripture, and Colet soon attracted a large following, some of whom would become leaders in the English reformation. In reading Paul, Colet discovered the idea of justification by faith.

As in Italy, humanism in England was very much an affair of the laity, and the greatest of the English humanists was a man who refused to enter the priesthood. Thomas More (1478- 1535) studied law rather than theology and became a member of Parliament in 1504. He had given serious thought to the priesthood, but decided that he was not called to the celibate life. This did not mean, for More, that he was not called to be religious, however. After his marriage in 1505 he tried to make his home into a religious and educational center. He led an informal group of scholars dedicated to the classics and to educational reform. One of England's best Greek scholars, More even taught his daughters to read and write Greek and Latin. This was a bold and controversial act in an age in which women were thought to have inferior minds, but his daughters disproved popular misogyny when they became active participants in the intellectual life of the More circle.

More defended the humanists from critics at Oxford, asserting that while no one needs to know Greek in order to be saved, secular education does train the soul in virtue." In addition, More rejected the scholastic method, preferring that students encounter the scriptures and the church fathers directly, he argued that students must be well-trained in the liberal arts and ancient languages before they can really understand the scripture and the fathers. More gave literary shape to his proposal for a humanistic reform of church and state in his famous *Utopia*, written after 1509 and published in 1516. *Utopia* was offered as a model for a truly Christian society where people lived according to both natural law and the gospel. In *Utopia*, all people were to be educated, laws were to be just, and Christian charity would be commonplace.

King Henry VIII was attracted to the talented and articulate More who soon became a trusted royal advisor. In 1529 More replaced Cardinal Wolsey as Lord Chancellor, the highest office in England, but three years later he resigned his office over a dispute concerning Henry's treatment of the church. When he refused to sign the act of Supremacy in 1534, which will be discussed in a later chapter, More was imprisoned in the tower of London for over a year. He found comfort in his faith and his studies. Refusing to violate his convictions, More was beheaded on July 6, 1535, demonstrating that humanists could also be martyrs.

Humanism was also influential in France during this same period. One of the first great French humanists was Jacques LeFevre Etaples (1460?-1536), also known as Faber Staupulensis, who was influenced by Nicholas Cusa and Marsilio Ficino. LeFevre visited Italy in 1491-92 and associated closely with the Platonic Academy. After a religious experience in 1507, he devoted himself to sacred studies, using the tools of humanism. Like Colet in England, LeFevre sought to uncover the true meaning of the scriptures without relying on a tradition he considered corrupt and barbaric. LeFevre affirmed in good humanist fashion that the church should teach nothing about God that is not found in the scriptures themselves. His 1512 translation of the Pauline epistles included his commentary in which he stressed that salvation does not come through good works but only by the grace of God.

LeFevre was a brilliant Latin scholar who devoted his attention to the study of the Vulgate. He was aware that the Vulgate text had been corrupted over the years, and he sought to return it to its original reading. In 1509 he published a critical edition of the Psalms that included five different Latin traditions in a single volume. Although intended as an aid in understanding the official Bible of the church, this *Psalterium quincuplex* highlighted the fact that significant variations existed in the Latin text, undermining confidence in the received tradition. LeFevre was also very fond of the French language and concerned about the education of common persons; therefore in 1525 he published a French translation of the Vulgate versions of the New Testament and Psalms. He also wrote a number of biblical commentaries in French. Like More, LeFevre remained a loyal Catholic despite opposition by some of the French bishops over his scholarship.

LeFevre was the most prominent of a group of scholars and reformers known as the *Cercle de Meaux* (Circle of Meaux). The bishop of Meaux, Guillaume Briçonnet and Marguerite d'Angouléme (1492-1549), one of the most powerful women in the sixteenth century, led the Circle of Meaux. Marguerite d'Angouléme was the sister of the French King Francis I, and she became the Queen of Navarre, in southern France, in 1527. Included in the Circle of Meaux was Guillaume Budé, a Greek scholar who encouraged Francis I to found the Collége de France as a center for the pursuit of wisdom and knowledge.

The Circle of Meaux worked to correct church abuses in southern France, and promoted Christian piety and morality. Education of the laity was a key feature of this reform effort, and the scholars at Meaux worked diligently to bring the liturgy, scripture, and devotional tradition of the church to the average parishioners. Although few of the Meaux circle joined the Protestant movement, the Inquisition eventually crushed the group despite the efforts of Margaurette.

In the 1520s French translations of the Bible were forbidden because of the revolutionary nature of a direct encounter with scripture. After the Inquisition moved against the Circle and put pressure on the Queen to resist heresy, she used her power and influence to support the Protestant Reformation in France and neighboring Switzerland.

Erasmus

The prince of the humanists was the illegitimate son of a priest in Rotterdam in the Netherlands who would gain a European-wide fame unlike any of his contemporaries. Desiderius Erasmus (1466?-1536) was educated at Deventer by the Brethren of the Common Life, an organization of laymen, primarily merchants, who tried to live a serious Christian life without taking monastic vows. Their approach to the Christian life, living devoutly in the midst of daily life, was very congenial to the humanist enterprise. The Brethren introduced Erasmus to the study of literature, but the life of a scholar without a patron can be difficult, and so Erasmus entered a monastery in 1487. Unascetic and social by temperament, Erasmus felt no real calling to the life of a monk, and after being ordained a priest in 1492 he became the secretary for the bishop of Cambrai in 1493. His new position gave him leisure and opportunities to study.

He began to gain a reputation as a humanist scholar in 1500 when he first published his *Adages*, a collection of ancient proverbs and wise sayings. He intended the *Adages* to improve the moral life of students while improving their Latin skills. In 1503, he published a popular guide called *Enchiridion Militis Christiani* (the Handbook of the Militant Christian) to show how an ordinary person may live as a serious follower of Christ. In contrast to medieval devotional guides, the *Enchiridion* stressed the value of life in the real world and downplayed religious ceremonies, the sacraments, and mystical experiences.

The true Christian, for Erasmus, lives a moral life based on the teachings of St. Paul. The true Christian has a practical religion devoted to avoiding evil and doing good, not to extensive prayer, emotional devotion, or ascetic practices. He develops similar themes in his *Colloquies*, which started as exercises in teaching good Latin grammar, but grew into incisive critiques of European religious and social corruption. Erasmus ridicules in particular popular superstition and devotion to relics as magical amulets. He equated much of medieval devotion with outright paganism. For Erasmus, like the Brothers of the Common Life, Christianity is an inward and spiritual matter, not a thing of ritual observances. Charity and morality, not pilgrimages and vows, were the proper ways to follow Christ, for Erasmus.

In 1499, Erasmus first visited England where he became close friends with Thomas More and John Colet. Colet encouraged him to devote his talents to the study of holy writings rather than just the pagan philosophers, and to master the Greek language. From 1500 to 1506 Erasmus perfected his knowledge of Greek, and in 1506 he visited Italy where he received his doctorate in theology from the University of Turin, one of the few universities to value humanism. He returned to England from 1509-1514 where he lectured on Greek at Cambridge. He lived with More during this time and encouraged him in the writing of *Utopia*.

At the same time, Erasmus produced his most famous critique of the Christian society of his day, *Moriae Encomium* or Praise of Folly. In the guise of a Praise for Folly, Erasmus pillories many of the practices of his day, particularly abuses of religion. He even pokes fun at scholars like himself and his friend Thomas More. "They add, they alter, they cross something out, they reinsert it, they recopy their work, they rearrange it, they show it to friends, and they keep it for nine years: yet they are still not satisfied with it. At such a price, they buy an empty reward, namely praise."[7]

Not everyone appreciated Erasmus' wit and his critique of abuses and follies. The Netherlands, where he lived from 1514 to 1521, was relatively tolerant, but the opposition of theologians and church officials there forced him to seek refuge in Basle. He had to leave there as well in 1529 because of the conflicts arising over the Reformation. Despite being offered the cardinal's hat, his writings were always in danger of being censored, and he often feared the Inquisition.

Erasmus' most influential, if not his most popular, work was his *Novum Testamentum Graeca*, first published in 1516. With careful scholarship, Erasmus published the first edition of the New Testament based on Greek manuscripts. This was the first time that the original Greek New Testament had been widely available in Europe since the days of the Roman Empire, and it created a great sensation among scholars. Erasmus carefully noted the numerous places where his Greek manuscripts differed from the official version of the Bible, the Vulgate. Although it was later determined that Erasmus' own manuscripts were corrupt, his critical edition stimulated the great period of Bible translation during the Reformation. Editions of the works of the church fathers and a paraphrase of the Pauline epistles would follow.

Erasmus has often been considered a forerunner of the Reformation because of his opposition to medieval superstition and his sincere desire that faith be based on scripture alone, but he never broke with Roman Catholicism. He remained a sincere Catholic who sought to remove all forms of fanaticism from Christianity. He longed for a temperate and understanding faith freed from sectarian squabbles. Christianity is a matter of following natural law and the commands of the gospel, especially the law of love, not doctrinal uniformity and oppression.

In fact, Erasmus vigorously opposed Luther and consistently fought for a unified church as the only hope for peace in society. He understood the danger of religious warfare and continually urged Christians to follow the Prince of

---

[7] Erasmus, "Praise of Folly," trans. and ed. John P. Dolan, *The Essential Erasmus* (New York: Meridian, 1964) 140-41.

Peace not Ares, the god of war. Erasmus' attitude was consistent with the basic humanist approach to church reform. Humanists throughout Europe tried to work within the Catholic Church to remove a number of abuses and promote an ideal of Christianity based more on learning and morality and less on ceremonialism and asceticism. They were optimistic that with proper education the human mind could understand what God requires and the human will could accomplish it. As such, they believed that all people should read the Bible for themselves instead of depending on tradition and authority. In our next section, we will meet a second generation of humanists who would take many of the same ideas and apply them in ways that horrified men like Erasmus and More.

Part 2

The Protestant Reformation

IN THE PREVIOUS chapter we examined some of the efforts to reform the medieval church as the feudal order broke down. Most of the reform efforts tried to correct moral and ecclesiastical abuses without seriously challenging the structure of the Western church. The humanists, for instance, used their urbanity and wit to ridicule religious devotions that appeared to them more superstitious than pious, while the concilliarists sought to restrain the power and corruption of the renaissance papacy. With the exception of the radical Hussites, the late medieval reformers wanted to preserve the unity of the church and its position within society while purifying both church and society of abuses and immorality. However, the church as an institution had grown increasingly rigid and resistant to change.

A new call for reform, voiced by an obscure German monk early in the sixteenth century, would shatter the old order. By the middle of that troubled century, Western Christianity would be divided into two camps that persist to the present: Catholicism and Protestantism. The reforming effort that splintered the church marks such a turning point in Western history that many know it simply as the Reformation, as if no others ever took place.

A number of things contributed to the Reformation of the sixteenth century, and it is worthwhile to note briefly some of them here even though we cannot take the space to go into them in detail. At the time of the Reformation, Europe experienced a major economic transition from feu-dalism to an early form of capitalism fueled in part by colonialism. The old system of nobility crumbled as wealth began to be measured in terms of mney and commerce, rather than land and retainers. Kings became indebted to bankers, such as the Fuggers of Augsburg, and peasants saw their traditional rights eroding. Discontent was evident throughout Europe, but especially in the Holy Roman Empire. People directed much of their discontent towards a church that used a variety of means, such as church fees and tithes, to bring money into Rome. The call for a break with Roman and clerical privileges was well received by the growing middle class as well as by many secular rulers.

Moreover, the aggression of the Ottoman Turks imperiled the eastern portion of the Empire. The city of Constantinople fell in 1453, and much of the old Byzantine Empire came under the rule of Muslims. The Turks even threatened the city of Vienna in the heart of Central Europe. The struggle with the Muslims prevented the emperor Charles V from dealing with the Protestants the way his predecessors had dealt with the Hussites.

A third major factor in the spread of the Reformation was a new invention that allowed words and thoughts to be spread over a vast area at a low cost. The printing press ushered in the era of popular media and propaganda, and the reformers effectively used the new tool in their efforts to redefine the church. In short, the tender was there for a major conflagration, but a young German monk named Martin Luther would light the fire.

Chapter 9

The Reformation in Germany

Martin Luther (1483-1546)

IN 1505, THE son of Hans Luder, a modestly prosperous miner, was studying law at the recently established University of Erfurt. Hans had impressed upon the boy the need to be a success in the world, but as young Martin was walking one day a thunderstorm suddenly came up. Lightning struck the ground near him and threw him to the ground. In terror the student cried out to heaven, "St. Anne help me! I will become a monk." His statement marked the first great turning point in the life of a man who would later reject the cult of the saints and monasticism itself.

Over his father's strenuous objections, Martin Luther kept his vow. He turned away from the study of law and joined the Augustinian canons at Erfurt. Luther diligently followed the routine of prayer seven times daily, and sought to control his sinful desires through frequent fasting. He engaged in intense self-examination and confession, exhausting himself and his confessor in the process. Many have written about the holiness of God, but Luther felt deep in his soul that holiness is accompanied by the feeling of worthlessness. The awareness of God's holiness and human sinfulness grew in the young monk.

Despite his efforts at being a good monk, he always had doubts. Did I fast enough, did I pray enough, did I do enough to please God? He observed all of the rituals of the church, but found no peace in them. How can we be forgiven for every sin if we cannot even remember all of our sins? What hope does sinful humanity have before a righteous God?

In 1510 Luther was sent to Rome to help argue a legal case in which the order was involved. His supporters hoped that the journey to the holy city would ease his inner turmoil. He went to the shrines, walked up the Vatican steps, and paid for prayers and blessings, but nothing helped remove the feeling of his complete unworthiness. Not only did the pilgrimage not salve his troubled soul, he lost some of his faith in the church itself when he saw first hand the greed, lust, and luxury in Rome. He saw how the money of simple peasants in Germany enriched the palaces and tombs of popes and cardinals in Renaissance Italy.

Justification by Faith

Despite his spiritual anguish, Luther advanced in his studies, and in 1511 his order sent him to the University of Wittenberg, a new university founded by the Elector of Saxony as a way to increase the prestige of his principality. The following year Luther became a Doctor of Theology and began lecturing on the scriptures. His confessor, a wise older monk named Staupitz, thought this new task would help get Luther out of his spiritual depression. Engagement with the scripture would indeed lift Luther out of his spiritual malaise, but it did not have the effects Staupitz anticipated.

The pivotal moment came when Luther was preparing lectures on the Psalms and the letters of Paul, particularly Romans and Galatians. At some time between 1516 and 1519, Luther came to a profound spiritual insight while struggling over Paul's statement that "the righteous shall live by faith." Years later, Luther reported that he had always identified God's righteousness with God's wrath. He knew from personal experience that no one can be truly righteous before God:

> My situation was that, although an impeccable monk, I stood before God as a sinner troubled in conscience, and I had no confidence that my merit would assuage him. Therefore I did not love a just and angry God, but rather hated and murmured against him. Yet I clung to the dear Paul and had a great yearning to know what he meant. Night and day I pondered until I saw the connection between the justice of God and the statement that the just shall live by his faith. Then I grasped that the justice of God is that righteousness by which through grace and sheer mercy God justifies us through faith. Thereupon I felt myself to be reborn and to have gone through open doors into paradise.[8]

Luther looked upon God in a whole new way. This was not the God who demanded human perfection, but the God who loved creation enough to

---

[8] Quoted in Roland Bainton, *Here I Stand: A Life of Martin Luther* (Nashville: Abingdon Press, 1973) 49.

suffer and die for sin. Righteousness is the work of God alone; it is not something sinful humans can do.

Luther made a radical break with the dominant theology of the late medieval church. The *via moderna* theologians that Luther had studied, such as Duns Scotus and Gabriel Biel, argued that salvation was essentially based on human merit. According to this theology God had made a deal with humans; if they did what was in their power for salvation, God would save them. In other words, God requires that we do what we can do, most especially to love God above all created things, in order for us to be saved. Luther's new idea that Christians are justified by faith alone shattered the previous understanding of salvation.

According to Luther, humans can do nothing to earn salvation. We are too sinful even to make the first move toward salvation. Although no human can claim any merit or stand justified before the holy God, this same God, through the sacrifice of Jesus imputes his righteousness to sinful creatures. We are proclaimed righteous through the gracious mercy of God, and become aware of this justification through faith alone. For Luther all Christians are both righteous and sinners at the same time. Luther's insight that sinners are saved by faith undergirded his entire theology and became the distinguishing feature of Protestantism. Much of the church's sacramental system was rejected in favor of faith alone since religious works such as penances, sacraments, or pilgrimages did not save people's souls. Furthermore, for Luther all Christians equally sin before God. Therefore saints also sin and lay persons are also priests.

The Indulgence Controversy

So far, Luther's story is one of personal intellectual and spiritual development. The story might have stopped there, but around the same time the young doctor of theology became publicly embroiled in one of the most controversial issues of his day, namely the selling of indulgences. We have seen that the church of the fifteenth and sixteenth centuries spent lavishly on artwork and architecture. Not only the popes, but also cardinals and archbishops competed in adorning their cathedrals and palaces. Moreover, church leaders involved themselves in the numerous petty wars that plagued Italy during the Renaissance. Beauty and political involvement were expensive, and the church could not get sufficient income simply through pious offerings or feudal endowments. One of the new creative ways to raise funds was through the sale of indulgences.

Since the early Middle Ages the church had taught that even though a person's sins have been forgiven in this life, there was still the possibility that penance might be required in the afterlife before one could enter paradise. Purgatory was the place where a soul suffered in order to be purified before entering into heaven. In the late Middle Ages, the papacy approved the idea that people could be relieved of some of the pain of purgatory through an indulgence. Originally a bishop or pope granted an indulgence in order to relieve someone of a difficult penance imposed in this life. For instance, a sacrificial gift to the church could substitute for the penance of going on a pilgrimage. Over time, the papacy reserved the right of granting an indulgence, and in the fifteenth century connected the idea of the indulgence with that of a penance to be paid in purgatory. In other words, the late medieval church taught that an indulgence could release a person from the sufferings in purgatory. In theory the sacrifice of paying for an indulgence replaces the sacrifice of suffering in purgatory, but in practice it took the form of selling salvation to people who lived in fear of the afterlife.

Just as Luther achieved his theological breakthrough, Albrecht of Brandenburg became the new archbishop of Mainz, and the papacy granted him permission to sell indulgences to pay off his debts. Albrecht employed a popular and effective indulgence preacher named Tetzel who preached that his indulgences would forgive all sins and bring release to relatives in purgatory. He used a sliding price scale according to social status so that it cost twenty-five florins for bishops to receive forgiveness, but only three for merchants. Even poor peasants could buy some time off of their future suffering. Tetzel urged the crowds to listen to the cries of their loved ones. Your mother is suffering; are you so hard hearted and greedy that you will not pay for her release? How could they free their loved ones from the fires of purgatory? Simply by buying an indulgence, Tetzel assured his listen-ers. "As soon as a coin in the coffer rings, a soul from purgatory springs."[9]

As a priest, Luther saw members of his flock spending their limited incomes on the indulgences offered by Tetzel. In confession, some told him that they did not need to do the penance he imposed because they had already purchased their indulgences. On 31 October, 1517, the eve of All Saints Day, Luther proposed a public debate on the subject. Scholars frequently held debates in those days, and it was customary to post a debate topic on the door of the castle church. Luther drew up ninety-five proposi-tions against the sale of indulgences, nailed them to the door of the church, and offered to debate

---

[9] Quoted by Bainton, ibid., 59.

them with anyone who would defend indulgences. Luther attacked indulgences from a number of sides, but there were four main notions. (1) Indulgences endanger people's souls by giving them false security. Instead of repenting of their sins and turning to God, people paid cash for forgiveness. (2) The pope has no authority over purgatory. (3) If the pope can save souls from suffering, then he should do it free of charge out of Christian charity. (4) Indulgences were impoverishing Germans for the sake of glorifying Rome.

Many people date the beginning of the Reformation to the posting of the *Ninety-five Theses*, but it does not appear that Luther intended them to generate the controversy they did. They are rather dry and scholastic. What happened? Others who were also concerned over the state of the church in Germany translated the *Theses* into German and used the new printing press to distribute them widely. In response, church officials attacked Luther in print and in sermons. Luther had demanded a debate, but it soon became a debate argued in the popular media.

As the controversy warmed and grew increasingly public, the pope sent Cardinal Cajetan to change Luther's mind, if not his heart. The monk and cardinal held a clandestine meeting that went poorly. The cardinal appealed to Luther to give up his fight and submit to the authority of the church. Luther insisted that the church instead submit to the authority of scripture. It was a fight over which is the prime value: unity or integrity. The church wanted to call Luther a heretic; however, he had already won the support of the elector of Saxony and other powerful Germans.

The Break with Rome

Luther finally got his longed for debate when John Eck (1486-1543), a theologian at the University of Leipzig, accepted Luther's challenge for a formal debate on the issue of indulgences. It was set for July 1-4, 1519 at Leipzig. Luther arrived with 200 armed students and his trusted colleague Philip Melanchthon (1497-1560), who taught Greek at the Universi-ty of Wittenberg. All were aware of what happened when Hus had gone to debate his theology at the Council of Constance. Eck was also provided with a large body guard. Eck proved a formidable opponent, and in the course of the controversy he argued that Luther's statements reflected the ideas of the convicted heretics Wyclif and Hus. He backed Luther into a corner. If he denied those statements, he risked undermining his opposition to indulgences, but if he affirmed them he risked being labeled a Hussite. While ecclesiastical and secular authorities looked on, Luther asked for time to prepare a response. He went to the library and read the official chronicle of the Council of Constance. When he returned to the debate he shocked everyone, including Eck, by declaring that Hus was right and the Council had erred. Friends and enemies named Luther the Saxon Hus.

Things moved rapidly after this. Luther's writings, written in a lively German, sold all over Germany, but the church took action to stop him. On June 15, 1520 Pope Leo X issued the bull *Exsurge Domine*, which condemned Luther on forty-two counts of heresy and gave him sixty days to recant or be excommunicated. Luther publicly burned the bull along with a copy of the canon law to show that the church, not Luther, needed reforming.

That same year, Luther wrote four important works that would prove that he was more radical than even the infamous Hus. In *An Address to the German Nobility* Luther challenged the idea of papal supremacy and argued for the priesthood of all believers. He went a step further in *The Babylonian Captivity* by attacking the sacramental system itself along with monastic vows and clerical celibacy, thus undermining the entire medieval church structure. In *Against the Execrable Bull of Antichrist* Luther took the bold step of declaring that the papacy itself was the antichrist, the diabolical agent working against Christ in the world. The last of the 1520 works was *On the Freedom of the Christian*, one of the great documents celebrating the freedom of conscience and social responsibility. On January 3, 1521, the pope, whose authority Luther no longer acknowledged, formally excommunicated Luther.

Luther might have suffered the fate of earlier reformers, such as Hus or Savonorola, but he had a powerful protector in Frederick, the Elector of Saxony. The newly elected Holy Roman Emperor, Charles V, was also at first reluctant to move against Luther and cause civil war in his realm, particularly at a time when he needed support in his crusade against the Turks. In 1521, Charles called for an imperial Diet to meet at the town of Worms in order to get the taxes and men he needed to wage war against the Muslims. On April 23 and 24, 1521, Luther was called before the Diet and given the choice of either recanting or facing arrest and possible death. The papal representative asked him if he repudiated his books and their errors, but Luther replied that he could not and would not recant anything unless convinced "by Scripture and plain reason." According to some accounts, he ended by stating, "Here I stand. I can do no other. God help me. Amen."

Toward the end of the Diet, Luther was officially declared a heretic and outlaw, but by that time he had been safely hidden away by the Elector of Saxony in the Wartburg Castle where he lived disguised as a knight. While in seclusion in the Wartburg, Luther began his monumental translation of the scriptures from the original Greek and Hebrew into German so that brewers and merchants could read the Bible for themselves. Luther's writings against the medieval church and his heroic stand at the Diet of Worms excited the imagination and the hopes of many in Germany. The second generation of humanists, scholars such as Melanchthon and Calvin, flocked to his cause. Already in 1521 Melanchthon produced the first Protestant systematic theology, the famous *Loci communes*, based primarily on scripture. Melanchthon also followed the practice of Luther and Erasmus in publishing biblical commentaries that rejected the medieval practice of looking for four senses of scripture. Instead he dealt mainly with the literal reading of the text, inaugurating a new approach to theology and exegesis.

Not only intellectuals and preachers joined Luther's crusade. Some of the lesser nobility, such as Ulrich von Hutten, saw the battle against corruption as a chivalrous way to regain the prestige they were losing to the growing power of the state. Some of the higher nobility, such as the Elector of Saxony, on the other hand, saw this as a way to assert sovereignty within the Empire. Luther's exaltation of the role of the ordinary Christian in the priesthood of all believers attracted merchants and various tradesmen. Many of the peasants saw Luther as one of their own, courageously defending the rights of the commoner against the power of the church.

Luther's words helped ignite a firestorm of discontent that was united only in its opposition to the church. In saying that Luther's activities touched social needs and desires we should not overlook the fact that many people genuinely believed his message. We should also remember that many faithful and intelligent people, such as Erasmus and Thomas More, genuinely rejected it. For Luther and his followers, though, the break with Rome was now complete, and Western Christendom would never be the same.

Marriage and Family

Luther and his colleagues agreed that the Augustinian cloister should disband, and that the monks should be allowed to marry. Monasticism, according to Luther, was based on the false premise that celibacy was a higher calling than married life; that monks are more holy than married persons. Originally, the word "vocation" or calling referred to the taking of monastic vows, but for Luther, every Christian has a vocation in life, a calling by God. Although this idea has been watered down through the years, we still refer to careers as vocations, based on Luther's idea.

In particular, Luther viewed marriage and parenthood as holy vocations. Some historians credit Luther with defining the modern idea of family. The status of ordinary wives was elevated, and the pastor's wife had a distinctive role in the Christian community. Rather than women being viewed as the source of sin, as in much earlier Christian theology, they were soon portrayed as agents for God's grace in the home. Men and women did not have to deny their sexuality in order to pursue holiness. In fact, marriage may even be more holy than celibacy since it is in some ways more difficult, as Luther discovered through personal experience.

In 1523, a group of nuns in a nearby village wrote Luther for help in escaping their cloister. It was a capital offense to kidnap a nun or help her break her vows, but Luther carefully arranged the plans. A local merchant hid twelve nuns in his wagon and brought them to Wittenberg. Luther prayed that "God grant them husbands lest worse befall," and went to work to arrange marriages. All but one found husbands. Her name was Katherine von Bora, a woman of twenty-six, almost too old to get married. She let it be known that she would marry no one but Luther himself.

Although Luther had resolved to remain a bachelor, in 1525 he and Katie married. Family life had an effect on Luther and his theology. He once said that no one should preach about Christ and Mary until he has learned to hang diapers on the line like Mary and Joseph had done for the infant Jesus. It was for his own children that Luther wrote "Away in a Manger" to teach about the earthly life of the savior. Luther continued to preach, teach, write, translate, and compose while Katie took care of Luther, the family, and the numerous refugees that sought shelter at the abbey, which the Elector gave them for a home. In his on-going battle with the pope, Luther said that it was right that the pope should not marry because he did not deserve marriage.

The Radical German Reformation

Luther believed that his reform was a reform of church doctrine. He wanted to call the church back to what he believed was the true teaching of Christ contained in the Bible. In particular, he emphasized the doctrine of justification by faith alone and the full righteousness of Christ that saves the elect. Church practices should not interfere with this fundamental theological point; therefore Luther wanted to remove the language of sacrifice from the Mass, abolish indulgences, reduce the number of the sacraments to the two instituted by Christ himself, and abolish all idea of salvation through works of piety.

However, things that did not contradict scripture or interfere with faith could be tolerated, at least for a while. Luther's reformed version of the Mass, for instance, was very similar to that of the Catholic Church. He translated portions of the service into simple German and removed sacrificial language, but for the most part the Mass remained. Luther also did not object to most of the church's ceremony and decoration, such as clerical robes, candles in church, or religious artwork. Such things could help educate the simple folk, he said. What remained important was whether such aids actually communicated the true doctrine. Not all of Luther's followers agreed.

Andreas Bodenstein, more commonly called Carlstadt (1480-1541), was a colleague of Luther's at the University of Wittenberg who had assisted Luther in the Leipzig debate. While Luther lived in seclusion at the Wartburg Castle, Carlstadt became the leader of the Reformation in Wittenberg. Carlstadt condemned Catholic worship more severely than Luther, and he understood the Reformation slogan *sola scriptura* (scripture alone) differently than Luther. Carlstadt preached that only the things permitted by scripture are allowable. Scriptural justification must exist for all aspects of Christian worship.

While Luther was away, many students at the university and some of the townspeople in Wittenberg agreed with Carlstadt and began disrupting Catholic religious services; mocking priests and monks, desecrating altars, and smashing statues of the saints. On Christmas Eve, 1521, Carlstadt took a bold step and presided at the Eucharist service without his priestly vestments. He reduced the words of the service to the basic words of scripture, and he gave lay persons both the bread and the wine. He renounced the idea of priesthood and proclaimed that the minister merely administrated the Eucharist. In other words, Carlstadt served communion like the Taborites of old. The next day he took an even more radical step against the traditional view of the priesthood and announced his engagement.

Around this same time a group of religious enthusiasts who had been expelled from the village of Zwikau arrived in Wittenberg. They preached that the Holy Spirit was still active in the church giving revelation to prophets, just as in the days of the New Testament. These self-styled prophets preached against infant baptism, religious artwork, and the power of priests. Carlstadt and even Melanchthon were at first attracted to the prophets, when Luther heard what was going on back home, he immediately left the safety of the Wartburg and returned to Wittenberg where he asserted his authority. He took direct action against the Zwikau prophets, whom he accused of thinking that they had swallowed the Holy Spirit "feathers and all." He proclaimed in no uncertain terms that the only revelation of God is in the scriptures, and he then convinced the secular rulers that it was dangerous to allow prophets to preach. The Elector had the Zwikau prophets removed from his realm. Luther then turned his attention to Carlstadt and his methods.

In 1523, he published two works: *On Civil Government* and *On the Order of Worship* in which he offered his views on the proper ordering of church and society. The state, with the assistance of the church, should take on the task of improving morals and social life. The church should preach and properly administer the sacraments but avoid the iconoclasm and radical changes at Wittenberg. Carlstadt eventually fled to Switzerland and joined the Reformed movement there, of which we will hear more about later.

The Great Peasants' War

German peasants had a long list of legitimate grievances against the German nobility, especially the bishops, and they saw Luther's teaching as an ally in their cause. In 1525, the same year Luther married, some of the peasants began to organize and demand the restitution of their ancestral rights: such as the right to freely gather wood and hunt in the forests. In March, they published the *Twelve Articles of the Peasants*, which was filled with quotations from Luther and scripture. They began to arm themselves and prepared to take their rights by force if they were not restored freely. In April, Luther wrote *Admonition to Peace* in which he urged the authorities to listen and help the peasants. Instead the nobility turned to war to crush the peasants' movement.

Thus began the largest and most disastrous peasants' rebellion in European history, the great Peasant's War of 1525. Luther heard the rumors of rioting peasants sacking monasteries and pillaging cathedrals. Always mindful of earthly authority, he was horrified. In May, he wrote a tract titled *Against the Robbing and Murdering Hordes of Peasants* which urged the nobility to kill without mercy the rebellious peasants. He argued that God had established civil authority, thus Christians must obey those authorities even when they are unjust. Christians have no right to rebellion, only to prayer, Luther said. The nobility needed little encouragement from Luther to slaughter the peasants, which they did with great efficiency and cruelty, but Luther lost the support of the masses because of that pamphlet. Lutheranism would never reach the heart of the German peasants.

One of Luther's bitterest enemies was neither a Catholic theologian, nor a rebellious peasant; it was a fellow reformer and former priest named Thomas Müntzer (1488-1525). He was a brilliant, courageous, and compelling preacher whom Carlstadt converted to the Reformation in 1520. For a couple of years Müntzer preached in Zwickau, Bohemia and Thuringia, and in 1523 he published the first complete liturgy in German. Around this time, though, he broke with Wittenbergers, claiming that Luther was perverting the gospel and not following scripture. He called Luther "Brother Fattened Swine" and "Brother Soft Life" because justification by faith alone seemed too easy. Luther also trusted too much in the German princes and too little in God.

Most important, Müntzer believed that he was a prophet living at the end of time. The apocalyptic struggle between the children of light and the antichrist had begun, and God was sending prophecies and visions to his chosen agents, like Müntzer. He filled his sermons with images of destruction culled from the prophecies of John and Daniel, but it was not always clear whether the pope or Luther was the antichrist. Regardless of who the antichrist was, Müntzer clearly saw himself as the leader of the children of light. He joined in the Peasant's War, announcing that it was the final struggle between Christ and Antichrist. Unfortunately for him, the eschatological army of righteousness was defeated at the battle of Frankenhausen. The prophet, found hiding in a barn, was tortured and executed by the German nobility led by the Protestant prince, Philip of Hesse.

Chapter 10

The Swiss Reformation

AS MÜNTZER REALIZED, the Reformation in Germany depended heavily on the rulers of the many small sovereign principalities that made up the Empire. If a prince, such as Philip of Hesse, joined the reform, then his realm became Protestant. Thus Saxony, Hesse, Brandenburg, and the Palatinate joined the Protestant cause, but Bavaria and the Hapsburg lands remained Catholic. In fact, Lutheran princes coined the word Protestant when they made a formal protest at the Diet of Speyer in 1529 and insisted on their right to determine the religion of their subjects. After a period of civil war between principalities of differing religions, this practical solution was agreed to in the Peace of Augsburg in 1555. The religion of a region would be determined by the religion of the ruler according to the formula *cuius regio euis religio* (whoever rules determines the religion). The solution established the pattern of territorial churches in Germany, known as *Landeskirchen*, which secular lords controlled.

Zwingli and the Reformation of the Cities.

The progress of the Reformation was quite different in the free imperial cities of western Germany and the city-states of Switzerland where the burgher class was the major force behind the Reformation. These self-governing cities had elected town councils and provided for their own defense and social services. Unlike Luther who was quite conservative politically, the reformers in Switzerland often combined classical republican ideals of citizenship with religious reform along humanist lines. The churches that would eventually emerge from this Swiss-centered reform are simply called Reformed churches in contrast to the Lutheran churches. Sometimes they are referred to as Calvinist, but the word Reformed is more appropriate since they predate Calvin.

The most important of the early reformers in Switzerland was Ulrich Zwingli (1484-1531) who convinced the city council of Zurich to embrace the Reformation in 1523, roughly at the same time that Luther and Melanchthon tried to bring some order to the Reformation in Wittenberg. Zwingli was a humanist and Greek scholar who became a priest in 1506, serving as the pastor of Glarus. At that time Swiss soldiers were valued throughout Europe as paid mercenaries, and from 1513-1515 Zwingli served as a military chaplain for a company of Swiss mercenaries serving Pope Leo X. As chaplain he began to despise the practice of Swiss men fighting for foreign governments and instead promoted the idea of patriotism, fighting for one's own country.

In 1516 he was appointed preacher at the popular Einseldin shrine. In that year he obtained a copy of Erasmus' edition of the Greek New Testament and began to read the scripture in its original language. Eventually he learned Hebrew as well. As with many reformers, Zwingli's encounter with the Bible in its original languages changed his views on many religious practices. Like Luther, he used his pulpit to oppose simony and the sale of indulgences. Soon he gained a reputation as an engaging and energetic preacher. Crowds flocked to Einseldin, not so much to worship at the shrine as to hear Zwingli rail against church corruption.

In 1518, Zwingli was elected the people's preacher at Old Minster church in Zurich, and the following year he broke with church tradition by preaching directly from the New Testament without using the prescribed lectionary lessons. He preached verse by verse from beginning to end, using the opportunity to attack church abuses, such as simony, but he also began to attack old and accepted doctrines of the church such as purgatory, the invocation of the saints, and monasticism. When some of the citizens of Zurich publicly broke the required Lenten fast in 1522 by eating meat, Zwingli defended them on the grounds that ceremonial fasts are unbiblical. The bishop protested, particularly since Zwingli's followers openly ridiculed Catholics, but the Town Council supported the fast breakers and rejected the bishop's authority in the matter. In Zurich and elsewhere in Switzerland, the Reformation and the drive toward political independence went hand in hand.

By the beginning of 1523 the religious controversy caused by Zwingli's preaching had grown so disruptive that the Town Council called for a public disputation to decide a number of issues related to church law. Zwingli represented the side that called themselves evangelicals, meaning gospel-based. The vicar of the Bishop of Constance represented the Catholics, but the

Council forced the Bishop to base his arguments on scripture rather than church tradition or authority. The Council's demand essentially silenced him in the debate; therefore the Council declared Zwingli the winner and decreed that the sole basis of religious truth is the Bible, which teaches that salvation comes by faith alone.

Accordingly, indulgences, prayers to the saints, required fasts, clerical celibacy, monastic vows, and the papacy itself were all rejected. Zwingli opposed clerical celibacy, in part because scripture does not command it, and in part because he knew from personal experience how difficult it was to remain celibate. He confessed that he had broken his vow on a number of occasions. In 1524 he married Anna Reinhard, a widow with whom he had been involved for two years.

Zwingli's theology rested on two major principles: that only what scripture clearly states is lawful for the church, and that religious authority rests with the community as exercised through legitimate civil authority. For Zwingli and the Reformed tradition, reformation must include a reformation of society as well as of the church. Zwingli won a second disputation held on October 26, 1523, and pushed the Council to approve of serving the wine as well as the bread in the Lord's Supper, which Zwingli argued was merely a memorial meal. The Council then decreed that his new catechism for clergy was to be used to retrain priests and preachers who chose to remain in Zurich. In 1525, the Council officially abolished the Mass in Zurich. They also removed pictures and images from churches because Zwingli convinced them that the Ten Commandments forbade images. Iconoclasm (image breaking), motivated by a literal reading of the biblical law, became a distinguishing feature of the Reformed tradition.

These ideas spread to neighboring Swiss cantons. In 1528 the city of Bern held a similar disputation, and soon that city joined the Reformation. The practice of public debates demonstrates both the Protestant stress on the priesthood of all believers and the humanist confidence in human reason. Soon after Bern went Reformed, Basle, St. Gall, Schaffhausen, and Constance followed. The preaching and teaching of a woman reformer, Katherina Zell, in large part won the imperial city of Strasbourg for the Reformation. The scholarly and irenic former Dominican, Martin Bucer (1491-1551) became the leader of the church in Strasbourg and tried to unite the local Protestant churches through his Tetrapolitan Confession in 1530. Bucer would die in England while assisting the Protestant cause there.

The Colloquy of Marburg

By 1529 most observers clearly saw that the attempt to reform Christianity would lead to war on a major scale. Pope Clement VII (1523-34) sent his legate Campeggio to the Nürnberg Reichstag in 1524 to insist that Luther be arrested and his movement squashed. The emperor Charles V, though, remained reluctant to bring his rebellious subjects back to obedience to the Holy See by force since he needed the support of the Elector of Saxony.

Campeggio organized a Catholic League under Duke George, a rival of the elector John of Saxony. The pope also created an Italian League that included France, Venice, and Florence to put pressure on Charles. The Protestant prince Philip of Hesse, who had led the suppression of the peasant's rebellion, formed a Lutheran League, a military alliance of the Lutheran principalities. Since war appeared imminent, he also wanted to form a strong alliance among all Protestants in central Europe; therefore he strongly urged Luther and Zwingli to join their efforts in a common Protestant cause. He arranged a theological colloquy between the Swiss and the German reformers to meet at Marburg in 1529.

Luther and Zwingli disagreed on a number of matters and also distrusted one another personally. Luther was inclined to dismiss Zwingli as a dangerous radical like Carlstadt with whom he had earlier fought in Wittenberg. Zwingli felt that Luther remained too Catholic, and had not fully accepted his own teachings on the authority of scripture. For Zwingli, Luther's stress on the freedom of the Christian from the law seemed to open the door to immorality and lawlessness. Luther felt certain that Zwingli's literalistic approach to scripture would bind humans to a new legalism and moralistic works righteousness.

Most importantly, the two theologians disagreed completely on the meaning of the Lord's Supper. Although Luther rejected the official Catholic teaching on transubstantiation, the complete transformation of the bread and wine into the real body and blood of Christ, he did believe strongly in the real physical presence of Christ in the Holy Communion. The bread and wine remained bread and wine, but in the context of worship Christ's body and blood were also present to be eaten by the believer.

Zwingli argued that Luther's belief made an idol of the altar. He made a sharp distinction between the symbol and the thing symbolized so that the bread and wine merely represented Christ's body and blood symbolically. The Holy Communion was thus a memorial, a reenactment of the Last Supper so that the worshiper would remember Christ and believe in him. The Lord's

Supper would be the major dividing point between the Lutherans and the Reformed at Marburg, and for decades later.

When Luther and Melanchthon arrived at the meeting, Luther took a knife and carved the words (in Latin) "This is my body" on the table. In this instance, he was the literalist because for him these words of Jesus meant just what they said. Zwingli tried to argue that Jesus meant "this represents my body," but Luther would not accept Zwingli's argument. The man who had defied the emperor and the pope at the Diet of Worms did not intend to bend on an important theological point just to form a military alliance. Zurich and Wittenberg remained divided and vulnerable.

In Switzerland the Reformation was opposed by the five forest cantons of Lucerne, Zug, Schwyz, Uri, and Unterwalden who formed a "Christian Union" in alliance with Hapsburg Austria in 1529. A major battle was fought at Kappel on October 11, 1531. The battle in part resulted from Zurich's use of economic pressure to force other cantons to accept the Reformation. The Catholic cantons responded by attacking an unprepared Zurich. Zwingli managed to raise an army and even led them into battle, but he was captured, killed, and dismembered. Zurich remained Protestant.

Religious Warfare in the Empire

The Holy Roman Emperor Charles V ruled an empire larger than Charlemagne's, but the pope refused to crown him until he promised to move against the Protestant heretics. Charles, as mentioned previously, felt reluctant to do this since there were Turkish armies in Hungary and Austria. Finally he agreed to hold a special meeting of the imperial Diet at Augsburg to settle the religious issue in 1530. Each party prepared a statement of their beliefs in the hope that a reasonable compromise could be reached. Philip Melanchthon drew up the Lutheran statement. The Augsburg Confession of 1530 tried to present the essential beliefs of the Lutherans while giving as much ground as possible for agreement with the Catholics. Melanchthon's document in either its original or altered form would remain the standard confession of faith for Lutherans down to the present. Martin Bucer presented the Tetrapolitan Confession of the south German (Imperial) cities, which was closer to the theology of Zwingli, but the Catholic representatives rejected both confessions and insisted on complete submission to Rome.

The Protestant princes and cities formed the Schmalkaldic League in 1531 for mutual defense in case of war. The League was a powerful force until its leader, Philip of Hesse, became involved in a bizarre scandal. Like many princes, Philip married a woman for political reasons, and, like most rulers of the day, he had numerous concubines. Since his conversion to the evangelical cause, however, his conscience bothered him. He thought that if he was married to the one woman he loved, he could be faithful to her. Luther advised him against divorce since that was against God's law, but pointed out that the Old Testament allowed bigamy. Therefore Luther encouraged Philip to secretly marry the woman he loved, even though this was illegal in the Empire. The carefully laid plan fell apart when the girl's mother bragged about her daughter's change in status and Philip's first wife publicly complained. When word of the bigamy and Luther's role in it got out, it destroyed Philip in the Empire and weakened the League.

The League was crushed militarily at battle of Mühlberg in 1547, but the Catholic victory did not end the religious struggle. A number of councils tried to reconcile the Protestants and Catholics theologically (Hagenau, June 1540; Worms, 1540; Regensburg, April 1541), but they reached no agreement. Luther rejected Melanchthon's efforts at compromise with reform-minded cardinals, and the papacy refused to accept recommendations made by regional councils. Charles forced Pope Paul III to call a general council, which met at Trent beginning in 1546. We will look at this council in detail later.

When he became frustrated with the slow progress of the Council, Charles declared the Augsburg Interim of 1548. With the Interim he tried to pacify the Protestants by granting the cup to the laity, allowing clerical marriage, and limiting the authority of the papacy in the Empire. Reichstag adopted the provisions of the Interim on June 30, 1548, but Rome immediately denounced them. Such tokens could no longer satisfy the Protestant reformers either. Soon war broke out again, this time led by the Lutheran princes of northern Germany. The treaty of Augsburg 1555 finally brought peace by acknowledging that no final religious solution could be attained. The treaty recognized as legitimate the Lutheran religion, defined by the Confession of Augsburg, in lands ruled by Lutheran princes in 1552. The Reformed churches, as well as more radical movements, were still outlawed.

Geneva

The Reformation in Switzerland began with Zwingli in Zurich, but Calvin's Geneva would become the most important Reformed city and the center of Protestantism for decades. The conversion of Geneva to Protestantism began with a rivalry between the canton of Bern and the Dukes of Savoy for control of the *Pays de Vaud*, the region around Geneva. When Bern became Protestant in 1528, the town leaders tried to introduce the Reformation in neighboring Geneva as a way to bring Geneva under the authority of Bern. They encouraged a French Protestant named Guillaume Farel (1489-1565) to preach the Reformation. Farel had studied at the University of Paris and had been a member of the humanist Circle of Meaux, mentioned previously, but he had been forced to flee France because of his radical preaching. He was on the Inquisition's list of suspected heretics, so he fled to Basle and then to Strasbourg where he worked with Bucer. Using Strasbourg as a base, Farel managed to convert several small French-speaking Swiss cities to the Reformation during the period 1528-32. Then he went to Geneva where the merchants were in the process of gaining their independence from their bishop-lord. Protestant ideas had already made their way into Geneva before Farel's arrival. In fact, the city was divided between Protestant sympathizers and loyal Catholics. Women as well as men actively participated in the great religious debate.

Marie D'entiere (dates uncertain), the wife of a Reformed preacher, had been abbess of a convent before she converted to Protestantism. She actively promoted the cause verbally and in print. In fact, she wrote the first history of the progress of the Reformation in Geneva as a propaganda piece in 1536. She and other women tried to convince the nuns in a local convent to leave their cloister and join the Reformation. The abbess there, Jeanne de Jussie, eloquently defended the faith of the nuns and argued that for many women the convent was much better than marriage. The debate over whether the Reformation enhanced or reduced the status of women in Europe continues among scholars today. Clearly the separate paths of de Jussie and D'entiere demonstrate that women played active roles in the religious controversy of the sixteenth century, and made independent choices of their own. For her part, D'entiere later discovered that the Reformed Church could also enforce patriarchal values. When she criticized Geneva's clergy in the 1540s and argued from scripture for women's right to preach, the Protestant rulers of Geneva banned her works. This early heroine of the Reformation eventually fled Geneva and died in obscurity.

Geneva was in turmoil in the 1530s. Farel and his assistant Olivet were forced to flee shortly after he began preaching, but he returned in 1534. When rioting broke out in January 1534 the Town Council decided to hold a debate to settle the religious issues. Farel argued the Protestant side, but the debate ended in rioting. The city leaders decided the time had come to drop their alliance with the Catholic city of Freiburg and accept some religious reforms. In the summer of 1535 Farel and his supporters took the initiative and seized Geneva's churches and its cathedral. The rioters began breaking religious images and publicly defying canon law. The next year the General Assembly voted for reformation.

Calvin

As these events were taking place, a young French lawyer named John Calvin (1509-64) was passing through Geneva. Farel recognized Calvin's considerable gifts and approved of his theology, so he convinced Calvin to stay in the city as a preacher and teacher of theology even though he had never been ordained. Calvin pushed for a full reform in Geneva. The Council should not stop with simply getting rid of the bishop and smashing images of the saints; its citizens and government should be radically reformed on biblical principles. Calvin produced a confession of faith, the *Articuli de Regimine Ecclesiae*, which Calvin intended to govern the religious life of Geneva. Threatened by war from Catholic Savoy and splintered by internal dissent, Calvin required that all the citizens of Geneva sign a Protestant confession of faith. Leaders of Geneva eventually accepted his radical idea; therefore every resident of the city with a right to vote had to swear to a Reformed confession of faith or leave the city. Geneva was to be a holy city united under the Reformed Church.

Other than Martin Luther, John Calvin was the most important individual in the Reformation. In some respects he may have been even more influential than Luther because Calvin gave a lasting and effective organization to the Reformed church. His theology would be the basis for Protestant worship and theology for centuries after his death, and his vision of the godly city inspired later religious and political movements in Europe and America. Before moving ahead with the story of Calvin and Geneva, therefore, it seems appropriate to take a look back at Calvin's formative years. Although he will always be associated with Switzerland, Calvin's story begins in France.

He was born in Picardy, and studied the liberal arts in Paris from 1523 to 1528. During that time, he changed his name from Cauvin to Calvin. His father intended for him to pursue a career in the church, perhaps as a canon lawyer, and he had secured a fee-paying benefice for his son when the boy was only twelve years old. The benefice meant that Calvin received the revenues from a congregation even though he was not serving as the priest. This was one of the types of abuse that reformers such as Zwingli criticized.

After his time in Paris, Calvin studied law at Orleans and Brouges for four years. As a student, Calvin displayed a keen intellect and appeared to have a future as a scholar rather than strictly as a lawyer. His first published work, for instance, was a commentary on the Roman philosopher Senecca. However, he shared many of the views of the Circle of Meaux, discussed in a previous chapter, and in 1534 Calvin broke with the path his father had chosen, resigned his benefices, and became a Protestant. During the persecution following the placards incident when someone in Paris posted a number of placards attacking the Mass as idolatrous, Calvin fled to Switzerland. As we have seen, Farel persuaded him to remain in Geneva and put his intellect and eloquence to work for the Reformation there.

Calvin's Geneva

After the Genevan Council accepted his plans for religious life, Calvin was clearly the leader of the Genevan church. He immediately faced a battle with the secular rulers over the issue of excommunication. Calvin stressed the importance of keeping sinners and unbelievers from taking Holy Communion. While the Council agreed that only the righteous should sit at the Lord's table, they disagreed over who should decide on excommunication. True to their Zwinglian roots, the Council asserted that it was the civic leaders' responsibility and right to determine which citizens were not worthy of taking communion, but Calvin asserted that this was an issue for the church. When the controversy grew heated, Calvin promptly excommunicated one of the leading citizens of Geneva. The Council responded by exiling Calvin.

From 1538 to 1541 Calvin lived in Strasbourg ministering to the French-speaking people there. He felt relatively happy to be working in Strasbourg with Bucer, but things were going badly in Geneva. The city was falling under the domination of Protestant Bern, and much discord existed in town among the residents. Furthermore, Cardinal Sadoleto had published a very eloquent appeal for the Genevans to return to Rome and reject the evangelicals.

With some hesitation the council asked Calvin to write a reply to Sadoleto, and then invited him to return to Geneva and take charge of the city's religious life. Calvin returned in 1541, and the Council promptly approved his religious ordinances that insured clerical control of the church. Under Calvin's guidance, they established the Consistory as the governing body for religious affairs. The clergy and town officials made up the Consistory, which oversaw the affairs of church and the moral life of the town. The Consistory had the power of excommunication and could recommend sinners for secular punishment.

The Consistory demonstrated its power when some of the leading citizens opposed Calvin's measures in 1547. On the recommendation of the Consistory, the town council executed Gruet, the most vocal of the rebels, for disturbing the peace. Even more significant was the execution of Michael Servetus (1511-1553). Servetus is famous as a brilliant medical researcher who helped establish the role of the heart in circulation, but he was also a religious thinker. He accepted the reformers' principle of *sola scriptura*, but he argued that the Bible does not establish the doctrine of the Trinity. Jesus may have been God's special agent, but he was not God incarnate. The biblical phrase "Father, Son, and Holy Spirit," according to Servetus, does not mean that God is one in three persons. Servetus published his views, earning the animosity of the Inquisition in Italy and the anger of the Protestants as well. Calvin preached against Servetus' ideas and made it clear that such heresy would not be welcome in Geneva, but the Unitarian theorist decided to publicly challenge Calvin's authority.

Servetus had enough courage to show up in worship in Geneva one day. Calvin recognized him and had him brought before the Consistory. They convicted Servetus of denying the Trinity and handed him over to the magistrate for punishment. Calvin argued that Servetus should be hung as a traitor, but the officials preferred the old practice of burning heretics at the stake. Most of the Protestant leaders, such as Bucer and Bullinger, approved of the magistrate's actions, but voices of dissent rang out. One former minister in Geneva, Sebastian Castellio, wrote a tract protesting religious persecution. When you burn a heretic, he said, you do not save a soul; you only kill a man.

The execution of Michael Servetus reminds us that the Reformation was not about freedom of religion and an end to religious persecution. Rather, the Reformation struggled to reform church and society. The people who carried out the reforms accepted the idea that church and state should work together to enforce religious truth.

Calvin's Theology

Calvin's influence spread far beyond Geneva, and his reputation soon made the city a mecca for Reformed preachers and theologians. Calvin's sermons became very popular and spoke directly to the concerns of the day.

His students wrote down his sermons as he preached them, and, after some editing by Calvin, they were widely published. He also founded the Genevan Academy in 1559 to train preachers and teachers. Calvin always viewed himself as a biblical commentator, and his commentaries and lectures on the Old and New Testaments were also read widely. His most influential product, though, was his *Institutes of the Christian Religion*, a work that went through several revisions. He published the first edition in 1536 as an apology for the evangelical cause in France. As such, the first edition was an extensive confession of faith argued from scripture. Calvin sought to explain the Reformed faith and demonstrate that the Protestants were not dangerous, and that King Francis should tolerate them. Calvin substantially revised the *Institutes* in 1539, while in exile, and he continued to revise it until 1559.

The final edition was less an apology than a systematic statement of Reformed theology. Calvin's legal mind is evident in this monumental work. Unlike Luther, Calvin had little taste for paradox, or the inner struggles of the soul. He did not believe that God is hidden within revelation, as Luther proclaimed, but instead asserted that the scriptures are clear and understandable to any intelligent reader. Calvin intended the *Institutes* to help make clear what the scriptures teach. Revelation, both in nature and in scripture, gives an incomplete, but still trustworthy knowledge of God, humankind, and duty. Although Calvin's approach differed somewhat from Luther, he accepted more of Luther's teaching than Zwingli had. For instance, he stressed the importance of the Eucharist, and he made justification by faith central to his thought. Calvin agrees with Luther and the church father Augustine that humans are saved only by grace. Calvin also argued that the divine law still has an important role in human life. Obedience to God is a basic human duty that binds all people, even pagans; however, such religious devotion does not procure salvation. Humans are saved only by the grace of God.

Calvin's name has become linked with the doctrine of predestination even though he did not invent the idea. We saw it earlier in Hus and Wyclif who argued that the church is the body of the elect. The idea of predestination flows from the belief in the power of God to effect God's will and the belief that sinful humans cannot earn their own salvation. If salvation is entirely a gift of God; then it is also entirely the work of God. Therefore those who are saved, are saved by God. By implication those who are damned, are damned by God.

Calvin made clear the logic of this double-predestination and, unlike Luther, connected it with God's governance of the universe. For reasons humans cannot understand God decreed election before Creation. In other words, as Calvin's students would assert later, Christ died only for the elect, not for everyone. It should be noted, though, that it was Calvin's successors who made the doctrine of predestination the centerpiece of Reformed theology.

Why then do people do good works if it does not affect their salvation? According to Calvin, they do good because it is their duty to do good. There is no salvation without works because those who are saved are given the ability to follow the fundamental laws of God. For Calvin, the law has three functions: it convicts people of their sin; it restrains the vice of unbelievers; and it shows believers how they should live.

Calvin, more so than Luther, looked to the Bible for the rules on how to govern and establish the true church. He believed that Christianity should be based on the Old and the New Testaments, and he remained convinced that the New Testament presented a model of the church that was Presbyterian rather than Episcopal. In other words, a council of clergy and other elected officers should control church affairs, not a single bishop. The church should be republican in structure, just as the Swiss towns were. The republican structure gives the people, including lay persons, much more say in church government than had been previously the case. Such a voice in church affairs often leads to a call for a voice in political affairs. The monarch of France was right to see in Calvinism a threat to royal absolutism.

Moreover, Calvin also accepted the Old Testament idea that God punishes sinners and rewards the righteous in life. Sinners will suffer, and the righteous, including merchants and the bourgeoisie, will prosper if they stay faithful. Calvin's theology, contrary to what one might expect, produced the most activist form of Christianity in Europe during this period. In the nineteenth century the sociologist Max Weber even claimed that Calvinism created the modern work ethic. You do not work for a heavenly reward, rather you work because it is your divine duty to work. The Calvinist work ethic was a necessary, but not sufficient, cause of the rise of capitalism, according to Weber.

Chapter 11

The Radical Reformation

THE LUTHERAN AND Reformed traditions are often referred to as the Magisterial Reformation because the reformers willingly used the power of the state to promote religious reform. Luther, Melanchthon, Zwingli, and Calvin did not reject the medieval Catholic notion of the Christian society; they merely disagreed on how such a Christian society should be organized. Other reformers were more radical in their application of biblical principles. For the most part, they had less interest in apocalyptic prophecy and violence than Thomas Müntzer, and more interest in a literal application of the New Testament for the Christian life.

Although many different types of radical reformers existed, they are joined under the general term Anabaptist because most of the groups rejected infant baptism. The Anabaptists generally called themselves brother and sister and their communities the "gathered church," but their enemies called them Anabaptists, those who rejected baptism. Like the Unity of the Brethren sixty years earlier, these believers refused to participate in the coercion of the state. They rejected military service and the swearing of oaths; therefore the civil authorities viewed them as dangerous. Many of these communities rebaptized their converts, like the Donatists had done back in the fifth century. The Roman Empire outlawed such rebaptism in the days of Augustine, and in the sixteenth century rebaptism again became a crime punishable by death in the Holy Roman Empire and elsewhere in Europe.

Anabaptist Theology

Although Luther and Zwingli strongly opposed religious radicals, Anabaptist theology and practice actually grew out of the teaching of the evangelical reformers. They fully accepted the Reformation's call of *sola scriptura*, to go directly to the Bible as the only guide of the Christian life, but in doing so, they found things in the Bible they thought contradicted the practices of the magisterial reformers. Most important, they believed that the Christian church should be entirely separate from the state and should live by the higher righteousness presented in Jesus' Sermon on the Mount. This included the acceptance of martyrdom.

Despite the great variety of radical movements, we can identify a number of characteristics common to most of the Anabaptist groups in the sixteenth century. They asserted that the New Testament alone is normative for the church's doctrine, ethics, and polity. They used the historical Jesus as the model of the Christian life, in particular his rejection of violence. In contrast, they read the Old Testament allegorically or spiritually, not literally, since it had been supplanted by the new teaching of Jesus. The Anabaptists exercised a strict discipline that included an emphasis on living simply and loving one's enemies. They banned evil doers from fellowship, but argued that neither the state nor the church should persecute them. Last, they rejected systematic theologies, creeds, and confessions of faith in favor of the words of scripture alone.

Swiss Evangelical Anabaptism

Although Thomas Münzter is sometimes depicted as an early Anabaptist, the Anabaptists really emerged in Zurich during the 1520's when Zwingli led the Reformation there. Balthasar Hubmaier (1485-1528), a priest and doctor of theology, introduced the Reformation in his parish of Waldshut in northern Switzerland. Hubmaier openly allied with Zwingli in 1523, but in the October debate of 1523 he disagreed with Zwingli over the issue of baptism. In his pamphlet *On the Baptism of Believers* in 1525, Hubmaier asserted necessity of personal faith for baptism, thus denying the validity of infant baptism. He also advocated for the peasants during the peasant's rebellion, and may have written the Twelve Articles of the Peasants which was used as a manifesto for the rights of the peasants. Unlike Müntzer, though, Hubmaier did not take up arms in the struggle, and he survived the war. However, he was burned at the stake in Vienna in 1528.

Among the early converts to the idea of believer's baptism in Zurich were the ex-priests George Blaurock (1492-1529) and Felix Manz (1500?-1527). Along with the humanist, Conrad Grebel (1498-1526), a member of one of Zurich's leading families, they challenged Zwingli's religious reforms. They argued that Zwingli had not gone far enough in purifying the church of superstition and idolatry.

As we have seen, Zwingli had established the precedent of religious debates which were to be decided on the basis of scripture alone. Some of the Anabaptist leaders debated Zwingli on 17 January 1525 on the topic of infant baptism. Baptism was a vital issue because it marked a person's entry into the church and the state. Most people widely accepted that society needed citizens who were also Christians, but the Anabaptists rejected this idea. In defending infant baptism, Zwingli argued that the Old Testament ritual of circumcision justified Christian infant baptism. The baptism of infants was a sign of the New Covenant, and was necessary to build up a Christian commonwealth. The Anabaptists, on the other hand, rejected such a use of ancient Israelite ritual and instead insisted on a literal reading of the New Testament, which nowhere affirms infant baptism.

Although some in Zurich felt that Zwingli argued from tradition rather than scripture, the City Council remained unconvinced by the Anabaptist arguments. For the magistrates, the stability of the civic order was at stake. The following day, at Zwingli's urging, the Council ordered all unbaptized children to be presented within eight days or the parents would be punished. The Council also outlawed unauthorized preaching and worship in Zurich. In Reformation Zurich, only Zwingli's theology would be tolerated.

On January 21, 1525 at a house owned by Manz' mother, Blaurock took a momentous step and allowed Grebel to rebaptize him. He in turn baptized Grebel and fifteen others. Their rebaptism radically applied the Protestant idea of the priesthood of all believers, and clearly rejected the authority of the Reformed ministers and the city council. Despite the prohibition of unauthorized preaching, the Anabaptists held revivals in the regions around Zurich and baptized their converts. Zwingli vigorously opposed the Anabaptists, but failed to convert them.

In 1526 the Zurich Council ordered that Anabaptists be drowned. Felix Manz was the first to suffer this fate, a cruel mockery of their practice of baptism by immersion, on January 5, 1527. As usually happens in the history of Christianity, the effort to suppress the Anabaptists by force failed. In fact, the movement quickly spread throughout central Europe as Anabaptists fled persecution. Hubmaier took the movement to Moravia where he met with great success until his arrest by Hapsburg authorities.

Persecution and Spread of the Movement

The early Anabaptists sent out numerous itinerant missionaries, some of them former priests and humanists, others simple tradesmen and women. They used the printing press to spread their views. In various cities in Switzerland, the Anabaptists debated in formal disputations with Reformed theologians, but none of the Swiss cities officially endorsed their views. Many radicals, like the early Christian martyrs, used their executions to witness to their understanding of true Christianity. Protestants and Catholics could agree on one thing, it seems, namely the persecution of the Anabaptists. The Imperial Diet of Speyer in 1529 revived Roman law against rebaptism and decreed death for those who rebaptized. Melanchthon's Augsburg Confession expressly condemns the Anabaptists. Blaurock was burned at the stake in Tyrol in 1529.

One of the most important sects to emerge from early Anabaptism was the Hutterites, named for their organizer Jacob Hutter (d. 1529). The Hutterites emerged as a separate community after a division among the Anabaptists during a meeting at Nikolsburg in Moravia. Hubmaier had convinced the Lutheran parish there to embrace Anabaptism, but he offended many fellow believers when he promoted a limited involvement in civil affairs, including military service. His opponents, led by the apocalyptic prophet Hans Hut, argued for complete pacifism and communalism. The Hut contingent left Nikolsburg and founded a pacifist community at Austerlitz in 1528. It quickly grew to several thousand members, but suffered from internal divisions. Hutter took over leadership of one group and established an effective and profitable communal system. The Hutterites thrived in Moravia until the onset of the Thirty Years War.

Many of the Hutterites found refuge in Hungary and the Ukraine where the need for industrious and peaceful peasants outweighed the desire for doctrinal purity. In the nineteenth century some Hutterites immigrated to the western United States, but even in the land of religious freedom they experienced interference from their neighbors and the government because of their communal lifestyle. Today a large Hutterite community exists in Western Canada.

Revolutionary Anabaptists

Not all preachers of the radical reformation supported pacifism. Apocalyptic revolutionaries, like Müntzer, read the book of Revelation as a clarion call for a violent overturning of the current order. Others viewed the church as the new Israel governed by a new Moses, or a new Joshua. All those who opposed the true church of God should be destroyed. We met similar views among the Taborites in Bohemia, but they resurfaced during the Reformation.

Melchior Hofmann (d. 1543) was such an apocalyptic prophet. He converted to Lutheranism early, in 1522, and became a reforming preacher. In 1529 he moved to Strasbourg where the Anabaptists converted him, and he soon started proclaiming that the Last Judgment would be in 1533. Not only would Christ come shortly, he would arrive in Strasbourg. Rather than heeding his dire warnings of doom, the authorities arrested him for disturbing the peace. Hofmann escaped imprisonment and fled to Friesland where he amassed a following. As the fateful year approached, more people joined his cause.

In 1533, after Hofmann had returned to Strasbourg where he had been imprisoned, Jan Mattys (d. 1535) took over the apocalyptically minded group in the Netherlands. Some of his followers gathered in Münster, a city in the midst of religious turmoil. Although Münster was the seat of a bishopric, one of the preachers in town, Bernhard Rothmann, had adopted Lutheranism. As the town council debated the religious questions and the bishop gathered troops to reclaim his see, Pastor Rothmann joined the Anabaptists in 1533. Mattys began sending his followers to Münster. Among them was the charismatic figure Jan Bockelson of Leyden (d. 1536).

Bockelson worked as a tailor and began having visions after moving to Münster. The city quickly became an Anabaptist haven and Mattys urged the true believers to defend themselves and their faith by the sword. On February 25, the Anabaptists, under the leadership of Bockelson and Rothmann managed to take over the town council. They set about creating the purified kingdom of God on earth in anticipation of the imminent return of Christ. Münster was the new Jerusalem predicted in Revelation. They banished from the city those who opposed the rule of the saints, and confiscated their property. Many of the merchants had already vacated the city, leaving wives and daughters behind to care for their property.

By now the bishop was encamped outside the walls with an army to besiege the town. The prophet Mattys, convinced of his divine calling, sallied forth like Gideon, but the Catholic forces soon slaughtered him. After the death of the Mattys, the prophet Jan became more radical. He proclaimed himself the king of the New Jerusalem and instituted forced sharing of property. He also used the Old Testament to justify polygamy. He and his closest followers took other men's wives as their own, often against the women's will. Jan became increasingly tyrannical as the siege continued and famine threatened. He began to execute his opponents publicly.

Finally, in 1535, a resident of Münster betrayed the saints when he showed the besiegers a way into town. The bishop's forces stormed the town and killed hundreds of Anabaptists. King Jan was imprisoned and executed in January of 1536. The kingdom of God at Münster ended in disaster, but it would stand as a symbol of the dangers of religious radicalism for centuries.

The Mennonites

The disaster at Münster did not destroy Anabaptism in the Netherlands. The message of biblical simplicity and communal love continued to appeal to the weavers and other common workers in the Low Countries. One of the most important converts to the movement was Menno Simons (1496-1561) who had left the Catholic priesthood in 1536 after he rejected the doctrine of transubstantiation and the validity of infant baptism. He joined the Anabaptist ministry in 1537, after the Münster debacle.

As an itinerant preacher and tireless writer, Simons worked to rehabilitate the Anabaptist movement in the Netherlands and recall the faithful to their original pacifism and biblicism. His book *Foundation of Christian Doctrine*, published in 1540, became a definitive text for his followers, now called Mennonites. Simons once pointed to the contrast between himself and ministers in other churches. They became wealthy through their false preaching while the Anabaptist commitment to the truth leads to persecution.

By the end of the decade, the Dutch leaders recognized that Anabaptists in general were law-abiding, industrious, and peaceful people. Eventually they were granted freedom of religion and flourished in the Netherlands. In the late seventeenth century, William Penn invited Anabaptists from all over Europe to come to his colony in America where they could find land and peace. Prominent among the immigrants were the Mennonites. In the twentieth century, American Mennonites were notable for their world-wide relief effort, especially in times of war.

Spiritualists

A number of thinkers and preachers developed Reformation tenets in a radical, individualistic direction, quite different from the communalism of the Anabaptists. They are sometimes called mystics, spiritualists or individualists, but no single term adequately fits such diverse thinkers. Many of the spiritualists were humanists who took the anti-institutional tendency of the Reformation to its logical conclusion. Erasmus had argued for decades that morality, not ceremony was important. Luther had proclaimed that faith, not works, saves one's soul. Zwingli and his followers asserted that it was the spiritual meaning of the sacraments that mattered, not the material elements.

The spiritualists went a step further and announced that all that matters is internal faith, not outward observances. Even such things as the sacraments, preaching, and church fellowship are irrelevant.

John Denck (1495-1527) was a humanist who joined the Anabaptist cause. He led a major Anabaptist synod held in Augsburg in 1527, but in his writings he stressed the supreme value of the inner Christ; the word of God within every person. Christ within was more important than church discipline, baptism, or legalism. George Fox would revive Denck's idea a century later.

Other religious thinkers of the era were influenced by the philosophy of the pioneering medical experimenter Paracelsus (1493-1541). Opinion is still divided over whether Paracelsus was a genius or a charlatan, but he exerted an enormous influence in Reformation Europe. While the Reformers rejected the authority of tradition in Christianity and openly rejected the works of the scholastic theologians, Paracelsus publicly ridiculed traditional medical authorities. Luther encouraged people to focus on their own experience with God; Paracelsus urged physicians to study living human beings rather than ancient textbooks. While teaching medicine at the University of Basle in 1527, Paracelsus burned the works of Galen, the standard Greek authority in medicine. Paracelsus also introduced chemistry into medicine, beginning the long history of drug therapy in modern medicine. Paracelsus based his medical theories on an understanding that the human being is a microcosm of the universe. He searched for the cosmic harmony that would produce health and happiness.

Rational spiritualists, like Sebastian Franck (1499-1534), applied Paracelsian theories to the human soul. Franck rejected formalism and dogmatism in religion in favor of spiritual experience. For him, the Bible is primarily a spiritual book that must be read allegorically for its spiritual message. Christ is the Logos, the rational soul that is common to all humanity and revealed in history. Debates over the nature of Christ and proper worship ultimately mean nothing since what is most important is seeing the Logos in the microcosm of the individual. Franck was one of the first Christians to argue publicly for the value of comparative religious study since the divine Logos is revealed in all religions.

Less anti-ecclesiastical and more influential was Caspar Schwenkfeld (1490-1561) who promoted a form of Christianity based primarily on the Gospel of John. In some ways a forerunner of the Pietists, Schwenkfeld disagreed with Luther on a number of points. Primarily he emphasized piety over doctrine, and instituted a strict discipline among his followers. He was both individualistic and tolerant of others, and tried for a while to mediate between the Lutherans and Zwinglians on the issue of the Lord's Supper. For him, the most important aspect of Holy Communion was the spiritual experience of the participant rather than the doctrine of what happened to the elements. He also proposed the idea of the celestial flesh of Christ, which was different in essence from his earthly flesh; therefore when believers partake of the host in Communion, it was different from eating Christ's earthly flesh. The Lutherans and Reformed both opposed Schwenkfeld's more idiosyncratic ideas and rejected his efforts at mediation, but he did gather a body of mystical minded believers who eventually made their way to Pennsylvania.

Types of Christianity in the Reformation

Ernst Troeltsch, an early twentieth-century theologian, philosopher and historian, theorized that three basic "types" of Christianity exist. The first and most prevalent is the church type. Churches, according to Troeltsch, seek to bring society fully under the sway of institutional Christianity. For churches, religion provides a major source of social control and improvement; therefore churches tend to be universalizing, seeking to bring all citizens under their sway. As an inevitable result, churches must make moral and doctrinal compromises with society. In the sixteenth century, Lutheran, Reformed, and Catholic churches were all of the church type of Christianity, and violently competed for the control of Christendom.

The second type, for Troeltsch, is the sect. Sects are small bodies of dedicated believers who to greater or lesser degrees have rejected the dominant society. Sects by their nature are fringe movements. Sometimes they aggressively seek converts; other times they withdraw from the outside world, but they always maintain strict boundaries between who is in and who is not. All of the Anabaptist groups belong to the sect group, and the rejection of infant baptism was the symbolic means of rejecting the idea of Christendom.

The third type is the mystical type. Mystics tend to be highly individualistic, even when they form communities of the like-minded. They also tend to be anti-institutional and anti-dogmatic, focusing instead on personal religious experience or enlightenment. Within twenty years of the posting of the *Ninety-Five Theses*, all three of Troeltsch's types emerged and flourished in Reformation Europe. The churches, however, because of their universal claims, generated much of the conflict of that troubled century as each church tried to become the only church. As the decades passed, exclusivity and confessionalism were wedded to military might as states attempted destroy heresy.

Chapter 12

The Spread of the Reformation and the Wars of Religion

THE REFORMED CHURCH (Calvinism) was the most dynamic Christian movement in the latter part of the sixteenth century, and became the focal point of numerous bloody conflicts. Thanks to the efforts of Calvin and his successor Beza, Geneva became the center of a European-wide effort at reform for more than a generation. Evangelists and pastors studied at the Academy, and those who could not travel to Switzerland studied the Institutes and biblical commentaries. Geneva's presses put forth a continuous stream of Protestant literature and biblical translations, including an English version of the Bible that remained the most popular Bible in England for over two generations. Geneva also actively supported the efforts of reformers in France, the Netherlands, and the British Isles. In all three areas, reformation led to warfare.

The Huguenots

France in the last half of the sixteenth century was not the powerful nation it had been in the time of the Avignon papacy. Near constant warfare with England, Spain, and Italy exhausted the country. Francis I (1515-1547) had managed to bring the French church largely under royal control with the signing of the Concordat of Bologna in 1516, and as long as Francis ruled, Protestantism made little headway. Even his sister, the Queen of Navarre, was forced into silence. However, a leadership vacuum occurred in France after the death of Francis. The succeeding Valois kings were generally sickly and died early so that for the rest of the century a regent rather than a monarch ruled France. The Queen mother, Catherine d'Medici, served as regent for three young French kings. During the decline of the monarchy, Protestantism gained power.

As in other regions of Europe, Reformed theology and middle class capitalism went hand in hand in France. Reformed theologians offered a new capitalist ethic that validated the profit motive and charging of interest. They departed dramatically from medieval religious reforms that generally promoted the ideal of poverty. French Protestants were called Huguenots, a term of obscure origin, and had close ties to John Calvin, himself a religious exile from France. By the middle of the sixteenth century, the Huguenot population was growing rapidly, especially among the merchant and artisan class. The first general Reformed synod held in 1559 shows the strength of French Protestantism where some 2000 congregations were represented.

· The Protestants were strongest in the towns of southern France, such as La Rochelle, and Meaux in the area where Marguerite of Navarre had been most influential. This was also an area of France that had long asserted independence from the French king in Paris. In the Middle Ages, it had been the home of the great Albigensian heresy, and in the sixteenth century the center of the Protestantism. Once again, religious reform was used to assert independence from the centralizing tendencies of the French monarchy.

Persecution

The crown was aware of the connection between reform and political independence, and the first persecution of Protestants began in 1534 and increased in intensity through the years. The Reformed church in Meaux fell to the Inquisition in 1546, and fourteen members of the church died following torture. When Henry II came to the throne in 1547 he increased persecution, legislating severe penalties for such things as eating meat during Lent and attending secret worship services. He set up a special court for heresy, ominously named the Burning Chamber.

Although the French govern-ment was more centralized than the Holy Roman Empire at the time, the local nobility still had a great deal of power and authority. One powerful noble family was the Guise who controlled much of northern and eastern France, and who remained staunchly Catholic. The Guise rose in power under Henry II who appointed several members of the family to high office. Charles, as the archbishop of Reims, was the primate of French church. He urged the king to set up a French Inquisition modeled on its more famous Spanish ancestor.

Henry II could not move as strongly against the Protestants as he would have liked, because of his on-going wars with the Hapsburgs of Austria. In 1559 the signing of the treaty of Cateau-Cambressis finally ended the wars. France appeared to be on the brink of a glorious future, but King Henry died in a joust while celebrating his daughter's marriage. During the ensuing period of chaos and struggle for the throne, the noble families of France used religion as a weapon of dynastic politics.

Control of religion and control of the nation linked in a deadly struggle that nearly destroyed the nation. The Guise were initially in the strongest position because a member of the family, Mary, the Queen of Scots, was the wife of the new king, Francis II, who was only fifteen. Mary's powerful uncles took this opportunity to institute harsh measures to stamp out Protestantism, but many in France saw their repressive measures as a threat to Frenchmen in general. A rival noble family, the Bourbons, defended themselves and took up the Huguenot cause.

The Huguenots Fight Back

Calvin's successor in Geneva, Theodore Beza (1519-1565), aggressively promoted French missionary activity and developed a new doctrine of Christian revolution. Beza argued that true believers must be ready to defend the cause of Christ with fire and sword. They may even oppose the legitimate government if it acts against the gospel. The call for citizens to rebel against their rulers in the name of religion differed greatly from Luther's views on civil obedience. The Protestants initiated the first action in the French wars of religion. The Bourbon prince Louis de Condé and other nobles participated in the conspiracy of Amboise. The conspirators attempted to kidnap the young king in March of 1560 in order to put a Bourbon on the throne. The conspiracy failed and several of the participants were executed.

When Francis died in 1561, the new king was Charles IX (1560-1574), a relative of the Bourbons. His mother was Catherine d'Medici (1519-1589) who managed to secure the role of regent, making her the effective ruler of France. Catherine wanted both to preserve the Valois dynasty and avoid a civil war over religion. Influenced by the broad-minded statesman, Michel de L'Hôpital, she called the Colloquy of Poissy in September 1561 in order to resolve the religious question. Beza himself took part in the proceedings and initially very persuasively presented the Huguenot cause before the Catholic bishops. However, when he publicly denied the real presence of Christ in the Eucharist the bishops realized there could be no real agreement between

Protestants and Catholics. The Colloquy failed to achieve its goals, but it did lead to the Edict of Toleration in January of 1562. Through the Edict, for the first time, Protestants received some freedom of worship.

Catherine's edict of toleration appalled many of the Catholic nobility and monarchs of Europe. How could a ruler make peace with heretics? The Guise responded violently in March 1562 when the Duke of Guise was on a hunting trip with 200 armed knights. When they entered the town of Vassy, they discovered a Huguenot congregation at worship. They slaughtered them. Thus began at least seven major periods of religious war in France. There is not space to go into the details of all of the wars, but we can briefly examine some of the major events. A Protestant killed the Duke of Guise in 1563 in response to the slaughter at Vassy. The leader of the Protestant nobility, Condé, died in battle in 1569. Gaspard de Coligny (1519-1572) took over the leadership of the Protestant cause and negotiated the Peace of St. Germain en Laye.

The agreement granted the nobility freedom of worship and commoners were allowed two places of Protestant worship in each province of the kingdom. Moreover, the Huguenots could have four fortified cities (La Rochelle, Cognac, Montauban, and La Charité,) for their defense. This was a version of the *cuius regio* policy in Germany, and Catherine accepted it in part as a way to oppose the growing influence of Catholic Spain. Furthermore, a marriage was arranged between a sister of King Charles and Henry of Navarre, a Huguenot leader. The wedding was to be held on August 18, 1572.

The Saint Bartholomew's Day Massacre

It appeared that peace had come to France, but now Catherine feared that the Bourbons would take the throne away from her family. The Guise persuaded her to take radical action to destroy the power of the Bourbons. First, there was a botched attempt to assassinate Admiral Coligny. When that failed, apparently in desperation, Catherine authorized the Guise to attack Huguenots in Paris on St. Bartholomew's Day, August 24, 1572. The setting was the celebration of the marriage that was intended to bring religious peace, but the gates of Paris were closed as royal troops entered under Guise leadership. Terror ensued.

Even in religious wars, the St. Bartholomew's Day Massacre was a scene of unprecedented cruelty. First Coligny was killed in his bed, and then rioting troops murdered men, women, children, and infants suspected of being heretics. A contemporary reported that "One little girl was bathed in the blood of her butchered father and mother and threatened with the same fate if she ever became a Huguenot." When it was over, more than six thousand subjects of the king lay dead in Paris. By the time the killing had stopped in the countryside some twenty thousand were dead. An indication of the depth of religious hatred at that time is the fact that Pope Gregory XIII struck a memorial coin to celebrate the massacre. However, the massacre had not crushed the Huguenots as planned. Warfare continued and grew more bitter.

The Edict of Nantes

The new king, Henry III (1574-1589), grew tired of the incessant religious and civil warfare, and attempted a smaller version of the St. Bartholomew's Massacre to crush Guise in Paris. The plot failed, and he fled the capital. He joined forces with Henry of Navarre, a Huguenot leader. Shortly after, Henry of Guise was murdered and a mad friar assassinated the king. Thus two of the three Henries who claimed the throne were dead, and Henry of Navarre emerged as the new king of France, Henry IV (1589-1610). To the surprise of all, a Protestant was now the king of one of the largest and most powerful nations in Christendom. However, when Spanish troops from the Netherlands attacked France in 1590, Henry saw that his country would be more secure from foreign invasion and civil war if he converted to the Catholic Church, which he did in 1594. Legend has it that he said, "Paris is worth a Mass." It is unclear if his conversion affected his religious beliefs, but in 1598 Henry ended the prolonged wars of religion with the Edict of Nantes that granted full toleration to the Huguenots.

The Low Countries

The Netherlands present a slightly different story. When Charles V gave up his throne in 1556, he divided his large realm between his sons. Ferdinand received Austria and became the Emperor, but Philip received the wealthiest lands in Europe: Spain and the Netherlands (formerly Burgundy). Philip II (1527-98) was a product of the Spanish Reformation and convinced of the divine right of kings. He hated heresy and continued his ancestors' practice of enforcing religious conformity throughout his realm. He also used the wealth of Spain to fight for Catholicism throughout Europe. Unfortunately for Philip, Protestantism had found fertile soil in the merchant and artisan classes of the Netherlands. There was also much Anabaptism, especially among lower classes. By 1562, there was a strong Reformed minority, particularly in Holland.

Philip attempted to squash this dissent by forcing his subjects in the Low Countries to conform to Catholicism. He named his sister Margaret, the Duchess of Parma, as the regent of the Netherlands, and appointed a committee of advisors to rule the region. The most important of the advisors was the royal minister, Cardinal Granvelle (1517-1586). The pope allowed Cardinal Granvelle to redraw ecclesiastical jurisdictions, creating eleven new dioceses and three archdioceses, all under the direct control of the monarch. Next, Granvelle increased the authority of the local Inquisition to stamp out heresy.

Philip's efforts to increase his authority over his subjects in the Low Countries led to a rebellion among the nobility who thought their traditional rights were being threatened. The nobles were led by a capable and powerful prince named William of Orange (1533-1584) who joined the Reformed church in 1573. However, even prominent Catholic nobles, such as the counts of Egmont and Horn, supported the opposition to Granvelle. Together they forced Margaret to remove Granvelle from office in 1564, but Philip soon tightened the reigns again. He insisted on the eradication of all heresy. This time the lesser nobility, including Louis of Nassau, openly dissented and presented a formal protest against Philip's religious policy in 1566. Called the Beggars (*les Gueux*) the protesting nobles led a general rebellion among the people in August of 1566. The popular rebellion was clearly iconoclastic and Calvinist in spirit, and was directed against Catholic churches as well as against the Spanish rulers. In response, Catholic and moderate nobles returned to Spanish loyalty in 1567. The stage was set for another destructive religious conflict.

The violence quickly escalated, and Philip commissioned the Duke of Alba (1508-1582) to crush heresy with the aid of nine thousand Spanish soldiers. Alba completely controlled the Low Countries from 1567-1573. He ordered the execution of more than a thousand rebels, including the Catholic nobles Egmont and Horn. In order to pay his army, Alba imposed heavy taxes that eventually alienated the merchant class. Just as Alba thought he had the situation under control, a new rebellion broke out under the leadership William of Orange and his brother Louis of Nassau. A group of patriots or pirates, depending on one's politics, known as the Sea Beggars harassed Spanish shipping, and in 1572 captured the important city of Brill. Soon the Beggars controlled Holland, Zealand, Friesland, and Utrecht.

In 1572, shortly before the St. Bartholomew's Day Massacre, the French king, Charles IX, had been prepared to send French troops to help the Dutch rebellion; however, the massacre caused a change in policy toward all Protestants. The civil war continued without French assistance. The Spanish were generally victorious, but could not control the wealthy northern cities. Spanish atrocities, such as the sack of Antwerp in 1576 and the "pacification" of Ghent, united both the north and south against Spain. Finally, the titular ruler of the Netherlands, Don John of Austria accepted terms of peace. He removed the hated Spanish troops in March of 1577.

It was evident that religious and civil peace could not be maintained in the Netherlands; therefore in 1579 the region was divided into a Catholic south (modern day Belgium), ruled by the Hapsburgs in Spain, and a Reformed north (Holland) which received independence. The independence of Holland led to the growth of the Dutch Reformed Church in the northern Provinces, under William of Orange.

The University of Leyden was founded in 1575, and, unlike most universities of the day, it was largely tolerant in theological matters. In 1577 William took the surprising step of extending religious protection to the Anabaptists. He was the first ruler to promote religious toleration for all Christians. From that day to the present Holland would be a haven of toleration for religious dissidents. Trade, not theology, remained foremost on the minds of the leading citizens of Holland in the seventeenth century.

The Synod of Dort

One major theological controversy in Holland erupted just decades after the country gained its independence. Jacob Arminius (1560-1609) was a native of Holland whose parents had been killed in the wars of religion. He received his education at the University of Leyden, and from 1582 to 1586 he studied in the Reformed academies in Geneva and Basle. Therefore Arminius had an impeccable Reformed pedigree. One of his teachers was Theodore Beza who refined Calvinist doctrines, particularly the doctrine of predestination. Beza made predestination the center of his theology and connected it to creation itself. Almost from the beginning, Arminius disagreed with Beza, particularly on the issue of predestination. Eventually Arminius' opposition to Beza's ideas on divine election led to a split in the Dutch Reformed Church.

In 1687 Arminius began a fifteen-year pastorate in Amsterdam where he was esteemed as a preacher and pastor. In 1603 he was chosen to be the professor of theology at the University of Leyden where his views angered Franciscus Gomarus, one of his colleagues. Gomarus stridently advocated an extreme form of predestination that claimed that divine election was determined even before creation. In fact, according to Gomarus, God allowed the Fall of Adam and Eve in order to implement the plan of election. God's has absolute sovereignty, and no human should question the fact that God had established the world in order to save some souls and damn others. Moreover, Gomarus taught, only those who hold to orthodox doctrine in all details should be considered truly Christian.

Gomarus' perspective horrified Arminius because he felt it made God the source of sin. In essence, according to Arminius, this understanding of predestination meant that God caused the fall of humankind in order to save some and damn others as a proof of God's sovereignty. We cannot go into all of the nuances of the debate, but Arminius argued that believers are predestined to salvation through Christ whom God appointed as the redeemer. Faith in Jesus Christ is the one requirement for salvation, and God, in eternity, has foreknowledge of those who will believe and those who will not. He knows who will be saved and who will be damned, but the individuals themselves choose their eternal destiny. The choice to believe comes through the power of the Holy Spirit at work in the scripture and in the church, but the individual must cooperate in salvation.

Arminius carefully formulated his position in order to avoid the notion of salvation by works, even by the "work" of believing, but in the confessional strife of the period, compromise was not possible. In 1610, after the death of Arminius, his supporters drew up a "Remonstrance" that stated their beliefs. Essentially it argued that Christ died for all people, not just the elect, but only believers receive salvation. Salvation comes through grace alone, but individuals can resist God's grace. They may even fall from grace by their own choice.

The Arminian controversy became a political issue. Republicans, such as the great jurist Hugo Grotius (1583-1645), tended to be Arminians. They allowed the local magistrates greater say in the running of churches, and resisted the centralizing policies of Maurice of Nassau. The republicans were also willing to make a treaty with Catholic Spain. Maurice, who used the militia to install Contra-Remonstrance magistrates and pastors in a number of Dutch cities supported the more doctrinaire Calvinists. Some of the Arminian leaders were imprisoned, exiled, or beheaded.

In order to decide the religious controversy, the States General of Holland called for a synod which met at Dort from November 13, 1618 to May 9, 1619. Since signers of the Remonstrance were viewed as defendants rather than participants, it is not surprising that the Synod of Dort condemned Arminianism as a heresy. The ninety-three canons of the Synod of Dort became the basic texts for Reformed theology for the next 200 years. Particularly influential were five points adopted on April 23, 1619 as a basic definition of distinctive Calvinist theology. They are: (1) election is unconditional; (2) Christ died only for the elect; (3) humankind is totally depraved without grace; (4) grace is irresistible; and (5) the saints will persevere to the end.

The Reformation in Scotland

The third country where the Reformed church would achieve dominance was Scotland. Although Scotland lacked the powerful burgher class and civic life that we associate with Calvinism in sixteenth-century France and Holland, the Reformation here was also tied to the quest for political independence. Scotland was still a relatively wild and poorly educated country in the sixteenth century, and the clan leaders feared English dominion, particularly with the powerful Tudor monarchy on the throne. The king of Scotland, James V (1513-1542), of the Stuart line, looked to France for help in resisting England, and so he married Mary of Lorraine, a member of the Guise family. James V's daughter Mary (1542-1587) was in turn betrothed to the future King Francis II, and sent to France for her education. In 1558, Mary Stuart became the Queen Consort of Francis, but her husband died two years later. In 1561 Mary, educated by Catholics in France and a member of the most aggressive and powerful French Catholic family, returned to her homeland as queen to find the Reformation proceeding in full force and fury among her subjects.

The first reformation preacher in Scotland, a Lutheran named Patrick Hamilton, had been burned at the stake in 1528, but the reform effort continued to gather support after his death. In 1543 the Scottish parliament authorized the translation and public reading of the Bible. The next year, though, the primate of Scotland, Cardinal Beaton moved to repress Protestant activities. The popular Reformed preacher George Wishart was burned in 1546. Rather than crushing the Reformation, Beaton's activities led to open rebellion. He was murdered, and rebels took his episcopal castle, St. Andrews, the same year.

St. Andrews briefly served as a refuge for Protestants, among them a young reformer named John Knox (1513-1572). When the French came to the aid of the king and recaptured St. Andrews, Knox was forced to serve as a galley slave for nineteen months. After he secured his freedom, he spent five years in England as a Protestant minister. When Mary Tudor took the throne in England and began to persecute Protestants, Knox fled to Geneva.

Knox's Rebellion

John Knox was a devoted disciple of Calvin, and helped with translating the Bible into English. The Geneva Bible, as it was popularly called, also stressed Protestant ideas with a clear and readable translation. For instance, the Greek word for "bishop," *episcopus*, was translated as "overseer" rather than bishop. Knox and his colleagues believed that episcopacy leads to religious tyranny and did not want to see bishops in the Bible. While in Geneva, Knox also developed his idea of a Christian revolution. Christians should rebel against an unchristian ruler, which for Knox meant a Catholic monarch. Furthermore, when Mary assumed the throne, Knox argued vehemently that it was an abomination of God's law for a woman to rule a country. Thus on two fronts, Knox urged the Scots to rebel against the Queen. Many of the nobles listened to this encouragement because they feared that Mary, one of the Guise, would let France take over their country completely.

Knox was back in Scotland in 1559. He preached at Perth where his sermons incited a mob to destroy a local monastery. Mary of Lorraine, the regent, saw this as an act of rebellion and called upon French troops to quell it. Rather than ending the rebellion, her actions led to civil war in many parts of the country. Church property suffered greatly from the rioting and iconoclastic Protestants. Just when the Protestant cause seemed lost, in 1560, the English sent troops to assist Knox. A treaty was signed with France assuring Scottish independence.

John Knox thus became not only a religious reformer, but also the leader of a successful revolution. He wrote a confession of faith for Scottish Protestants that Parliament approved by 1560. Parliament also renounced obedience to the pope and forbade the Mass under penalty of death. The following year, Knox's *First Book of Discipline* was presented to Parliament, and the church was organized along Reformed lines throughout the kingdom. Ministers and elders ruled parishes, not bishops. Knox called his version of the Consistory the "Session" and granted it full power of excommunication. A General Assembly was put in charge of the national church.

In 1564, Knox's plans for Reformed worship were legislated. True to Reformed principals, Parliament outlawed religious practices and holidays not ordained in the Bible. The liturgy was to be based on the words of scripture and free prayer by the minister. Knox also issued a call for national education and poor relief, which unfortunately was not fully put into place. Rather than redistributing the wealth of the church to the poor, the Scottish nobility took this opportunity to confiscate church lands for their own use.

Still, the emphasis placed on reading the scripture in the Scottish church did lead to a general increase in literacy and education around the country.

After Mary was implicated in a scandal that included adultery and the murder of her second husband, Lord Darnley in 1567, she was forced to abdicate the throne in favor of her infant son who was crowned James VI. Mary's old nemesis, John Knox, preached Jame's coronation sermon. Mary fled to England. After one too many intrigues against her cousin Elizabeth, Mary was executed in 1587. Many Catholics viewed Mary, Queen of Scots, as a martyr, but Scotland would remain staunchly Calvinist and Presbyterian for hundreds of years.

Chapter 13

The Reformation in England

IT IS DIFFICULT to define just what makes Protestantism protestant, or the Reformation a reformation. Many scholars, particularly Protestant theologians, define the Reformation in terms of specific doctrines, especially justification by faith through grace. Often this theological definition is used to exclude the radicals from the true Reformation. Sometimes scholars define the Reformation in terms of modernization. In other words, the Protestant churches were those that decisively broke with medieval tradition, however, certain Protestant churches maintained a strong sense of continuity with the church's long history and rich tradition.

Part of the difficulty in defining the Reformation is that many different reformations occurred in different areas of Europe. We have already examined the unique characteristics of the Reformation in Germany, Switzerland, France, Scotland, and the Netherlands. Now we turn our attention to England, which has a unique religious history because, unlike other Protestant churches, the Church of England broke its ties to Rome and adopted some Reformed doctrines while maintaining Catholic structure and piety. Furthermore, in England we see most clearly the combination of politics and theology that helped determine the fate of the Reformation. Outside of Scandinavia, England was the only country where the monarch and bishops encouraged the Reformation. Elsewhere in Europe, Catholicism, episcopacy, and monarchy went together. "One King, one Law, one Faith" was the working principle of most European monarchs long before Louis XIV coined the phrase. Most monarchs and their aides believed that allowing the people religious choice would encourage them to insist on having a voice in government, a view feared by all absolutists.

Henry VIII, Defender of the Faith

Initially the union of monarchy and Catholicism was the view of King Henry VIII (1509-1547). Well educated and proud of his theological training, in 1521 Henry put his name to a tract, *Assertion of the Seven Sacraments*, written against Luther. In gratitude for the monarch's public affirmation of the Catholic faith, Pope Leo X officially proclaimed the King of England, "the Defender of the Faith," a title that English monarchs continue to hold. When the Reformation began to sweep across Europe, all expected that Henry would join Francis, Charles, Ferdinand and the other kings in opposing it vigorously. Indeed, Henry had Lutheran books confiscated and burned. In 1527 the government burned William Tyndale's early English translations of the Bible, and the Zwinglian agitator John Firth was burned at the stake in Smithfield on July 4, 1533. In pursuing suspected heretics, the King of England acted like the other kings of Europe, but Henry wanted a divorce. His efforts to be rid of his wives opened the door to the Reformation in England; therefore we cannot understand the English Reformation without peeking into the king's bedroom.

Henry was a young and handsome man when his father arranged for him to marry Catherine of Aragon in 1509. Catherine was part of the powerful Hapsburg family, and a relative of the emperor Charles V. It was hoped that this political marriage would cement ties between England and Spain at a time when England remained in conflict with France and Scotland. Unfortunately, some had doubts about the legality of the marriage since Catherine had been briefly married to Henry's older brother, Arthur, who had died before he could succeed his father as king. Canon law forbade a man to marry his brother's widow, but Henry VII had prevailed upon Pope Julius to grant a special dispensation so that young Henry could marry Catherine. Catherine bore Henry six children, only one of whom, a girl named Mary, survived. As king, Henry VIII desperately wanted a male heir for his throne in order to secure his dynasty. He was convinced that Catherine, who was growing older, could not do this; therefore he consulted his closest advisor, Thomas Wolsey (1474-1530).

Attempts at Divorce

No one considered Wolsey a religious man, but he was a capable servant to the king, so Henry made him Archbishop of York in 1514 and then Lord Chancellor in 1515. Wolsey also became a cardinal in 1515. When Henry tired of Catherine and fell in love with Anne Boleyn, one of his wive's ladies in waiting, he turned to his most trusted councilor Wolsey for help. He resolved to divorce Catherine and marry his beloved, a scheme Wolsey supported because it would break the alliance with Spain. Wolsey wanted England to join with France and Venice in resisting the power of Charles V.

Unfortunately for the Lord Chancellor, in 1527 Catherine's nephew, the Holy Roman Emperor Charles V, had invaded Italy. Thus the pope was literally under the power of the emperor, and Charles did not desire his Aunt Catherine to be declared unmarried and her child illegitimate. Furthermore, Pope Clement found himself in a difficult legal position. Dispensation had been granted so that Henry could marry his brother's widow, but now Wolsey argued that the marriage with Catherine should be annulled because it was not a legal marriage. Cardinal Wolsey, the second most powerful man in Britain, tried for three years to secure Henry's divorce, but he failed. Henry charged his chancellor with treason, and the Cardinal died while awaiting trial.

Thomas Cromwell (1485-1540) now became one of Henry's most trusted advisors, and Thomas More, the humanist reformer whom we met earlier, was named Lord Chancellor in 1530. Henry called Parliament to meet late in 1529, and with the help of More and Cromwell, he convinced Parliament to enact a series of laws intended to reduce the authority of the pope in England. First, Parliament abolished a number of fees charged by the church for services such as burials. Next, the clergy had to acknowledge the King of England as their Supreme Head, "as the law of Christ allows." The forced acknowledgment directly assaulted papal supremacy, but Pope Clement still refused to grant Henry's divorce.

In 1533, Henry tried a new tactic. He appointed Thomas Cranmer (1489-1556), a professor at the University of Cambridge, as the new archbishop of Canterbury. Like many of the theologians at Cambridge, Cranmer had Lutheran leanings and supported Henry in the struggle with the papacy. After consulting with the universities, Cranmer decided that Henry be allowed to divorce Catherine. As the primate of the church in England, Cranmer declared the marriage annulled and allowed Henry to marry Anne. When the pope declared Cranmer's actions illegal and threatened excommunication, Henry signed the Act of Supremacy (1534) making the king, in essence, the pope for the English church.

Royal Supremacy

In the Middle Ages popes such as Innocent III had used the threat of excommunication and interdiction as a way to bring princes to their knees, but no longer. The state was becoming absolute, and the Lutheran princes in Germany had shown that Protestant rulers could successfully reject papal authority. Henry, though no supporter of Protestant theology, used the Reformation for his own ends. Thomas More, however, remained faithful to the Catholic Church and refused to sign the Act of Supremacy. In 1535, the King executed him for treason. Because of his faithfulness and courage, More was declared a Catholic martyr. Bishop John Fischer and the Carthusian monks of London met similar fates as Henry enforced his supremacy over the church.

Thomas Cromwell, who became Henry's vice-regent for ecclesiastical affairs and the King's principal secretary in 1535, created the new idea of royal Supremacy over the church. Cromwell was influenced by the medieval philosopher and reformer Marsiglio of Padua who argued for the secularization of ecclesiastical property. For Marsiglio, there could only be one ultimate authority in a realm, and it must be the secular authority. One can also perceive echoes of Wyclif's ideas in Cromwell's actions. He moved quickly to dissolve some 800 monastic houses and transfer their income to the state. In all, Cromwell uprooted about nine thousand monks and nuns, although he pensioned off some of the elderly. As in Scotland, the poor did not benefit from the seizing of church property since most of it found its way into the hands of the nobility and the crown. Many an ancient abbey became a manor house for a British squire.

Henry and his Wives

By 1536 Henry thoroughly controlled the Church of England; however, the Defender of the Faith continued to have marital difficulties. Anne Boleyn's time as queen was short. Shortly after the wedding she gave birth to a child, Elizabeth, but Henry had found a new lover, Jane Seymour. Anne was convicted of adultery, on charges that were probably false, and beheaded on May 18, 1536. Henry married Jane only two weeks later. She bore him his only male heir, Edward, four months after the wedding.

When Jane soon died of natural causes, Cromwell arranged a marriage to Anne of Cleaves for political reasons, but Henry was disappointed in Anne's appearance. When Cromwell resisted Henry's plans to divorce Anne, whom Henry claimed he never "knew," he quickly arrested Cromwell and had him beheaded in 1540. Archbishop Thomas Cranmer obligingly annulled the marriage to Anne so that Henry could marry Catherine Howard in August. In November of the following year, she was charged with committing adultery with her cousin. This time the charges were probably true, and she was beheaded in January 1542. The aging king's final wife was Catherine Parr whom he married in July 1543. She managed to survive until Henry's death in 1547, but bore no male heir.

Obviously, theology played little role in Henry's great search to establish himself as an absolute monarch in England, and to secure a male heir. Henry may have rejected the authority of the pope, but he remained theologically Catholic. In 1539 he proclaimed the Six Articles Act that declared that transubstantiation was a required dogma, priests could not marry, and the laity could not receive the cup at communion. Those who denied the Real Presence of Christ in the Holy Communion were burned to death and their property confiscated by the government. Prison terms and various tortures were decreed for holding to a number of Protestant doctrines. Henry was not sexist when it came to persecuting heretics. Anne Askew was burned in 1546 because of her views on the Holy Communion.

The English Bible

Despite Henry's violent opposition to Lutheranism, Protestant reformers worked in England. We have already seen that a native reform movement occurred at Oxford early in the century, and that Thomas More supported an Erasmian type of reform. In the 1520's a number of scholars and priests secretly read Luther's works in England. Some of them were capable and shrewd enough eventually to attain high office, and all were associated with the effort to produce and publish an English version of the Bible.

As early as 1522, William Tyndale (d. 1536) resolved to translate the New Testament into English, using Erasmus' 1516 Greek New Testament. In 1524 Tyndale consulted Martin Luther, who was busily creating a German Bible. He published his first English translation in 1525. The new English translation was a major advance from the older Wyclif translation made from the Vulgate. Despite the archaic spelling, one can still hear the charm of Tyndale's rendering of Paul's words, "Now therefore as electe of god/ holy and beloved/ put on tender mercie/ kyndnes/ humbleness of myndes/ meknes/longe sufferynge/ forbearynge one another/ & forgevynge one another." For the next ten years, Tyndale remained in Europe and continually improved his translation. He also translated portions of the Hebrew scriptures, and wrote a number of polemical pamphlets against King Henry and Cardinal Wolsey.

When Thomas More replaced Wolsey as Lord Chancellor, he condemned both Tyndale's religious pamphlets and his translation. More had been a close colleague of Erasmus and an advocate of biblical studies, but he feared the effect of Tyndale's decidedly pro-Reformation translation and commentary; therefore he worked to keep the Tyndale Bible out of England. In 1535 Catholic authorities arrested Tyndale in Brussels. The English crown felt no distress when he was strangled and then burned at the stake, but his translation continued to exert an influence after his death.

Miles Coverdale (d. 1568) built on Tyndale's work to produce the first complete English Bible in 1535. Mindful of Tyndale's fate, John Rogers published his version in 1537 under the pseudonym Thomas Matthew; therefore it is known as the Matthew Bible. Thomas Cromewll licensed for sale both the Matthew Bible and the Coverdale Bible, and in 1539, in part to satisfy popular demand, Cromwell commissioned a new translation by Coverdale. The new translation was to be a large book for public use in English churches. Because of its size, people called it the Great Bible. Archbishop Cranmer added a moderately Protestant preface to the 1540 version. The Great Bible was to be placed in every parish church so all people could read it. However, it created so many disputes and calls for reforms among the laity, who were now debating theology and biblical interpretation, that King Henry feared the Great Bible would lead to rebellion. He eventually outlawed the public reading of Scripture, and removed the Great Bible from the churches. In 1546, it was made illegal to own or read either the Matthew Bible or the Tyndale New Testament.

The Book of Common Prayer

As head of the church, Henry did make an effort to reform worship in England. For one thing, he wanted his subjects to quit praying for the pope, and he decreed that worship should be in English rather than the traditional Latin. His motivation probably came more from nationalist rather than religious concerns. He gave the task of developing new worship materials to the scholarly Cranmer who published the first English version of the Great Litany, based on the medieval Sarum missal, in 1544. Royal command required its use in all churches.

Cranmer eventually produced *the Book of Common Prayer*, which is one of the enduring masterpieces of the English language, and one of the most controversial works of the Reformation. The original prayer book was fairly conservative and based on medieval Latin litanies. It instructed the priest to wear the traditional vestments, elevate the host during the Eucharist, and contained prayers for the dead and other "Catholic" features. Later editions would be more clearly Protestant. In England, the struggle to establish Protestantism focused on the prayer book.

Three of Henry's children, all from different mothers, would eventually sit on the throne. Henry's idea that the king determines the religion of the realm held through the years, and the religious nature of England changed with each succession to the throne. Edward VI (1547-1553), the son of Jane Seymour, was Protestant; Mary (1553-1558), the daughter of Catherine was Catholic; and Elizabeth I (1558-1603), the daughter of Anne Boleyn, was a Protestant.

Reformed England

Henry VIII tried to maintain a Catholic Church without the papacy, but England became clearly Protestant with the accession of Edward VI as king in 1547. Edward was just a child and also sickly; therefore much authority fell to his advisors. Nobles in favor of the Reformation held power in the king's privy council and at court. In particular, the last wife of Henry, Catherine Parr, supported the reforming ideas of Cranmer and encouraged the young king to extend the Reformation. In 1547, Parliament repealed many of the heresy laws and restrictions on the reading of scripture that had been in force in Henry's reign. Thanks in part to the influence of the king's uncle, Edward Seymour, earl of Hertford and now Duke of Somerset, Edward's reign saw a sudden increase in Calvinist and Reformed influence in England. A number of reformers from all over Europe, including the Polish preacher Jan Laski (1499-1560), came to England to promote their cause.

Somerset, with the king's permission, also moved to confiscate even more church property. Endowed masses for the dead, known as chantries, were abolished and the income seized by the crown, as were hundreds of smaller organizations, such as chapels and almshouses. In 1548, the crown embraced iconoclasm, and images were ordered removed from churches. The following year, the Church of England took a step that was generally one of the first actions taken by Protestant reformers; priests were allowed to marry. Such radical changes enacted on a national scale were bound to create confusion and controversy. Discontent was compounded by the crown's efforts to enclose common lands, thereby reducing the rights of peasants, and by

Somerset's failed efforts in foreign policy. There were uprisings in England, particularly in the north. The financially and politically astute John Dudley, earl of Warwick, became the new regent in 1550 after overthrowing Somerset.

Dudley, now the Duke of Northumberland, continued his predecessor's effort to remake the Church of England after the model of Strasbourg and Geneva. Martin Bucer, the head of the Reformed Church in Strasbourg, was invited to England to assist the Protestant cause. He published *Censura*, a detailed critique of Cranmer's prayer book from a Reformed perspective, in 1551. His critique led to a revision of the *Book of Common Prayer* the following year that removed many ceremonial features, such as anointing with oil and exorcism, which the Reformed considered superstitious. Moreover, the Eucharist clearly became a Protestant service using a table rather than an altar. The words of the communion service favored a Zwinglian understanding of the sacrament as a memorial service. Traditional vestments were forbidden, and ordinary bread was required for the communion. Dudley issued the new Bucer-inspired Prayer Book in 1552.

After the death of Henry, the Archbishop of Canterbury, Thomas Cranmer became openly Reformed in his own theology. In 1552 he composed a statement of faith for the Church of England, the *Forty-Two Articles of Religion*. The privy council submitted the articles to a board of theologians that included John Knox. Upon their approval, the king made the *Forty-Two Articles* the law of the land in 1553. Moreover, Cranmer also filled episcopal vacancies with reformers such as his old friend Hugh Latimer.

In 1553 it appeared that England had become the first monarchy to become thoroughly and irrevocably Protestant, but then the seventeen-year-old Edward became deathly ill. At the urging of Dudley, Edward named his cousin, and Dudley's daughter-in-law, Jane Grey, as his heir. When Edward died on July 6, 1553, Lady Jane was hastily crowned, but the nobility and the people did not accept her. Mary Tudor, the daughter of Henry VIII and Catherine of Aragon, used popular support and Spanish troops to secure the throne. Parliament reversed the earlier actions of Cranmer and declared that Mary had indeed been born legitimate. Lady Jane was imprisoned and eventually executed.

Mary Tudor and the Return to Catholicism

Mary had been raised in Spain and was very devout. Upon taking the English throne she immediately repealed most of the Protestant legislation of

Edward VI. Plans were made to reconcile England to Rome along the lines already established in Spain and France, whereby the monarch acted as the effective head of the church, but obedience was formally given to the papacy.

Soon after becoming queen, Mary married the son of Charles V, soon to be Philip II, the King of Spain and the Netherlands. The marriage had great political advantages because it allied Mary with the most powerful nation in Europe, but she failed to calculate for the animosity her subjects felt toward Spain and any form of foreign control. Spain in the 1550s was at its zenith, with an empire encompassing much of the New World as well as the old, but the English feared that Philip would simply add England to his vast domains.

Cranmer and the leading reform-minded bishops were imprisoned, and Catholic bishop Gardiner was made Lord Chancellor. About 800 Protestant agitators read the writing on the wall and fled to the mainland. These Marian Exiles found refuge in the Reformed centers of Geneva, Basle, and Strasbourg. Incidentally, Lutheran areas did not welcome the Marian Exiles since they were Reformed rather than Lutheran in doctrine. Among the exiles was John Knox. In Geneva, they drank deeply of Calvinist theology from Calvin himself, and they grew increasingly hostile toward their ruler at home. While in Geneva, they also produced a new and inexpensive English Bible, known as the Geneva Bible, which would be the most popular English translation until the more famous King James Bible superceded it.

England was officially restored to the papacy in November 1554, after intense negotiations to limit the power of the pope within England. Parliament received Reginald Pole (1500-1558) as a papal legate. He assured Parliament that those church properties that the crown had confiscated and given to members of Parliament would not be taken away. When Parliament restored papal authority over the church, Pole absolved the nation of heresy. At his request, Parliament also restored the old laws against heresy. The actions of Cromwell, Cranmer and Edward were abolished, and the persecution of heretics began almost immediately. Among the first was John Rogers who had produced the Matthew Bible. Former bishops Latimer and Ridley were among the seventy-five persons burned in 1555. Their heroism became legendary in England and began to rouse opposition to the methods of Mary and her officials.

Persecution under Mary

Mary Tudor had a particular reason to get rid of Thomas Cranmer since he had declared her a bastard when he annulled her mother's marriage. Rome excommunicated Cranmer on November 25, 1555, and Cardinal Pole became the new Archbishop of Canterbury. Cranmer, the dedicated royalist, faced an interesting dilemma. During the reign of Henry he had maintained that the monarch completely ruled over the church, but what if the monarch restored the papacy, as Mary had done? By this time Cranmer was a convinced Calvinist, but his lord was a Catholic. At one point, Cranmer submitted to the royal will and signed a statement of recantation. Pole, Archbishop Gardiner, and Mary hoped that such an action might convince others to give up their heresy, but as his execution neared, Cranmer gathered his courage and took back his recantation. Thus he was sentenced to death by burning rather than simple beheading. As the flames rose, the author of the *Book of Common Prayer* held out his right hand with which he had signed the recantation. He watched as it was completely burned off so he could die with a clear conscience.

In all, over 300 persons were executed under Mary, making it one of the worst religious persecutions in English history. As we have seen, a number of nobles faced the stake, but most of the convicted heretics were peasants or working class. Rather than crushing heresy as intended, the persecution made Mary increasingly unpopular among the people who began calling her Bloody Mary.

In 1563, John Foxe (1516-1587) published his collection of stories of the Marian persecution under the title *Acts and Monuments*. Usually called *The Book of Martyrs*, his work graphically portrayed the torture and execution of the Protestants, urging the reader to remain steadfast in the face of persecution. It became one of the most read books in the English language, and fueled English animosity toward Catholicism and Spain for over a century. In the Anglo-American world, the popular imagination associated Catholicism with tyranny.

The Elizabethan Settlement

Mary died after only a five-year reign, and England had a new monarch as well as a new religion. Elizabeth I was Protestant and returned to some of the policies of her half-brother Edward. Her chief advisor in these matters was William Cecil (1520-1598) who assisted Elizabeth in her shrewd policies. As the daughter of Henry VIII, she knew first hand the dangers of being queen, so she moved very cautiously. However, Protestant nobles and commoners dominated Parliament, and insisted on moving quicker toward reform than Elizabeth would have liked.

First came the New Supremacy Act in 1559 that made the queen the supreme governor, but not the head, of the Church of England. Her authority was officially limited to matters of governance and polity rather than faith. A Book of Common Prayer was prepared that was intentionally ambiguous on several very controversial points, such as the presence of Christ in the Eucharist. The new Act of Uniformity in 1559 commanded the use of this prayer book, and the wearing of vestments in all parish churches. In short, during the first years of Elizabeth's reign Parliament found a way to compromise Protestant and Catholic sentiments. The Church of England, or Anglican Church, was no longer under the authority of the pope, and a number of Catholic practices and views were abolished, but certain marks of the old Catholic worship remained. In this respect, the English church looked similar to the Lutheran one, although it was theologically more ambiguous.

The Thirty-Nine Articles of Religion

Matthew Parker (d. 1575) was made the new Archbishop of Canterbury, the religious head of the Anglican Church. He was a scholarly and moderate Protestant who tried to steer the church away from both militant Calvinism and Catholicism. Under his leadership the *Forty-Two Articles of Religion* were reduced to thirty-nine statements that all English priests must accept. Extreme Zwinglian statements were removed in order to give as much common ground as possible for moderate Catholics to join the church while keeping the church Protestant. These Thirty-Nine Articles remain the basis for Anglicanism today.

Parker also established the Anglican episcopacy in apostolic succession, using bishops who had survived the Marian persecution. In contrast to Reformed theologians, Parker believed that the rule of bishops was biblical and should be preserved; however, he attempted to reform the episcopacy from a number of abuses, and make sure that all bishops were true to Protestant beliefs. By 1563 the Church of England was fully established.

The Elizabethan Settlement was a largely successful compromise that preserved much of the old catholic worship and church structure, while putting the essential features of Lutheran/Reformed theology in place. For instance, there were no longer seven sacraments, but priests still wore robes and consecrated the Eucharist at an altar. People could believe that the Eucharist was a memorial meal, or that they were receiving the actual body and blood Christ. Sanctuaries could have statues, but prayers to the saints were reduced. The *Thirty-Nine Articles* clearly forbade devotion to the Pope and asserted justification by faith, but remained rather vague and silent on a number of disputed points. The Elizabethan Settlement tried to appeal to the broad common ground in religion, the so-called *via media*, but extremists on both sides rejected the prayer book and the *Thirty-Nine Articles*.

Opposition

The settlement helped prevent the kind of religious warfare seen in France, but it did not fully satisfy all parties. On the one hand, the Elizabethan Settlement existed under constant threat, or so it seemed, by a resurgence of Catholicism. In 1570, Pope Pius V officially excommunicated Elizabeth and began to forment rebellion in England. The greatest threat to Elizabeth's throne came from outside England in 1588 when Philip II sent his famous Armada to try to reclaim his hold on England and restore Catholicism. His opponents in the great sea battle, Sirs Walter Raleigh and Francis Drake, found inspiration in their fight both by their devotion to the queen and by Foxe's *Book of Martyrs*. Their surprising, to some divinely providential, victory reduced the Catholic threat to an occasional act of intrigue such as Guy Fawke's failed effort to blow up Parliament.

More serious was the threat to the settlement from a number of Protestants, especially the Marian exiles who had returned from Switzerland. They wanted to see the full implementation of the Reformed system that Calvin had instituted in Geneva and Knox was creating in Scotland. Full implementation meant the complete abolition of saints days, clerical vestments, religious images, and even the semblance of the Catholic Mass. Most important, they wanted to get rid of bishops. They found the episcopacy tyrannical, unbiblical, and idolatrous. Some of the Protestants who had stayed in hiding during Mary's reign also felt that Elizabeth had minimized their sacrifice. Puritanism emerged from these circles toward the end of the century.

Thomas Cartwright (1535?-1603), a leading opponent of Elizabeth's system, taught divinity at the University of Cambridge in 1569 when he began agitating for the dissolution of the episcopacy. Cartwright believed that the New Testament depicted a non-hierarchical ministry where all priests were essentially the same. The church should be governed by ministerial conferences, known as presbyteries. Cartwright's ideas gained support in various places around England through the publication of *An Admonition to Parliament* in 1572. Even the current Archbishop of Canterbury, Edward Grindal, was sympathetic to the Presbyterian movement. In part because of his sympathy, Elizabeth suspended him from his duties. Supporters of the idea of episcopacy included the gifted Richard Hooker (1553-1600) whose *Laws of Ecclesiastical Polity* argued that while God did not ordain episcopacy directly, it was the best form of government to avoid both papal tyranny and Protestant fanaticism.

In 1583, Elizabeth elevated John Whitgift (1530-1604) to the position of Archbishop of Canterbury because of his vigorous and eloquent opposition to Presbyterianism. Whitgift had already managed to deprive Cartwright of his professorship and his income, leaving him to wander Europe as a Presbyterian activist. Throughout the 1580s and 1590s Whitgift used the courts to stamp out the increasingly vocal Presbyterians. He ordered all clergy in England to (1) observe all of the rubrics of the prayer book, including kneeling and wearing priestly vestments; (2) accept royal supremacy over the church; (3) acknowledge that the *Book of Common Prayer* contains nothing contrary to Scripture; and (4) sign the *Thirty-Nine Articles*. About 400 ministers refused to abide by these rules. The great opposition to his orders forced the archbishop to allow limited non-conformity.

Puritanism

Whitgift used the term "Puritan" as a derogatory label to describe those who hoped to purify the church of supposed idolatrous practices and theology. The movement was also associated with efforts to purify the moral lives of Christ-ians according to a certain understanding of biblical teaching. Historians debate whether the term "Puritan" is useful since it encompasses so many different types of anti-episcopal agitators and popular reformers. It has, however, become so familiar that it will be used here to describe Calvinist-leaning church reformers in England during the reigns of Elizabeth and her immediate successors, the Stuart kings.

Among them were Robert Browne (1550?-1633), a former student of Cartwright's, who urged the faithful to separate from the established church. Inspired in part by Dutch Anabaptism, these separatists attacked Anglicans and Presbyterians alike. The leaders of a separatist congregation in London were hanged in 1592 for denying the right of the queen to govern the church. In response to the separatist challenge, Parliament passed laws forbidding unauthorized worship services and compelled church attendance in parishes. Increasingly, the Puritans drew on the revolutionary theories of Beza and Knox as their struggle continued into the next century. Eventually, this religious and social conflict would break out in civil war.

Elizabeth's successor in 1603 was James Stuart (1603-1625), the king of Scotland. He was James I in England and James VI in Scotland. James had grown up in the midst of Scottish Presbyterianism, and was familiar with its impulse toward rebellion. He had not forgotten that the Presbyterians had forced his mother, Mary, to abdicate her throne. He was afraid they would try to do the same to him. However, the Puritans in England assumed that their new king was a true Scottish Presbyterian.

At his coronation some one thousand clergymen presented James with a petition for church reform called the Millenary Petition. Among its provisions, the petition called for a presbyterial form of government, similar to that already established in Scotland. A theological conference was held in the king's presence in January of 1604. James decisively rejected the Puritan position, reputedly saying, "No bishop, no king." He strongly believed that episcopacy and royal authority went together. The King of England should rule like King David in the Bible and answer to none but God. James also insisted on uniformity in the church, and in 1610 he imposed the British episcopal system on Scotland over the objection of his subjects there. He also ordered his High Commission to hunt down non-conformists.

The king's one concession to Puritan sensibilities was the commissioning of a new translation of the Bible into English, the so-called King James or Authorized version; however, even here his motives were to preserve episcopacy. The popular Geneva Bible had written bishops out of the New Testament, and James wanted that corrected. There was much popular opposition, initially, to the conservative Authorized Bible, but gradually it became the most widely used English Bible.

Separatism

The Puritan congregation of John Robinson (1575?-1625), which met in Scrooby, read the signs of the times. They believed that they were witnessing the first signs of the prophesied tribulation of the Last Days, so they resolved to flee England where the servant of the Antichrist sat on the throne. They became pilgrims, religious travelers, who first went to Holland where they found freedom of worship. Among these exiles was the theologian William Ames (1576-1633) who argued that the faithful should establish independent churches that somehow remained connected to the Church of England. Ames' *Marrow of Theology* became the standard textbook for Puritan pastors in England and America. He gave a classic exposition of the Puritan attitude toward the Bible when he wrote that the Bible is "a perfect rule of faith and morals" and should be the only basis for the church's doctrine and worship.

Dutch Anabaptists convinced a portion of the congregation in exile, led by John Smyth, that the scriptures do no contain infant baptism, so they created the first English Baptist church while in Holland. True to Separatist teaching, they also acknowledged no church structure above the congregation. The general freedom of Dutch society frightened many of the English Puritans, however. They wanted freedom to worship in their way, but feared that their children would run wild and that Dutch luxury and immorality would seduce their children. Some of the Puritans made plans to put an ocean between them and corrupt Europe.

Protestantism and English Society

King James had shrewdly and successfully laid the groundwork for absolutism in his realm. Through various tactics, he had wrested control from the House of Commons, which was composed largely of Puritan-leaning middle class men of property. He had given bishops great authority over their dioceses and appointed men loyal to him to episcopal posts. He even tweaked the noses of the Puritans with his promotion of games and amusements on Sundays. His *Book of Sports* issued in 1618 was anathema to the Puritans who insisted that Sunday be purified from secular pleasures. James also refused to assist the Protestant powers who engaged in the Thirty Years War.

Although James found success in most of his religious policies, popular discontent, led by the Puritan middle class, was rising. When his son, Charles I (1625-1649), took the throne in 1625, he crushed Puritan hopes by reaffirming the Acts of Supremacy and Uniformity. One way Charles decided to handle dissenters was to let them immigrate to the colonies in New England. In 1629 the king chartered the Massachusetts Bay Colony whose governor, John Winthrop, sought to make it into a "city on a hill" for the whole world, especially England, to see.

Present day popular opinion of Puritans is that they were dour people resisting progress and pleasure. H. L. Menken once said a Puritan lived in terror that someone somewhere was having a good time. Although the Puritans promoted moral discipline and piety, they were hardly reactionary. In the early seventeenth century, the Puritans agitated for progress and experimental science. The middle classes, the squires, merchants and artisans heavily supported the Puritan cause. They called for reform of the educational system and established the most progressive English school of the day, Gresham College, in order to educate bright men who could not afford to attend the university.

By and large, Puritans advocated the theories of Francis Bacon who urged people to ignore traditional answers and examine things experi-mentally. By overcoming prejudice, one could find truth. Within Puritanism, the quest for religious autonomy and purity was combined with the quest for rational science and technology. Reform of the church was joined with a desire to reform society through technology and education. Bishops, courtiers, petty lords, tradition, and royal absolutism all seemed to stand in the way of social and moral progress.

In the 1620s and 1630s Puritanism became a potent force in the British Parliament, and Charles rightly saw it as a threat to his absolute authority. In 1633 the king appointed as Archbishop of Canterbury William Laud (1573-1645) who was a friend and advisor of Charles. As the bishop of London, Laud had tried to suppress Puritanism in his diocese. He was such a brilliant and energetic defender of episcopacy and tradition that he was once even offered a cardinal's hat if he would convert to Roman Catholicism. He refused the offer, but he was no Calvinist. In fact, he promoted Arminianism, a Protestant theology that rejected the idea of predestination. According to Laud, humans cooperate with God in salvation, and the church aids them in that quest. Laud also valued ceremonialism in worship, asserting that religious ritual was one of the ways to please God and cooperate in salvation. In general, Laud believed strongly in the literal sense of the *Thirty-Nine Articles* and insisted that others do likewise.

Laud and the Parliament

Charles gave Laud the task of making his church uniform in practice and doctrine. As archbishop, he demanded that priests wear the prescribed vestments and follow the entire liturgy. He persecuted those who refused to conform. He also made it illegal to worship in private homes, distribute Puritan literature, or separate oneself from the Church of England. He was imperious, pompous, and much hated. In 1629, Charles dismissed the Parliament because it opposed him, and Archbishop Laud became the symbol of royal tyranny for many members of Parliament. Although Laud's persecution of non-conformists under the Stuarts was less severe than that of Mary Tudor, the Puritans had been nourished on Foxes' *Book of Martyrs*. They gloried in the stories of faithful Protestants being abused and murdered by Catholics. They easily saw a new threat in the Arminian Bishop Laud who displayed "popish" tendencies.

Initially the controversy aroused by Laud was fought in the churches, but the archbishop made a fatal error when he tried to bring the Church of Scotland into full conformity with England. The Scots saw Laud's actions as a threat to their liberty and an affront to the laws of God. In 1638 the Presbyterians in Scotland, with the encouragement of the lords, openly rebelled over the religious issue. Charles moved to crush the rebellion by force, but the king could not settle the dispute alone. Much to his displeasure, he had to call a Parliament to raise taxes and an army. John Pym led this Parliament, and he was a Puritan layman who was very hostile to the policies of Charles and Laud. Charles immediately disbanded the Parliament, now known as the Short Parliament, but was soon forced to reassemble the body.

The Civil War

The second meeting of Parliament is called the Long Parliament because it stayed in session until 1653. Parliament asserted its own power and attempted to make the king respond to the legislative desires of the Parliament. When Catholics in Ireland rebelled against the crown in 1641, Parliament grew more radical. Charles tried to disband the Long Parliament by force, but his attack led to open rebellion by the Puritans. Acting on its own authority, Parliament arrested Archbishop Laud for treason in 1641 and executed him four years later. Soon England became involved in a complex Civil War between the king and Parliament. In the end, the king lost the war in 1644, and lost his head in 1649 when Parliament convicted him of treason against the nation. The first regicide by a representative body in European history foreshadowed the French revolution 140 years later, but this revolution was conducted in the name of God.

The Westminster Assembly

In 1643, Parliament abolished the episcopal system and set about creating a new church order. One hundred and twenty-one ministers and thirty laymen assembled in Westminster to take on the task of reorganizing the church and its doctrine. The Westminster Assembly included Puritans of congregationalist persuasion and even some moderate Episcopalians, but by and large was composed of presbyterians. The assembly developed a presbyterian form of church government that Parliament partially implemented in 1646. *A Directory of Worship* that was less ceremonial, more wedded to the words of scripture, and provided some opportunity for extemporaneous prayer replaced *The Book of Common Prayer*. The assembly also presented Parliament with a confession of faith that the Scottish General Assembly accepted in 1647. In a slightly revised form, the English Parliament approved it in 1648. The confession affirmed a number of key points of Reformed theology, and would remain the standard statement of faith for Presbyterianism in Scotland and America down to modern times. Two catechisms were also prepared. The longer one was for the training of clergy and for preaching, and the shorter for educating children.

Although these theological statements were not universally accepted by all Puritans, and certainly not by everyone in England, they exerted a profound influence on English and American Protestant thought for the next century. First and foremost, the Bible became the source and norm for doctrine, worship, and morality. Next was predestination. Because of Adam's sin, all humans are hopelessly lost in sin and cannot save themselves. They are utterly depraved, but after the fall, God elected some to be saved. Saving some was part of God's providence, and God's reasons are ultimately inscrutable. Salvation comes not from the covenant of works, but through the covenant of grace. This covenant theology in part mitigated the arbitrariness of election. God had made a covenant with humankind by which they should live and find salvation. In Reformed theology the individual must be turned from the world and sinfulness and toward God. This comes through the gracious action of God, but the believer must experience it. The experience of conversion or awakening is itself a sign of one's election.

The architect of Parliament's military victory was a moderate Puritan named Oliver Cromwell (1599-1658). Cromwell was a solidly middle-class Calvinist who believed that an army should be inspired by devotion to the country and to the Lord. He created the New Model Army, made up of volunteers who advanced in rank by merit instead of through by birth and favoritism. He filled his devotional manual for his troops with Old Testament quotations about the Lord's army smiting evil doers. The New Model Army smited King Charles, then smited the rebellious Irish Catholics, and in 1653 smited Parliament itself, which had proven incapable of ruling the country. The army made Cromwell the Lord Protector of England in 1653. During the period of war and chaos, a number of radical groups had emerged in England, such as the Levelers and Diggers, who pushed for such things as the right to vote for every person regardless of social status. Some of the religious radicals even asserted that the Protestant idea of the priesthood of all believers meant that women have civil rights equal to men. Such notions appalled the Lord Protector, and he crushed the radicals by force.

Cromwell found it difficult to rule England. The structures were not in place for a fully representative government, even though Puritan theology supported such a plan. Economic and social conditions in England worsened during the Interregnum. People chafed under the imposed Puritan morality and wanted to have popular entertainments restored. Cromwell's son tried to continue the revolution after his father's death, but England in 1660 was ready for a return of the kings as long as there were constitutional protections against tyranny and guarantees of a limited religious toleration. The people wanted neither the high episcopacy of Laud, nor the strict moralism enforced by the Puritans.

Chapter 14

The Catholic and Counter-Reformations

SO FAR SECTION two has focused primarily on the development of the Protestant Reformation, but the Roman Catholic Church also experienced a major reformation during the sixteenth century. Roman Catholicism and Protestantism both grew out of medieval Western Christianity, and in different ways used that common heritage to create the churches we know today. Protestants, to greater and lesser degrees, rejected many of the practices and beliefs of the medieval church, while the Catholic Church tried to maintain greater continuity with the immediate past, but it could not do so without reforming itself and defining many doctrines.

When Martin Luther called for a public debate on a number of controversial points, many of the doctrines had not yet been officially defined by the Roman Catholic Churc. Issues such as justification and were still open questions in 1517, and Luther's writings encouraged the Catholic Church to reconsider its teaching and practice. So far in this section, we have seen how Catholic rulers often responded in violence to the Reformation. Now we will see how the Catholic Church reformed internally and sought to regain territories lost to Protestantism.

Names are important and can be controversial, particularly in historical studies. Older, mainly Protestant textbooks refer to this subject as the Counter Reformation. The phrase indicates that the reform of the Catholic Church primarily responded to the Protestant Reformation and was directly opposed it. While there is some justification for this view, it is far from adequate or accurate. As indicated in a previous chapter, there was a reform effort taking place within the Catholic Church long before the time of Luther. Spain had already solidified its own unique reform by 1500 and would lead the effort to bring Europe back to Rome. There were other independent efforts elsewhere in Europe which we will examine in more detail below. Therefore it is more accurate and less biased to refer to the Catholic Reformation, a phrase that includes the efforts at reform within Catholicism before 1517 as well as those taken in direct response to the Protestant challenge.

Reform in Italy

Many of the financial and moral abuses in the church, including those connected to the Vatican, occurred in Italy, but Italy was also the setting for some of the more creative and dynamic reforming efforts of the period. Particularly important was the creation of the "oratories." These were similar in spirit to the pious institutions associated with the Brethren of the Common Life in the Netherlands decades earlier. Priests and lay persons worked together to promote personal piety and acts of charity. They cared for orphans, lepers, and others afflicted by incurable diseases, such as the new scourge of Europe, syphilis.

The Oratory of Divine Love, established in 1497 by a disciple of Catherine of Genoa, was the prototype for this piety of active mercy. The Oratory movement spread to Rome where Gaetano da Thiene (1480-1547), the future Saint Cajetan (not to be confused with Cardinal Cajetan who opposed Martin Luther) and Giovanni Caraffa (1476-1559), the future Pope Paul IV, established the Theatines Order in 1526. This was a reforming order similar in character to predecessors in the Middle Ages. The Theatines focused on the strict observance of priestly vows, including the vow of poverty. The founders of the order gave their property away for the benefit of the poor in their diocese, and they resigned their benefices. They were priests who chose to live like monks under the authority of a strict superior who regulated an ascetic lifestyle of fasting and prayer. The Theatines did not withdraw from the world, however. Instead, they pursued their pastoral duties and cared for the sick and poor in their area. By their example and admonitions, they hoped to improve the quality of the clergy throughout the church.

After the sack of Rome by imperial troops in 1527, the Theatines moved to Venice, a city-state where the Reformation was making inroads. There Caraffa helped gather a group of Catholic reformers that included the senator and future cardinal Gasparo Contarini (1483-1542) and Reginald Pole, the future Archbishop of Canterbury. Contarini promoted the idea that the best way to reform the church was by reforming the bishops themselves. Rather than living as lords and princes, bishops should devote themselves to their religious duties. For Contarini, in order for true reformation to occur, the church leaders needed spiritual reformation. Those entrusted with the office of bishop must be worthy of that office. Contarini, though not a priest, was a worthy opponent of Martin Luther, and a persuasive advocate of Catholic doctrine.

The Italian reform took hold under pontificate of Paul III (1534-1549) who appointed several reformers as cardinals. Among them were Contarini, Sadoleto, Caraffa, and Pole. Contarini and Pole acknowledged that the Lutherans had reacted to a number of real abuses in the church, and that the best way to fight Protestantism was to reform Catholicism.

In a 1537 report, *Consilium de emendanda ecclesia*, written largely by Contarini, the cardinals presented a critique of the church and a plan for reform. In general, they blamed the Reformation on the greed and luxury of the popes, cardinals, and bishops. Moreover, Contarini exhorted the pontiff: "A pope should know that those over whom he exercises this rule are free men; not according to his own pleasure must he command, or forbid, or dispense, but in obedience to the rule of reason, of God's command, and to the law of love."[10] The proposed reform followed the lines Contarini had outlined a decade earlier; namely that church leaders must be spiritual leaders rather than princes. The church as a whole should embrace voluntary poverty and work with renewed vigor to care for the souls entrusted to it. Along with Pole, Contarini sought to restore the Protestants to the Roman Church through reconciliation. At Ratisbon in 1541, he and Philip Melanchthon made great strides toward achieving a common understanding of justification by faith and the proper role of works in the Christian life, but Catholics and Protestants alike rejected their statement as compromising the faith.

How to deal with the Protestant heresy caused a division among the reforming cardinals. Should they follow the conciliatory path of Contarini and find ways to welcome Protestant insights and concerns, or should they rely on the traditional approach to heresy? Caraffa, the ascetic and zealous founder of the Theatines, saw no reason for compromise. In 1542 he reorganized the Roman Inquisition to focus on Protestantism. Under his leadership Protestantism was largely exterminated in Italy. In 1555 he was elected Pope Paul IV and made sure that there would be no compromise with Protestants. As pope, though, he proved so autocratic and ineffective that the people of Rome cheered his death in 1559.

---

[10] Leopold von Ranke, *History of the Popes: Their Church and State* (New York: 1901) 1:102.

One of the most enduring of the new reforming orders was the Ursulines, established in 1535 by Angela Merici (1474-1540) after she received visions during a pilgrimage to the Holy Land. Merici intended that her order would provide for virgins who would live in their own homes. Thus it was named for the legendary St. Ursula who was reputed to have been martyred along with several of virgins by the Huns in the fifth century. The Ursulines devoted themselves to charity and the education of girls. Pope Paul III approved the order in 1544 without the requirement of monastic vows. As often happened to women's orders, though, the loose arrangement of the Ursulines concerned many church leaders. In 1572 Gregory XIII required vows and enclosure. Eventually it became a full-fledged monastic order, but continued in its primary mission of educating women.

Matteo di Bassi of Urbino (1495?-1552) was a Franciscan who wanted to return to the original Rule of St. Francis. In the 1520s Matteo dedicated himself to absolute poverty, the mortification of the flesh and its desires, and missionary work. Three companions joined him in this quest for the apostolic life, and they adopted coarse robes with a distinctive hood (cappuccio). It is ironic that this ascetic order may be best remembered now for their innovative way of brewing coffee, but the Capuchins were one of the most successful new orders of the sixteenth century. They excelled in preaching, and did much to strengthen Catholicism and popular devotion in southern Europe.

In 1541, the third general of the order, Bernardino Ochino, converted to Protestantism, an event that nearly led to the suppression of the order. Ochino's spiritual pilgrimage led him to Zurich and ultimately to the Anabaptists in Moravia. The order survived the scandal, and by 1550 the Capuchins had over 25,000 members who devoted themselves to extreme poverty and the spread of the gospel. After Gregory XIII allowed the order to go international in 1572, it became an effective agent for regaining areas lost to Protestantism.

The Jesuits

The most important figure of the Catholic Reformation was undoubtedly Ignatius Loyola (1491-1556), a knight turned saint. Unlike the leaders of the Catholic Reformation in Italy, Loyola was neither a humanist nor a theologian. He was a Spanish knight filled with the ideals of chivalry that were popular in Spanish literature of the time. Ignatius might have become a real-life Don Quixote, but in 1521 a cannonball injured his leg during a

French invasion. While he slowly recovered, Ignatius had little reading material other than lives of the saints and the *Life of Christ*, written by a Carthusian monk named Ludolph. He converted to a new form of chivalry, and decided to become a knight of Christ dedicated to the service of the Virgin Mary.

In 1522, he traveled to the shrine of Mary at Montserrat, left his weapons at the altar, and assumed a beggar's attire. For about a year in nearby Manresa, he put himself through a series of very harsh penances, contemplated Thomas a'Kempis *Imitation of Christ*, and experienced visions and raptures. During his time of inner preparation, Ignatius developed a new type of devotion, which he describes in his 1548 book *Spiritual Exercises*. The book presents a detailed guide for spiritual devotion conducted under the tutelage of a spiritual director. The long series of exercises leads the pilgrim into a new life of complete obedience and devotion. The disciple uses his imagination to relive the life and sufferings of Christ, and gives his life entirely to the Lord. Everything is to be sacrificed for the glory of God. Unlike the spiritualist Protestant sects, obedience to the pope and a willingness to go wherever called were cardinal signs of one's devotion to Christ and his church.

Ignatius himself went to Jerusalem with the intention of serving as a missionary to the Muslims as a Franciscan, but that order rejected him as a dangerous fanatic. Undaunted, he returned to Spain in order to receive an education. He quickly advanced from the boy's school in Barcelona to the premier universities of Alcal and Salmanica from 1525 to 1527. Ignatius gathered a following among the students and introduced some of them to his exercises, but his activities raised the suspicions of the Inquisition. He was briefly imprisoned as a suspected heretic in 1528.

After his release, he traveled to France where he studied at the University Paris, just at the time that Calvin was leaving. One of the great ironies of history is that for a brief while the architect of Reformed theology and the leader of the Catholic Reformation could have been schoolmates. While at the university, Loyola again gathered a following of students, including Francis Xavier, the great missionary to India and Japan. At Montmarte on August 15, 1534 Loyola and his companions vowed to become missionaries to Turks, but they also resolved to finish their studies before embarking on their mission.

In 1537 they went to Venice with the hope of sailing for Jerusalem, but war prevented them from departing. The small group sought priestly ordination, and began to work among the poor and in hospitals. Around 1539, they found their way to Rome, and in 1540 formed the Society of Jesus, or as the order is more popularly known, the Jesuits. In addition to the usual religious vows, the Jesuits took a special vow of strict obedience to the papacy. At the same time that Henry VIII broke allegiance to the papacy and Luther was referring to the pope as the antichrist, the Jesuits made absolute obedience to the Holy See one of the bedrocks of their order, which was officially sanctioned by Paul III in 1540. One of the major innovations of this new order was that the members did not observe regular hours of worship and prayer, nor did they wear a distinctive habit.

The Jesuit Order had two main strengths that would make it one of the most effective orders of the modern period. First was the process of preparation. Using the *Spiritual Exercises*, every member repeated the spiritual journey of Ignatius, and was thus internally formed according to Ignatian ideals of obedience and devotion. There was also a two-year novitiate following by extensive academic and spiritual training. Second was the constitution of the order, which was based on contemporary military structure. The Society had an autocratic General assisted by four subordinates, who together could depose him. Next in the hierarchy were the Provincials appointed by the General to oversee each district. The order embraced rational planning and it spread rapidly in Italy, Spain, and Portugal.

Although originally intended as a missionary order to convert the Muslims, the Society of Jesus quickly became the vanguard of the effort to win Protestant rulers and people back to the Catholic Church. They did this through extensive preaching, the use of the confessional, and especially the education of the upper classes. The Jesuits were great educational innovators in the sixteenth century, and the upper classes of Protestant and Catholic Europe sent their sons to Jesuit schools. While there, the boys were educated in Catholic doctrine and frequently won for the church. As we shall see later, the influence of the Jesuits in the courts of power eventually led to their downfall.

The Council of Trent

Ultimately more important than the various new religious orders and the work of the Inquisition in reforming the Catholic Church was the great church council that Paul III called at the insistence of Charles V. Since the conciliar movement of the previous century, the papacy remained suspicious of church councils, but Charles felt that a council was the only way to restore the religious unity of his realm and avoid civil war. He eventually persuaded the papacy to organize such a council, and through a monumental act of diplomacy the great Catholic monarchs agreed on a time and place for the meetings. Once it began, war frequently interrupted the council. It met at Trent in 1545-47, moved to Bologna in 1547-1549, and met again at Trent from 1551-1552. After a long hiatus, it reconvened at Trent from 1561 to 1563 as a continuation of the original council rather than a new council.

In all, twenty-five plenary sessions and hundreds of committee sessions convened where theologians debated both Catholic doctrine and practical strategies for reform. The Council of Trent experienced great difficulties and suffered from disputes between the Italian and Spanish representatives. Despite its claims to be ecumenical, Trent represented a rather small section of the Western church. Although called to settle the Protestant question, Protestants did not participate in the council. Despite its limits and difficulties, though, Trent would have a greater impact on the Catholic Church than any council between the Fourth Lateran Council of 1215 and the Second Vatican Council of the early 1960s.

Most of the major doctrinal decisions were made early in the council, and these decrees clearly rejected Protestantism, of all kinds: Lutheran, Reformed, and Anabaptist. Among the most important of the doctrinal decrees were (1) justification is by faith formed by love, not by faith alone; (2) salvation comes through an acquired and inherent righteousness, not through an imputed righteousness; (3) there are seven sacraments exist; (4) the Latin Vulgate is the only canonical text of scripture; (5) the unwritten "apostolic" tradition has authority in interpreting scripture; (6) the church, not individuals, determines orthodoxy; (7) penance involves satisfaction as well as contrition and confession; 8) in the Mass the elements are transubstantiated into the body and blood of Christ, and the Mass is a sacrifice of Christ; 9) private Masses are commended; 10) the liturgy must remain in Latin; and 10) the cup is denied to the laity who receive the full sacrament in the bread. The church had disputed some of these items before Trent, and the more conciliatory cardinals, such as Contarini and Pole opposed the decrees. Carafa won on the major doctrinal matters. Catholicism was to be clearly distinguished from Protestantism.

Trent also instituted a number of disciplinary reforms, inspired by Contarini, that centered on making the local diocese subject to the local bishop. Reform was not as thorough as many would have liked, but considering the vested interests of the participants, it was more extensive than most had hoped. Among the reforms approved at Trent were that bishops should be primarily pastoral leaders of dioceses who call regular diocesan councils. Bishops must reside in their see, and every diocese must have a theological seminary to train priests if no university exists. Moreover, fewer clerics were allowed to be exempt from episcopal control, thus eliminating the plague of vagabond priests complained about in every country in Europe since the Middle Ages. The papal curia was reduced and cleansed of many abuses as well. All in all, Trent was a remarkable achievement, and its decrees became the law of the Catholic Church until modern times. Trent offers a summary of the distinctive features of the Catholic reform of the sixteenth century that (1) focused on clarifying and defending Catholic teaching against the new Protestant ideas; (2) concentrated on improving the morality and discipline of the clergy, including the bishops; (3) stressed piety and charity among the laity; and (4) supported papal supremacy.

Charles Borromeo (1538-1584), an Italian nobleman related to the d'Medici family was one of the most important figures in the final stages of Trent. At first he might appear to be an odd choice for a church reformer since the career of the young Borromeo seemed to exemplify nepotism and simony in the church. When he was only twelve he was placed as the abbott of a wealthy Benedictine abbey controlled by his family. He studied theology and prepared to advance in the church, but his rise was accelerated after his uncle became Pope Pius IV in 1559. Before Borromeo reached age twenty-three, he was appointed papal legate of Bologna, Romagna and the March of Ancona, protector of Portugal, the Low Countries, Switzerland, the Franciscan Order, the Carmelite Order, and the Knights of Malta, and made a cardinal. In many ways he was a typical renaissance Italian prince, living in a lavish palace and entertaining on a grand scale. His only real contribution to the church or the world as a young cardinal was as a patron of learning, but then he set to work on the final session of the council of Trent.

Personally pious and reasonably intelligent, Borromeo wrote the catechism of the Council of Trent. He also supervised a major renovation of the liturgy and church music. In 1563 he was consecrated Bishop of Milan, a city that had not had a resident bishop for nearly a century, but he did not enter his see until 1566. When he took over his duties, Borromeo proved to be exactly the type of bishop envisioned by the reformers at Trent. He reorganized the diocesan finances in order to give more assistance to the poor, insisted on children in the parishes being educated according to the catechism, established schools and libraries, and confessed his own sins daily. His efforts at bringing the entire diocese under his episcopal control led one disgruntled priest to attempt assassination. Until his early death, Borromeo worked tirelessly to implement the reforms of Trent, in particular raising the educational level of the clergy.

Mysticism

The resurgence of Roman Catholicism in the late sixteenth century included more than just administrative reform of the church and a better definition of Catholic doctrine. A new flowering of mystical piety, particularly in Spain, also fueled it. As we have seen, mysticism is not very concerned with institutions and theological debates. Instead it focuses on personal religio us experience. In this way, it can be very similar to the concerns of the Protestant reformers, and Catholic mysticism made its way into Protestantism in the late seventeenth century. Mysticism, in general, though, is usually united to asceticism, that is the practice of self-denial; therefore mysticism thrives in a monastic setting. By and large, genuine mysticism is much more at home in Catholic monasticism than in Protesantism with its call for full involvement in the world and its fear of works righteousness.

The greatest of the sixteenth century mystics was Teresa of Jesus of Avila (1515-1582) whose works *Way of Perfection, Interior Castle*, and *The Life of Teresa by Herself* continue to be read by Christian and non-Christians interested in the spiritual life. Teresa was a member of an old Spanish family, and educated by nuns dedicated to the Spanish style of reform. In 1535, she entered the Carmelite order at Avila, which was an unreformed convent following rules much laxer than the original Carmelite rule. Twenty years after entering the convent, Teresa experienced a conversion to the perfect life while meditating before a statue of Jesus being scourged. She began to mortify her flesh and soon began having mystical ecstasies.

She founded her own monastic house following the strict Carmelite rule in 1562, despite much opposition from both her male and female superiors. She wrote *Way of Perfection* to instruct her nuns in austerity, mortification of the flesh, and prayer. Her reforming efforts eventually developed into a separate stricter branch of the Carmelites, known as the Barefoot Carmelites. During the struggle to establish her order, Teresa's mysticism grew deeper, and in 1572 she experienced the spiritual marriage with Christ. Her reputation for sanctity attracted many followers who longed to experience complete union with Christ. Interestingly, her greatest disciple was a man, John of the Cross (1542-1591), who wrote the famous work *Dark Night of the Sou* that explores the issue of spiritual dryness and depression as one advances toward mystical union.

Popular Roman Catholicism in the post-Tridentine church produced a host of capable and energetic men and women who sought to make Christianity a living reality for ordinary people. One of these was Frances de

Sales (1567-1622) who managed to win Savoy, near Geneva, back to Rome by demonstrating the moral and charitable aspects of Roman Catholicism. His book *Introduction to the Devout Life*, published in 1609, promoted the idea of Christian perfection for the laity. Even a common person could live a holy life without becoming a nun or monk. His work was immensely popular, even among Protestants. Although Protestant and Catholic theologians continued to hurl polemics at each other for centuries, as the years progressed some believers began to find some common ground liturgically and devotionally between the two branches of Christianity, using the writings of de Sales and Teresa for inspiration. However, tensions were still high early in the seventeenth century, and in 1618 they broke out in war.

Chapter 15

The Final Wars of Religion

BY 1555 GERMANY was largely Protestant. Most of the secular rulers had embraced the new faith as had most of the people. Catholicism was preserved mainly by the ecclesiastical rulers, the archbishops of Mainz, Trier, and Cologne, some powerful dukes in the south, most notably Duke Albert V (1550-1579) of Bavaria, and, the Hapsburg emperors. Protestantism in Germany was not fully united, however. In addition to the division between the Lutherans and the Reformed, a number of bitter theological controversies that arose after the death of Luther in 1546 divided the Lutherans.

Lutheran Divisions

Many of these controversies surrounded Philip Melanchthon who continued to attempt reconciliation with both Catholics and Reformed. His later editions of the *Loci communes* and the 1540 edition of the Augsburg Confession seemed to modify Luther's teaching on justification and the sacraments. Melanchthon tentatively proposed that humans do cooperate with the Holy Spirit in justification and that the presence of Christ in the Eucharist is more a spiritual than a physical reality. During the Augsburg Interim, Melanchthon also allowed the use of a number of practices other Lutherans considered dangerously Catholic. On the issues of justification and worship, Melanchthon was called a crypto-catholic, but on the issue of Holy Communion, he was called a crypto-Calvinist.

Matthias Flacius (1520-1575), a professor of theology at the new Lutheran University of Jena, took the lead in opposing Melanchthon and his supporters, the Philipists. In polemics, theological works, and his monumental church history, the *Magdeburg Centuries*, Flacius and his colleagues vigorously promoted Gnesio-Lutheran (true Lutheran) orthodoxy and opposed all forms of compromise with Catholicism and Calvinism.

Andrea Osiander (1498-1552), the publisher of Copernicus' work on the solar system, also began a controversy when he proposed that justification makes sinners actually righteous through the indwelling of Christ, rather than being merely proclaimed righteous. At times the Lutheran dispute led to the persecution and torture of suspected heretics, but in 1577 a number of theologians met to resolve their differences. The fruit of their efforts was the Formula of Concord, a statement of Lutheran theology that rejected the extremes on both sides of the debate while defining the difference between Lutheranism and Calvinism.

In 1580, the fiftieth anniversary of the Augsburg Confession, the Formula was published in the *Book of Concord* along with three ancient ecumenical creeds, the original Augsburg Confession, Melanchthon's *Apology*, the Schmalkald Articles, and Luther's Small and Large Catechism. The *Book of Concord* would become the basis for Lutheran theology down to the present. Fifty-one princes, officers of thirty-five major cities, and over eight thousand Lutheran ministers signed the *Book of Concord*. It helped heal divisions among Lutherans, and ushered in the era of Lutheran Orthodoxy, but it did not solve all religious problems in Germany.

Bohemia

Calvinism made inroads in the Empire during this period of theological strife. The Reformed churches were not recognized in the Peace of Augsburg, thus they had no legal status, but they continued to attract converts. In 1559, the elector of the Palatinate, Frederick III (1559-1576), shocked Europe by adopting Calvinism and granting toleration to the Reformed Church in his realm. Heidelberg quickly became the intellectual center of Reformed theology in the Palatinate, and it was there that irenic theologians prepared the Heidelberg Catechism of 1562 for use in educating the laity. Calvinism was also advancing in Hungary, Poland, and Bohemia.

The Utraquist Church in the late sixteenth century had become basically a Lutheran Church, although many conservative Utraquists rejected Protestantism and returned to the Catholic Church. The Unity of the Brethren, on the other hand, moved closer to the Reformed Church, particularly as represented by Martin Bucer. In order to present a united front against the Catholic overlords of Bohemia, particularly in the face of determined activity by the Jesuits, the Utraquists, Reformed, and the Brethren in Bohemia presented Emperor Maximillian with a joint *Confessio Bohemica* in 1575. The emperor gave a verbal promise to respect freedom of religion for those who adhered to the confession, but he broke his word in Bohemia and forbade the Brethren to hold public worship or print books.

Maximillian's successor, Rudolf II, made Prague his capital and spent great sums of money on making it the intellectual center of the scientific revolution, but he had political difficulties in his realm. He initially gave the Jesuits a free hand in trying to make Bohemia Catholic again, even allowing them to violate royal laws. However, he had difficulties with his aggressive brother Matthias, the king of Hungary, who wanted to be emperor. In order to secure the support of the Protestant nobility in Bohemia and Moravia, Rudolf signed a letter granting freedom of worship in 1609. This move by the emperor angered the Jesuits and other Catholics in the imperial court, and gave fuel to Matthias' efforts to have Rudolf declared insane. Rudolf was soon deposed, and when Matthias became the king of Bohemia, he made it clear that there would be no toleration of heresy. Protestants were removed from office; Protestant children were taken from their parents and educated by the Jesuits; Protestant services were interrupted and churches destroyed.

The religious tensions in Prague were the worst they had been since Hussite days. The Protestant Estates (the nobility, clergy, and merchants) met in 1618 and drew up a list of grievances to present to the new emperor and soon-to-be king of Bohemia, Ferdinand. When the emperor's appointed representatives refused to deliver the document, some of the Protestant nobles threw them out of the window of Hradcany Castle. This second Defenestration of Prague led to open revolt as the Protestants established their own government and exiled the Jesuits and the archbishop of Prague. Thus began one of the longest and most destructive conflicts in European history.

The Thirty Years War

The following year, the Czech nobility declared Emperor Ferdinand, a tyrant, and they offered the Bohemian crown to Frederick IV of the Palatinate. Frederick led the Protestant League, participated as a devout member of the Reformed Church, and was the brother-in-law of James I, the King of England. He was crowned on 31 October (Reformation Day) in 1619, but contrary to his expectations, the Protestant kings and princes of Europe did not support the Bohemian rebellion. The army of Jan Tserkales, Count of Tilly destroyed the Protestant forces at the battle of White Mountain, near Prague, on November 8, 1620.

Through harsh repression of religious dissidents, Catholicism was reestablished in Bohemia and Moravia, and the nobles loyal to the Hapsburgs confiscated the estates of the rebels. Among them was Albrecht von Wallenstein who would successfully lead the Catholic forces later in the war. Similar measures were employed in Austria. As the Hapsburgs exerted control over Hungary, Calvinism was similarly repressed there.

Emperor Ferdinand issued his Edict of Restitution on March 6, 1629. All Catholic Church property that had fallen into Protestant use (churches, cathedrals, abbeys, etc.) since 1552 was to be restored, and Protestants living under Catholic rulers were expelled from those realms. The only religion other than Catholicism to be tolerated in the Empire would be Lutheranism as defined by the Book of Concord.

In many ways, the story of the Thirty Years War does not belong in a history of Christianity. Despite the fact that religion played a role in the conflict, the war was really a war of dynastic competition among the leaders of Europe. At one point, Cardinal Richelieu of France negotiated an alliance with the Ottoman Turks against the papacy and the empire. Religion was clearly not first in the minds of the contestants. In any event, the war had three distinct stages. From 1625-1629 the emperor was largely successful in capturing Protestant lands in the Empire, but he lost many of those gains in the next six years when Sweden, under Gustavus Aldophus, came to the fore. An avowed Lutheran, Gustavus had no qualms about an alliance with Catholic France, but he did refuse to acknowledge the Edict of Restitution in the lands he conquered.

In the final phase of the war (1635-1648), France asserted the greatest influence, but in the end the war ground down to an inconclusive ending. Finally exhausted by the ceaseless conflict, the warring parties agreed to a settlement. Their diplomats met at Westphalia where they negotiated peace treaties that were signed on October 27, 1648. Politically, the Peace of Westphalia permanently altered the Holy Roman Empire. The independence of Switzerland and Holland was recognized. The Empire became the Holy Roman Empire of the German Nation and the sovereignty of the individual states was confirmed. Brandenburg, Austria, Sweden, France, and Bavaria all gained territory. On the religious issue, the peace of Augsburg was reaffirmed. Those states that were Protestant in 1624 could remain Protestant. The Edict of Restitution was revoked and the Reformed Church was accorded rights for the first time. The Peace of Westphalia was at best a compromise. Europe remained divided by religion, but the era of religious warfare had given way to the era of war between nation-states.

Conclusion

The Protestant Reformation began with one man's struggle over sin and salvation. It ended with a conflagration that nearly destroyed Europe. Although much of the history of the era is filled with war, persecution, and religious hatred, it was also a period of significant religious activity. It was an era of saints, martyrs, and mystics. The Protestant reformers, whether Lutheran, Calvinist, or Anabaptist, responded to the corruption of the late medieval church by breaking away from Rome and creating new ecclesiastical institutions. Reformers within the Catholic Church created new religious orders, inspired renewed popular devotion, and corrected many ancient abuses. It was a time of serious debate over the nature of the church and the meaning of scripture that produced profound theological insights and serious attempts to mold a Christian society. The Reformation sanctioned the strivings of many in Europe to break free of the old feudal order with its privileges and obligations in favor of dynamic industry and experimentation. The Protestant belief in the priesthood of all believers exalted family and secular vocations.

However, the shattering of the unity of the church continued as Protestants disagreed among themselves over the meaning of scripture and the proper form of the church. Protestant clergy and magistrates proved to be as skillful in the art of persecution as their Catholic counterparts. Throughout its history, Protestantism continueed to splinter as the Protestant dynamic continued to encourage men and women to challenge ecclesiastical authority and church tradition.

The Reformation also led to a major renovation of the Catholic Church, helping it to break away from some of the more egregious abuses of the Middle Ages. Reform-minded bishops and cardinals labored hard to reduce the greed of the church and to improve the morality and educational level of the clergy. The Catholic Church became better disciplined and focused more on its essential religious mission after Trent. Thanks to this reforming effort, the church was better prepared to face the new political situation as the nation-state replaced the Empire and the pope ceased to be a major political figure. In Catholic Europe, the era of the Reformation saw a renewal of spirituality and piety that made the church stronger than ever. Western Christianity had survived, and even thrived, in the midst of reformation, division, war, and persecution. The next question would be whether it could handle the unique challenges of the Enlightenment.

Part 3

Religion of the Heart in the Age of Reason

THE FIFTEENTH AND sixteenth centuries opened with calls for reform in the church. The reforming effort led to the Reformation, which in turn led to warfare throughout Europe. By the beginning of the seventeenth century, Christianity, which had once helped create and unify European culture, had become a major source of division and war. It took Europe decades to recover from the horrors of the Thirty Years War, a conflict that marked a watershed in Western history. The Treaty of Westphalia and the restoration of the Stuart kings in England helped settle the political side of the conflict; however, prolonged years of religious conflict and persecution raised profound questions about the nature of religion, and the relationship of the church and state. Treaties and armies could not settle religious questions nor satisfy religious yearnings. In the decades following the war, philosophers and preachers alike expressed ideas that eroded the foundations of the Constantinian church. In sanctuaries, halls of government, and even in coffee houses and salons, men and women debated the meaning and proper role of religion in a world enlarged by discoveries and enriched by technology.

It is no surprise, then, that the eighteenth century would also see a number of creative reforming movements in the Western church and in Western society. The most famous of the movements is the Enlightenment, which transformed politics, fashion, science, and education. A second movement also had a profound impact on life and culture, but historians have largely overlooked it. This religious revival and reformation effort goes by a number of names and had diverse manifestations, but we can describe it by the general name Heart Religion. Heart Religion would change the nature of both Protestantism and Catholicism as the churches struggled to make Christianity relevant to the changing circumstances of common people, and to set up a bulwark against atheism and loss of faith. As we shall see, the Enlightenment and Heart Religion shared many goals, but by the end of the eighteenth century, these two great streams of Western culture would take opposing stands. The eighteenth century closed with the French Revolution, and a growing sense that the Age of Reason had supplanted the Age of Faith. The events and ideas of the eighteenth century sowed the seeds for the ambiguous role of religious faith in the modern world of science and commerce.

Chapter 16

Creating a Christian Society in the Old World and the New

IN MUSIC AND art history, the period 1600-1750 is termed the Baroque Age. Within Catholicism, it could also be termed the Jesuit Age since the Society of Jesus proved to be the most dynamic force in the Catholic Reformation. As early as 1559, 1,000 Jesuits were living in some 100 foundation houses. By the time Pope Clement XIV suppressed the order in 1773, there were 23,000 Jesuits whose influence was felt in every major court in Catholic Europe. At that time, the Jesuits operated 800 or more schools with over 200,000 students, most of whom came from the leading families of Europe. General Acquaviva in his *Ratio atque Institutio Studiorum Societas Jesus* in the 1580s expressed the Jesuit ideal of education. It was an elitist education designed to keep the upper classes faithful to the Catholic cause. The Jesuits used advanced methods to teach the liberal arts, religion, the new sciences, and good manners to the upper classes of Europe. Even Protestant rulers sent their children to be educated by the Jesuits.

Unlike many religious reformers through the ages, however, the Jesuits did not oppose all sensual pleasures or advanced learning. In fact, the Jesuits lived among the more cultured and educated members of European society, and actively encouraged religious decorative arts. Jesuit theology stressed the divine order of the cosmos and viewed human creativity as an important expression of religious faith. Their motto *"Ad Majorem Dei Gloriam"* could well have been the motto for the entire Baroque Age in which visual and musical beauty attempted to overwhelm the senses with the glory of God and the story of salvation. Baroque played on the full range of human emotions in an attempt to lift the believer toward heaven. In an age when science was advancing a mechanistic view of reality, the Baroque celebrated the supernatural. Baroque painting and architecture had its greatest impact in Catholic countries, but its influence is seen even in the work of Christopher Wren in England.

Perhaps the greatest legacy of the Baroque Age is its religious music. Baroque music, largely produced by Catholic and Lutheran composers, stands in exuberant contrast to the austere psalmody of the Puritans. Unafraid to touch the deepest chords of the human soul, Baroque music appeals to the full range of emotion to strengthen the soul's union with its Savior. One of the innovations of the Baroque Age was the sacred cantata, an unstaged religious opera that uses beauty as a means to evangelize. The cantata would become known as the oratorio because the Oratorians, a religious order founded by Filippo Neri, used the form so extensively. The Oratorians used beautiful music as a way to win people back to the faith. The masters would be Joseph Haydn ("The Creation" 1798), Johann Sebastian Bach (St. John's Passion 1724; St. Matthew's Passion 1727), and George Fridrich Handel. Händel alone wrote thirty-one oratorios including *Esther* (1718), *Saul* (1739), and the *Messiah* (1742), which has become a musical and religious tradition for millions in the West.

Poland

The seventeenth century saw the Roman church slowly winning back some of the lands lost during the Reformation. The most notable example is Poland, a nation that was being politically dismembered during the eighteenth century. Poland had no strong central government because the powerful local lords had successfully resisted the rising tide of absolutism that was winning the day in the West. Poland's nobility, therefore, could protect a number of religious groups that found toleration nowhere else in Europe. Members of the Unitas Fratrum found refuge here when persecution raged in Bohemia. The Lutheran and Reformed churches established a strong foothold in Poland, building on the work of Jan Laski. In addition, native Orthodox and Catholic populations remained. Even the anti-Trinitarian followers of Fausto Sozzini (1525-1562) found a degree of toleration in Poland that the rest of Europe denied them.

One of the first great ecumenical statements, the Consensus of Sandomier, a mutual protection agreement between Lutherans, Reformed, and the Brethren, was signed in Poland in 1575. By the end of the sixteenth century, it appeared that Poland would follow northern Europe and become entirely Protestant; however, several things conspired to bring Poland back to Rome. The energetic activity of the Jesuits won a number of powerful nobles back to Catholicism, and encouraged persecution of Protestants and Soccinians. Another important factor occurred during a war between Sweden and Poland. The monastery of Czestochowa valiantly and successfully resisted a Swedish siege in 1655. Queen Louisa Mary of Gonzague decided that the Black Virgin of Czestochowa had ensured the victory, so she placed the entire nation under the Black Virgin's patronage. Her decision led to an outpouring of popular support for the Virgin. Catholicism and nationalism were joined, leading to renewed persecution of Protestants. In 1717 non-Catholics were denied legal rights. In the eighteenth century, as Poland was being squeezed between Orthodox Russia and Protestant Prussia, Catholicism became a mark of national pride, and in the twentieth century Poland would remain one of the most devout Catholic countries in Europe.

Catholic Missions

The Jesuits were also great innovators in the mission to non-Christian peoples. Closely tied to the courts of Spain and Portugal, Jesuit missionaries went wherever European merchants and explorers went. A spirited, and at times bitter, competition existed between the Jesuits, Franciscans, and Dominicans for new mission fields. Francis Xavier (1506-1552) became the patron saint for many Catholic missionaries because of his heroic and innovative work in Asia. He went to India in 1541, and found particular success among the lower castes. There he established a church among the Paravas people and promoted the ordination of local Indian priests. In 1549, Xavier went farther East and found creative ways to adapt Christian rituals and doctrines to Japanese thought-forms and customs.

Inspired by his remarkable success among the educated classes, he set out for China in 1552, but he died without reaching the Celestial Empire. The mission in Japan was reserved for the Jesuits, and it continued to prosper after his death. One of the feudal lords, a *daimyo*, was baptized in 1567. By 1582, reports showed that there were some 150,000 Japanese Christians in 200 churches. Six years later Japan received its first bishopric. In the first half of the seventeenth century, however, the shoguns of Japan crushed the fledging church as part of a nationalistic campaign against foreign influences. Christianity was outlawed in the 1630s, and thousands of Christians were killed in popular uprisings or executed by the rulers in Japan as they closed its doors to the West and its religion. However, thousands of Christians in the mountains near Nagasaki secretly kept the faith well into the nineteenth century.

Although Xavier did not make it to China, the Jesuits did bring Christianity to the Chinese Empire when the Portuguese established a trading center at Macao, near Canton. The most effective and creative of the missionaries to China was the Jesuit Matteo Ricci (1552-1610) who arrived in Macao in 1582. There he offered his expertise in mathematics, astronomy and geography for the service of Chinese officials. They found his service so valuable that they allowed him to live in the Forbidden City, Beijing, where he educated himself in Chinese classics, making a careful study of Confucian writings. Ricci found ways to express Christian doctrine in terms acceptable to the followers of Confucius, and even created a Christian version of the rituals used to honor one's ancestors, a vital part of Chinese culture. In effect, Ricci made it possible for one to remain faithful to the Chinese heritage and Confucian way while becoming a Christian. Many prominent officials converted as a result, and by 1700 over 200,000 Christians lived in China with their own native bishops. The Jesuits were even entrusted with the task of revising the official Chinese calendar for the emperor; however, the Chinese mission was doomed to fail, largely because of a change in papal policy.

Ricci's Confucian-Christian rites were the source of a controversy in Europe that lasted for nearly a century. The "war of the rites" started in 1643 when the Dominicans argued to the papacy that Ricci's rites encouraged idolatry and syncretism, the blending of Christianity and paganism. Scholars all over Europe rallied to the defense of the Jesuit rites. Even the Protestant philosopher Leibnitz joined the debate, arguing that the West could learn much from the wisdom of the East without losing saving faith in Christ. Unmoved by such appeals, the papacy condemned the practice of accommodating Christianity to local cultures in 1704. A papal delegation that was sent to Beijing to investigate the Jesuit mission angered the emperor K'ang Hsi so much that he expelled all missionaries who refused to use the Ricci rites. The final blow came in 1742 when Benedict XIV issued the bull *Ex quo singulari* forbidding the use of the Chinese rites. The bull halted the Chinese mission. In 1814, as part of an anti-foreigner policy in China, all Christian missionaries were expelled from the Empire.

Catholic Missions to the Americas

The most successful French missionary to North America was the Jesuit Jean de Brebeuf (1593—1649) who worked among the Huron in Ontario. He baptized about a thousand converts during his short career, and built five chapels. Brebeuf found his inspiration in Francis Xavier, and like the great missionary to the East, Brebeuf sought to communicate the gospel in the idiom of the local people. A Christmas carol Brebeuf wrote in the Huron language illustrates his effort: "Within a lodge of broken bark/The tender Babe was found/A ragged robe of rabbit skin/Enwrapp'd His beauty round;/But as the hunter braves drew nigh/The angel song rang loud and high/Jesus your king is born, Jesus is born/In excelsis gloria." Brebeuf urged missionaries to live with the natives, even eating foods they found repulsive. The Iroquois captured Brefeuf in 1649 during a war with the Huron. His courage during his long and vicious torture so impressed the Iroquois that they paid him the ultimate compliment. They ate his heart after he died.

The story of the Spanish conquistadors and their brutal treatment of the native peoples of the Americas is infamous. Frequently missionaries assisted in the subjugation of the native population; however, that was not always the case. The Dominican priest Bartolome de las Casas stands out as a notable exception. He moved from slaveholder to a liberator and advocate for native rights. His father had sailed on Columbus' second voyage to America, and brought back an Indian slave to serve as Bartolome's pageboy. As a young man Bartolome came to America and became a planter and slaveholder on the island Hispaniola. When he became a priest, he ministered to the Spanish colonists, planters like himself. In 1514 he had to preach on an assigned text from Ecclesiasticus: "The sacrifice of an offering unjustly acquired is a mockery," and suddenly he saw the situation of the natives in a new light. He realized that he mocked God by living off of the land and labor of the Indians.

Shortly after, he returned to Spain to plead the cause of the native peoples. The newly crowned King of Spain, Charles V, passed laws intended to protect the natives, and he eventually gave Las Casas a colony on the coast of Venezuela where he could create a new type of community among the natives. The community was to be based on love rather than fear, but it failed miserably in part because of the attacks of local slave holders. Las Casas then retired to a monastery where he wrote the monumental *Brief Relation of the Destruction of the Indies*, published in 1552. The thesis of the work is simple: the Spanish were cruel oppressors and the natives were noble savages. He asserted that the Indians were superior to the ancient Greeks and Romans, and had developed utopian republics in the wilderness.

His compelling account of the abuse of the native peoples led to some changes in Spanish policy, but ultimately his attractive myth of the noble savage did the natives little good. It contrasted too sharply with the popular stories of human sacrifices and inhuman cruelties among the natives, some of which were also true. Las Casas also made one tragic proposal in his defense of Indians. If slaves are necessary for the economy, he asked, then why not bring Africans over to the new world to work the plantations and the mines? Two years later, in 1518, Charles V authorized the use of Africans as slaves in the New World. Although Las Casas repudiated his suggestion later, the damage was already done.

The Jesuits conducted the boldest and most successful mission to the native peoples of America. They were granted land along the Parani River between Paraguay and Brazil in order to build an experimental Christian commonwealth in 1610. They established a number of communal societies, called Reductions, among the Guarani people in order to prove that the natives could be Christianized and civilized according to Western standards without violence. The Republic of the Guarani was a remarkable state by any standards. All of the residents had full access to education, health care, and a means of labor. The Jesuits taught agriculture and manufacturing in addition to religion, and the region prospered.

At its height in the mid-eighteenth century, the Republic had 350,000 residents, but it had also earned the jealousy of greedy plantation owners in the vicinity. In 1750 Ferdinand VI of Spain deeded part of the Reductions to Portugal. Soon armed conflict broke out between Portuguese colonists and the Guarani. After the Jesuits were expelled from Spain in 1767, the Republic of Guarani was violently crushed. The Jesuit Reductions were a remarkable attempt to build a Christian commonwealth, but other such efforts also took place in the seventeenth century. During this period, some Protestants wanted to reform church and society completely.

The Puritans in New England

Throughout its history, America has been the home and the inspiration for religious experimenters and seekers of all kinds. America offered the promise of a new beginning, an opportunity to create or recreate the church in its purity. Of course, as many have discovered, one cannot entirely escape the past even when fleeing to a new land. The new churches and religious movements that flourished in America still retained close historical connections with the European world. The Puritans offer a case in point. We last saw the Puritans in the context of the English Civil War when Parliament rebelled against King Charles' religious and domestic policies. In the years of religious struggle leading up to the Civil War, significant numbers of Puritans chose to leave England, because they saw it as the corrupt Babylon mentioned in the Bible. They fled to a new land where they could worship as they believed God intended. The Puritans felt strongly that they were living in the last days before the triumphant return of Jesus.

The Separatist congregation led by John Robinson in Scrooby Manor was a group that read the signs of the times. As the laws against nonconformity grew more severe, Robinson and his followers believed they were witnessing the first signs of the final tribulation. Therefore, in 1609, they left England where the man they considered the servant of the antichrist sat on the throne. Thus they became Pilgrims, religious travelers who had fled to a new land. First they settled in Leyden in tolerant Holland, where they found freedom of worship, but the general freedom of Dutch society frightened them. So they made plans to put an ocean between themselves and corrupt Europe. They secured passage on a ship of the Virginia Company, the Mayflower, and set sail on 6 September 1620.

Their ship was bound for the new colony of Virginia, but whether by chance or the grace of God, it was blown off course and landed in Cape Cod in early November. The Pilgrims defied the terms of their agreement with the Virginia Company and the King's charter by settling in what would later be called Massachusetts. Before they departed the stinking, tiny Mayflower they sealed a solemn Compact to order their new life together. William Bradford, Miles Standish, and other Pilgrim names would become part the American identity because of their heroic efforts in the first winter of their colony. It was a "starving time" when nearly half of the small colony died, but discipline and faith brought them through. In the spring some of the few Indians in the area, including Squanto and Massasoit, befriended them, and helped the settlers adjust to a new climate.

The Plymouth Bay Colony was intended to be a society of the saints, but it should be noted that sinners as well as saints lived in Plymouth. For instance, in 1642 the magistrates executed Thomas Graunger on charges of bestiality, which specified that he had intercourse with "a mare, a cow, two goats, diverse sheep, two calves, and a turkey."[11] They also shipped Thomas Morton back to England after he set up a Maypole at Merry Mount. The problem was not just the maypole, however. Morton also sold guns and alcohol to Indians, and arranged sexual liaisons for the white settlers. Despite such distractions, by 1630 Plymouth Bay colony had grown to 300 persons, and was prosperous by colonial standards. Soon it would be overtaken by another Puritan Colony—Massachusetts Bay Colony.

In 1630, King James was persuaded to allow some of the most bothersome Puritans to set up a royal colony in the New World. It seemed like a good solution to a number of problems. They would be out of England, but England would benefit from their colony. Within a decade 1400 settlers had joined the new Massachusetts Bay Colony. In another decade it would boast 20,000 residents, almost all loyal Englishmen. For religious settlers fleeing England, the biblical story of ancient Israel became their story. They had experienced the Exodus from Egypt when they fled the corruption of England. America was their Promised Land where they could set up a society based on God's laws just as the Israelites had covenanted at Shechem. The Puritan leaders were determined to avoid the mistakes of ancient Israel. In the Promised Land of America, God's people would remain faithful to God's law for the good of society.

The Puritans in Massachusetts Bay officially remained loyal to the Church of England, but they rejected the church's bishops. Instead of bishops, they governed their religous life through the congregational system, and ordained their own ministers without episcopal approval. They also tried to govern their society by a literal understanding of the Bible. John Winthrop, a Cambridge graduate, became the leader of the new venture. He was a vigorous and capable leader who outlived three wives and had a total of sixteen children. Winthrop staked out the capital village of Boston carefully, placing the green and the church in the center of town. He wanted Boston to be a "city on a hill" shining a light of righteousness to guide England to the true path. The arrangement would become the norm for New England villages where the church was the symbolic and functional center of the village.

The Puritans in America were Reformed in theology. They believed that the Bible was a clear book which set forth God's will for all to read. Both the Old and New Testaments regulated personal life, church life, and civic life. All persons had rights and duties in the Puritan state, but only converted men

---

[11] Martin Marty, *Pilgrims in Their Own Land: 500 Years of Religion in America* (New York: Penguin Books, 1984) 61.

could vote and hold office. The arrangement had to be modified in the 1660s with a Half-way Covenant that allowed morally upright, but unconverted men to hold public office. The Puritans also advocated the theology of the biblical book of Deuteronomy that proclaims that if the nation lives obediently it will be blessed; if not, it will be judged and punished. The idea governed much of the penitential system of the Puritans and explains why they considered blasphemy such a serious offense. Individual sins, even secret sins, could destroy the whole society. Year after year on election days New England preachers called the citizens to repent or face God's righteous judgment. These jeremiads (named for the prophet Jeremiah) continually called people to remember that the original purpose of New England was to be a model for the entire world to see.

The other side of this deuteronomic theology, though, was equally important. The Puritans believed that the saints would be blessed in the present life if they lived obediently. The blessings of holiness, such as food, shelter, and family may be enjoyed with thanksgiving as long as they did not interfere with devotion to God. Riches were not evil in themselves, as the church has often taught, but they could become a temptation to turn from God. Therefore the Puritans were in a bit of a bind. They had to enjoy God's blessings without renouncing the world. The sociologist Max Weber called their situation "worldly asceticism," and he credited this perspective on wealth and duty for creating the necessary conditions for the capitalist ethic.

Winthrop was representative of the Puritan "godly magistrates" who created the New England way of life, a life dedicated to sobriety and stability. For example, Winthrop and his first wife Margaret lived so devoted to order and stability that they covenanted to think only of each other between five and six o'clock on Mondays and Fridays. The idea of the covenant helped set the Puritans apart from Calvin. Calvin's theology leaves one with the distinct, although not accurate, impression that God is a puppeteer in control of every historical moment. The Puritans modified Calvin's theology with the notion of the covenant based on the covenants God made with Noah, Abraham, Isaac, and Jacob in the book of Genesis. According to New England theologians, God always works through covenants. Even the laws of nature were part of God's covenant. God could have structured the world in any way, but God made a covenant that the world would predictably work in a certain way. The laws of nature were thus part of God's providence.

Like their European predecessors, though, the settlers of New England lived in an enchanted world. God's providence governed, but forces of evil still filled the world. Early New Englanders lived in a wilderness filled with demons and magic that preyed upon their psyche. The wilderness called to them and repulsed them. The devil was alive and well in New England, and the settlers had no doubts about the reality of a burning hell. They delighted in the thought that their persecutors would suffer in eternity, but they lived in fear that they or their children might as well. Despite the assurances that God would be faithful to the elect, they feared the seductions of Satan. The only way to fight the devil was with constant vigilance—of oneself and one's neighbor. Vigilance could lead to savage persecution, such as the famous witch trials in Salem in 1692. However, the more threatening forms of dissent did not involve demonic forces; they came from within Puritanism itself. Despite their best efforts to create a stable and uniform society, the Puritans in New England faced dissent almost from the beginning of their settlement.

New England Dissenters

Roger Williams (1604-1683) was a strict Calvinist who took Puritan theology to logical extremes that threatened the New England system. For one thing, Williams questioned the right of European kings and Parliaments to give away lands that God had given to the Indians. In Rhode Island, he insisted on establishing a legal covenant with the Indians to purchase their lands regardless of what the king said. He established friendships with the natives, and was one of the few Puritan leaders to learn native tongues. Massachusetts land owners and farmers did not want to hear such talk about aboriginal peoples having natural rights to their land and language.

As a pastor, Williams also insisted on strict biblical purity in his congregation. Women had to wear veils in church, for instance. At one point he felt so distressed that his wife had remained friendly with impious persons in his congregation that he refused to say table grace with her at mealtimes. Such austerity was disturbing, but even more troubling was Will-iams' argument that it was useless, perhaps even sinful, to try to force the unconverted to live under the gospel law. Williams maintained that since true Christian action comes only from a Christian heart, it was wrong to force unbelievers to go to church or observe Sabbath laws. Each person must make up his or her own mind based on rational argument. Truth will win in the competition of ideas; therefore ideas must not be restricted.

Williams was called to be the preacher at Salem in 1633 and soon attract-ed the ire of Winthrop and the leading citizens of Boston. Such radical ideas, although consistent with Reformed theology, would unravel society as the New England magistrates understood it. Williams was banished from Massachusetts. In the competition of ideas, civil authority won out. Everyone expected that Williams would go back to England, but he chose the wilderness. He left Boston in October 1635 and barely survived a bitter winter.

When he arrived at Narragansett Bay in April 1636, he named his new city Providence. Williams put his convictions into practice and built his new Rhode Island colony on the principle of religious toleration. It was the first such colony in America, and it soon attracted dissidents of all stripes. He allowed the residents of Rhode Island to express all manner of unorthodox views while he debated his own notions of biblical truth with them. He was frustrated that the truth did not always win such debates or convince his hearers, but he made the step few Europeans or Americans could imagine. He clearly separated government and religion, for the good of the Christianity.

The Antinomian Controversy

The next great dissension in New England involved a midwife named Anne Hutchinson(1591-1643) who was convinced of Puritan truth, but used that truth to challenge the religious and civil authorities. In her case, the issue was two-fold. Did the covenant of grace include the law and good works? This was the so-called antinomian question. Hutchinson seemed to deny the power of the law for those who were converted. Whereas Williams argued that church laws did not bind unbelievers, Hutchinson proclaimed that it was believers who were not bound to those laws.

The other issue was whether women could be called by God to interpret scripture for men. Anne Hutchinson said yes. Governor Winthrop said no. She was tried in 1635 on the grounds that she did not honor her superiors. Hutchinson defended herself brilliantly, using Puritan arguments against the clergy who had preached them, but then she went a step too far. She claimed that she received direct inspiration from the Holy Spirit. Such a claim conjured up images of the chaos of Münster in the minds of the magistrates, and Hutchinson was quickly convicted of "enthusiasm." They shipped her off to join Roger Williams in Rhode Island. Eventually, she moved to Long Island where the natives killed her a few years later. Her fate was vindication enough for Winthrop that God had agreed with his judgment.

Quakers

Another group of Christians was even more disturbing to the Puritan order than Roger Williams or Anne Hutchinson. They spoke the same language as the Puritans and pursued many of the same ends, but what were the New Englanders to make of a group of people who were directed by an inner light rather than scripture, who shouted and ranted in the street, who proclaimed God's coming destruction of Boston and its residents, and announced the imminent return of Christ? Today most people think of the Friends as quiet people who sit silently in church and refuse military service, but people in colonial America considered them dangerous criminals. The Society of Friends will be discussed in more detail below, but a few words are necessary now to understand the hostility of the Puritans.

The Friends preached a doctrine of radical equality for men and women. All persons have direct access to God; therefore people have no need for priests, preachers, or even churches. All persons are friends; therefore one should use the familiar "thee" and "thou" for all persons of whatever social rank. Friends refused to remove their hats for dignitaries since they recognized no worldly dignity. Since they also believed they were the true prophets of the coming millennial age, many early Friends accepted imprisonment and beatings as a blessing from God. One woman shocked an English village by marching stark naked into the middle of church to symbolize the nakedness of the soul before the coming judgment of God.

In 1656 two Friends, Ann Austin and Mary Fisher, arrived in Boston with their eschatological pronouncements. They were immediately escorted out of town, but the Friends kept coming. Massachusetts tried dumping them all on Roger Williams who had no sympathy for their doctrine, but grudgingly accepted them as residents. However, many Friends felt called to bring the inner light into the Puritan darkness. Soon the Puritans resorted to more dramatic and painful measures. They bored through their tongues, cut off their ears, fined them and whipped them for insolence and blasphemy. The punishment only seemed to encourage the Friends to preach more vigorously. Finally from 1659 to 1661 the Boston authorities hanged four Friends for disturbing the peace. Less than forty years after fleeing the persecution of the bishops in England, the godly magistrates of New England killed others because of their faith.

One of those executed by the godly magistrates was Mary Dyer (1610-1660), a friend of Anne Hutchinson who had lived for years in Boston. She became convinced of the truth of the inner light during a trip to England.

Upon her return to New England, she began to criticize openly the Puritan leaders. They responding first by telling her husband to control her better. When he failed to do so, they shipped her off to Rhode Island. She came back. They banished her again, but again she returned. At one point, they stripped her to the waist and tied her behind a cart in order to whip her throughout town. That only inspired her zeal. In fact, she preached as they whipped her. When she broke her exile a fourth time the authorities decided that she must die. They hanged Mary Dyer on the Boston Commons in 1660. Rather than squelching dissent in New England, the event turned public opinion against the clergy and civil authorities in New England. It even got the attention of King Charles II who outlawed hangings for religious dissent.

Quakers were the most dramatic dissenters in New England, but Baptists became another problem for one very simple reason. They were Separatists who taught that only adult believers should be baptized. This was a direct challenge to the unified society that Winthrop and company were trying to build in New England. How could Massachusetts build a society if people attended a separate church instead of attending the established one? How could the magistrates guarantee that the citizens heard the proper sermons about heaven, hell, salvation, and their civic duty? How could children be raised without being baptized? Who were these Baptists to decide that the educated, landed elite of Boston, Salem, and other communities were not Christians?

Part of what made the Baptists a problem was that they, like Roger Williams, came out of Puritanism, but took Puritan propositions to conclusions contrary to those of the mainstream. They came from the Separatist branch of English Puritanism that had decided to make a clean break with the Church of England instead of reforming it. English Baptists soon made their way to America, and in 1639 Roger Williams helped John Clarke (1606-1676) establish a church and the town of Newport in Rhode Island as a center of Baptist activity. From this base in Newport, Clarke tried to convert the residents of Plymouth and Massachusetts. His actions led to fines and imprisonment for himself and his followers. Unlike the Friends though, Clarke had no taste for martyrdom. He challenged Puritan rule through the press, not the gallows. In 1652, he published in London *Ill News from New England*, which publicized religious persecution in New England.

More troubling to New England society than Clarke's activities, though, was the news in 1654 that the president of Harvard College, Henry Dunster, had become a Baptist. Even one of the mainstays of the Puritan establishment was not safe from dissent. It seemed like the city on a hill was crumbling almost before it could be established. Greater threats to the Puritan way lay ahead.

Chapter 17

The Enlightenment

IT MAY APPEAR strange to include a chapter on the Enlightenment in a book on Christian history since the Enlighteners were often bitter enemies of the church, but in many ways the Enlightenment also began as a way to reform Christianity in the light of the emerging science. The type of Christianity proposed by the Enlighteners was a far cry from that of the Puritans, to be sure, but individuals like John Locke and Thomas Jefferson were very concerned about religious matters. Whereas the Puritans wanted to purify Christianity from idolatry and insincerity, the Enlighteners hoped to purify religion itself from superstition and intolerance. As the quest for a rational religion developed, however, the Enlightenment grew increasingly hostile toward the traditional church and paved the way for public atheism. The story is important for our history because the questions raised against traditional Christianity defined the religious and theological issues of the nineteenth- and twentieth-centuries.

As with all major social and intellectual movements, there was not a single Enlightenment. The Enlightenment included a wide variety of thinkers and writers who maintained a loose social connection primarily in England, France, and America. They united in their self-conscious attempt to create a modern culture guided by science and reason rather than tradition and superstition. The cornerstone of the movement was freedom of inquiry and discussion. Such discussion took place in coffee houses ("penny universities"), fashionable salons, clubs, scientific societies, and public lecture halls rather than in universities. Subjects of inquiry ranged from new agricultural methods and technology to the nature of virtue. The pagan classics were rediscovered and reevaluated positively as an antidote to excessive piety and dogmatism. Moreover, there was an awareness that modern discoveries were significantly changing how the world should be viewed.

The Scientific Revolution

When people speak of the Copernican Revolution, they refer to the Polish astronomer's theory that the earth revolves around the sun rather than the sun around the earth. Little was made of Copernicus' theory as spelled out in *De revolutionibus orbium coelestium* (On the revolution of the celestial spheres) for more than half a century after his death. Copernicus offered his heliocentric (sun-centered) model of the universe as a simpler view of the cosmos than the complex Ptolemaic system, but Copernicus' theory was little better at predicting the precise positions of the heavenly bodies than the typical model. Copernicus' model also had the further disadvantage of contradicting the common sense perception that the sun moves and the earth stands still. It is not really surprising that intellectuals like Martin Luther ridiculed the heliocentric theory. As late as 1620, the great educational reformer Comenius could dismiss the Copernican theory as philosophical rather than practical. In short, Copernicus' magnus opus did not set the world on fire when it appeared in 1543.

The work of Johannes Kepler (1571-1630) and Galileo Galilei (1564-1642) moved the heliocentric theory to center stage in an intellectual debate with profound implications for Christianity and world history. Kepler and Galileo benefited from the revival of ancient mathematics in the sixteenth century. The works of Archimedes, Euclid, and Pythagoras were published in the sixteenth century, and scholars discovered that physical properties could be mathematically described. Galileo used the new mathematical power to discover the physical laws of falling bodies, shattering traditional Aristotelian ideas about motion. Kepler used the new math to discover the laws governing the motions of the heavenly bodies themselves. Between them, our view of the world would be forever changed. First we will look at the heavens and then the earth.

Kepler assisted the great astronomer Tycho Brahe (1546-1601). Emperor Rudolf II, who used astrology to rule the empire, patronized Brahe. Brahe was a master of astronomical observation and calculation. His charts of the stars and planets were by far the most precise up to that time, and they clearly revealed the inadequacies of both the Ptolemaic and Copernican systems. After his death, the great Brahe would be overshadowed by his apprentice who took his observations and applied them to the Copernican theory.

It had been assumed from ancient times that since the circle is perfect the planets must have a circular orbit. Kepler worked on his calculations for years, focusing on the difficulties of the orbit of Mars, but he could not make the calculations work using circular orbits. Eventually it dawned on him that the planets revolve with a non-circular orbit. He mathematically demonstrated that the planets revolve in an ellipse with the sun at one focus of the ellipse. Using the ellipse model, Kepler found that he could demonstrate mathematically that the planets do indeed revolve around the sun in a consistent and predictable fashion. His years of observation and calculation resulted in three simple laws of planetary motion that worked for all known planets. He published his results in 1609 in a book appropriately titled *Astronomia nova*, the new astronomy.

For Kepler, this was a divine revelation. Pythagorean mysticism that saw sacred value in numbers attracted him, and he also accepted Neoplatonic thought that viewed the universe as a shadow of the ideas thought by God. His calculations seemed to verify these philosophical notions since the cosmos could be understood in terms of simple numerical ratios. Furthermore, the first of God's creations rests at the center of the universe: the sun, the giver of light and life. Kepler was further gratified to see that the ratios of the distances of the planets from the sun matched musical harmonics. For him, there really was a music to the spheres, a music that only God could hear.

Kepler's laws of planetary motion created a sensation among those with the ability to understand his mathematical argument. He provided evidence that proved the universe itself was orderly, predictable, and far larger than previously imagined. Even comets could be explained by natural laws. God did not sent comets as omens, rather they were celestial objects following a predictable orbit. Moreover, Kepler's theory gave the first solid evidence that Copernicus was right. The earth does move. Unfortunately, Kepler's own work proved so difficult that few appreciated what he had accomplished.

One who did understand the significance of Kepler's work was an Italian mathematician and philosopher who began a raging controversy over the nature of the universe and the relationship of science and religion. Galileo taught at the University of Padua, and, like many thinkers of his generation, he found many gaps and errors in Aristotle's natural philosophy. Aristotle had said that an object needs a continual force to keep it going, but Galileo theorized that in a perfect vacuum an object would continue moving in a straight path for all time. His idea of inertia went along with Kepler's understanding of planetary motion. Once God had set the planets in motion, they would continue in motion eternally.

Galileo also began an intense observation of falling objects and discovered that objects accelerate toward the earth at a standard rate. In other words, one can predict the speed of a falling object according to the height from which it falls. His theories and observations were immediately useful in the new field of military ballistics, but they had broader implications. According to Galileo's experiments, all physical objects obey the same laws of nature. Nature is both predictable and measurable. His insight launched the great scientific endeavor of measuring all that can be measured.

Philosophers and mathematicians like Descartes discussed Galileo's writings on physics and experimentation, but his observations of the heavens became a topic of popular interest. Galileo had read about a new invention that could allow one to see great distances. In 1609 he made his own telescope and turned his gaze to the heavens above. What he saw there astounded Europe when he published his findings in a little worked titled *Sidereus nuncius*, the Starry Messenger. The heavens were not perfect as had long been assumed. Venus and Mercury had phases, just like the moon. Saturn appeared to have bulges (his telescope was too weak to see the rings clearly), and little planets circled the major planets. His observations were as disturbing as the discovery of a New World had been in a previous century. More things existed in heaven and on earth than had been dreamt of by philosophy or mentioned in the Bible.

Unlike Kepler, Galileo wrote for the educated layman, and before long he became a European-wide celebrity. His observations offered further support for the Copernican theory since the phases of the inner planets could only be explained if they revolved around the Sun and not the Earth. Soon, however, the Dominicans in Italy began to attack his writings because they contradicted Aristotle and the Bible. The theologians feared that Galileo's approach would undermine the whole Thomistic theological system that underpinned the Catholic Reformation.

The controversy came to a head in 1616 when Galileo was summoned to Rome to defend his views. Although he convinced many philosophers and theologians at the Vatican, the Copernican theory was officially condemned on the grounds that the Bible says that the earth does not move. The Catholic Church rejected Galileo's argument that the Bible speaks metaphorically in matters of natural science. Despite their judgment, Galileo continued his research and writing, and in 1632, he produced *A Dialogue on Two World Systems* in which he attacked the Aristotelian view of the universe. The Inquisition examined him again, and forced him to withdraw his opinions.

Although he complied, they placed him under house arrest, and many of his books were put on the *Index of Forbidden Books.*

Galileo would be revered by the Enlighteners as a martyr for modern science, a thinker who discovered the truth about the natural world and boldly defended it in the face of the church's obdurate opposition. For many, the Galileo affair would be symbolic of a perpetual struggle between science and religion, freedom of inquiry and the Bible. However, Galileo himself viewed his work as consistent with Catholic teaching. In letters and publications, he argued the theologians had obscured the truth of the Bible by forcing certain interpretations on a few biblical passages that could be explained in other ways. Theologians should learn science from the scientists, but instead some "make a shield of their hypocritical zeal for religion. They go about invoking the Bible, which they would have minister to their deceitful purposes."[12] For Galileo, and many who followed him, God had written two books of revelation, the Bible and Nature. The former should be studied for salvation, the latter for understanding the physical world. It is "contrary to the sense of the Bible and the intention of the Holy Fathers" to invoke the authority of scripture "in purely physical matters where faith is not involved."[13]

The treatment of Galileo by the Holy See cast a shadow on the development of theoretical science in southern Europe, and Protestant propagandists used it in the north as an example of Catholic "tyranny." Despite their biblicism, the Puritans in England encouraged technological and scientific endeavors during the seventeenth century, arguing along with Galileo that God had been revealed in nature as well as in the Bible. As we have seen, the Reformed view of providence and covenant was consistent with the new theory of universal laws of nature.

Francis Bacon (1561-1626) heralded the rapid progress of science as a sign of the inbreaking of the long-awaited millennial dawn. Bacon's method of inquiry focused on the careful collection and analysis of data rather than building grand theoretical systems. He warned against prejudices, particularly popular opinion and traditional authority, that cloud reason and prevent the discovery of reality. Theological prejudices should be avoided as well. Nature and the Bible can be understood clearly if one employs the right method, and keeps the mind free of prejudice. Moreover, since God created humans just

---

[12] Galileo Galilei, "Letter to the Grand Duchess Christina," in *Discoveries and Opinions of Galileo*, trans. and ed. Stillman Drake (Garden City NY: Anchor Books, 1957) 179.

[13] Ibid.

below the angels and made them the pinnacle of creation, humans should neither revere nor fear nature. God, through science, shows humans how to master nature and harness its power for human happiness and progress. By joining human effort to God's providential will, a new and better world could be created.

Social and Intellectual Reform

Seventeenth century utopian literature, such as Bacon's *Solomon House* and Andrea's *Christianopolis*, offered a vision of a perfect Christian society where piety and progress joined, but the world remained a difficult place. In 1620, Europe erupted in warfare that raged for a generation. The great educational reformer John Amos Comenius (1592-1670) witnessed much of the turmoil of a violent age. He was a priest in the Unitas Fratrum who had played a role in the Bohemian rebellion that precipitated the Thirty Years War. In the months following the Protestant defeat at White Mountain, Comenius lost his wife and children and had to abandon his home. While in hiding and suffering from grief and depression, he wrote one of the great critiques of Western culture. Like John Bunyan's *Pilgrim's Progress* half-a-century later, Comenius' *Labyrinth of the World and the Paradise of the Heart* takes the reader on a tour of society that reveals all of the sham and empty values of the world around him. Comenius' view of the world is filled with violence, selfishness, cruelty and misery. He does not even spare marriage the critic's harsh glare. The only hope for individual happiness is to turn away from the values of acquisition and ambition and find one's paradise within the heart. There one can find eternal truths and lasting happiness. Comenius represents a bridge between the activism of the Puritans and the heart religion of the Pietists.

Comenius was more than a social critic with mystical leanings. He also stood at the forefront of pedagogical reform. He attempted to apply Bacon's empirical and practical methods to education. He urged parents and teachers to view children as young plants that will grow naturally if given gentle care and guidance rather than treating them like wild beasts that need to be tamed and broken. Schools should be fun places where students discover the joy of learning about the world around them rather than "slaughterhouses of the mind."

Comenius' approach to education came from his theology. He abandoned the notion of utter human depravity and argued that Christians should give more attention to the redemption given by Christ than to the fall of the race in Adam. For Comenius, salvation is possible for all; therefore all children (rich, poor, male, female) must be educated in Christian values and modern science. Such an education would reform all of society, reducing the misery of poverty and warfare. Through education and genuine faith, Christians could transform the labyrinth into an earthly paradise.

Comenius tried to create a philosophy that would embrace all wisdom (*pansophy*) and essential knowledge leading to social reform. His more famous contemporary, René Descartes (1596-1650), took a different approach to the intellectual problems of the day, and in the process inaugurated modern philosophy. Descartes had served for a time as a soldier, but he retreated from the turmoil of the world into the sanctuary of his own reason. One mark of genius is the ability to perceive problems more clearly than others have, and Descartes clearly perceived that the modern world shattered old certainties. Each new discovery undermines an old certainty. Even the evidence of the senses was continually proven to be unreliable. For Descartes, it is useless to simply shout old propositions louder and call that a quest for truth. Instead, he tried to find what we can know for certain by first doubting all that can be doubted.

His *Discourse on Method* (1637) takes the reader step by step through a process of shattering illusions of certainty. Everything accessible to the senses is subject to doubt, but there is one thing that no one can honestly doubt: his or her own existence. "I think therefore I am," Descartes decided, and he used the assertion as the first axiom in an elaborate mathematical proof of the existence of the visible world. He also sought to prove the existence of God without relying on revelation or the authority of the church's dogmas. His confidence in reason alone to find the truth became a hallmark of the Enlightenment even though Locke had the greater influence on Enlightenment philosophy. Although Descartes maintained that his philosophy supported Christian doctrine, a claim echoed by Melabranche, his method undermined confidence in tradition and revelation.

Baruch Spinoza (1632-1677) used Descartes' method to argue for a radically different way of viewing God and revelation than that of Judaism or Christianity. His ideas made him an outcast in his day, but they eventually led to some of the most creative philosophical thought of the nineteenth century. Spinoza's family had fled Portugal for Holland when the Jews were banished from that kingdom in the late sixteenth century. As a child, Spinoza proved to be a brilliant Hebrew student who mastered the great Jewish religious and philosophical works at a young age. He moved on to read even works of Calvinist theology and Descartes' philosophy. Like Descartes, he found no certainty in the truth claims of religion, but mathematics gave Spinoza a model of truth. Therefore he applied the method of geometric argument to the problems of philosophy and theology. He also subjected the Bible to a rigorous historical and philosophical examination that led him to reject the idea that God gave scripture through direct revelation. Such activity led to his expulsion from the Amsterdam synagogue in 1656.

Unwilling to compromise his beliefs in order to secure a teaching post, Spinoza supported himself by grinding lenses while continuing his investigations. He built a reputation as an insightful interpreter of Descartes, but in his most controversial work, *Tractatus theologico-politicus*, published anonymously in 1670, Spinoza went well beyond Descartes and argued that the traditional understanding of God is fundamentally flawed. There is no distinction between divine and created substance. All that exists, is part of God. God and nature are the same.

The Age of Newton

We do not have enough space here to go into the whole history of the rise of modern science, but scientific progress occurred rapidly in the seventeenth and eighteenth centuries. New technologies led to new industries creating new sources of wealth, especially in England and France. New instruments unlocked an unknown and shocking microscopic world. Many of the secrets of the human body were unveiled and chemistry moved from magic to science. The new science came from more than just observation and invention, however, there was a theoretical transformation as well.

Isaac Newton (1642-1727), a professor of mathematics in England, published one of the most important scientific works of all time in 1689. His *Principia mathematica* built on the work of Kepler and Galileo and offers an elegant theory of the physical universe. Newton theorized that all matter exerts a force that he called gravity. Everything pulls on everything else in proportion to its mass. The stars are no different from objects on earth. Everything that has mass exerts gravity in a predictable and measurable fashion. Others provided the experimental and observational data to support Newton's theory, and within fifty years it had gained general assent. Newton's laws of gravitation would be the basis for physics until a Swiss patent clerk named Einstein shocked the world with his relativity theory over 200 years later.

Newton did not write his work for the average reader, but others took on the task of popularizing his theory. Thanks in part to their efforts, the shy and scholarly Newton became an international celebrity, and a symbol of rationality for the Enlightenment. The poet Alexander Pope even put Newton into the scheme of divine revelation: "Nature and Nature's laws lay hid in night: /God said, let Newton be! and all was light." Newton was used as the prime example of the ability of human reason to understand the universe.

The Enlighteners, however, overlooked Newton's own religious convictions. He was convinced that history works according to a divine law just as the physical cosmos does, thus he spent much of the later years of his life carefully examining biblical prophecies in order to unravel the mystery of the end-time. Although people often overlooked or dismissed his religious conviction, it was fundamental to his scientific endeavors. He, like most of the scientists of his generation, saw no contradiction between the revelation of God in scripture and in nature. Rational beings could discern both because God guarantees that both remain unchanged.

Although Newton was a sincere believer, he was not orthodox according to traditional standards. In his examination of scripture and nature he became a convinced unitarian. Jesus was a prophet of God, not God himself. God, for Newton, is the supreme creator who established the laws of nature and history, and who will judge all persons in the end. Jesus was God's messenger and revealer. His unitarian perspective caused some controversy among theologians in England, but the biggest conflict Newton faced was with a German philosopher named Gottfried Wilhelm von Leibniz (1646-1716).

In an age of genius, Leibniz stands out as a prodigy. He had an encyclopedic knowledge, and was a brilliant mathematician in addition to being a philosopher. He and Newton both claimed, with justification, to have invented calculus, but more important for our purpose was their debate over the nature of God and the universe. Newton believed that the universe could not continue to function unless God intervened from time to time. Such interventions were not miracles; they were part of God's providence and demonstrated that God actively engaged in creation. This idea connected Newton's view of history as God's plan to his view of the universe as God's creation.

Leibniz shared Newton's mechanistic model of the universe, but he rejected the idea that God functioned like a watchmaker who had to keep winding the watch. He argued that Newton's idea implied imperfection on the part of God because God had failed to create a perfect universe. In contrast, Leibniz asserted that God does not intervene. The cosmos functions according to God's eternal, unchanging laws of nature without direct intervention on the part of God. Moreover, the universe as we know it is the best of all possible worlds. Although imperfections exist in the cosmos, it has been created in such a way as to allow the maximum amount of goodness with a minimum of evil.

Deism

Descartes, Newton and Leibniz all remained Christians, although not quite orthodox in their beliefs. In fact, Leibniz labored for years in a vain attempt to reconcile the Protestant and Catholic churches on the basis of his understanding of the essential aspects of their faith. Their theories, though, gave support to a new religious movement that emerged in England in the seventeenth century. Deism in part responded to the long wars of religion and the continuing religious squabbles of the time. Many persons, including John Locke (1632-1704), who may be considered a first cousin of the Deists, blamed religious wars on disputes over dogma. Since priests and theologians could not prove beyond a reasonable doubt their peculiar doctrines, they had to force others to assent through the threat of punishment.

According to the Deists, institutional religion, with its competing sects and conflicting rituals, came from priests asserting their power over others. The key to ending religious conflict, then, would be to strip away useless dogmas and return to the original rational religion. All of the controversies over the Incarnation, the proper mode of baptism, and the role of bishops could be dispensed with as irrelevant or irrational. Doctrines contrary to reason should be abolished.

For Locke, the great architect of empiricism, the solution to religious controversy in the West was to return to a simple and rational reading of the New Testament. There he saw Jesus depicted as God's Messiah, the prophet who pointed the way to salvation. Locke himself accepted the idea of prophecy, and remained attached to Jesus as the revealer of God's will. Christians should unite behind the central revealed truth that Christ came to show humans the way to live.

The Deists went farther than Locke in reducing religion to a basic set of beliefs. Some Deists argued that scripture distorts an original religion common to all humans. They theorized that all humans have an innate knowledge of the creator. If priests did not interfere, all people would honor the creator in a similar fashion. The Deist used so-called primitive peoples discovered in the New World as examples of humans who lived according to a natural religion common to all. According to Herbert of Cherbury (1583-1648) natural religion has five basic doctrines: 1) There is a God revealed in creation. 2) God deserves to be worshipped. 3) God has given a natural moral law for people to follow. 4) The soul is immortal. 5) In the afterlife the good will be rewarded and the evil punished. Notice in his list the absence of a sacred scripture and the idea of redemption.

In works such as John Toland's *Christianity not Mysterious* (1699), the Deists sought to remove what they considered superstition from the Christian religion and restore it to its original truth. Seen from this perspective, Deism was a reform movement similar to many types of Protestantism that claimed to be returning to primitive Christianity. For the Deists, though, the original religion was not Christianity or Judaism. They claimed that miracles, sacraments, rituals, blood sacrifices, and metaphysics distorted the true message of Christianity, and kept people in darkness and ignorance rather than freeing them through the truth.

The process of perverting the original Christian message reached its height in the Middle Ages. Luther and the reformers had begun the process of enlightenment, but only modern people had the wisdom and courage to reject superstition. Matthew Tindal (1655-1733) asserted in his work *Christianity as Old as Creation* that the original religion was woven into the fabric of creation itself. If people could be freed from the obscurantism of religious authorities, then they would see that all religions are essentially the same, and thus end all religious fighting. Tindal also highlighted one of the great problems in Christian apologetics, namely a troubling circularity of argument. He condemned those who try "to prove the Truth of a Book by the Truth of the Doctrines it contains, and at the same time conclude those Doctrines to be true, because contained in that Book."[14]

Tindal was in many ways a sincere reformer, but for many people, the rejection of Christianity was also a rejection of conventional morality. This was the age of Casanova, Don Giovanni, and *Dangerous Liaisons*. By the end of the century, music had also become secular. Mozart found more inspiration from Freemasonry than Christianity, and his successors focused on opera rather than cantatas. Posterity replaced salvation as the ultimate goal of artists and writers.

Ironically, Deism inspired research into comparative religion that eventually disproved the basic Deist claim that a common core exists in all religions, but that would not become evident until the nineteenth century. In the eighteenth century, Deism moved from a movement of radical free-thinkers to an acceptable belief among the educated elite of the West because

---

[14] Matthew Tindal, *Christianity as Old as Creation* (London: 1730) 186.

many saw it as consistent with the new scientific world view. Moreover, Deism allowed individuals to repudiate the oppressive policies of the institutional church without rejecting God and religion. Deist ideas even affected those who remained loyal to the established churches. The Whig bishop John Tillotson (1630-1694) was such a figure. A collection of his sermons published in 1704 was one of the most widely read books in England and America. Moderate Christian Deism or Latitudinarianism was a potent force in colonial America, particularly among the planters of Virginia, most notably George Washington and James Madison.

It seemed to many educated observers in 1750 that the Age of Reason had triumphed; however, one of the Enlightenment's own luminaries sounded the death knell of the Enlightenment's trust in reason. David Hume (1711-1776) was a Scottish philosopher more at home in France than in Britain. He was one of the great historians of his age, and possessed lucid philosophical insight. He boldly challenged one of the basic texts of the Enlightenment, Locke's *Essay Concerning Human Understanding*. Hume demonstrated that knowledge of the external world is not as certain as Locke assumed. We only know sensations such as colors and textures. We cannot prove that our sensations represent real objects, nor can we prove cause and effect with certainty since we have no sensory knowledge of the future. For Hume, humans have no basis to deduce metaphysical claims about God from physical effects. Hume's radical skepticism dealt a fatal blow to Deism, and in many ways to the Christian tradition of natural theology. When first published such ideas were not fully appreciated, but they would awaken the great philosopher Immanuel Kant from his "dogmatic slumbers." As we shall see, Kant tried to limit reason in order make room for faith, but we must hold that for later in our story.

Religious Toleration and Disestablishment

One of the most significant features of the eighteenth century was the rise of religious toleration in many areas of Europe and America. People generally blamed the wars and devastation of the previous century on fanaticism. People felt that a civilized society needed moderation and toleration. John Locke gave an early expression to the new perspective in his *Letter Concerning Toleration* (1689), which promoted the idea that religion must succeed by persuasion rather than coercion. The killing of heretics harms society more than any heretical idea could. Pierre Bayle (1647-1705) attacked one of the fundamental pillars of Western political theory and practice since the time of Constantine when he publicly defended the civil rights of atheists. Belief in God and membership in the church do not guarantee morality, Bayle pointed out, nor does atheism guarantee immorality. A nation of atheists may be just a moral as a Christian or Muslim nation. In other words, religion should not be seen as the glue that unifies society. Religion is a purely personal and private matter.

The political path to toleration was not smooth. Toleration emerged in England because of the history of the last Stuart kings. Following the death of Cromwell in 1658, the Puritan Commonwealth collapsed. In 1660 Charles II was welcomed to the throne with the assistance of the Presbyterians in Parliament, but the bishops soon regained their power. The initial result of the shift in power was a new Act of Uniformity that required episcopal ordination, and an oath of assent to the Prayer Book for all parish priests. Many ministers refused to obey, and were forced to leave the Anglican Church as dissenters or noncon-formists. The Earl of Clarendon, the royal chancellor, pushed through several laws, known commonly as the Clarendon Code, designed to crush religious nonconformity for good. Dissenters were denied the right to public worship, and could not serve in government. Parliament's suspicion of the king's Catholic leanings led to the Test Act that required participation in the Anglican sacraments for all who wanted to hold public office. The Test Act ruled out Baptists, Presbyterians, Catholics, and Deists among other non-comformists.

The Clarendon Code harassed, imprisoned, and financially ruined many non-conformists. The next Stuart king, James II, was Catholic and he pushed for some toleration of dissent, primarily for the benefit of Catholics in England. In 1688, he put seven bishops on trial because they refused to support his Declaration of Indulgence. His heavy-handed effort to insure toleration for one religion caused popular opinion to turn against him, and both Whigs and Tories believed that the rights of all Englishmen were in danger as long as a Stuart held the throne. The response was the Glorious Revolution when Parliament offered the crown to James' son-in-law, William of Orange. The new king issued the Toleration Act that allowed dissenters to worship under certain restrictions. Latitudinarian bishops, such as Tillotson and Stillingfleet, supported the principal of toleration in England into the eighteenth century. The Glorious Revolution caused a problem, though, for some Anglican priests. The clergy had sworn allegiance to James, and some felt that they could not give allegiance to a new king while the old one lived. They were called non-jurors and lost their posts.

The Holy Experiment in Colonial America

The path to religious toleration in the United States was unique in part because colonial America was a scene of extraordinary religious diversity. The Puritans in New England were largely successful in their attempt to establish religious conformity, but that pattern did not repeat itself for the rest of the colonies. Attempts to establish the Anglican Church as the only legal religion in the southern colonies largely failed because the scattered nature of the population was not conducive to an Anglican parish system. Furthermore, the southern planters needed workers and so overlooked religious irregularities. Thus, a wide variety of dissenters called the southern colonies home. Also, the lack of clergy meant that most settlers in that region had little or no contact with organized religion of any kind.

The colonies between New England and the South, the so-called Middle Colonies, were also home to a variety of religious groups. This was most notable in Pennsylvania, founded by the brilliant Quaker leader William Penn (1644-1718). Penn's father had served with distinction as a vice-admiral in the British navy, but William was not a military man. He was one of many tortured souls in the seventeenth century who became religious seekers. Penn found his solace with the Society of Friends. With his connections in the royal court and his education, Penn assisted the Friends as they sought religious toleration in England; however, many Friends saw clearly that America might be a safer haven than England. When the king offered Penn a colony in America as payment on a large debt owed to his deceased father, he accepted it in order to provide a refuge for the Friends. All persons regardless of their religious beliefs could live in Penn's Woods (Pennsylvania).

Not since Roger Williams had left Massachusetts to found the small Rhode Island colony had anyone attempted such a "holy experiment" as Penn proposed. He intentionally recruited various German sects, such as the Mennonites, who had suffered years of persecution, and offered them freedom to live separate lives according to their own customs. People spoke German as widely as English in eastern Pennsylvania in the eighteenth century.

Philadelphia, the capital of the colony, soon grew to be one of the most important colonial cities. Pennsylvania, contrary to expectations, proved to be the most prosperous colony in America. Penn's "holy experiment" demonstrated that complete religious freedom did not have to rend the fabric of society. The framers of the Bill of Rights for the new United States of America used his model. Far from leading to social chaos and irreligion, the freedom of religion in Pennsylvania and New Jersey helped make the middle colonies a central setting for one of the great revivals of religion in American history, the Great Awakening, which we will discuss later.

Disestablishment in America

Latitudinarianism in New England was known as Liberalism. The Liberals rejected much of traditional Reformed theology, and placed responsibility for social harmony on individual virtue rather than on the fear of God. The role of religion was not to ward off the wrath of God on a sinful community, but to help each individual find ways to strengthen society. Long discussions of personal and public morals filled liberal sermons. Virtue, not piety, was the goal of their religion. The Liberals did not feel that they were in any way rejecting the tradition of their Puritan ancestors. Rather, they were winnowing away the chaff of Calvinism. Their fathers and mothers had had the courage to give the Bible to the people and to break away from bishops; the Liberals claimed they had the courage to dismiss with dogmatism and hell-fire preachers.

Benjamin Franklin (1706-1790) shared liberal views. He ridiculed traditional religion with its reliance on prayer and ritual to influence the deity. When New Englanders left on an ill-advised crusading attack on the French at the fort of Louisbourg in 1775, he playfully ridiculed the effusion of prayers which preceded the campaign, saying that if the adventure did not succeed he would have only "an indifferent opinion of Presbyterian prayers." His Poor Richard stood for the old Puritan virtues of hard work, thrift, and common sense rather than prayer, piety, and conversion. However, Franklin saw more good in Christianity than many Deists did, and he proposed that religious instruction be required in the public schools. In his 1749 *Proposals Relating to the Education of Youth in Philadelphia*, Franklin put forth his theory of Public Religion. The new type of religion would retain the value of Puritanism without the vices. It would inspire a common morality among the youth that a strong society needed, but we must note that his public religion is Christianity stripped of its defining doctrines. All that is left is civic morality. In other words, Franklin proposed that the children of Philadelphia be taught moderate Deism in the schools.

One of the most religiously minded of the American Deists was Thomas Jefferson (1743-1826) who was passionately concerned about theological issues even though he rejected the institutional church and its rituals. After a thorough study of theology, he soundly rejected Calvinism, even in its

Unitarian form, but he remained convinced that Jesus had been the perfect religious teacher. Jefferson believed that Jesus' teachings should be the basis for society and individual life. In his later years, he carefully prepared a work that he believed gave the true story of Jesus' life and teaching. Essentially, he severely edited the four gospels and brought them into one narrative with all miracles and improbabilities removed. Jefferson's Jesus makes no claims of divinity, but he does promise eternal life to those who follow his teaching. The summary of this teaching is "love your neighbor as yourself."

Jefferson was willing to tolerate all religions, even those he personally abhorred, confident in the belief that in the end this simple teaching of Jesus would become the rule for all reasonable and moral persons. The reliance on human reason rather than revealed truth is evident throughout the documents of the American Revolution and formation of the Republic. For instance, the Declaration of Independence refers to "the God of nature and nature's God" not to the Father, Son, and Holy Ghost of traditional Christianity.

Deists such as Jefferson and Franklin aggressively promoted religious toleration in America, but toleration was also encouraged by the fact that at the time of its founding the United States was the most religiously diverse nation since the days of the Roman Empire. Each colony and most villages had already come to grips with the reality that no one religion numerically dominated. Although Anglicanism had been established in Virginia and the Carolinas, by 1776 the Anglican Church was one of the smallest denominations in the southern colonies. The Congregationalist Church was established in New England. Their ministers were supported through tax revenues and were seen as quasi-political figures. However, even the Puritan town of Boston had to make room for Timothy Cutler's Anglican congregation, Chauncy's Brattle Street Liberal church, and scores of Quakers and Baptists. Pennsylvania had virtually every Christian sect known at that time. It would have been impossible for any single Protestant church to unify a colony, much less the nation.

Diversity prevented any one sect from becoming dominant, but more important, it demonstrated that the society could survive with a mishmash of churches. Pluralism brought a whole new set of problems to society, but it did not destroy the fabric of society as many preachers had claimed. Instead, each church learned to promote its own cause in the new marketplace of religion. By 1776 most of the American churches had accepted free-market competition as the new reality for religion. Parishes were gone. Evangelists and competition for members would remain. Religious minorities, such as the Presbyterians, Baptists, and Methodists welcomed the new situation and fought along with Deists and Liberals to protect it.

Thomas Jefferson consistently advocated a full separation of church and state, and was one of the first to broach the issue politically. During the American Revolution, he introduced *A Bill for Establishing Religious Freedom in Virginia* that proclaimed "that all men shall be free to profess, and by argument to maintain, their opinions on matters of religion, and that the same shall in no wise diminish, enlarge, or affect their civil capacities."[15] However, Patrick Henry vigorously opposed the measure and it did not pass until 1786. The issue of religious establishment came up again in the Constitutional Congress, but the Constitution itself said nothing about religion. That was left to James Madison's Bill of Rights in 1791. The first U.S. President could confidently tell a group of Jews that America would allow no religious persecution. People who had been hounded out of nearly every "civilized" country in Europe welcomed this answer. The United States became the first secular government in the West.

Enlightened Despotism

In Continental Europe religious toleration was promoted by a generation of monarchs devoted to the pragmatic goals of the Enlightenment. The most powerful of the Enlightened despots was Frederick the Great of Prussia (1712-1786) who made his young kingdom into one of the most important European powers. Frederick viewed all religion with disdain but granted religious toleration to his citizens over the opposition of the Lutheran Church and the Holy Roman Emperor. He also promoted education, decreed freedom of the press, and abolished torture, but serfdom actually grew more oppressive during his reign. Most ominous for the future history of Germany, Frederick actively promoted military service and nationalism as substitutes for religious devotion. His sanctification of the militaristic state yielded bitter fruits in the twentieth century.

The most dramatic change in religious policy came in the Austrian Empire. Since the Reformation, the Hapsburgs had been the leading supporters of Roman Catholicism in central and southern Europe. The empress Maria Theresa shared her family heritage, but her son Joseph had a different mindset. Although he was probably as sincere in his personal beliefs

---

[15] Thomas Jefferson, "A Bill for Establishing Religious Freedom in Virginia," in *The American Reader: Words that Moved a Nation*, ed. Diane Ravitch (San Francisco: Harper Collins, 1990).

as any eighteenth-century monarch, Joseph II (1741-1790) was also sincerely committed to the ideals of the Enlightenment. He strongly disagreed with his mother's various attempts to suppress religious dissent because it wasted valuable human resources that the state might need later. Persecution also offended the patience of God.

When he became the sole ruler of the Empire in 1780, Joseph aggressively, even autocratically, pursued his liberal goals. He instituted compulsory education, reformed taxation, closed a number of non-productive monasteries, and abolished religious censorship. More significant for our story was his *Patent of Toleration*, issued in 1781, that gave legal rights to non-Catholics in Hapsburg lands for the first time since 1627. He granted Jews a degree of toleration denied them elsewhere in Europe. Joseph's reforms were not warmly received, however, his successor modified or abandoned many of them.

The most violent process of church reform pursued by enlightened despots came in Holy Russia. Over the centuries the Russian Orthodox Church had developed a messianic mission tied to the Russian nation. Moscow was proclaimed the Third Rome after the fall of Constantinople to the Turks in 1453. Under Ivan the Terrible, Russia began to develop a powerful monarchy, but it remained the least educated kingdom in Europe. Even priests were largely illiterate; therefore the church attached great importance to the rituals of the liturgy. Such devotion to the ritual was even greater among the large peasant class.

During the reign of Patriarch Nikon (1605-1681) ancient rituals were challenged. Nikon wanted to make the Patriarch in Moscow the final authority over all the Eastern Orthodox churches. In pursuing his policy, his scholars found many places in the divine liturgy where Russian practice differed from the Greek originals. Some things were as minor as how many fingers to hold up when giving the blessing, but in a culture that ascribed divinely ordained status to every detail of the liturgy minor elements had cosmic importance. When Nikon insisted on reforming the liturgy many monks and priests, the Old Believers, broke away from the Patriarch and the Tsar. They were brutally suppressed, some even burned at the stake.

Eventually, Peter the Great (1672-1725) granted toleration to the Old Believers. The schism often strikes Westerners as a strange tempest in a teapot, but it shared some of the features of the Puritan revolt. Both the Old Believers and the Puritans believed that the right to worship is an essential part of the Christian faith, and that God decreed the form of worship. For the Old Believers this meant following the rituals of their ancestors while for the

Puritans it meant renouncing traditional worship and religious art. For both, worship was a matter of life and death.

Peter made many substantive changes to the Russian Orthodox Church in his process of westernizing his empire. He insisted on higher education standards for the clergy, and completely subordinated the church to the state by abolishing the office of Patriarch. From 1721-1917 a Holy Synod controlled by the Tsar, rather than an independent Patriarch, led the Russian Orthodox Church. Many conservatives strongly opposed Peter's westernization, particularly his decision to abandon Moscow in favor of St. Petersburg, but Catherine the Great (1729-1796) continued his westernizing trend. She was a German and a Deist who was the darling of the French Enlightenment. She increased the power of the state by confiscating church lands and closing hundreds of monasteries. In the process two million serfs became the direct property of the state. Most of them found their condition worse under the Tsar than under the church. Catherine opposed superstition and allowed the nobility and state servants to express radical views on religion, but she did not push for full toleration in her lands. She found that the church could be a useful ally in the dangerous game of politics.

France and the Radical Enlightenment

The Enlightenment in France took a more aggressively anti-Christian stance than in England and Central Europe. Inspired by Pierre Bayle's scathing critique of Protestant and Catholic repression and superstition, the French Enlighteners, called *philosophes*, used wit, sophistication, and literature to undermine the church's power and authority.

The voice of these *philosophes* was François Marie Arouet, better known as Voltaire (1694-1776). Voltaire was a member of the rising bourgeoisie who resented the inherited power of the nobility and the clergy. He was also a poet-philosopher who supported himself quite comfortably by his writing. For a time, he was an historian of some note, and he encountered Deism and Newtonianism while in London. In 1738, he published a work that popularized Newton's theories and promoted empiricism against the dominant Cartesian rationalism. He also spent three years in Potsdam as a companion of the enlightened despot Frederick the Great. In short, he worked at the epicenter of the Enlightenment, and he used his writings to attack the Catholic Church for being obscurantist and reactionary. He promoted the view that Christianity, hopelessly corrupted by priests and kings, was bent on destroying science and all human improvement. He urged his readers to "crush the infamous," meaning the church. Christianity, in his view, was too closely tied to fanaticism and intolerance to be allowed to survive. In his masterful work *Candide* (1759), Voltaire also ridicules the optimism of Leibnitz who argued that this is "the best of all possible worlds." *Candide* is an anti-utopia similar to *Labyrinth of the World* in which the hero witnesses all of the irrational pain and cruelty of human society. Unlike Comenius, however, Voltaire's character does not find solace in religion. In fact, religion causes much suffering. Candide finally builds a small, tolerant community apart from the barbarism of religion.

Voltaire feared atheism almost as much as Catholicism, but some of his companions and followers cheerfully embraced atheism. Denis Diderot (1713-1784) believed that Deism was just a way-station for those without the courage to be atheists. Diderot was urbane, well read, and uniquely skilled at avoiding censorship. He claimed that he rejected religion in order to liberate humankind to achieve greatness. His *Encyclopedia* (1751-1772) contained articles on a wide range of subjects, including detailed drawings of new inventions and technological advances, but it was more than a reference work; it was a tribute to human creativity and genius. Diderot drew heavily upon Bayle's *Historical and Critical Dictionary* to ridicule the ignorance and cruelty of religious people and conventual morality.

More theoretical than Diderot was the atheist theorist Claude Adrien Helvetius (1715-1771) whose work *Of the Spirit* (1758) attacked the very idea of the soul. He rejected Descartes' assertion that matter cannot think, and instead proposed a completely naturalist view of human life. Moreover, self-love, not religion really leads to virtue. His idea became the basis for the capitalist system of free enterprise in America. Anticipating Jeremy Bentham, Helvetius also argued that social utility should be the only judge of virtue. From his perspective, the church had no utility and thus should be destroyed. In America, the patriot Thomas Paine led the radical Enlightenment.

The French Revolution

The Enlightenment helped create the first two great revolutions in modern Western history. America had the luxury of creating a new government in a new nation with few deeply rooted traditions. The revolution in France, on the other hand, was a bitter civil war against institutions that had helped define the French nation for centuries. We did not have space here to recount the details of that conflagration; however, a few words are necessary to show how the revolution affected Christianity in France. The revolution began when Louis XVI was forced to call a meeting of the Estates General, an assembly at which the rising bourgeois class was given a voice. Within a month, the Estates General became the National Assembly, assuming great legislative powers. The first violent act of the revolution took place when the Parisian crowds stormed the hated Bastille prison on July 14, 1789, an event that led to peasant and proletariat uprisings throughout France. Before long, the National Assembly controlled the country and attempted to crush all remnants of feudalism including the Catholic Church.

The National Assembly followed the example of Henry VIII during the Reformation and confiscated all church-owned lands, nearly one-fifth of the property in France. Tithes were abolished, and in 1790 the monasteries dissolved because they were deemed to have no social utility. In July, the Civil Constitution of the Clergy radically reorganized the church. The old dioceses were redrawn along the same lines as the new civil governmental depart-ments. The government paid clergy, but not through direct means. The pope lost administrative authority in France, and even parish priests were to be elected by the people. When the Vatican refused to sanction the arrangements, the National Assembly required that all clergy sign an oath of obedience to the state. Although many of the poor parish priests had agitated for years for radical reform of the Catholic Church, the outright rejection of papal authority was a step too far. About two-thirds refused to take the oath and thus they became opponents of the revolution. The following year, French citizens received complete religious freedom.

In 1792, the Revolution took a more radical turn in the face of growing opposition from the monarchies surrounding France. The royal palace was stormed and the king imprisoned by the Commune of Paris. On 21 September 1792, the National Convention declared the monarchy ended and established a republic. In January of 1793, the king and queen went to the guillotine and soon the Revolution slipped into the Terror when the Committee for Public Safety under the orders of Robespierre instituted a brutal repression of all opposition.

As a symbol of the radical break with the Christian past and the instauration of a new era, the Convention replaced the old church calendar with a new Revolutionary Calendar. The birth of Jesus was no longer the focal point of history. Instead, years would be calculated from the start of the Republic, September 22, 1792 (1 Vendémiaire, Year I). National memorial days replaced Christian holy days, including the Sabbath. The week would be ten days with a three-week month. In violation of the earlier guarantee of religious freedom, all churches were closed on 3 Frimaire, Year II (November

23, 1793). The following year, a new religion was proclaimed in revolutionary France: the Worship of the Supreme Being, Wisdom. The new religion was part of Robespierre's goal of uniting France in a common Deist worship complete with rituals to celebrate virtue and wisdom. Christians and atheists who refused to bow at the shrine of wisdom and the revolution were led to the guillotine.

The new cult failed to unite France or insure the success of the Revolution. The country rapidly slid into chaos and anarchy. Finally, Napoleon Bonaparte, the most successful general of the revolutionary armies, took direct control of the government. In a Concordat signed with the papacy in 1801, Napoleon partially restored the power of the Catholic Church. Church and state would cooperate in the running of the church, although the state reserved a veto power. In 1804, the pope participated in the coronation of Napoleon as the French Emperor, but Napoleon placed the crown on his own head. For many in the West the chaos of the revolution and the rise of Napoleon marked the end of the Age of the Reason. The early Enlightenment had claimed that the end of traditional religion would mark the end of fanatical strife; however, the French Revolution proved that the cult of reason could also demand human sacri-fices.

Chapter 18

Religion of the Heart

THE SEVENTEENTH CENTURY was more than a time of intellectual and
scientific daring; it was also a time of religious seeking and experimentation.
Far different from the anti-mystery prejudices of the Deists were the mystical
writings of medieval spiritual guides, such as Meister Eckhart, Johannes
Tauler, and the Rhineland mystics who experienced a popular revival in the
seventeenth century. At the same time that the Enlightenment was heating up,
mysticism became popular among clergy and laity as new forms of devotion
and theology developed. Much of the interest in mysticism was motivated by a
desire similar to that of the Deists: to integrate new intellectual developments
with a useful understanding of God.

The turn to religious feeling developed into various forms of experiential
religion in Germany after the Thirty Years War. The word Pietism describes
a wide variety of movements and persons who attempted to breathe new life
into Protestantism in the late seventeenth and early eighteenth centuries. An
elastic movement, Pietism would have an effect on Christianity far beyond
the borders of Germany, reaching as far as Russia in the East and America in
the West where it would be called evangelicalism. By embracing the emotional
and ineffable, the religion of the heart presented an approach to Christianity
resistant to the attacks of radical Enlighteners and helped preserve
Christianity in a secular age.

Revival of Mysticism in Europe

One of the most controversial and creative of the new mystical writers
was Jakob Böhme (1575-1624), a shoemaker in Görlitz in Silesia. Böhme had
a number of mystical experiences that he recorded in his first work, *Dawn*

(*Aurora oder die Morgenröte im Aufgang*), in 1612. The authorities in Silesia considered it dangerous, and they ordered him to stop writing; however, he began writing devotional tracts again in 1618. Soon he began traveling throughout central Europe to promote an inner spiritual reform based on his provocative ideas.

Essentially, Böhme proclaimed that God the Father is the ground of being and the incomprehensible abyss. The Father is unfathomable but learns to know himself through the Son who is divine Wisdom. The Father then expresses himself in creation through Spirit. The Spirit in turn illuminates the individual human soul, which must make an act of the will to choose between God and Satan. The soul must choose to be consumed by the fire of Christ's love. When it does so, it then comes to know itself through a feeling for life, which is ultimately more important than reason or dogmatic truth.

Böhme has a strong pantheist streak, but he remains distinct from most pantheists in his idea that the will is the ultimate principal in the universe. Mystical union comes when the human will joins the divine will, creating an almost overpowering feeling of life. Böhme's writings, especially his *Magnum Mysterium*, would be read by Spinoza and Newton, but they would truly bear fruit much later in the philosophies of Hegel and Schilling in the nineteenth century. More immediately, Böhme's writings generated a renewed interest in religious experience and a longing for a direct encounter with the divine.

Almost as radical as Böhme was Valentin Weigel (1533-1588), a Lutheran pastor of a country parish. Few people knew Weigel's own theological speculations until the publication of his *Dialogues des Christianismo* after his death. Weigel rejected Lutheranism's stress on the objective aspects of Christianity, and instead embraced an entirely subjective approach. All that matters for salvation is the experience of Christ within the individual. The sacraments, preaching, and even the church have no role in faith. In fact, they can interfere with true faith, which is the soul's personal union with God through Christ. Although Weigel's views were extreme and roundly condemned in the seventeenth century, they influenced many later Pietists, particularly mystically-minded separatists. Of greater impact, though, was Johann Arndt (1555-1621), a Lutheran theologian attracted to late medieval German mysticism, particularly the works of Tauler and Thomas a' Kempis. Arndt's *True Christianity*, published in 1610, was a favorite among the Pietists.

The Inner Light of the Quakers

By an entirely different path, a young man in England came to conclusions similar to Weigel's during the days of the Puritan commonwealth.
George Fox (1624-1691) was the son of a weaver in Leicestershire. At the age
of nineteen, he permanently turned his back on official Christianity when he
saw several professed Christians indulging themselves at a drinking party. He
became a religious seeker until 1646 when he had a transforming experience
that convinced him that divine revelation comes to all believers. He recorded
that at that time, "I was taken up in the love of God, so that I could not but
admire the greatness of His love. While I was in that condition it was opened
unto me by the eternal light and power, and I saw clearly therein that all was
done, and to be done, in and by Christ."[16] For Fox, every person has an inner
light of truth which is Christ within. The following year he began preaching
in marketplaces and barns without official sanction. He found the confusion
of the English Civil War to be a ripe time to introduce his ideas publicly. He
told his listeners that rituals and ceremonies mean even less than even the
most extreme Puritans thought. True sacraments are entirely spiritual;
therefore there is no need to use water, wine, or any physical aid in worship.
He also proclaimed that by following the Inner Light, one could achieve
complete victory over sin. Furthermore, since each person has Christ within,
it is wrong to be servile to others. Therefore he condemned slavery and even
the rituals of self-abasement, such as bowing or removing one's hat, that are
common in Western society.

The charismatic Fox attracted a devoted following. In 1652, he organized
the Society of Friends in northern England. The movement grew rapidly
despite, or perhaps because of persecution by the Commonwealth. Within a
decade some three thousand Friends had been imprisoned, usually for
disturbing the peace. The early Friends received the derisive name Quakers
because millenary zeal often inspired them, and they shook violently when
they were touched by the Spirit within. By 1666, the basic features of the
Friends' organization were in place including the monthly and yearly
meetings. The Toleration Act of 1689 gave the Friends in England their first
degree of toleration after years of persecution. Everyone in England who
promised to be loyal to the monarchs and reject the pope and distinctively
Catholic doctrines, such as prayers to the saints, was granted freedom of
worship.

---

[16] George Fox, *A Journal or Historical Account* (Philadelphia, 1831) 1:76.

Quietism

The longing for spiritual experience and mystical union developed in a different form in seventeenth century Catholicism. Miguel de Molinos (1640-97), a Spanish priest, became a celebrated confessor and spiritual guide in Rome beginning in 1663. Cardinals and prelates were among those whom he guided. They protected him when both the Dominicans and Jesuits accused him of heresy after he published *Spiritual Guide* in 1675, a work in which he recommended the prayer of acquired contemplation and the complete indifference of the soul. He practiced a form of mystical detachment similar to that of Tauler in which the spiritual pilgrim seeks a perfection of perpetual union that transforms the soul into God. The soul must rest entirely in God. Since external observances, mortifications, and desires can hinder the soul's union, the pilgrim must go beyond the attachment to the church and devotion to Jesus into a union with God that totally annihilates the will. His type of mysticism would be called Quietism because of its stress on the passive nature of the soul. Although Molinos' *Spiritual Guide* was not condemned, he did get into trouble when nuns under his care began to refuse to observe the daily office and house discipline. He was finally imprisoned in 1685, and his unpublished letters and instructions to his spiritual disciples were condemned.

The writings of Molinos influenced the French mystic Madame Guyon (1648-1717). Born Jeanne Marie Bouvier de la Mothe, Madame Guyon lived unhappily married to Jacques Guyon. She found solace in religion, and after her husband's death in 1676, she gave herself over completely to religious devotion following the teachings of Molinos. A Barnabite friar, Father La Combe, became her confessor and spiritual guide. The two of them traveled throughout southern France and northern Italy for five years spreading the idea of Quietist mysticism. For Guyon, the goal of religious devotion is a contemplation that needs no concepts, an experience in which God completely overpowers the soul. As the soul progresses in devotion, it reaches a stage of complete indifference. The shifting sands of life cannot affect the soul at rest in God. The soul should be indifferent to salvation itself and remain entirely passive in God's being. Ultimately one "cannot tell whether the will of the soul is become the will of God, or the will of God become the will of the soul." She published her views in a widely-circulated book titled *A Short and Very Easy Means of Prayer* in 1688. Guyon's teaching and activities aroused the suspicions of the church authorities in France, and they imprisoned her twice on heresy charges. Despite the opposition of some in the church, Guyon was very influential in royal circles.

One of her major supporters was the Archbishop of Cambrai, François de Salignac de la Mothe, better known as Fénelon (1651-1715). Fénelon was one of the great spiritual leaders of the seventeenth-century French church. In 1678 he had been given charge of educating recent converts from Protestantism, and in 1685 was sent to convert the Huguenots. He was also chosen to be the tutor to the grandson of King Louis XIV. He opposed Louis XIV's absolutism and tried to instill in the future Louis XV the conviction that the true measure of a king is justice not conquest. His 1687 *Treatise on the Education of Young Women* remains a benchmark in the progress of Western education.

Fénelon defended Guyon and her teaching for a number of years, earning the enmity of Jacques-Bénigne Bossuet (1627-1704), the primate of France, who began opposing Guyon in 1694. At the conference of Issy, Guyon and her teaching were condemned, and she was arrested. She would be released in 1702, living the rest of her life in relative obscurity. Fénelon was forced to sign the articles of Issy condemning Quietism. In 1697 he published *An Explication of the Maxims of the Saints* in which he tried to distinguish between true and false mysticism. Bossuet attacked his work, and shortly after Fénelon was banished from the royal court. He submitted to the Vatican in 1699, and thereafter focused on improving the spiritual condition of his own diocese. Fénelon wrote some devotional works, the most popular of which were his letters of spiritual advice published after his death. Those who knew him remembered him as a graceful and gentle aristocrat who had great insight as a spiritual guide. He could gently encourage and admonish a friend by saying, "I will pray Him to take pity upon your weakness, and do you good in spite of your resistance to Him. For myself, I will not forsake you."[17] The careers of Fénelon and Guyon demonstrate both the longing for spiritual experience in the later seventeenth century and the church's fear that unrestrained spiritual movements would damage the institutional church and undermine the state.

The Jansenist Controversy in France

The concern for conformity in the church in the sixteenth century manifested itself during the long reign of Louis XIV who fought a long battle

---

[17] Thomas S. Kepler, ed. *Selections from the Writings of Francois Fenelon* (Nashville: The Upper Room,[1980]) 31.

with the papacy over the issue of supremacy of the church. In 1682, the "Sun King" encouraged the French clergy's Four Articles of Gallicanism that asserted that councils of bishops are superior to the papacy, and that the King of France is supreme in his realm. Gallicanism, which had medieval roots, attempted to do in France what Henry VIII had done in England, but Louis did not wish to break completely with the papacy and alienate powerful church leaders in France. He eventually bowed to the authority of the papacy and withdrew the Gallican Articles in 1693.

Louis' desire to have complete mastery over the religious life of his subjects manifested itself in another way on October 18, 1685 when he revoked the Edict of Nantes that had guaranteed limited freedom of religion for the French Protestants. He wanted "one king, one law, one faith" in France. However, such absolutism came at a price. Thousands of Huguenots fled France, many of them leaders in industry and finance. The kingdom lost needed resources. Those who could not flee faced harassment and abuse, treatment that caused many of his subjects to view the king as a tyrant. Other monarchs feared that Louis desired to return to the failed policies of the sixteenth century, particularly when he launched a persecution against Protestants in recently captured territories.

Louis also violently opposed a theological movement within French Catholicism known as Jansenism. Cornelius Jansen (1585-1638), the bishop of Ypres, began a reforming effort with his massive, 1300-page work *Augustinius*, a summa of Augustine's theology published posthumously in 1640. Jansen was a noted scholar who carefully studied all of the available works of Augustine of Hippo, and found in them a doctrine of grace at variance with that taught by contemporary Jesuits. Jansen vigorously promoted a doctrine of predestination based solely on God's grace. Humans are completely corrupt and unable to save themselves; therefore salvation lies only with God. Furthermore, God's grace is irresistible. If God chooses to save, God will; therefore Christians are saved entirely by the choice of God. Luther and Calvin had read Augustine in a similar way; therefore the Jesuits denounced Jansen's work as Protestant by the Jesuits. However, Jansen and his followers remained firmly attached to the Catholic Church.

Jansen's teaching convinced Jacqueline Marie Angelique Arnauld (1591-1661), and she combined it with an austere piety similar to the Puritans. She was the abbess of the Cistercian convent of Port-Royal-des-Champs not far from Paris where she made Jansenism the rule in her cloister's school. The school at Port Royal trained many of the French nobility, particularly those opposed to absolutism, and thus helped spread Jansenism and join it to political movements. Mother Angelique's brother was Antoine Arnauld (1612-1694), who became a doctor of the Sorbonne in 1643. He became the public leader of the Jansenist movement, and he challenged the theology and practice of the Jesuits relating to confession and communion. His polemical pamphlet, *On Frequent Communion,* attacked what Arnauld perceived as the excessive lenience of the Jesuits, and warned of the danger of taking communion without having properly confessed and received true absolution. Arnauld's enemies at the Sorbonne compiled a list of five propositions supposedly taken from *Augustinus,* which they managed to have the Holy Office condemn in 1653. Three years later, Arnauld was removed from the Sorbonne and eventually found refuge in Brussels.

Jansenism had some important converts and defenders, among who was the great mathematician Blaise Pascal (1623-1662). Pascal had an intense religious experience "in the year of grace 1654" when he encountered "the God of Abraham, Isaac, and Jacob" in a deeply personal manner. As a result, he became associated with the convent of Port Royal where he used his considerable talents to defend the Jansenist cause. His *Lettre provinciales* ridiculed the Jesuits as hypocritical and argued instead for the rigorism of the Port Royal model. Pascal left Port Royal in 1658, but continued to explore the nature of religion. He never completed his most famous work, *Pensees.* Pascal recorded his thoughts about religion on numerous note cards that were discovered in his room after his death. In his notes Pascal struggled with his scientific inquiries and his religious faith. His experience was a microcosm of the age, and his assertions continue to provoke thought. He tried to demonstrate the limits of human reason and the need for saving faith. Ultimately happiness does not lie in reason but in faith. For him, the heart has reasons that the mind knows not.

Jansenism soon became associated with anti-monarchical movements within the *parlements* of France. As such, Louis XIV hated the movement. With some pressure from the king, the French bishops insisted on uniformity in 1661. Mother Angelique and many of her nuns carried on a valiant passive resistance to the king, the bishops, and the papacy itself, but in August 1664 royal troops closed the convent, and the nuns were dispersed to other convents. In 1710 the convent itself was destroyed, but the Jansenist controversy continued after the death of the original instigators. In 1699, Pasquier Quesnel, a friend of Arnauld, published *Moral Reflections on the New Testament* in which he called for a thorough reform of the Catholic Church, including the use of a presbyterial form of government. Such "Protestant" ideas shocked many in the French church, but the Jansenists had support at high levels, including Cardinal Louis Antoine de Noailles (1651-1729) who became the Archbishop of Paris in 1695. He resisted the king's efforts to suppress Jansenism, but in 1713 he was forced to publish the papal bull Unigenitus that condemned 101 propositions taken from Quesnel's treatise. Noailles pointed out in vain that many of the condemned propositions were in fact direct quotes from Saint Augustine himself. Over the course of the century, Jansenism became largely a political movement of opposition to absolutism.

Pietism in Germany

Pietism originated in the Lutheran Church in part as protest to Lutheran Orthodoxy. Orthodoxy itself had developed out of the conflicts within Lutheranism following the death of Luther. As we saw in a previous chapter, these conflicts led to the production of the Book of Concord, which served as a theological agreement between the various parties. Within the theological schools Orthodoxy attempted to define this Lutheran doctrine in very precise terms. Lutheran Orthodoxy appeared similar to medieval scholasticism in style and methodology, but remained strictly Protestant in doctrine.

The Book of Concord, in particular the Augsburg Confession, was viewed as almost equal to scripture in authority. Furthermore, this definition of theology attempted to clarify and even magnify differences between Lutheranism and Calvinism. The effort to establish an unambiguous statement of belief was one answer to the anxieties of the age. Orthodoxy promoted the idea that scripture is the infallible norm for faith and conduct. The scripture is clear, coherent, and contains all that one needs for salvation. Moreover, no possibility of new revelations or direct mystical experiences exist because the Holy Spirit is tied to the written and spoken word of scripture. According to the Orthodox view, the most important role of a pastor is to give a careful exposition of the Bible and defend it against fanaticism and heresy.

Orthodoxy also stressed the idea that salvation is entirely the work of Christ because the human race has become hopelessly corrupted through sin. Those who will be saved are saved by the election of God. God's word given in sermon, sacrament, and scripture calls humans into salvation through grace. Good works come only after conversion and must spring from a good conscience. As Orthodoxy gained control over theology schools and pulpits, theological disputes and polemics became the principle subject matter of sermons and publications. Many serious-minded individuals felt that

Orthodoxy had substituted its form of rationalism for the living faith of Luther, and in the process had lost Christianity's true promise for transforming lives.

Philip Jakob Spener (1635-1705) may rightly be called the father of Pietism. Spener had a strong religious up-bringing and was very well-read as a child. He was familiar with a number of Puritan authors, such as Bayly and Baxter, and shared their concern that faith should lead to a changed life. Spener also read much of the mystical literature of the day, particularly the works of Tauler, Arndt, and Böhme. Moreover, unlike the Orthodox, Spener had an appreciation for the left-wing of the Reformation, including spiritualist authors such as Denck, Schwenkfeld, and Hut. Spener served as a minister in Strasbourg in 1663, and then in Frankfurt in 1666. As a pastor he felt called to renew the Lutheran church and make it more meaningful for the common person.

Spanner's ideas and methods for reform gained a large audience after 1675 when he published *Pia Desideria* (Pious Desires), a short piece on the need for reform in the German church. This work had originally been a preface to a new edition of Arndt's *True Christianity*, which was an exposition of Luther's Small Catechism. In *Pia Desideria* Spener asserted that the clergy wasted time on religious controversies and polemics while ignoring the most important aspects of Christianity: faith and love. He then offered six concrete proposals that would become the basis for Pietism and evangelicalism in general. In brief, Spener proposed that the church should:

1. Encourage people to read the Bible alone and with fellow Christians
2. Recover the priesthood of all believers by forming small devotional groups
3. Acknowledge that Christianity is not a matter of learning but of service
4. Resolve church disputes by prayer, not by argument
5. Reform ministerial training so that pastors receive training in holiness as well as theology
6. Make preaching simple and edifying for the laity.

The underlining theme of the six proposals is that the church should make religion an active and effective force in the lives of common persons. He believed that he was simply continuing the work begun by Martin Luther of restoring faith to the laity. Luther had focused on doctrine; Spener would focus on lifestyle.

The most important and controversial institution to emerge from Spener's reform was small, voluntary gatherings of lay persons to pursue piety. The groups went by a number of names such as conventicles, *collegia pietatis* (colleges of piety), and *ecclesiolae* in *ecclesia* (little churches within the church). Wesley called his conventicles "bands" and "classes," but the purpose of the various groups remained essentially the same. An intimate gathering of devout persons and seekers could strengthen one another in their religious lives.

The conventicles began in 1670 as an outgrowth of Spener's adult education classes on Luther's Smaller Catechism. At first they met in Spener's home, but the authorities soon forced them to move into the church building. We can see echoes of the *devotia moderna* in Spener's conventicles, and like their medieval forebears these separate gatherings aroused opposition within the church. The conventicles were thought to undermine social classes and the distinction between the laity and the clergy. Increasingly, conventicles were forbidden in various parts of Germany and Scandinavia. For instance, the Swedish Conventicle Act of 1726: "forbade, under threat of heavy fines, the assembly of men and women, old and young, and acquaintances and strangers in private homes for the purpose of cultivating piety or worship."[18]

Such laws slowed Pietism in several regions, but Spener continued his efforts despite opposition. He and his followers were frequently accused of promoting separatism from the state church, a very serious charge following the Peace of Westphalia. However, Spener's ideas appealed to a significant number of the nobility in the Empire, and in 1690 he was given the important position of chaplain to the elector of Brandenburg, soon to be the first king of Prussia. He was instrumental in the founding of the University of Halle in 1694, which became the center of Pietism.

The most important convert to the Pietist cause was a young teacher of philosophy and theology at the University of Leipzig named August Hermann Francke (1663-1727) who in 1686 became an active participant in the *Collegia Philobiblica* (gathering of Bible lovers) at the university. Carpzov, one of the leading Orthodox theologians founded leadership, but when Francke took over the group, he followed Spener's advice to focus on devotional rather that philological study of the scripture. He also read and promoted a variety of spiritual writings including the works of Molinos, though he never became a Quietist.

---

[18] William E. Petig, *Literary antipietism in Germany During the First Half of the Eighteenth Century* (New York: P. Lang, 1982) 25.

In 1687, Francke experienced a dramatic conversion while at Lüneberg as he prepared to preach his first sermon on John 20:31. As he struggled with the text he came to the humbling conclusion that he did not have the faith about which he needed to preach. That evening, he experienced a deep spiritual struggle over his faith until he finally experienced a breakthrough to grace and peace. The aspect of struggle (*Bußkampf*) and breakthrough (*Durchbruch*) became standard features of Pietism after Francke published his struggle for faith. He soon became one of the most popular professors at the university; however, his devaluing of theology in favor of piety and spiritual experience aroused opposition among the Orthodox, including his old mentor Carpzov. In 1692 Francke was forced to resign his post, but Spener managed to secure an appointment for him as a pastor and teacher in the town of Halle. Spener's program of reform impressed King Frederick I of Prussia. He saw in it a possibility for healing the divisions between the Lutheran and Reformed in Prussia, and for improving the moral lives of his people. As pastor in Halle, Francke received the daunting task of reforming a town that had 200 houses and at least thirty-seven brothels. Francke reinstituted the oft-neglected practice of regular visitation of his flock, through which he instructed his parishioners in the faith and helped care for any physical needs they may have. In 1695, Francke began his Institutes with a school for poor children that met in his home. The following year he founded his influential paedagogium and an orphanage. Francke's renovation of the educational system influenced the Prussian school system.

The diverse activities of Francke point to the essential features of Pietism at Halle where he emphasized life after justification. A minister should first preach for conversion, but then focus on the renovation of life. In some ways Halle Pietism can be viewed as a Lutheran version of Calvin's emphasis on the law as a goal for social life. Pietist sermons stressed the subjective effects rather than objective ground of faith, placing more emphasis on the work of the Christian than the work of Christ. The believer must be reborn or regenerated to a life of piety and morality, and the minister should encourage this rebirth and growth through personal example rather than relying solely on the preached word. Pietism created a new model for the ministry, the pastor as example, friend and guide. Pietist pastors were expected to be living examples of the Christian life and to establish close, personal relationships with their parishioners. This model of ministry eventually became the norm in America.

Pietism addressed many social problems of the day in terms of individual morality, and the image of the Pietist as the stern moralist remains to the present day. Franke particularly condemned sloth. He assured his followers that at the Last Judgment they would have to give an account of every moment of their time and the way they had used it. Focus on the Christian life was not entirely individualistic, though. Halle Pietism stressed social improvement as well because the life of the Christian involves love for one's neighbor. Pietists established countless welfare and charitable organizations, particularly orphanages and schools for the poor. Halle would also take on the task of spreading Christianity to the world. The first Protestant missionaries left in 1705, and the story of Halle's endeavors inspired the later mission efforts of the Moravians and the Baptists.

Theologically, Pietism set the stage for the subjectivity we will examine later when we discuss Schleiermacher in the nineteenth century. Pietism also led to renewed interest in the Bible, and helped encourage the development of biblical criticism, most notably in the work of Albrecht Bengel. Unlike the Orthodox, the Pietists stressed devotional rather than doctrinal reading of scripture. One should read the Bible to find solace or encouragement, not to find hairs to split or verses to hurl at one's enemies. Some Pietists could even say that one must distinguish between the kernel of the Bible and its shell, focusing attention on what nourishes and leave the rest aside until later. Their approach to the Bible would take a decidedly unpietistic turn in the work of Ritschl and Harnack in the next century.

From Prussia the movement spread throughout Germany, although it met great resistance in Saxony. Thus Pietism became a reforming effort of great proportions in Germany and beyond. It adapted the structure of the church to meet its immediate mission and found new ways to minister in a world rapidly changing through the rise of capitalism. In some ways, the Pietist movement re-christianized Germany just prior to the rise of the Enlightenment, significantly affecting the nature of the Enlightenment in Germany. As with most reform efforts, however, Pietism lost much of its initial vigor and flexibility by mid-century. Theologically and institutionally, it became rigid in its application of Spener and Francke's original ideas. Pietists turned increasingly legalistic and openly hostile to new ideas generated by the Enlightenment. The case of Christian Thomasius (1655-1728), a leader of the early Enlightenment, illustrates this history nicely. Thomasius was an early defender of the Pietists and taught at Halle, but he turned against the Pietists when he saw that many of the pastors and teachers developed a new dogmatism and legalism. Halle, which had once led the fight for academic freedom, removed the rationalist philosopher Wolff from his position at the University in 1723, but in 1740 Frederick the Great reappointed him. Soon the University of Halle, once the leading proponent of a religion of the heart, became the center of rationalism in Germany.

Radical Pietism

Not all Pietism was of the Spener-Halle variety. As with most reform movements, Pietism encouraged theological and institutional innovation. Some of that innovation went in ways quite contrary to the original intentions of Spener, and led to outright separation from the established church. One of the most controversial of the radical Pietists was Johann Konrad Dippel (1673-1734), an alchemist and lay theologian. Like the old Waldensians, Dippel believed that the fall of the church came in the time of Constantine when the church received secular authority. According to Dippel, since that time Christianity and the church have been separate entities. True Christianity is not the church because the church stresses dogma and doctrine while Christianity is a matter of ethics and living. Dippel protested that Lutheran Orthodoxy was simply a different form of the Inquisition.

He also rejected the traditional understanding of the Atonement as a substitutionary sacrifice. No one can give a vicarious atonement, nor would the God of love demand a blood sacrifice. Rather, Dippel argued, Christians should view the death of Christ as a model of God's great love that all should imitate. Such views created a storm of controversy as Dippel traveled throughout central and northern Europe. He was forbidden to publish on theology, and was imprisoned for seven years on the island of Bornholm in Denmark. Rejected by Pietists and Orthodox alike, Dippel's views gained new currency in nineteenth century liberalism.

Gerhard Tersteegen (1697-1769), another radical Pietist, had an entirely different spirit than the bellicose Dippel. Tersteegen converted at age twenty. He then retreated into solitude and earned his living as a ribbon weaver. Since he refused to take communion with the unconverted he separated himself from the state church. His piety was highly individualistic and interior, and his most enduring contribution to Christianity is numerous hymns and poems that celebrate the individual soul's encounter with the divine. People admired Tersteegen for his gentle spirituality, and he eventually gathered a community called Pilgrim's Hut that voluntarily supported him so he could minister to them full-time. As part of his spiritual care, he translated Quietist literature and biographies of mystics, making a variety of mystical literature available for Protestantism.

Another influential separatist was Gottfried Arnold (1666-1714) who had been a deeply pious and reclusive youth. While serving as a tutor in Dresden from 1689 to 1693, he joined Spener's conventicle, which at that time included Francke. Despite Spener's urging Arnold decided not to become a pastor. Instead he chose to reform Christianity through scholarship. For a while he lived in Quedlingburg (1693-1697) where a number of self-proclaimed prophets had gathered. There they received revelations and experienced ecstasy. Many radical Pietists, such as Gitchel, rejected marriage as sinful and urged celibacy as the only path for the true Christian, a view that Arnold supported for a time. Arnold received an appointment to the University of Giessen in 1697, but he resigned the next year because of religious scruples, an action he defended in a published apology that brought him a great deal of criticism, even by his former mentor, Spener. Arnold then returned to Quedlinburg where he generated additional controversy over his refusal to take Holy Communion.

Arnold's marriage in 1701 angered many of his former radical colleagues who sensed that he was becoming more mainstream. The next year he was made a royal historian, and in 1705 he was ordained in the Lutheran Church. Although he had moderated some of his earlier radicalism, he continued to criticize the institutional church. His most famous work *Unparteiische Kirchen- und Ketzer-Historie* (Impartial History of the Church and Heretics) was published in 1700. His was a groundbreaking piece of historical writing because Arnold gave a sympathetic ear to heretics. He argued that the early church leaders at first attacked errors in doctrine, but soon they began to attack whatever they did not understand. Eventually the Orthodox became the true heretics because they tried to crush the truth and impeded free inquiry. However, despite persecution there remained a succession of "witnesses of the truth" through ages that kept the apostolic tradition of personal faith and freedom of conscience alive. The church must listen to the voice of those condemned as heretics because they may have preserved the true church.

His attitude offended many Pietists, but the Lutheran Orthodox were most bitter towards Arnold. Colerus, in 1718, proposed the following epitaph:

Here lies Gottfried Arnold, not so much a theologian, as the bitterest enemy of orthodox theologians; the persistent defender of heretics, the stupid repristinator of mystical theology, perhaps the first of all distorters of church history. He had mixed religion or none at all.

Henceforth he is commended to God's judgment. Wanderer, go hence![19]

Württemberg Pietism

Less controversial than radical Pietism or even that of the Halle variety was the form of Pietism promoted in the area of Swabia, a region that had been devastated by war and oppressed by the ruling dukes. Duke Karl Eugene (1737-1793) demanded very oppressive taxation until his second wife Franzika exerted a moderating influence. She inspired him to work with Pietist pastors to improve the physical and spiritual condition of his subjects. Pietism had already become firmly entrenched in the region by that time. Conventicles were established in several villages during the 1680s and at the University of Tübingen in 1705. This Tübingen Pietism was less legalistic and conversion oriented than that of Halle, but it was so strongly established there that the Enlightenment never really took hold at the university.

Bible study was the heart of Württember Pietism, especially in the days of Johann Albrecht Bengel (1687-1752). Unlike his older contemporary Francke, Bengel experienced no *Bußkampf*, nor could he remember having not been pious. He entered Tübingen as a student in 1703, and after graduating he lectured at the university for five years. In 1713, he became a local pastor, but continued to pursue his biblical studies. When he read the recently published Oxford Greek New Testament, he became very disturbed over the large number of textual variants indicated. Convinced that the Bible held a system of divine revelation, Bengel felt called to establish a reliable biblical text that accurately reflected the original manuscripts. He began this daunting enterprise in 1715, but his Greek New Testament was not ready for publication until 1734. In many ways his publication marks the beginning of modern textual study of New Testament because Bengel included a separate volume of critical apparatus. His *Gnomon Novi Testamenti* (Key to the New Testament) of 1742 presented his rules of textual criticism, many of which textual critics still use.

Württemburg produced its own creative theologians, the foremost of whom was Friedrich Christoph Oetinger (1702-1782) who experienced conversion in 1721. Oetinger turned away from Orthodoxy while at the university and studied the rationalism of Leibnitz and Wolff. Their mechanistic and deterministic view of the cosmos did not impress him, and he rejected their

---

[19] F. Ernest Stoeffler, *German Pietism During the Eighteenth Century* (Leiden: Brill, 1973) 176.

philosophy as lifeless and unchristian. He then discovered the ideas of the mystic Böhme which sent him on a religious pilgrimage to the major Pietist centers of Halle, Jena, and Herrnhut. He even studied the Jewish Cabbala for a time.

According to Oetinger, philosophy is the history of Mystery striving to know itself. In other words, history is God's process of self-understanding and actualization. Deity is perfect Act, not Being, thus God is life and participates in time, space, and history. Moreover, spiritual rebirth is really the recovery of the lost Adamic knowledge of God's purpose and presence in the world. Rebirth leads to peace and righteousness as the regenerated person participates in the harmony to which the cosmos tends. In general, his theology hoped for the eschaton when all things will be restored.

Oetinger was very well-read and open to secular philosophy which he reinterpreted it through biblical images. He also placed a high premium on experimental science, which he viewed as a rethinking of the thoughts of God. Furthermore, he argued that Christians must either refute or accept philosophy, but they cannot simply ignore it. Oetinger's own writings went under censorship and some books banned. Though he had very little influence in his own time, he was a direct forerunner of the great philosopher Hegel and all theologians who seek to integrate scientific inquiry and biblical truth.

Zinzendorfian Pietism

One of Francke's students at Halle became the most important, albeit controversial, theologian and church leader produced by Pietism. Nikolaus Ludwig Graf von Zinzendorf (1700-1760) was raised in his grandmother's castle according to Pietist principles. Later in life he could recount several religious experiences he had while only a child, and he criticized rigid Pietists for insisting on a painful conversion struggle. For Zinzendorf, Christianity must be accepted in childlike faith, not with a bitter struggle. He was also a leading proponent of heart religion, which he offered as a vital alternative to the rationalism of both Orthodoxy and Deism. Heart religion views religion primarily as personal experience rather than rational discourse. Naturally, most of Zinzendorf's literary production he would be in the form of hymns and sermons rather than systematic theology

As a student in Halle, Zinzendorf experimented with various types of conventicles and mission societies among his friends. He felt convinced that true Christianity must be expressed in open and intimate personal relationships with fellow believers. Though he studiously avoided separatism and made a point of always taking Holy Communion from the local parish minister, Zinzendorf insisted that voluntary associations of believers made up the heart of the church.

As a German count, Zinzendorf was expected to enter into state service, but he always pursued his religious activities even while at the University of Wittenberg. In 1722, he purchased the Berthelsdorf estate from his grandmother and made plans to establish Halle-style institutes there, beginning with an orphanage. He called a popular Pietist preacher as the pastor and placed the estate under care of a Pietist sympathizer. In the summer of that year, a small band of religious refugees sought shelter on the Zinzendorf estate. They were emigrants from Catholic Moravia who claimed to be descendants of the old Unity of the Brethren. With Zinzendorf's permission, they built a village named Herrnhut (The Lord's Watch).

In 1727, after a period of intense religious controversy, Zinzendorf presented the residents with a list of rules to govern both the social and religious life of the new community. It was to be an *ecclesiola* within the Lutheran Church. The Moravians could thus revive some aspects of their old church without separating from the legally established religion. Herrnhut's constitution made it clear that its primary purpose was to promote religion among its residents and in the wider world. Zinzendorf had created a unique form of the Pietist conventicle. An entire village had become a religious community

The first Moravian missionaries were sent out from Herrnhut, in 1732. Leonard Dober, a potter, was given the task of preaching the gospel to the slaves of St. Thomas. Within twenty years hundreds of Moravian missionaries went to Greenland, Surinam, South Africa, Egypt, and Russia among other places. Under Zinzendorf's influence, the Moravians developed a mission-strategy that was based in heart religion. The missionaries did not need to convince the people philosophically of the existence or attributes of God, nor did they need to change the culture of native peoples; rather, they merely told the evocative story of Christ's loving sacrifice for all humans. By the time of Zinzendorf's death, the Moravians were widely regarded as the most dynamic force in Protestant missions

In 1741 Zinzendorf traveled to Pennsylvania to examine the work recently begun there. He even traveled into Indian country to examine the mission enterprise. While in Pennsylvania, Zinzendorf called several ecumenical meetings of the various German-speaking churches and sects, a gathering he called the Church of God in the Holy Spirit. This was the first ecumenical church council in America, and although it failed to produce a

German Protestant church in America, it demonstrates Zinzendorf's lifelong commitment to church reunification. Shortly after, in 1744 and 1745 he articulated his "Tropus" concept, an early denominational theory that argues that each historical church has its own special gift from God and should be valued. While in America, Zinzendorf also helped organize the community of Bethlehem in Pennsylvania, which would be the center of Moravian activity in America.

Zinzendorf promoted several intriguing and controversial notions. According to Zinzendorf, the Holy Spirit should be worshipped as the mother of the church. His followers also developed a stable communal social structure that gave almost equal authority to women and men. The piety of the Moravians focused intensely on the suffering of Jesus and the soul's desire for union with him; however, their richly evocative hymns about the atonement gave much fuel for the fires of controversy that surrounded the church during Zinzendorf's life.

Zinzendorf also rejected the legalism of Halle, embracing the idea of free grace promoted in the Augsburg Confession. For the Moravians, the Christian life is to be a life of sober joyfulness and celebration. However, they could not avoid controversy. The opposition to Zinzendorf was so great that when word reached Halle that its former pupil was organizing the Germans in America in 1742, Henry Muhlenberg (1711-1787) left for Philadelphia to save Pennsylvania from Zinzendorf. Muhlenberg successfully took his assigned pulpit away from Zinzendorf and proceeded to organize the Lutheran Church in America along Halle Pietist lines.

Chapter 19

Methodism and the Great Awakening

UNDOUBTEDLY, THE MOST important movement related to Pietism was the Methodist movement of John Wesley (1703-1791). Methodism developed in England, but it would have its greatest impact on the United States where it would be a major source of evangelism, moralism, and social activism in the nineteenth century. Movements as diverse as revivalism, Pentecostalism and the Social Gospel, which we will study later, can be traced to the Methodist movement. The origin of Methodism can be found in the biography of an intense young man at Oxford who sought peace for his own troubled soul, but first we should look at the world that Wesley inhabited.

Industrial England

England experienced the blessing and curse of the Industrial Age first. The island experienced a population explosion beginning in the latter part of the seventeenth century that led to a tremendous increase in the size of its major cities. Several factors contributed to the population increase, including a more reliable food supply and a decrease in mortality rate. By 1700, the population was increasing at almost a geometric rate, and the surplus population began crowding into the slums of the cities. The increased demand for coal and ore, as well as newly developed methods of mining, accelerated the mining industry, producing large mining and manufacturing cities such as Bristol and Newcastle.

In 1769, Isaac Watts introduced his steam engine and British industry exploded in productivity, but the life of the working poor turned bleak and meaningless. The strange hostility of the city slum with its grinding, dehumanizing isolation and poverty replaced the traditional life of the village, with its predictable patterns, intricate relationships, and rituals. Even the nuclear family fell apart as mothers, fathers, and children were forced to toil twelve or fourteen hour days in the factories, mines, and even on the streets. A new distilled liquor, called gin, became a common way for people of all ages to blunt the misery of their lives. In such conditions domestic violence was accepted, alcoholism and crime normal, and prostitution pervasive. This was the life so graphically chronicled in the etchings of Hogarth: a life of chaos, social disruption, ignorance, and fear. Western history had never seen anything like the life of the industrial city, and the traditional church had few answers to the new problems. While the amateur, bourgeois philosophers of the Enlightenment enjoyed the comforts of mass production, and sat in coffee houses debating how to create a new society, the Methodists went into the coal fields and slums to offer a new life to those clinging to the lowest rungs of society.

John Wesley (1703-1791) was the fifteenth child of Samuel and Susanna Wesley (1669-1742). His younger brother and co-worker, Charles, was the eighteenth and penultimate of the children. Although Wesley's grandfathers had been dissenters with Puritan leanings, Samuel and Susanna remained firmly attached to the Anglican Church. Samuel was the rector of the country parish of Epworth, and his wife helped keep the family together with frugal housekeeping and strict discipline. She was the dominant influence in John's life, helping to shape not only his austere personality but also his Armenian theology. His own writings show that no other woman was so close to his heart.

John Wesley was made a priest in 1728 while studying at Oxford. Shortly after, he became an active member of a small religious society started by his brother. It was similar to hundreds of religious groups in England modeled on Spener's colleges of piety. The members pledged themselves to pursuing a serious and devout life filled with prayer, Bible-reading, fasting, self-examination, and concrete acts of Christian charity, such as visiting prisons. Other students at Oxford derisively called them the Holy Club or the Methodists because of the rigidity of their religious approach.

One of the key converts to the Holy Club was George Whitefield (1714-1770), whom we shall meet again in America. Whitefield grew up in relative poverty and gave up a career on the stage in 1735 when he experienced a new birth. He would have a profound impact on Wesley's career even though the two great evangelists had bitter disagreements over the issue of predestination. Whitefield remained a staunch Calvinist while Wesley embraced Arminianism.

The Holy Club became interested in General Oglethorp's great philanthropic plans in the New World. Oglethorp founded a colony, named for King George, that would be a haven for debtors, orphans, and other poor souls who needed a fresh start. In 1735, Charles and John Wesley sailed for Georgia. Their pilgrimage changed the course of Western religious history, and brought together German Pietism and English Methodism. On board the ship with Wesley were twenty-six Moravians who were also bound for Georgia to conduct missions to the natives and slaves. Wesley felt that the Moravians had an assurance of salvation and a peacefulness that he lacked. He was particularly impressed with how calmly the Moravians behaved during a storm that frightened even seasoned sailors. Never one to waste time, Wesley took advantage of his contact with the Moravians to improve his German, translating a number of Zinzendorf's hymns and sermons while on board. In Georgia, Wesley met the Moravian leader Spangenberg who asked him if he knew Christ in his own heart. It would be years before Wesley could answer yes to that question.

Wesley found life difficult and unrewarding in Georgia. He approached his ministry with great zeal, preaching often and establishing religious societies, but he met with little success. His attempts to impose strict Anglican worship and rigid moralism offended many. One person who was deeply attracted to him, though, was Sophie Hopkey, the daughter of a prominent colonist. Sophie regularly attended Wesley's religious meetings and made it clear that she was available for marriage. After some months of dithering, he finally rejected Sophie, who quickly married another suitor. When she stopped attending Wesley's religious meetings, he denied her Holy Communion. His denial caused such uproar in the colony that Wesley deemed it wise to return to England. He sailed on February 1, 1738, distraught over his failure and his sense of unworthiness.

Back in London, Wesley spent time with Peter Böhler, the Moravian who led the Fetter Lane Society. Böhler impressed on Wesley the need for assurance of faith and the experience of Christ in one's own heart as the way to overcome sin. On May 25, 1738, after a serious illness, Wesley attended a meeting of the Aldersgate Street religious society where he heard Martin Luther's preface to *The Commentary on Romans*. As he heard the words about God's grace, he felt his "heart strangely warmed." He later recorded that "I felt I did trust in Christ, Christ alone, for salvation." His breakthrough to the experience of grace permanently changed Wesley's life and ministry. Soon he began taking his message around to other religious societies.

Whenever possible, he preached the idea of personal salvation from Anglican pulpits.

In 1739 Whitefield invited Wesley to preach in the growing town of Bristol to the poor coal-miners and their families who were largely excluded from the fashionable life of the average Anglican parish. Shortly before, Whitefield had started holding open-air preaching services to reach the unwashed masses in the growing industrial metropolises of England and Wales. Although lacking Whitefield's great dramatic gifts, Wesley delivered a compelling message of salvation that had dramatic effects on the hearers. He, his brother Charles, and Whitefield became traveling evangelists, seeking converts wherever a crowd would gather. Thousands responded to their preaching, but for Wesley conversion alone was not enough; Christians should grow in faith and morality.

The Methodist Societies

After a period of conflict with the Moravians in the Fetter Lane Society and a serious falling out with Zinzendorf over the idea of perfection, Wesley withdrew from the Moravians in 1740 and began organizing his own societies. One of his key innovations was the establishment of "classes" of about a dozen people with a class leader. Class members had to pay penny dues and meet high standards of morality and piety. The classes were the backbone of the Methodist organization for decades and had a number of positive effects. For one thing, they developed many strong lay leaders who could effectively communicate to people of their own social and economic status. Close, personal contact was a necessary counterpoint to the large public revival services.

A second benefit was that the classes effectively strengthened moral life. They served as support groups for people trying to overcome alcoholism and sexual abuse. Moreover, they provided needed community and intimacy in the impersonal world of the eighteenth-century metropolis. They also helped provide necessary funds to support the Methodist mission. Wesley, like most of his contemporaries feared unrestrained religious enthusiasm, so in 1744 he instituted the annual conference of preachers in order to maintain discipline and order among his lay preachers. Ever sensitive to the need for organization, Wesley divided the preaching work into districts he called circuits. Traveling preachers staffed each circuit, most of them laymen who were not permitted to administer the sacraments. Each circuit also had a permanent leader called the superintendent who oversaw the work of the preachers. Wesley took a major step toward separation from the Anglican Church in 1784 when he helped ordain ministers to work in the New World. On Christmas Day of that same year the Methodists in America officially separated from the Church of England.

Charles Wesley strongly supported his brother's work, but he remained more closely attached to traditional Anglicanism. Eventually he settled in London and gave up the itinerant life. His greatest contributions to Western Christianity are his hundreds of beautiful hymns that speak of a warm and personal relationship with God through the atoning work of Christ. The eighteenth century was a golden age of Protestant hymnody when emotional depth and theological truth beautifully joined.

By 1760 there were some 30,000 people that paid penny dues and even more listening to Methodist sermons. In the second half of his life, Wesley increasingly devoted himself to the idea of Christian perfection or holiness of life. He strongly advocated to his followers that they could and should move toward a sinless state, even in this life. After having experienced salvation through a personal conversion, they should exercise themselves with strict discipline, prayer, and self-examination until they no longer consciously violated any law of God. His was a bold and innovative doctrine that remains controversial, but it would be a major force in the Methodist commitment to personal morality and social justice.

The Methodist movement had an effect on the church in England beyond its own members. A significant number of priests within the established church were sympathetic to the Methodist cause of converting sinners, but were unwilling to adopt all of their methods. The Evangelical Party, as it was called, included John Newton (1725-1807), author of one of the most popular hymns in the English language, "Amazing Grace." Newton was captain of a slave ship before his conversion. He gave up the slave trade and became the pastor of a congregation at Olney where he urged others on to a life-changing conversion.

The most famous Evangelical after Wesley was William Wilberforce (1759-1833), a man of substance and influence before his conversion in 1784. In 1787 he launched a long and ultimately successful battle against the inhuman practice of slavery. He argued tirelessly in every public forum from the pulpit to Parliament that slavery was an offense before God and humans. For Wilberforce, concern for people's souls also means a concern for their bodies as well. He first succeeded in abolishing the slave trade, and in the year of his death, 1833, Parliament proclaimed full emancipation in all British Colonies.

The Great Awakening

The Methodist evangelical reform provided an effective way for the church to adjust to the Industrial Age. It also contributed significantly to the revival of Christianity in North America known as the Great Awakening. As with most things in history, there is a debate over the Great Awakening. People use the term to describe a general revival of religion in colonial America in the early 1740s, but the revival was not called the Great Awakening until the next century. Some historians point out that the revival in the 1740s was more a series of isolated revivals rather than a single Great Awakening. As such, the phrase "Great Awakening" may be inaccurate and even misleading; however, the term does have some validity. The leaders of the revival sensed that this religious movement differed from the local revivals of religion they had experienced in the past. They had a general sense that this Awakening affected most of the colonies, and was in fact joining the colonies together. Also, the size of the Awakening astounded even its enemies. Reliable reports say that tens of thousands of people came to hear the evangelists. Moreover, this Awakening introduced a number of practices, such as itinerant preaching that would have a profound impact on American religion. In the 1740s American religion took its first definite turn toward the evangelicalism that would characterize it to the present day.

Religious revivals had occurred in New England before the Great Awakening. The term "Awakening" itself comes out of Puritan theology where it describes the moment when the elect awaken to their condition and become more sensitive to religion and the service of God. They are converted to a new life characterized by godliness. Such awakenings could be individual or affect whole communities. The Great Awakening would be seen as special because it affected so many over so large an area; however, it began like previous awakenings.

Jonathan Edwards

In 1729, Jonathan Edwards (1703-1758) took over as pastor of the Northampton congregation. Northampton was a small town in Connecticut, and like many towns in New England there was a general feeling that the old religious zeal of the original Puritans had been lost. It appeared to many that religion was in decline evidenced by the fact that few youths showed interest . in religion. Edward's grandfather, Timothy Stoddard, had pastored the Northampton congregation in the previous century, and had led a revival of religion in the 1670s. His grandson, Jonathan Edwards, would do much more.

Edwards may be the most famous clergyman in American history, other than living figures. Part of his fame rests on his shocking and compelling sermon, *Sinners in the Hand of an Angry God*, in which he tells the worshipers that "the God of Wrath holds them over the pit of hell like a spider. The wrath of God burns against them, their damnation does not slumber; the pit is prepared, the fire is made ready, the furnace is now hot, ready to receive them; the flames do now rage and glow."[20] That sermon is often held up as an example of the harsh and judgmental religion of the Puritans, but it actually marked a movement away from the typical New England sermon which consisted of a long (one or two hour) theological discourse. *Sinners in the Hand of an Angry God* is memorable because of its dramatic and emotional appeal. It attempts to convince the heart to place all trust in God's grace rather than convincing the mind to believe in a theological proposition.

Less dramatically, Edwards is known as one of the few great American-born theologians. Unfortunately his *Sinners* sermon has led to a caricature of Edwards as a verbal sadist attacking his congregation. He was primarily a scholar who was one of the first theologians to make use of John Locke's theory of knowledge. In fact, one of Edward's great contributions to theology was his careful analysis of religious emotions using Locke's epistemology. In 1746, in the wake of the Great Awakening, Edwards published his ground-breaking *A Treatise Concerning Religious Affections* in which he delineated twelve signs of genuine piety, the chief of which is love. This is a sophisticated theory of religious conversion, which translated the Puritan heritage for the eighteenth century. Edwards also kept himself informed of the revival of religion going on in Europe at the same time. The Pietists published numerous accounts of conversions and the spread of religion, setting up an extensive network of correspondence and publication that reached Edwards even in distant Connecticut.

In 1734 and 1735 Edwards gave a serious of sermons on justification in which he rejected the covenantal theology of his ancestors. He returned to the original thought of John Calvin and stressed the absolute sovereignty of God and God's hatred of sin. Edwards was not a dynamic speaker. Reports say that he focused his attention on the bell rope in the back of the church and spoke in a monotone voice without flair or dramatics, but his words painted a clear picture of the soul's damnation without the grace of God. A revival began among the youth of the church, which soon spread throughout the area.

---

[20] Quoted in Alister E. McGrath, *The Christian Theology Reader* (Cambridge MA: Blackwell, 1995) 362.

Edwards collected stories of the religious revival in Connecticut and published them in 1737 in a work titled *A Faithful Narrative of the Surprising Work of God in Conversion of Many Hundred Souls In Northampton, and Neighboring Towns and Villages*. His narrative spread word of the revival as far as Oxford where John Wesley read it.

The revival in Northampton, though, was not as permanent as Edwards had thought, and within a few years he ran into trouble with his own congregation. It reached a crisis in 1748 when he tried to overturn his grandfather's policy of open admission to Holy Communion and instead reserved Communion only for the visibly converted. The Northampton congregation refused to go along with his proposal and asked him to resign. Soon he lived in virtual exile at the Indian mission of Stockbridge, Massachusetts. However, he continued to write and publish. His reputation grew among the revival-minded clergy, and in 1758 he became the president of the recently established evangelical college in Prince Town, New Jersey. He barely had taken office, however, when he died from a small pox vaccination.

The Tennents

Less famous than Edwards but perhaps more important to the Great Awakening was the Tennent family in New Jersey. The Middle Colonies witnessed a massive immigration of Scots-Irish Presbyterians in the early eighteenth century. These were Scots who had accepted the king's invitation to settle in Northern Ireland following the English Civil War. Conditions in Ireland proved very difficult and thousands of Scots-Irish came to the New World. Most of them were Presbyterian with a strong suspicion of the Anglican Church, and an equally strong tendency to split into factions among themselves.

Already by the 1720s divisions occurred in America over whether candidates for ordination needed to subscribe to the Westminster Confession, or if the quality of a candidate's life meant more than his doctrine. William Tennent, Sr. supported the latter position. He was also a gifted teacher who trained several young men to be ministers, among them his three sons. His "log college" in New Jersey taught Greek and Latin, but also stressed the need for ministers to experience the conversion about which they would preach. This "log college" offered an alternative to Harvard and Yale, which Tennent felt had lost genuine religion, and provided an affordable education for ministers in the Middle Colonies. It would eventually become Princeton University.

Gilbert Tennent (1703-1764) was the most gifted of the three sons of William, and the most controversial Presbyterian preacher in the Great Awakening. Gilbert received a call to be a pastor in New Brunswick, New Jersey close to Raritan where the Dutch Pietist Theodore Jacob Frelinghuysen (1691-1748) preached on the necessity of personal conversion and holiness of life. Tennent heard Frelinghuysen preach and the sermon inspired him to make conversion the focal point of his own ministry. As his congregation grew, so did his reputation as an effective preacher. When the evangelist Whitefield came to preach in Philadelphia, he met with Tennent and other revival-minded Presbyterians, and encouraged them to spread the revival beyond their own parishes. Whitefield inspired Tennent to become an itinerant, and preach wherever he could find an audience, ignoring the presbyterial structure by intruding into other presbyteries without permission. He traveled as far north as Boston where he publicly criticized clergy educated at Harvard for being unconverted.

Unlike the eloquent Whitefield, Tennent was unsophisticated, belligerent, and crude, but his qualities appealed to the farmers and poor artisans in the colonies. He railed against ministers who substituted education and refinement for personal religious experience, and openly encouraged people to leave their congregations if the minister was not pious enough. In 1740, he created a firestorm when he preached a sermon titled "The Danger of an Unconverted Ministry" in which he warned the congregation that having an unconverted pastor could endanger their souls. Unconverted ministers were "Pharisees" and "hypocrites" who substituted education for salvation. He asked, "Is a dead man fit to bring others to life?"[21] Tennent urged the congregation to call only a converted minister, and he even encouraged the members to attend a different church if their minister was unconverted.

His sermon was published in Boston and Philadelphia in 1742, and contributed to the growing division within the Presbyterian Church between the New Side who favored revivalism and the Old Side who clung to the Westminster Confession. The New Side openly attacked the time-honored parish system inherited from medieval Catholicism, and encouraged the laity to choose their own church and own minister. By 1758, Tennent moderated some of the opinions expressed in the Awakening and helped reconcile the

---

[21] Gilbert Tennent, "The Danger of an Unconverted Ministry," in *The Great Awakening: Documents on the Revival of Religion, 1740-1745* (Chapel Hill: University of North Carolina Press, 1969) 91.

New and Old Sides, but he remained a leading voice in the emerging "free enterprise" approach to religion in America.

George Whitefield

The greatest of the Great Awakening preachers was George Whitefield (1714-1770), an English Methodist who had been a member of Wesley's Holy Club at Oxford. Whitefield had at one time considered a career on the stage, and he used his early training in dramatics to enhance his preaching. One British actor remarked jealously that Whitefield could move a crowd to tears simply by saying "Mesopotamia." Being cross-eyed, Whitefield had difficulty preaching from notes, so he dispensed with a manuscript, which was quite a departure from the typical Puritan or Anglican preaching. Ministers typically read carefully crafted theological or moral arguments, but Whitefield entertained and cajoled the people. Wesley recognized Whitefield's gifts and encouraged him to visit the Georgia colony where Whitefield decided to sponsor an orphanage.

Unlike Wesley who never returned to America, Whitefield devoted much attention to the colonies. He made several preaching tours in the major American cities, beginning in Charleston, South Carolina. His grand tour of 1739 and 1740 took him through much of colonial America as he preached in every major city, making him the first person to be easily recognized in every colony. Benjamin Franklin was skeptical of the exaggerated claims of the size of Whitefield's crowds, so when Whitefield preached in the main square in Philadelphia, Franklin personally calculated how many people the square could hold. He decided that 30,000 people attended the event, making Whitefield's sermon the largest public event in colonial history. Franklin was also wary of Whitefield's ability to raise money. He reported that he only took small change hidden in the lining of his clothes when he went to the hear Whitefield preach because he had heard how persuasive the evangelist could be. Despite his precaution, Whitefield's appeal to support his orphanage moved Franklin so much that he left without his money.

Wherever Whitefield preached, the Awakening took hold, and soon dozens of preachers imitated his style and method. Some of them significantly lacked skill and tact, however. Among them was James Davenport (1716-1757) who left his own parish on Long Island in 1738 to become an itinerant preacher. A graduate of Yale, he spoke at the commencement ceremony in 1742. He shocked everyone by attacking his former professors for being unconverted. Expelled from Connecticut, he soon gathered crowds in Boston where he assured his listeners that they could have full knowledge and assurance of their salvation if they experienced genuine conversion. Moreover, he claimed that he could personally tell who was converted just by looking them in the eye. He even went so far as to name some of the leading citizens of Boston as those who were going to hell. He was arrested for disturbing the peace, and convicted of slander. Davenport's excesses brought reproach on the Awakening in general. He came to his senses in 1744 and published a confession and retraction.

Effects of the Awakening

The Great Awakening helped unite the American colonies through a shared religious event, and also undermined traditional ecclesiastical divisions. For the evangelicals, doctrines and structures were less important than conversion. An evangelical Anglican, like Deveraux Jarratt (1733-1801) in Virginia, had more in common with a New Side Presbyterian or a New Light Congregationalist than with many clergy in his own church. On the other hand, the revivalists introduced new divisions in Christianity as they tried to reform and renew the church. The Awakeners, to lesser or greater degrees, attacked more traditional-minded ministers who valued doctrine and order more than individual experience. The Old Lights fought a losing battle to preserve the traditional ways. The Awakeners also encouraged individuals to make their own religious choices and leave their congregations if necessary. Isaac Backus (1724-1806) in New England left his Congregationalist Church and became a Baptist. He led the successful fight for the rights of Baptists and other separatist groups to enjoy religious toleration and exemption from church taxes.

Furthermore, intense conflict arose between those who wanted to reform Christianity through reason and those who focused on emotion. The rationalists, or as New Englanders called them, the liberals, objected to the way the evangelists stirred up the emotions of the crowds. The leading voices of opposition came from Charles Chauncy (1705-1787), pastor of the Brattle Street Church in Boston, and Timothy Cutler (1723-1765), a convert to Anglicanism. Chauncy and Cutler condemned the Awakening as a destabilizing force in society that undermined the social order and unleashed potentially dangerous emotions. In his 1743 work *Seasonable Thoughts on the State of Religion in New England*, Chauncy gathered every tale of excess he could find to ridicule this emotional outbreak, and show his readers the need for a reasonable religion. Chauncy asked if the Awakening could really be the work of God since it stirred up so much discord among people. True to his Latitudinarian sympathies, he argued that religion should unite people and produce a virtuous society. The itinerant evangelists were actually irreligious because they divided people according to sentiment, and undermined traditional authorities. He was particularly upset that women were being used as lay exhorters to encourage the revival. Chauncy's works helped pave the way for New England Unitarianism, which we will discuss in a later chapter.

Indeed, the Awakening did help demystify the clergy and promote the religion of the common person. As with Pietism elsewhere, the Awakening preachers found new ways to make religion a vital force in the life of ordinary citizens, and in doing so undermined the traditional authority of the clergy. Seen in this light, the Great Awakening was a religious prelude to the political revolution of 1776. It may also be blamed for the anti-intellectualism that dominates the history of American religion. More important for our story, though, the Great Awakening took the first major step toward the modern American religious setting where evangelicalism and freedom of choice in religion are the norm, and church divisions are less a matter of institutional structure than personal theology.

Conclusion

The 150 years from the ending of the Thirty Years War to the rise of Napoleon witnessed enormous changes in Western society and unprecedented challenges for Christianity. Christianity contributed to many social reform movements, but it also had to find ways to reform itself. Initially, effort suc-ceeded as mysticism and heart religion resisted rationalistic challenges to the faith and found ways to reach the middle and lower classes. Diverse experi-mentation created strains within the churches and rifts between individuals, but Christianity in 1750 was a strong and vibrant force. However, by the end of the century the church faced possible extinction.

The world was larger and more complicated in 1789 than it had been in 1650. Many fronts challenged Christian exclusivity. Denominations com-peted with one another and with new philosophies. World travel caused in-creased contact with other religions. The United States had created a secular government. France had created a new religion to celebrate the revolution. Deism and atheism had become fashionable among the upper classes in Europe, even among bishops.

As society grew more tolerant of other beliefs, Christians had to find ways to respond. There was a growing conviction that the great dramatist Gotthold Ephraim Lessing (1729-1781) offered the best perspective for the future. Christianity as a religion had preceded the writing of the New Testament and had survived for centuries without governmental assistance. Christianity is true, according to Lessing, because it meets the needs of human beings and society. Other religions may also be true, even if in an inferior sense. In *Nathan the Wise* (1779) Lessing dramatized his conviction that Judaism, Christianity, and Islam were variations of the same theme of love for God and neighbor. The following year, in his essay *The Education of Mankind*, he put forth the theory that history is a process of progress. The world's religions and sects make up part of that process. Christianity has helped educate the human race, but who can predict what the future might hold?

By the time of Napoleon, many people expected that Christianity would slowly die out and be replaced by philosophy, science, and the nation state. Overlooked were the great signs of vitality in many churches, particularly the evangelicals in America. Also overlooked by all but a few dreamers and thinkers was Christianity's internal drive for continual reformation and adaptation to changing social conditions. In the next century, Christianity would find ways to win the minds and souls of people without relying on the power of kings and the sanctity of tradition. Although Europe grew increasingly secular in the nineteenth century, for the rest of the world it could be called the Christian Century.

Part 4

The Nineteenth Century

THE NINETEENTH CENTURY was a dynamic period that continues to shape Western society and religion today. Prior to this time, the church had often struggled with kings and emperors over who would control the church and its symbols, but during the nineteenth century the modern state and nationalism competed with religion as the major motivating and unifying force for people. Throughout Christendom, the church lost direct political power as the state took over spheres of influence once dominated by the church, such as education and medical care. The American model of religious disestablishment gained ground in Europe over the course of the century, and by the end of the nineteenth century, Christianity faced a world in which the state was secularized and religion pushed out of public affairs. Moreover, the spread of education and the decline of ecclesiastical power allowed once forbidden ideas to be discussed openly and creatively throughout Europe. Some of these new ideas and philosophies were aggressively anti-Christian and atheistic; others inspired the most creative theological work since the days of Augustine.

During this same period industrialization took hold in Europe and America, bringing hitherto unimaginable material wealth, comfort, and technological advancement which challenged traditional Christian views on materialism. Industrialization also created new and horrifying conditions for those who crowded into the growing slums that seethed with pestilence and despair, and who were enslaved to machines and impersonal corporations. The new urban suffering challenged traditional Christian views on poverty and charity as well. Thanks in large part to the creation of efficient governmental bureaucracies and advanced technology, the European powers extended their control over the rest of the world through ruthless colonialism during this century. The subjugation of India, East Asia, Africa, and the Middle East brought vast wealth to Europe, especially England, and opened the door for the greatest numerical expansion of Christianity since the fourth century. The "white man's burden" to civilize and Christianize the nations of the world did bring Christianity to millions, but it also created problems that would plague the church in the next century as those nations threw off the yoke of European rule.

In addition to such sweeping political and social changes, Christianity also confronted new scientific and historical research. Geologists and biologists rejected traditional ideas about the origin of the earth and life itself. Astronomers demonstrated that the universe was far larger and older than anyone had ever imagined. At the turn of the century, a Swiss patent clerk showed that even the laws of physics are relative and exceedingly subtle. Some Christians responded in reverent awe at such revelations about creation; others rejected the new science as atheistic and unbiblical. Scholars subjected the Bible itself to careful scrutiny according to the new methods of historical and literary research. It, too, was shown to be relative and complex, a product of a particular ancient culture. For some Christians, biblical criticism opened up the Bible in new and marvelous ways that brought forth new revelations for the modern world. For others, biblical criticism was simply atheism and apostasy. During this age of rapid social change and theological controversy, new Christian sects and even new religions emerged and flourished.

Despite the evident signs of increasing secularization in Europe and the erosion of ecclesiastical authority and power, most observers in 1900 looked forward to the coming century as one in which the promise of Christianity would be fulfilled around the world. Liberals and conservatives, Protestants, Catholics and sectarians certainly disagreed on the best course of action and the proper way to reform church and society in the century ahead, but there was general confidence that the kingdom of God was at hand. Western society and Christianity (variously understood) steadily advanced toward creating a civilized world. The trenches of World War I would shatter the optimistic vision of the coming kingdom of God as the Christian monarchs and Christian democracies of Europe sacrificed their children in a futile apocalyptic struggle.

Chapter 20

Catholicism, Eastern Orthodoxy, and Nationalism

Political Changes

THE FRENCH REVOLUTION and the Napoleonic wars redefined European society and culture at the turn of the nineteenth century, but the defeat of Napoleon's grand French army by a coalition of patriotic forces led by Blücher and Wellington began a time of restored monarchies. The Catholic Church ardently supported the cause of restoration. "Throne and Altar" were to work together paternally to preserve peace and order in Europe. With the self-crowned emperor in exile, the Congress of Vienna met to redraw the political map of Europe; however, the Congress ignored the growing nationalist movements that the French Revolution had inspired throughout Europe. Greeks, Serbs, Croats, Poles, Czechs, Hungarians, Belgiums, Italians, and Germans agitated for national autonomy and limited democracy. The clamor exploded into revolution throughout Europe in 1848. Though the revolutions largely failed, patriotism continued to be a vibrant, and at times violent force in Europe, and a major threat to the Catholic Church.

Napoleon abolished the Holy Roman Empire, one of the dominant institutions of the Middle Ages, when his armies swept through Germany in 1806. Thirty-nine German states dominated by Prussia and the Austro-Hungarian Empire replaced the empire. Over the course of the century, Prussian kings, following the policies of chancellor Otto von Bismarck, successfully unified the German states into a single, powerful German Empire. The Hapsburgs were forced to grant limited independence to some of the powerful national groups in their empire, most notably the Hungarians. They lost their Italian possessions to the new unified Italian state created by

Mazzini, Garibaldi, and Victor Emanuel II. In 1870 the Papal States were brought into the new kingdom of Italy, and Rome, once the papal city, became the capital of Italy. The papacy lost all of its temporal possessions except for Vatican City.

By the end of the century the Catholic Church had lost virtually all of the political power it had enjoyed in the Middle Ages. Its power had been eroding since the days of Boniface VIII, but the final blow came in the nineteenth century. Napoleon willingly acknowledged the authority of the pope in some matters as long as he supported his plans, but when Pius VII opposed his divorce, Napoleon held him in prison for five years. The Congress of Vienna paid no attention to papal wishes when redrawing the map of Europe, and none of the European monarchs sent an army to save the pope from virtual imprisonment in the Vatican once Italy was unified. Still, the papacy and most of the Catholic bishops continued to support the monarchs. Moreover, as the pope lost a voice in European politics, he and his cardinals increasingly asserted papal authority over the church. The medieval idea of papal supremacy developed into the idea of papal infallibility in matters of faith and doctrine.

Conservative Reaction

Pius IX (1846-1878) was the pontiff during these difficult times. He had been an effective bishop and cardinal who held liberal sympathies before being elected pope in 1846. A capable administrator, Pius made the Catholic Church's government more efficient and effective. He also granted new rights to Jews living within the Papal States. However, the Italian Revolution of 1848 cut his liberal reform short when he was forced to flee the Vatican because of rioting crowds. He resolutely, but impotently, opposed the unification of Italy and the termination of the church's temporal authority. The faithful were forbidden to vote in Italian elections under threat of excommunication.

Convinced that new political and religious ideas threatened to destroy the church and European society, Pius attacked new modes of thought. The 1864 encyclical *Quanta Cura* included an appendix, the *Syllabus of Errors*, which listed modern evils faithful Catholics must reject. Included in the list of errors were democracy, secular government, freedom of worship, biblical criticism, socialism, atheism, pantheism, and liberalism. Priests, bishops, and theologians who had sympathies with modernism were disciplined and silenced. The *Index of Forbidden Books* grew accordingly large during Pius' reign.

By 1869, Pius felt confident enough in his control of the church that he called the first general council since Trent. The First Vatican Council consolidated much of the work of Pius, bringing the international Catholic Church firmly under the control of the Vatican. On July 18, 1870, the council agreed that in matters of faith and doctrine, the Roman pontiff speaks infallibly. However, Pius' reactionary politics and assertions of complete authority over the Catholic faithful generated opposition in parts of Christendom. In Germany, Bismarck used this issue to generate support for his *Kulturkampf* (Culture War) by which he tried to absorb Catholic institutions completely into the Prussian state. In France, anticlericalism continued to gain ground, and all parties generally assumed that one could not be republican and a faithful Catholic. Early in the twentieth century, the Fourth Republic created a secular state in France that took education and social services out of the church's control.

Catholicism in America

The *Syllabus of Errors,* which openly condemned of the American political system, especially the First Amendment, created a crisis for American Catholics and fueled the already prevalent anti-Catholic sentiment in America. Anti-Catholic prejudice had long been strong in America. Political parties, such as the Know-Nothings and the Nativists, with the stated intention of keeping immigrants, especially Catholics, out of America. They wanted to restrict immigration from Catholic countries, forbid the speaking of non-English languages in public places, and deny the rights of citizenship to "undesirable" elements.

Anti-Catholic rioting broke out in Boston in 1834 when a mob stormed an Ursuline convent in order to "rescue" the children from the nuns. In 1842, anti-Catholic rioting broke out in Philadelphia when Bishop Kenrick requested that Catholics in public schools be allowed to use the Catholic version of the Bible. A Protestant crowd decided to invade the Kensington area where a large number of Irish laborers lived. They managed to burn down thirty houses, a church, and a school during several days of rioting. When it ended, fifty were wounded and thirteen were dead. In light of such hostility, American bishops and priests had to deal gingerly with the *Syllabus of Errors* when it appeared.

American bishops also confronted the difficulty of blending Catholic immigrants from many countries and traditions into a single American church, while also convincing non-Catholics that it was an *American* church. Despite the litany of modern ills in the *Syllabus*, most American bishops agreed with John Ireland that "there is no conflict between the Catholic Church and America.... The principles of the church are in thorough harmony with the interests of the Republic."[22] James Cardinal Gibbons (1834-1921), the archbishop of Baltimore, did the most to create an American Catholic Church. In 1876 he published *The Faith of the Fathers*, an enormously popular apologetic for Catholicism that highlighted the theme of Americanization. While allowing parishes to be drawn along ethnic lines, the church hierarchy would be heterogeneous. He also supported efforts to adapt Catholicism to an American setting, such as using the parochial school system to educate Catholic children, and he encouraged active involvement in politics. Gibbons stated that "Loyalty to God, Church and to our Country! This is our religious and political faith."[23] With Gibbon's encouragement, Catholics supported American military activities, even the war against Catholic Spain. Within the church, Gibbons had to convince the Vatican that the separation of church and state was a good thing, at least in America.

Conservative bishops in Europe were shocked to see the modernism that they fought against in Europe being advocated by the church hierarchy in America. The Catholic University of America was accused of training priests to be liberal democrats as well as priests. Some of the church's adaptation to American forms of thought and life styles seemed to be a Protestantizing of Catholicism. The Americanization fight was brief and bitter, but Gibbons won in the end. Bishops, priests, and teachers were warned that strict limits existed as to how much the church could adapt to America. Becoming American did not mean becoming Protestant. The church's hierarchy, doctrines, and practices must be preserved, but there was no reason that Catholics could not endorse democratic politics or kill other Catholics in the name of America. The final victory for the American party came in 1908 when the papacy officially declared that America was no longer a mission field to be controlled from Rome. The American Catholic Church demonstrated that the Catholic Church could survive and even thrive in the midst of separation of church and state.

---

[22] Quoted in Sidney Ahlstrom, *A Religious History of the American People*, 2 vols. (Garden City NY: Image Books, 1975) 2:310.

[23] Marty, *Pilgrims in Their Own Land*, 282.

Catholic Piety

Despite, or perhaps because of the church's loss of political power, a popular Catholic revival occurred during the reign of Pius. Pius IX actively promoted the theology and philosophy of Thomas Aquinas as a bulwark against emerging atheist philosophies. The renaissance of Thomist and medieval scholarship bore rich fruit in the twentieth century. In 1854, without consulting his bishops, Pius declared the doctrine of the Immaculate Conception of Mary, which states that the Virgin Mary had been conceived without the taint of Original Sin. In other words, Mary was conceived and remained without sin. The doctrine was accompanied by renewed manifestations of the Virgin throughout the Catholic world, and an increase in popular devotion to the mother of Jesus. Pius also canonized numerous saints, many of whom served as exemplars of devotion to the Holy See and traditional values. In 1875, he dedicated the whole church to the Sacred Heart of Jesus, a relatively recent form of devotion that was gaining popular support.

The Romantic movement, which turned away from the adoration of technology and rationalism of the Enlightenment, aided the resurgence of Catholic devotion. Romanticism valued the irrational, emotional, and mystical over the scientific. This literary and philosophical movement flourished in Germany around the turn of the nineteenth century and soon spread to England and America. The Romantics valued dynamism, freedom, and creative will rather than formal structure. The whole universe, including the individual soul, is a source of wonder and revelation. Although many Romantics tended toward pantheism, seeing God and nature as one, others looked to history as the scene of the divine manifestation. For Johann Gottfried Herder (1744-1803) "religion can only be set forth in history," and in fact, the more human and individual religion is, the more it manifests the divine.

The Romantics turned away from classicism and saw the Middle Ages as the model era of harmony and beauty in the midst of storm and stress. The marvels of Gothic architecture, with its soaring heights and complex balance of opposing forces were again prized and emulated. The Catholic view of the Eucharist, in which God is embodied in matter, captured the Romantic longing to capture the infinite in the finite. The ancient liturgy spoke to the Romantic longing for meaningful tradition. In Germany Johann Adam Mühler (1796-1838) presented the Catholic Church as the true church because it alone guaranteed unity. It is the synthesis of all opposites and the full revelation of God. In America Isaac T. Hecker (1819-1888) made a journey from Methodism to Transcentalism and then to the Roman church in 1844. He founded the Paulist Fathers; a religious order dedicated to converting Americans to Catholicism.

Oxford Movement

In England, the Oxford Movement, also known as the Tractarian movement because it inspired ninety pamphlets on theology, ecclesiology, and church history, represented the new appreciation for the Christian past as a norm for the present. Some of the tracts attacked modern theology; others presented solid historical research on the early church's liturgy and theology. The Tractarians believed that England had fallen into apostasy by embracing liberal principles and modern thought. They blamed the evangelicals for splintering the church and stripping worship of its essential rituals. Their solution was a return to the ancient tradition of the church, particularly the golden age of the fourth century.

Edward Pusey (1800-1882) became the leader of "high church" Anglicanism, and worked to reinstitute monasticism and religious orders in the Church of England. John Henry Newman's (1801-1890) studies in ecclesiology eventually led him to reject the Anglican Church and join the Catholic Church in 1845. In 1879 his efforts to promote Catholicism in England earned him the title of cardinal.

Latin America

The French Revolution and Napoleon's empire had a more profound effect on South America than in the north since the kings of Spain and Portugal ruled that region. In 1808, Napoleon placed his brother Joseph on the Spanish throne, replacing Ferdinand VII; however, the local leaders in South America refused to accept Joseph's sovereignty. Instead local *juntas* governed in the name of the deposed king, often instituting more liberal policies. For decades conflicts arose between the old colonial families in America, the *crillos*, and the governmental and ecclesiastical officials sent from Europe, the *penisulares*. During the Napoleonic era the colonials gained strength, and when Ferdinand, who returned to the throne in 1814, tried to reassert Spanish sovereignty over the colonies, they began declaring their independence of Europe.

Chile, Paraguay, and Uruguay gained their independence by 1820. In the north, Simon Bolîvar led an army that defeated the Spanish forces and created the nation of Greater Columbia. Bolívar planned to unite most of the continent, or at least the Spanish speaking regions, into a single federal government, similar to the United States. The terrain disrupted communications and the fierce independence of the aristocratic families hampered his plan. Greater Columbia broke up into Colombia, Venezuela, Ecuador, Peru, and Bolivia. At the Panama Congress of 1826, the United States also intervened to keep South America divided. During the same period, Mexico fought a revolution led by Father Miguel Hidalgo y Costilla. Central America broke away from Mexico in 1821, and soon divided into five smaller countries. In 1825 Portugal recognized Pedro, the son of the King of Portugal, Joao VI, as emperor of an independent Brazil. Brazil became a republic in 1889.

The newly independent nations each had their own character and history. The ideals of the French Revolution influenced some of the leaders, and they sought to combine patriotism and republican government. Others were simply independent kingdoms or empires ruled much the way they had been before. A military aristocracy ruled many others. In most of the southern nations, perpetual conflict existed between the liberals agitating for a more democratic and open government and conservatives who reasserted royal power and prerogative. In many countries, a cycle of coups, *juntas*, revolutions, and dictatorships in which the great landowners, competed for control while the masses of rural laborers, mostly of Indian descent, continued to suffer.

The Catholic Church in Latin America suffered a similar conflict. As we have seen, the church hierarchy in Europe took a conservative or even reactionary stance against the French Revolution, and the papacy did not look favorably upon the move toward independence and republicanism in the Americas. Many bishops fled to Europe during the period of upheavals, deserting their flocks but preserving their lives and wealth. The pontiff, strongly encouraged by the monarchs of Spain, France, and Austria, insisted that American bishops be supplied from Europe and approved by the king of Spain. At one point there were only five bishops for the whole South American continent. For some twenty years, the church remained crippled since bishops were necessary for ordinations of clergy and confirmation of laity. It was only in the 1830s that Pope Gregory XVI (1831-1846) recognized the independence of the new nations. His recognition came in part because of his conflict with the governments of Spain and Portugal, which were enacting anti-clerical legislation at the time, but it was also due to his firm conviction that mission areas needed native clergy. During his rule, he established seventy new dioceses and appointed 200 mission bishops, most of them for the Americas.

Pope Gregory's activism laid the foundation for a Catholic revival in the twentieth century, but the church continued to decline during the nineteenth. Before independence, most of the Latin American priests were of mixed blood and close to the poor laborers and lower classes, while the bishops were closely related to the ruler aristocracies. Many of the priests had actively supported the revolutions, but in the decades following, the liberals attacked the privileges of the clergy. Most of the clergy, therefore, supported the conservatives while the liberals grew increasingly anti-clerical. By the end of the century, many liberals adopted the secularist philosophy of the sociologist Auguste Comte who argued that religion needed to be suppressed in order for society to progress.

Latin American governments became increasingly secular, and the church struggled to meet the spiritual needs of a mixed population that appeared to many priests to be only nominally Catholic. Native Indian and imported African beliefs and practices were often combined with Catholic rituals in creative religious forms that competed with approved Catholic doctrine. Four hundred years after Columbus, Latin America in many ways remained a mission field for the Catholic Church. By the end of the nineteenth century, it also became a fertile field for Protestant missions.

Eastern Orthodoxy

Lands once dominated by the Orthodox Church experienced much of the nationalistic fervor of the nineteenth and early twentieth centuries. As we have seen, the old Byzantine Empire and Orthodox kingdoms of Bulgaria and Serbia fell to the Ottoman Turks in the fifteenth and sixteenth centuries. The Turks used the Orthodox Church hierarchy to help rule the Christian population in their far-flung empire, and the church in many ways stagnated during this time. Corruption was rife, the law forbade expansion, and few great theological or intellectual movements emerged.

However, the Orthodox Church preserved its rich liturgy and iconography and continued to promote spirituality, especially in the monasteries. The church, with its air of mystery and antiquity, helped people preserve their ethnic pride and identity under Turkish rule. Thus, despite the inherent conservatism of the church's upper clergy, Orthodoxy became a factor in the rise of nationalism as the power of the Ottoman Empire waned in the nineteenth century. In fact, the revolution in Greece began at the monastery of Megaspelaion, and the patriarch, Gregory V, was hanged as an insurgent in 1821. Since the Turks still controlled the office of the Ecumenical Patriarch in Constantinople, the Greek Church was cut off from the Patriarch after the Greeks achieved independence in 1829. In 1833, the King of Greece officially recognized the independent Greek Church, a move that the Patriarch did not approve until 1851.

Serbia achieved a degree of independence from its Turkish overlords in 1817, and also organized a national Orthodox Church under the metropolitan at Belgrade. After the Russian victory over Turkey in 1879, the Serbian Orthodox Church became completely independent of the Ecumenical Patriarch. Bosnia and Herzegovina, under Austrian rule, also asserted political and religious independence in 1878. The history of Rumania is similar. Thanks to the military intervention of Russia, Wallachia and Moldavia separated from the Ottoman Empire in 1829 and united to form Rumania in 1862. The Ecumenical Patriarch in Constantinople officially recognized the independence of the Rumania Orthodox Church in 1885. The Bulgarian Church engaged in a much longer conflict with the Ecumenical Patriarch, and was not accepted into the Orthodox communion until 1945.

Nationalists insisted on having national churches that the Ecumenical Patriarch recognized, but did not rule. The churches were Orthodox but independent. The Slavophiles, on the other hand, saw Orthodoxy and Slavic identity as having a mystical bond. Orthodoxy would unite the Slavs the way Catholicism had once united western Europe. Even those who rejected the theology of the church were willing to use the church as a symbol of a glorious pre-Turkish past and an institution to promote a new national identity. Orthodoxy distinguished eastern Europe from Muslim Turkey and from the rest of Europe, divided between the Catholics and Protestants. For the most devout Slavophiles, like A. S. Khomiakov (1804-1860), the Slavic Orthodox Church had a divine mission to save all of Europe from Catholicism, Protestantism, and irreligion. Only the Orthodox effectively preserved both Christian unity and freedom in a spiritually grounded community or *sobornost*.

Vladimir S. Soloviev (1853-1900), a mystic, philosopher, and writer, believed that the Orthodox spirit could reunite all Christians, in fact, all humans in God's wisdom, Sophia. Soloviev rediscovered Orthodox spirituality after a youthful pilgrimage through atheism and philosophy. As he watched European developments in the late nineteenth century, he turned away from his earlier evolutionary view of the human spirit and embraced an apocalyptic perspective. The first reunification of the world would be through the antichrist. The faithful minority would unite in renunciation of the antichrist while awaiting the return of the true Christ.

The church-state situation was very complex in the Russian Empire where the church acted as an arm of the state, controlled by a tsar rather than a sultan. Alexander I had a personal religious experience, which led him to actively promote Christian renewal in his rapidly expanding realm. He saw the defeat of Napoleon as a Christian triumph, and convinced many of the European monarchs to form a "Holy Alliance" in which they swore to conduct their affairs in light of the gospel's "precepts of justice, Christian charity, and peace."

His successor, Nicholas, more interested in absolutism than holiness, saw the church as a potentially valuable ally since the tsar was viewed almost as a living saint. However, he also recognized that the church contri-buted to the backwardness of the nation. Priests were poorly educated and almost as superstitious as the peasantry. Therefore, he established theological seminaries and made the clergy salaried state employees.

C. P. Pobiedonostsev, the Procurator of the Holy Synod from 1880-1905, went even farther in making the church an arm of autocratic rule. He used repressive legal measures and the secret police to suppress political and theological dissent, encourage subject peoples to convert to Orthodoxy, and resist democracy. Radical political reformers, influenced by liberal ideas from the West, felt that the first step toward freeing Russians from autocratic oppression would be to abolish the church.

Russian Literature

In the midst of conflict over institutions and hierarchies, the church still had a powerful attraction, especially for Russian peasants, who venerated their icons and adored their saints. However, it was not only peasants who sensed that the spirituality of Orthodoxy offered answers, or at least the possibility of answers in an increasingly complicated world. Two of the great literary and intellectual giants of the nineteenth century, whom Orthodoxy profoundly affected, personify the creative clash of traditional Christianity and modernism.

Novels became a way to explore the mysteries of the human soul, the twin realities of good and evil, and the awful knowledge of mortality. Lev Tolstoy (1828-1910), best known for his novels *War and Peace* and *Anna Karenina*, pondered deeply the question of the Russian soul. He decided that the soul and the soil must unite. Although an aristocrat and an international celebrity,

Tolstoi turned his back on the glittering world of nineteenth century St. Petersburg, Berlin, and Paris in order to embrace a communal, agrarian life. In many ways, Tolstoi resembled his character Levin in *Anna Karenina* who finds stability, depth, and meaning while working alongside of his own peasants on his country estate. Tolstoi, though, rejected much Orthodox theology in favor of a non-sacramental, Christ mysticism expressed in absolute non-violence and non-participation in the state.

Perhaps the greatest novelist of the soul was Fyodor Dostoyevsky (1821-1888). While in exile in Siberia for ten years for subversive activities, Dostoyevsky became fervently attached to the Russian Orthodox Church and rejected westernization, especially the rationalism and adoration of technology that was pervasive in much of Europe. For Dostoyevsky, only traditional Christianity, particularly of the Orthodox variety, preserves the freedom of the will from the assault of totalizing philosophies and bureaucracies. In a parable in *The Brothers Karamazov*, the Grand Inquisitor, an official of the church, represents the state that wants to keep its citizens children. They need to be protected from the full implications of the freedom of the mind and soul. The Grand Inquisitor would even kill Christ to prevent him from pronouncing his words of existential freedom. At the end of the parable, Christ kisses the Grand Inquisitor, inviting him into a life of love rather than control.

Dostoyevsky also embraced the Christian doctrine of redemption and suffering, even for Raskolnikov, the character in *Crime and Punishment* who kills a man for apparently no reason at all. In stark contrast to Raskolnikov, is Aloysha, one of *The Brothers Karamazov*, who represents the radical love of Christ who loved even Pilate. Aloysha left the monastery in order to bring true spirituality into the world, and in the end was the only one of the four brothers who finds true happiness in the world. For Dostoyevsky, the modern world is dangerous to body and soul, but happiness comes when one loves the world with the love of Christ.

Chapter 21

Nineteenth-Century American Evangelicalism

THE RELIGIOUS SITUATION in America developed quite differently than in Europe. It was far less intellectual, liturgical, and mystical in character. Instead, evangelicalism was the primarily religious expression, and Christianity became part of the popular culture. Evangelicalism refers to a type of Christianity that focuses on personal conversion. It started in Europe with the Pietists and the Methodists but blossomed in the United States in the nineteenth century, and continues to shape American religious expression. The Methodists and Baptists were the two largest evangelical groups, but the vast movement spawned countless smaller churches. Even more traditional and liturgical churches, such as the Lutherans, adapted to the American evangelical style.

The Second Great Awakening

The period of the great evangelical explosion is generally known as the Second Great Awakening, which differed significantly from the Great Awakening discussed earlier. The Second Great Awakening was far less unified than the first, but it had a greater long-term effect on America. The First Awakening introduced the notion of itinerant evangelists and revivals; the Second Awakening institutionalized them as a regular feature of American life. The First Awakening introduced religion of the laity and personal conversion, but the Second Awakening canonized them. The First Awakening began the process of decentralization of church authority; the Second Awakening shattered Protestantism. The preachers in the First Awakening were university-educated and officially appointed ministers who questioned the need for such credentials. The preachers of the Second Awakening often had no such credentials and rejected those that did.

The Second Great Awakening began shortly after the end of the American Revolution, and it followed the frontier west as the new nation expanded. Although the Founding Fathers were relatively conservative, the American Revolution was one of the most radical events in Western history, and it had a profound impact on the American religious consciousness at the turn of the century. It was a Revolution accomplished by an ideology and rhetoric of freedom for the common man (not yet woman). The rhetoric of freedom from tyranny that had inspired people to endure economic deprivation and war, continued to inspire Jeffersonian and Jacksonian democrats to expand the franchise to those without property. The early republic was a period of popular rejection of constituted authorities in all walks of life, including religion. Populism is seen in evangelical religion where each individual has to make his or her own choice for salvation, and where anyone might receive a calling from God to preach the gospel.

The great populist preacher Lorenzo Dow (1777-1834) gives us a good example of the fusion between republican politics and evangelical religion, blending Jeffersonian language with evangelical fervor. He wrote:

> If all men are Born Equal and endowed with unalienable Rights by the Creator in the blessings of life, liberty and the pursuit of happiness—then there can be no just reason, as a cause, why he may or should not think, and judge, and act for himself in matters of religion, opinion, and private judgment.[24]

The antebellum period also saw radical demographic changes in America. In the seventy years following 1776 the population grew from 2.5 million to 20 million, largely from an amazing birth rate. America was the fastest growing Western nation, but did not become overpopulated. There was land, and the Americans were land hungry. The fact that natives were living on the land west of the Appalachian Mountains was unimportant to a people who had successfully defeated the British Empire. At one time 500 people a day were crossing the mountains, and it was hard to establish institutions of social control for such a mobile and independent people. Even the family became less stable as children packed up to seek their fortunes ever to the

---

[24] Quoted in Nathan Hatch, *The Democratization of American Christianity* (New Haven: Yale University Press, 1989) 37.

West. The Methodist preacher Francis Asbury (1745-1816) realized that European methods would not work in the American setting.

American Methodism

Asbury converted to Methodism at age thirteen, and he quickly put his oratorical talents to use as a Methodist exhorter and lay preacher. When John Wesley called for preachers to carry on the work in America in 1771, young Asbury volunteered to be a missionary. Methodist work in America at that time followed the pattern in England. Preachers tried to establish settled bands of devout believers who were moving on toward perfection. Such work requires a commitment to a particular location and close supervision; therefore the Methodist preachers tended to work in the few large cities of North America. Asbury immediately appreciated the differences between America and England. Outside of the Northeastern seaboard, America's population was widely scattered and virtually untouched by organized religion.

Asbury soon began recruiting young and energetic men who would "go into every kitchen and shop; address all, aged and young, on the salvation of their souls."[25] He put them on horses and set them traveling throughout America. These dedicated and poorly-paid "circuit rider" missionaries stayed with families that offered them whatever hospitality they could afford, which frequently meant a spot in the barn. Asbury himself gave testimony to trials faced by the circuit rider. By the time he died he had traveled nearly 300,000 miles by horseback, often without roads. He made forty trips across the Appalachian Mountains, a barrier most people would cross only once. He suffered constantly from a variety of physical complaints and exposure to the elements. He lived as austere as a Franciscan, and he expected his preachers to be likewise.

Asbury's preachers had little formal education, but they knew how to preach to the common people. The contrast between a circuit rider and a Boston clergyman could hardly have been greater. Methodist theology was simple enough for farmers and laborers to grasp. All people are going to hell unless they choose to accept Christ and be saved. If they choose to be saved, then Christ will help them stop sinning. On Asbury's orders, Methodist preachers avoided preaching about the Trinity or the Incarnation or many of the traditional themes of Christian theology. Salvation and sanctification

---

[25] Quoted in Mark Noll, *A History of Christianity in the United States and Canada* (Grand Rapids MI: Eerdmans, 1992) 171.

marked the sum of the message, but they gave that message in an endless number of variations with illustrations drawn from common life. Methodist preachers were not above using carnival to attract crowds. They told jokes and funny stories to get people interested, and then worked themselves up to a fever pitch portraying the fate of the damned and the reward of the saved. Sin and the devil were the enemy, but each person could win the battle. It was a theology well suited for a new republic exalted the common man.

Following the Revolution, Wesley sent Thomas Coke (1747-1814) to be the superintendent of the work in America. Upon his arrival, he called a general conference of Methodist preachers. The Christmas Conference of 1784 created the American Methodist Church, and instituted measures of which Wesley did not approve. Asbury and Coke were elected superintendents, and soon after Asbury took on the title of Bishop, much to the distress of Wesley. Bishop Asbury ruled with an unquestioned hand. He set the circuits, appointed the elders who supervised the lay preachers, and appointed his ministers however he desired. By the time of his death, Asbury was the most powerful religious figure in America; however, his movement was at the same time one of the most democratic on a local level. He built a church for the common people, and it grew rapidly. When Asbury first came to America there were four Methodist preachers and 300 members. By the time he died in 1816, there were 2,000 ministers and over 200,000 members in the United States.

Baptists

Almost as successful as the Methodists during the Second Great Awakening were the Baptists. The American Baptist tradition has its immediate roots in the First Great Awakening in New England when some of the Congregationalist clergy separated completely from the established church, and instituted the practice of baptizing only those adults who could honestly claim to have received saving grace. Adult baptism was for persons old enough to give assent to Christian beliefs, and who had experienced conversion in their own lives. Usually in the history of Christianity, such practices produce small, inwardly focused sectarian communities; however, the Baptists became one of the most aggressive conversionist movements in American history.

The reasons for Baptist success are similar to those of the Methodists. Both movements made effective use of lay preachers, established small congregations wherever a few people gathered, excelled in open air preaching services, and stressed the need for personal conversion and regeneration. Both were also aggressively anti-elitist. Baptist ministers were often barely literate, much less educated, and they preached to the ordinary individual. They dealt with the broad and bold themes of heaven, hell, sin, and salvation. Furthermore, the Baptists had no criteria for ministers other than recognition by a local congregation so anyone who felt the call to preach could start preaching. If people listened and converted, he or she was accepted as a minister. Baptists preachers usually supported themselves by farming, just as their flock did, thus they remained close to the masses. Anyone could begin a Baptist church wherever people desired salvation and baptism.

The methods of the Methodists and Baptists were ideally suited for the new republic, and they swept the country. In 1776 only 2.5 percent of the population were Methodist and another 17 percent were Baptists. By 1850, 34 percent were Methodists and 20 percent were Baptists, thus more than half of the population belonged to these groups. The Congregationalists and Anglicans had been 36 percent of the population in 1776. By 1850 they represented only 7.5 percent of the people. Clearly the American religious situation had shifted dramatically.

Restoration Movements

The Presbyterians rather than the Methodists or Baptists generated one of the most popular and ecstatic events of the Second Great Awakening, but James McGeady (d. 1817) and Barton Stone (d. 1844) were not typical Presbyterians. McGready was a Scots-Irish Presbyterian who took over three churches in southwestern Kentucky in 1796. In the summer of 1800 he began holding camp meetings, religious revivals lasting for several days. People would take a break between summer plantings, travel for miles to the service and pitch tents for shelter. Any number of lay and ordained preachers would hold nearly constant preaching services. Hundreds of people might attend during the week of meetings while the organizers tried to keep track of converts.

One of McGready's converts was Barton Stone who was serving the Cane Ridge Church. Stone announced a meeting to be held at Cane Ridge on August 6, 1801. Dozens of ministers from several denominations arrived for the occasion as did between ten and twenty-five thousand people. The revival lasted for a week, until provisions ran short. Participants described the event as a new Pentecost where thousands converted, often with dramatic emotional displays.

Cane Ridge began a new era in American religion, but was roundly condemned back East. To the established clergy and other intellectuals, Cane

Ridge was an outbreak of the Spirit all right, but of a diabolical spirit that robbed people of their reason. Cane Ridge represented their worst fears of the new popular religion being preached by the circuit riders. One critic charged that "more souls were begot than saved" during the revival, pointing out that the emotional display broke down traditional barriers of gender, class, and even race. The ignorant, poor exhorter could lead the prosperous landowner into an experience of salvation. The egalitarian promise of the Revolution was being felt in the Western revivals, but the controversy over the revivals led to a schism in the Presbyterian Church. The followers of Barton Stone separated themselves from the Presbyterians, and rejected all of the historical Presbyterian confessions in favor of following the Bible alone. They called themselves simply Christians.

Another important arm of the Second Great Awakening emerged independently of the Cane Ridge revival. Thomas Campbell (1763-1854) was a Scottish Presbyterian ministering in Northern Ireland before he emigrated to America in 1807, and settled in western Pennsylvania. Campbell thought that the historical creeds and confessions of the church created Christian division rather than union, so he preached that all Christians should share in the Lord's Supper together. When he was ejected from the Presbyterian ministry for heresy, he formed an independent association that promoted a new type of Christianity. He argued that the Bible was a reasonable book that any reasonable person could read and understand; therefore he saw no need for creeds or other human interpretations. God has spoken clearly, and the Bible lays down the rules for church practices. "We will speak when the scriptures speak, and remain silent when they are silent." With that simple phrase, Campbell abolished many traditional church practices, such as days of fasting and the use of musical instruments in worship. His approach to Christianity is called Restorationism because proponents assert that the only way to purify the church was to restore the apostolic church.

Campbell's son, Alexander, was less scholarly than his father, but more dynamic and consistent in his application of his father's principles. He convinced his father that infant baptism was not Christian, and in 1812 a local Baptist minister immersed all of the Campbells. However, even the Baptists were not biblical enough for Campbell. Father and son continued their independent evangelical work, and Alexander fought many public battles against atheism, Mormonism, Unitarianism, creedalism, sectarianism, emotionalism, and even slavery, but he was singularly unsuccessful in bringing about church unity. His non-creedal Christian Church became one of the first independent churches to be born in the United States. Eventually the Stonites and the Campbellites merged to form the Christian Church/ Disciples of Christ.

Revivalism and Benevolence Societies

In contrast to the separatism of Stone and Campbell, Charles Grandison Finney (1792-1875) brought revivalism into the Christian mainstream, and institutionalized the revival service in the rapidly growing regions of upstate New York and Ohio. Finney planned to be a lawyer, but instead became a preacher following a sudden conversion in 1821. Thereafter, he attacked sin like a lawyer prosecuting a client, and his confrontational style won many converts. He also actively encouraged women to convert their husbands and children, or at least to bring them to a revival where they could hear the gospel. The unconverted but wavering souls sat on the "anxious bench" while the preacher and congregation prayed for them to make the decision. Like Wesley in the previous century, Finney's success in moving people to a decision convinced him that Calvinism was wrong. In the new free-market of American religion, success provided its own justification.

Finney did more than just convert souls; he also advocated the idea that true Christians can become morally perfect with the help of Christ. For him, the keystone to perfection was "disinterested benevolence," the desire to reach out and help others without concern for one's own gain. New Haven Theology influenced Finney in this regard. Nathaniel William Taylor (1786-1858), a professor at Yale claimed that Jonathan Edwards inspired the New Haven Theology, but unlike Edwards, Taylor argued that after conversion a person does have the power not to sin, if the individual so chooses. Sinfulness is a matter a sinful acts, not a sinful nature; therefore, people have the power not to sin. Since the root of sin is selfishness, then those who practice disinterested benevolence can be free from sin. This theology found expression in the formation of voluntary societies of Christians practicing altruism. Wherever Finney preached, such benevolent societies blossomed.

The American Bible Society was formed to make sure that every American who could read had a copy of the Bible. From 1829-1831 alone the society printed and distributed over a million copies of the Bible. One in every thirteen Americans had a Bible, thus making the Bible the primary textbook for American education. In a similar vein, the American Tract Society published five pages a year per person in America. The tracts were inexpensive, popular, and covered a vast array of topics from eternal damnation to personal hygiene. During this period, phrases such as "cleanliness is next to godliness" began appearing in America. By 1830, a benevolence society existed for almost any social ill.

Connected to the concern for making the country religious and moral was an effort to educate the new nation. Except in parts of the South, people generally accepted that education and Christianity went hand in hand. If nothing else, people should be able to read the Bible. Moreover, education would help people move on to perfection since they would know what they should not do. The vanguard of the movement was the American Sunday School Union founded in 1824 to send educational missionaries into rural areas, and to publish Sunday School materials. As teachers worked to save the lost and help the saved move to perfection, they also taught reading and writing to thousands of lower and middle class children. By the end of the century over 70,000 Sunday Schools had been established. On the educational front, Finney also established Oberlin College as the first co-educational college in America.

Holiness

Phoebe Worrall Palmer (1807-1874) shared Finney's passion for evangelization and perfection. She launched the Holiness Movement, which made personal holiness the focus of the Christian life. Palmer was the wife of a physician in New York City, and both she and her husband were devout Christians. Like many Christians in ante-bellum America, the Palmers had experienced conversion, but longed for something more. In 1835, her sister reported that she had experienced the direct presence of the Holy Spirit. In other words, she experienced sanctification. Palmer longed for a similar deeper experience of God, and on 26 July 1837 she received it. From that time she believed that the Holy Spirit was in her life, and she began to spread the news to others. She became a leader in her sister's Tuesday Meeting for the Promotion of Holiness, and before long she led Thomas Upham, a minister, into the experience of the Holy Spirit.

This success convinced her that she was called to preach to both men and women about the joys of the Spirit. Contrary to tradition, she spoke in churches and other forums, and contributed to religious journals. In 1859, she published *The Promise of the Father* in which she argued vigorously for the right of women to preach in church. The Spirit can and does call men and women both into God's work. Her Holiness Movement, which began as a middle class benevolent movement linked to social reform gradually developed into Pentecostal Holiness, which will be discussed in a later chapter.

The Conversion of African Americans

During the first half of the nineteenth century, the number of Christians in America increased dramatically, in large part due to the aggressive and effective methods of the evangelicals. Much of this effort focused on people of European background who were at least familiar with Christianity and its teachings, but one large population in America came from a quite different background. Between the American Revolution and the Civil War, evangelicals turned their attention to the African slaves and successfully converted hundreds of thousands to Christianity. It is a history filled with spiritual triumph and bitter ironies.

Slavery was a part of the New World from the beginning of European settlement. The Spanish conquistadors immediately began enslaving native peoples to work mines and plantations, but that proved unprofitable. The American natives did not make good slaves for a number of reasons. They died quickly in captivity, largely due to the diseases of the Europeans; they could escape into the brush and return to the wild; and the Europeans had a much harder time breaking up the support structure of native communities. Early in the sixteenth century, Spanish and Portuguese authorities began exporting millions of Africans to labor in the New World. From the early days of English settlement, the Virginians used African slaves on their plantations. By 1776, North America had a large population of African peoples from many different tribes who followed different religious practices. They represented a pagan and foreign nation within the borders of·the United States.

It is important to understand the reality of slavery in America. Slaves were property who lived totally dependent on the master for all of the necessities of life. A slave might have a comparatively kind master, but that could change suddenly when that master sold the slave, or his children inherited them. Masters had full authority to beat, imprison, or starve slaves, and many masters reveled in their sadistic power. Rarely was a master punished for killing a slave. Moreover, one of the most dehumanizing aspects of American slavery, unlike slavery in the ancient world, was that marriage was not respected. In fact, according to law in most southern states, marriages between slaves had no validity, nor did the ties of parenthood. Bill Simpson told about the time his master moved from Georgia to Texas:

> Mother, she gave out on the way, 'bout the line of Texas. Her feet got raw
> and bleeding, and her legs swoll plumb out of shape. Then Massa, he jus take

out his gun and shot her, and whilst she lay dying he kicks two-three times...Boss, you know that man, he wouldn't bury mother, just left her laying where he shot her.[26]

Slavery posed problems for devout white Christians, particularly after the War of Independence. Basically two positions existed on the advisability of bringing the gospels to slaves. One was that religion could be dangerous. If the slaves were treated as persons with a soul, then they might become rebellious. They might think that since Christ died for them, then they were equal to the whites. They might even think that if there is a life after death, then why not die in a rebellion? So, it would be better for white masters to deny slaves access to Christianity. The other position was that slaves were indeed human, even if inferior to whites, and were in danger of losing their souls. Many evangelical whites felt that it was a grave sin not to try to save the souls of the slaves, even if their bodies were in chains. In order to make this point of view palatable to the owners, evangelicals asserted that religion would make the slaves more obedient and docile. Most theologians and preachers accepted St. Paul's admonition "slaves obey your masters" (Ephesians 6:5) as God's will for slaves with little discussion of whether it should apply in the modern world. A few Methodists urged emancipation in the eighteenth century, but that position was abandoned by the church in favor of evangelization. As time passed, evangelicals even argued that the potential for saving the souls of slaves justified the practice of slavery itself.

Slave Religion

The new evangelical churches offered both a genuine concern for the slave's human soul and an opportunity to express religion in their own way. Services were very emotional and focused on converting the sinner. Often during a revival service, a person would break through to a conversion accompanied by overwhelming joy and rejuvenation. He or she would be born again and might burst out with shouts or dancing. The conversion experience and accompanying emotional outbursts were common to whites and blacks, but the experience of slavery gave blacks a different perspective. Conversion meant that a person was a special child of God, no matter what hardship he or she endured on earth. Sometimes, it meant that the slave had a spiritual superiority over an unconverted master. There are several records of

---

[26] Quoted in B. A. Botkin, ed. *Lay My Burden Down* (Chicago: University of Chicago Press, 1945) 75.

slaves who converted their masters, and served as the religious leader for the owner and his family.

Both evangelical Christianity and African practices, such as rhythmic singing and chanting, shaped slave religion, but slavery itself left its mark on the religion. Once slaves learned what the Bible actually said, they found a different message than what the white preachers and owners had given them. It was reported that on one plantation the slaves sneered at the mistress who gathered them for prayer meetings because she always read "Slaves obey your masters" but never "break every yoke and let the oppressed go free" which they knew was in the Bible. Some of the slaves claimed the existence of two Bibles: the master's Bible and the real Bible. The real Bible told the story of the children of Israel whom the Lord rescued from slavery in Egypt. As the Civil War approached, slaves naturally saw the war as God's vengeance on their masters and the coming of promised deliverance. They could sing that God told Jeff Davis to "let my people go." In the context of American slavery, even the act of prayer or worship could be a significant act of defiance to the oppressor.

The Black Church

African Americans sometimes managed to form churches, such as the Baptist Church of Silver Bluff, S. C., which is credited with being the first black church before the Civil War (c. 1773). Of more lasting consequence was the work of Richard Allen (1760-1831), a former slave from Delaware. Allen bought his freedom and made his way to Philadelphia where a fairly substantial number of freed Africans lived. He saw a field ready for the harvest, and preached sometimes five times a day to the blacks in the city. He regularly attended St. George's Methodist Church where Africans were generally welcomed but segregated.

One day while Absalom Jones (1747-1818) knelt in prayer, white trustees physically removed him to the back of the church. When the congregational leadership supported the action, Allen and Jones led the black members out of the congregation. Despite the racism they experienced in Philadelphia, in 1793 the two friends worked to help the entire city during a fever epidemic. The next year Jones became the pastor of St. Thomas' Church, the first black Episcopalian congregation.

In 1793, Allen established the Bethel Church for Negro Methodists in Philadelphia. In 1816, the Pennsylvania Supreme Court ruled that the church could control its own property without oversight by white Methodists. During the course of the property dispute the Bethel Congregation and five other predominantly black Methodist churches left the Methodist Church and formed the African Methodist Episcopal Church in 1814. Allen became its first bishop in 1816. Other African American Christian organizations followed. Among them were several Baptist churches in the Northeast, some of which joined in the world mission efforts of the Protestants. Black missionaries traveled to Liberia, Sierra Leone, and Haiti. Lott Carey founded the First Baptist Church in Monrovia, Liberia in 1821.

Following the Civil War, freed blacks in the South quickly formed their own congregations and denominations entirely under black leadership. These churches emerged as the most stable and safe form of association for African Americans. Former slaves gained unaccustomed status and prestige, and soon demonstrated great leadership in difficult circumstances. Educated persons quickly rose to prominence within their churches and increased the educational level of their parishioners. The churches produced African American periodicals, provided economic opportunities, and created educational institutions. Among these leaders were women who felt the call to preach and advocate for the Gospel call of equality. Amanda Berry Smith (1837-1915), like Phoebe Palmer, experienced sanctification and brought her message to the public, speaking to interracial crowds on the joy and peace faith can bring.

Evangelical religion, in its many forms, was one way that the Christian message was adapted to the needs of a new nation. Egalitarian, emotional, and flexible evangelicalism spoke to whites and blacks in the United States, and helped form the American religious ethos. In Europe, however, there were different challenges and needs as intellectuals and pastors struggled to adjust to the rapidly changing modern world. The most influential response was liberalism.

Chapter 22

Liberalism

AS WE HAVE seen, the Enlightenment challenged traditional Christian views of revelation and the divinity of Christ, but for the most part Christians managed to adapt to many ideas and attitudes of the Enlightenment. Either by appeal to a religion of the heart or to a rational Christianity, the clergy and the laity found various ways to coordinate certain Enlightenment ideas and Christian faith. Both sides had extremists who insisted on either faith (defined as adherence to church doctrine) or reason (defined as empirical knowledge). The search for autonomy and free inquiry inaugurated by the Enlightenment, however, continued to flourish in the nineteenth century and raise new questions not easily answered.

German Philosophy

The philosopher who completed the Enlightenment and set the stage for the great philosophical and theological enterprises of the nineteenth century was Immanuel Kant (1724-1804) who had been schooled in the rationalist/optimistic school of Leibniz and Wolff. Leibniz used geometric logic to show that the world exists by necessity, and is thus the "best of all possible worlds." His followers believed that they could explain all reality, including God, through reason alone. Kant agreed with this perspective as a professor of logic at Königsberg in East Prussia, but then he encountered the skeptical philosophy of David Hume (1711-1776). Hume questioned the fundamental idea of cause and effect. According to Hume, we can only be sure of sense perceptions based on experience. We cannot directly prove cause and effect by perception alone. What appears to be cause and effect may simply be coincidence. Moreover, Hume questioned the notion of natural law. We cannot prove an event prior to experiencing it. We can only assert probability based on past experience.

Kant perceived that Hume's skepticism undermined all confidence in reason and science; so he reflected deeply and critically on reason itself. His inquiry resulted in three monumental works: *The Critique of Pure Reason* (1781), *The Critique of Practical Reason* (1788), and *The Critique of Judgment* (1790). Each critique addresses the ancient triad of the True, the Good, and the Beautiful, or put another way, the questions of what can we know, what should we do, and for what should we hope. Each critique had profound implications for religion and human life.

We cannot go into the intricacies of Kant's philosophy, but in brief, he argued that while all knowledge arises from sensory experience, sensory experience alone does not produce knowledge. Human reason is endowed with certain universal categories by which we make sense of the sensory world. We perceive the world in space and time because space and time are categories of our reason that we use to make sense of the world. They are universal and necessary categories that exist in our own minds. We do not learn space and time from the world, but we can understand the world because we have the prior capacity for perceiving space and time. In other words, we do not encounter the world directly, but only through categories of perception and analysis. Interestingly enough, Kant's attempt to ground scientific, objective truth on solid philosophical grounds actually elevated the role of the subject in addressing truth. Because of Kant, modern philosophy is deeply interested in the internal categories of the mind.

Kant divided human life into the sensory or phenomenal world that is subject to empirical examination and the moral or noumenal world in which the person is a moral agent. The great edifice of Christian metaphysics, including natural theology, was a misguided effort to understand what is inaccessible to the human mind. Religion, furthermore, has nothing to say about the natural world, other than what reason alone can discern. Therefore, no true conflict can exist between science and religion so long as each remains in its proper sphere. Kant thus put an end to the long tradition of natural theology that moved from the world of senses and causation to the suprasensible world of the final cause.

Kant found it impossible to prove an infinite cause (God) by finite effects (nature). Therefore Aquinas' famous proofs of the existence of God fail in their purpose, according to Kant. All that reason can know with certainty are things that are true by logical necessity, such as geometric proofs, and things verified by the senses, such as science. Religious claims about God can neither be proven nor disproven by reason.

Having established the limits of reason, Kant turned his attention to human social life and ethics. He examined what he called the practical reason which guides human affairs, and he attempted to ground ethics on principles as certain as those of mathematics. Moral principles should be universal principles that can be discerned through rational reflection. He proposed that moral obligations are by definition unconditioned (categorical). He rejected the dominant Enlightenment idea that morality is based on pain and pleasure. Instead, he tries to show that the concept of morality is based on the idea of "Ought," or duty. This world of the subject in relationship to other moral subjects within human society makes up real religion. Religion can acknowledge and even praise the rational law of the universe and posit a creator, but the real heart of religion lies in the moral law within each person. Organized religion exists to bring individuals into compliance with that moral law. It is not supposed to influence the deity to change that law, intercede in natural affairs, or hope for redemption and forgiveness. Christianity should be freed from superstition so that people can pursue the moral and ethical life, which is our surest knowledge of God.

Conservative theologians reacted with hostility toward Kant's philosophy, viewing it as just another form of deism or atheism, but Kant rejected their judgment. He established the true limits of reason to make room for faith. Moreover, Kant felt that his critique of practical reason established a new argument, although not certain proof, for the existence of God. The Categorical Imperative, or moral obligation, and the universal human sense of morality cannot come from sense experience or nature. It dwells within the human mind, and only the divine being could have established it there. The starry heavens above and the moral law within each person rather than miracles or revelation gave Kant evidence for the existence of God.

Hegel

Not everyone appreciated Kant's dualism, his separation of the phenomenal and the noumenal, the subject and the object. Georg Wilhelm Friedrich Hegel (1770-1831) possessed one of the great minds of all time, and produced an awesome philosophical system that tried to unite and explain the world of spirit and the sensible world. The essence of Hegel's thought is that reality is a continuum. The universe is connected; thus it is a mistake to try to understand reality as discreet particulars. We not only define a table by what it is, but by what it is not; in other words how it stands in relation to all else. Every positive statement involves a negation and every denial an affirmation. This produces the dialectic between what is and what is not. Through this dialectic human spirits come to understand the universal spirit. Nothing can be properly understood without the concept of time.

Theologically, God as the Infinite Spirit could only come into full actualization by creating that which is not God, namely the Cosmos. Through the encounter between God and the Cosmos, God becomes fully what God will be by encountering dialectically God's own negation and thereby producing a higher synthesis. Thus the whole history of the universe is actually the history of the Absolute actualizing itself through time. Hegel then constructed a system that illuminates the process of the Spirit emerging through history. The human spirit is part of the actualization of the divine Spirit, and as humans attain full self-consciousness as spiritual, noumenal subjects, they will discern the working of the Absolute in the cosmic history and knowingly participate in that process. Ultimately, the split between the knower and the known, the subject and the object, is overcome within the Absolute.

Hegel's scheme then, appreciates the Infinite within the Finite as Romanticism does, but there is also an awareness that this actualization of the spirit is not yet complete. Humans are thinking spirits who can have a higher fellowship with God as they participate in the actualization of God, but they are not yet complete in God. They participate in the negation of God, and thus are estranged from God and ultimate reality. Estrangement is a result of finitude, which is the cause of evil and human unhappiness. However, God and reality are reconciled through the working of nature. Everything moves toward this eventual reconciliation. Estrangement is overcome as humans self-consciously participate in the actualization of God in history. Hegel is one of the few modern philosophers to take seriously the doctrine of the Trinity as an ontological reality in God, as well as the resurrection of Christ as a cosmic event. Christ's return to God through the resurrection began a new phase of the actualization of Spirit by reconciling humanity with God.

Nineteenth-century Science

At the same time that Europe struggled with the philosophy of Kant and his successors, scientists uncovered a world unimagined by either Aquinas or Voltaire. By the end of the century, scientists determined that the earth was far older than previously believed, and that the universe was far larger.

Planets unknown to Kepler were found circling the sun according to the laws he had discovered. Geologists, such as Lyell and Hutton who set out to prove the historicity of the biblical flood and Noah's ark, concluded that there had been no world-wide flood upon which Noah could have sailed. Biologists and botanists further determined that there was a mind-boggling variety of species of living things that can hardly be catalogued, much less gathered in a single ark. Surprising new species of animals were discovered in areas previously isolated from Europe. At first the rush of discovery excited Westerners, including Christians who found confirmation for the immense power and wisdom of God in designing such a complex system. Gradually, however, these discoveries and theories eroded confidence both in the Bible as reliable history and in human nature itself. For centuries scientists had believed firmly in the stability of the species in a chain of creation, but the cross-breeding of species and new evidence of animal extinction raised serious questions about this theory. There was also the troubling evidence of old bones of extinct creatures who lived millions of years before the appearance of humans.

The biggest blow to received theories came from an Anglican cleric named Charles Darwin (1809-1882). Darwin was a botanist who enlisted as the science officer on board the *Beagle*. For two years he carefully collected and analyzed various species of plants and animals, as any good naturalist would do; however, he applied his probing mind to the data in a new fashion. In *The Origin of the Species*, published in 1859, he proposed an evolutionary theory based on survival of the fittest. The best adapted organisms survive and somehow transmit their adaptations to their progeny. Thus different species evolve in different climates and locales. Evolutionary theories had been current for some time in other fields, but Darwin was the first to apply them to biology and botany in a sweeping theory of selection.

His work created a minor uproar as scientists and theologians struggled with what his theory meant for long-cherished notions of the permanence and uniqueness of each species. Darwin always denied that he had removed the creator from nature, but many believed that atheism was the natural consequence of his idea. God did not make the polar bear white in order to be fit it for the arctic climates; the raw force of nature forced the bear to become white in order to survive. Nature, through violence and death, drives the evolution of the species.

The uproar increased when Darwin applied his theory to the human species in *The Descent of Man* in 1871. There he argued for the evolution of humans from primordial primates. He touched on the dignity of the human being and the reality of the soul. One of the great Princeton theologians, Charles Hodge (1797-1878), was the first to publish the thesis that Darwinism must be atheistic. Hodge's work unintentionally encouraged many Darwinists to embrace atheism, or at least to reject Christianity.

Schleiermacher

Although Hegel exerted a strong influence in his day, modern philosophy has been primarily a commentary or dialog with Kant. The first theologian to make Kant his starting point for understanding Christianity was Friedrich Daniel Ernst Schleiermacher (1768-1834) whose method dominated nineteenth century theology. Scheiermacher's father was converted by Moravians, and he sent his son to the Moravian school at Barby. While Schleiermacher valued the genuine piety he experienced among the Moravians, he left the school when he came to the conclusion that he could not accept the idea that Jesus was an atoning sacrifice to God. Later in life he would call himself "a Moravian of a higher order," meaning that he combined the Pietist emphasis on religious experience with Enlightenment philosophy.

Schleiermacher was a very popular preacher in Berlin for most of his career who actively participated in German social life. He worried that his educated peers glibly rejected religion without truly understanding what they were rejecting. In his 1799 publication, *On Religion: Speeches Addressed to Its Cultured Despisers*, Schleiermacher answered the typical Enlightenment criticism of religion by offering a new way of understanding religion itself. Contrary to what people think, including devout people, religion is not a matter of theological systems and doctrines, nor is it ethics. Rather, religion is something in the soul of the religious person; it is a feeling for the Infinite, the Absolute, and the Eternal. Religion is based on the intuition that the universe does fit together and make sense, and that the individual human is a part of the whole. This is what some called a "creaturely feeling," or a feeling of dependence on the Absolute. In a real sense, one cannot teach religion; one can only feel it. The aesthetic sense of beautiy is closest to the religious sense for Schleiermacher, but unlike aesthetics, religion moves humans to action. Religion integrates our mind and will, the transcendent and the immanent, the subjective and the objective.

The *Speeches* made Schleiermacher a celebrity in Germany, and over the years he slowly built an entirely new approach to Christian theology based on his initial turning toward the religious person rather than to written revelation. Schleiermacher followed Kant in rejecting traditional metaphys-ics.

Humans cannot know the essence of God; they can only know their experience of God through faith and in history. Faith is the starting point for theology, not belief in a particular dogma. Faith is an awareness and trust in the divine presence in human history and individual life. Furthermore, faith is a part of human life; therefore it is a part of the historical process. In order to understand Christianity, one must understand its history and relate that to the Christian conscious. History, not metaphysics, is the realm of true theology.

Schleiermacher wrote at the time when Christian Europe was just beginning seriously to confront the reality of sophisticated world religions. His existential approach to religion allowed him to see validity in all historical religions even while arguing for the superiority of Christianity. What makes Christianity superior is the person, Jesus of Nazareth, who redeems his followers with his message of divine grace. Original sin does not refer to some disobedience of the first parents that we inherit genetically. Original sin is the universal human awareness of human limitations and the inability truly to be good. This awareness of human failing leads to the human longing for redemption, which the Christian finds in Christ. Jesus is the model for humanity; he was a man entirely filled with the awareness of God so that he might be said to be the full revelation of God on earth. The early church's doctrinal statements about Christ attempted to express this awareness, but people do not need to accept them as factual statements about the nature of Christ.

Moreover, Schleiermacher separated theology and natural science. In 1829, while working on his great dogmatic work, *The Christian Faith*, he wrote that he wanted "to create an eternal covenant between the living Christian faith and an independent and freely working science, a covenant by the terms of which science is not hindered and faith not excluded." [27] Christians did not need to fear the discoveries of modern science that contradicted statements in the Bible. Science explains the workings of the natural world, and its findings should be accepted, but faith deals with the depths of the human soul. Faith deals with humankind's longings, hopes, and striving for goodness. Faith may motivate the scientist to pursue his or her inquiries into the hidden workings of nature. Faith brings individuals out of their self-centeredness and into the dynamic flow of cultural life as well. The

---

[27] Quoted in Claude Welch, *Protestant Thought in the Nineteenth Century*, 2 vols. (New Haven: Yale University Press, 1972) 1:63.

religious person does not reject culture or progress, but embraces both and transforms them through faith.

Biblical Criticism

Schleiermacher's theology encouraged a new generation of biblical scholars to read the ancient text without the need to defend Christian or Jewish orthodoxy. At the same time, other scholars revolutionized the study of history by approaching the past as scientists rather than moralists. They desired to understand the past on its own terms without making value judgments. They accepted that even morality is relative to time and culture because all things human are subject to change.

Biblical scholars likewise approached their primary text, the Bible, as a human product. As such, they studied the Old Testament as one of many sources for the history of Palestine. The Old Testament represents a relative truth held by one ancient people, and can be studied in the light of other ancient writings that archaeologists were unearthing. Biblical scholars devoted their lives to understand how the Bible came to be, rather than trying to show how the Bible should lead modern humans to salvation.

This historical-critical method of biblical scholars took decades to develop and remains controversial in many Christian churches. The roots of the new method go back to the Enlightenment when Baruch Spinoza (1632-1677) and Richard Simon (1638-1707) raised serious doubts about the ancient tradition that Moses wrote the first five books of the Old Testament, the Pentateuch. Both men pointed to evidence within the Pentateuch that indicated a date well after the conquest of Palestine for the final writing. In the eighteenth century, scholars struggled over establishing the text of the Old Testament itself in light of the thousands of variant readings in ancient manuscripts. Establishing as far as possible the most accurate Hebrew text did not solve all the problems with the Pentateuch, however. Careful readers have long noticed contradictions, repetitions, and changes in style that are hard, if not impossible, to reconcile with the traditional claim that Moses himself wrote those books.

Freed from the need to reconcile these differences, Julius Wellhausen (1844-1918) proposed a new theory on the origin of the Pentateuch. A single scholar did not write it. The Pentateuch is a complex union of four distinct ancient sources (JEDP), which in turn preserve much older material. Each source has its own style, purpose, history, and theology. Over 500 years separate J from P, thus the so-called books of Moses were produced over a period of many centuries. Wellhausen was convinced that in the Pentateuch one can see an evolution in the religion of Israel and their understanding of God.

The Life of Jesus

Schleiermacher called for Christians to focus again on the person of Jesus of Nazareth rather than the church's doctrines about Christ, and biblical scholars applied the historical-critical method to the New Testament. The apostolic status of the Gospel writers was generally rejected. Some of the letters attributed to Paul of Tarsus were also shown to have been written much later than 60 AD. F. C. Baur (1792-1860), influenced by Hegel's philosophy of history, emphasized conflict within the early church between Hellenism (Greek culture and philosophy) and Judaism. He distinguished between the theology of Paul, a Hellenistic Jew, and the original message of Jesus. The process of hellenization continued as the later books of the New Testament, such as the Gospel of John, reveal. For Baur, the New Testament was not the apostolic record of revealed doctrine, but a collection of documents of the early church that show how Christian doctrine evolved out of Greek philosophy, Judaic religion, and the teaching of Jesus. Jesus himself became a matter of intense concern in nineteenth century biblical scholarship.

Biblical scholars, following the early lead of the rationalist Hermann Samuel Reimarus, determined that since the gospels were written by the church and reflect the concerns of the church, they must be read critically in order to separate the church's theology from the historical Jesus. They determined that the Gospel of Mark is the oldest extant gospel and was the primary source for Matthew and Luke. Scholars also proposed that another source, called Q, contained many of the sayings of Jesus. Using Mark as a basis, some scholars tried to write historical accounts of the life of Jesus, just as if they were trying to describe the life of any other historical figure, separating fact from legend.

David F. Strauss (1808-1874) began a "quest for the historical Jesus" with his 1835 work, *Life of Christ*. Strauss' historical Jesus bore little relationship to the Christ whom the Protestant and Catholic churches worshipped. This Jesus had no idea that he was the unique Son of God, and he was not resurrected from the dead. Many more "Lives of Jesus" followed, all of which reveal as much or more about the theological presuppositions of the author than the person of Jesus.

Adolf von Harnack (1852-1930) extended the critical examination of Christian origins to the history of the early church. He sought to free Christianity from its bondage to a decayed Greek past, and to restore the pure message of the preaching of Jesus as the church moved into a new era. Harnack believed that biblical and historical scholarship would help the church recover the original teaching that is the "essence of Christianity."

Liberal Christianity

The effort to reform Christianity according to Kantian philosophy (there is no metaphysics), Schleiermacher's theology (Christianity is a matter of faith not dogmas), and the historical-critical approach to the scripture formed the basis for the dominant European theology of the late nineteenth century, Liberalism. The greatest architect of Liberalism was Albrecht Ritschl (1822-1889) who rejected metaphysics and supernaturalism in Christianity. Although a theologian, Ritschl mainly wrote historical works in which he raged against Catholics, Pietists, Lutheran Orthodox, sectarians, and all others who insisted on importing foreign mystical elements into the pure religion of Jesus. What did Jesus teach? Humans are reconciled to God through faith, and the kingdom of God is at hand. God's kingdom is an earthly kingdom that Jesus' disciples will create, not some kind of apocalyptic millennium. For the liberals, human happiness comes with the arrival of the kingdom of God when Christian values such as love, toleration, and brotherhood will reign throughout the world.

Liberals felt that the old doctrines of the church distracted Christians from their true calling. Salvation comes through active engagement in the work of the kingdom of God. Christians must set the standards of civility and openness to future progress for everyone in the world. Liberals rejected the supernatural in favor of the natural, the metaphysical in favor of the physical, prayer for action. Thus, in liberal thought, the monk praying alone in his cell represented the worst form of Christianity. God calls Christians to make the world a better place, and to do so with gentleness and civility. For Ritschl Christianity is not mysticism, sacramentalism, ritualism, or Pietism. It is not about biblical literalism. Following the teaching of Martin Luther, whom Ritschl studied in depth, Christians are most Christian when they have accepted their secular vocations on behalf of God's kingdom. The question that others would raise is what difference is there, then, between Christianity and European culture.

Transcendentalism

German philosophy inspired the transcendentalist movement in America. Ralph Waldo Emerson was a microcosm of the American religious quest before the Civil War. His father pastored the First Church in Boston, and he ardently defended traditional Calvinism against "the Learned, the Witty, and the Wicked." Emerson took a quite different path and eventually found his way to Harvard where the great Unitarian William Elery Channing (1780-1842) introduced him to a number of German books that forever destroyed Emerson's faith in traditional Christianity.

However, Emerson refused to give up on the idea of the human spirit/soul. Emerson resolved to find some way to preserve spiritual truth without the dogmatism of the New England way. He was ordained to be pastor of a Unitarian church in Boston, but was soon dismissed from his position when he rejected the Lord's Supper as a meaningless ritual. He went to Europe where he studied philosophy and art. When he returned to America, he felt even more convinced of the need to develop a new form of religion suitable for a new age. His religion would combine romantic sentiment for the sublime with a rational belief in the immortality of the soul and the universality of divine being. Emerson quit attending any church, but grew nostalgic about a heroic Puritan faith that he simply could not believe in. He developed his new approach to religion, Transcendentalism, through his essays and poems as he became the preeminent American writer of the period. Transcendentalism became a shelter for a large number of thoughtful persons who longed for a religious perspective, but who rejected both traditional religion and revivalism.

American Liberalism

Liberalism found willing adherents in the rapidly growing American cities of the late nineteenth century. The northern United States experienced a great economic boom following the Civil War, and within half-a-century was transformed from an agrarian to an urban society with an expanding middle class. The members of the new urban middle class wanted to enjoy the pleasures that urban life offered, but which their Puritan ancestors had forbidden. New ideas from Europe about philosophy, morality, scripture, and history were attractive as well as scary for the rising urban class who wanted to share in the glittering world associated with society and progress. They feared losing the meaning and stability offered by Christianity. Could one remain Christian without following the rigid, old fashioned, countryside faith?

A new generation of educated and articulate Protestant clergy rose to meet this challenge. Less scholarly than their German counterparts, these liberal preachers popularized and domesticated German theology. Horace Bushnell (1802-1876) introduced the new style of Christianity to America. He was one of the first Americans to draw upon the thought of Schleiermacher and the romanticism of the English poet Coleridge. In *Christian Nurture* (1847) he argued against the revivalists in favor of a gradual growing into the experience of God's grace, and he urged his listeners to seek the goodness of God in nature and in their families. Bushnell led the Protestant campaign to exalt the importance of the nuclear family as the heart of society. The family was a divine institution that must be defended against all enemies. Family, not church, became the center of religious life and social reform. Heaven became a perfect middle class home. The sanctification of family life commonly assumed today was largely the result of nineteenth century liberalism.

Connected with the sanctification of family came a change in the church's attitude toward women. Throughout the nineteenth century, except for a few brief periods of revival, women outnumbered men in American churches. For much of the Christian era women had been depicted by preachers and theologians as agents of sin tempting men into losing their souls. In the nineteenth century preachers lauded women as the moral exemplars of society. They gave religious and moral influence in the home. They were the quiet workers making America more civilized. Women in the growing middle class welcomed this message, and they flocked to hear liberal preachers. In the major metropolitan areas some preachers became celebrities, princes of the pulpit who entertained as well as educated their flock.

Henry Ward Beecher (1813-1887), a member of the great Beecher clan that included Lyman Beecher and Harriet Beecher Stowe, was the premiere liberal preacher. Beecher boldly proclaimed that the historical critical method of biblical scholarship would help people find the truth in the Bible. In the process, he also transformed Congregationalist theology. He presented God as a kind and loving father, not the stern, damning judge. He offered a patriarchal view of the deity, but Beecher based his conception of fatherhood on the ideal of a Victorian home life. Father is a strong but kind moral guide who gently calls his children into obedience. Beecher also transformed the role of Jesus. No longer was he the sacrificial lamb killed to justify God's wrath, nor was he the great Messiah at the end of history. He was now the brother of all people, the kind and loving symbol of how humans should live.

Liberal theology can be summarized in the phrase "the Fatherhood of God and the Brotherhood of Man." In Europe and America, liberalism was the dominant theological movement at the turn of the century. It embraced modern culture, and optimistically preached that the message of Jesus would continue to shape Western culture and create a just and loving world. Others saw liberalism itself as a threat to authentic Christianity.

Existentialism

One of the strongest voices of opposition to complacent, bourgeois liberalism was a Danish layman and writer who was virtually ignored in his time, but whose writings profoundly influenced twentieth century theology and philosophy. The son of a wealthy and devout Copenhagen business man, Søren Kierkegaard (1813-1855) knew very well that complacent bourgeois Christianity could mask but not heal the suffering of the human soul. Kierkegaard had an unhappy childhood and suffered from melancholy most of his adult life. He broke off an engagement to Regina Olsen because of his own internal torment. In short, he experienced a world quite different from that described by transcendentalists and liberals. The world is not a harmonious synthesis moving toward the ultimate recon-ciliation as Hegel had proposed. Rather it is an alien world with no place for humankind. Sin is the personal experience of this inevitable alienation, but the bourgeois culture of his day sought to avoid the reality of alienation by hiding behind masks of respectability and the enjoyment of life. Christianity had been co-opted by liberalism into assisting a false consciousness.

Kierkegaard uncovered the darkness of the human soul, and rejected the Hegelian system as unreal. True reality is existential; that is, reality is in the realm of existence not abstractness. Truth can only be found in the context of the knower, who is the real existing subject. Encounter with truth is not Schleiermacher's religious feeling or aesthetics; it is an honest confrontation with existential anxiety and despair over the awesome freedom humans have to create their own life and meaning. Ultimately, life is not based on dogmas, philosophical systems or social conventions. Life begins with a leap into the unknown, an existential choice that actualizes existence.

Kierkegaard identified three realms of life: the aesthetical, the ethical, and the religious. In the first realm, a person lives autonomously and for pleasure (whether sexual or artistic). The world is an object existing to satisfy the individual's needs. Thus the hero of the aesthetical world is the seducer; however, refined tastes belong to the aesthetic world as much as vulgar ones. Non-involvement and detachment, such as that of a scientist or art critic, ultimately mark the aesthetical realm.

To enter the ethical sphere, one must make a non-rational leap into involvement and responsibility. No logical necessity exists for doing so; one cannot ultimately define why someone should be responsible to another rather than only to oneself. Love is the hallmark of the ethical world in which one passionately involves oneself in the concern for another: whether for an individual or society at large. It is a concern beyond the concern of oneself. Camus and Sartre explored the ethical realm most deeply in the twentieth century. In Camus' *The Plague*, a plague in Oran destroys all of the normal conventions of society resulting in the isolation of the citizens. No logical reason exists why any one should help the plague victims, and yet many individuals in Oran make this choice, regardless of their theological and philosophical points of view. In making the choice to enter into the lives of the victims, and not simply adapt bureaucracies to handle the situation, ethical people find a new meaning in life. The ethical moves to action for others.

The religious realm produces infinite passion, or creates a passion for the infinite. Here Kierkegaard sounds like Schleiermacher, but he distinguishes between two types of religion: that of Socrates and that of Jesus. Socrates is the existential, dialectical teacher who first uses irony to destroy self-confidence in one's supposed knowledge, and then brings forth true knowledge from within, like a mid-wife. In Socratic religion, each individual ultimately contains the infinite within, and the infinite can be actualized. Jesus, on the other hand, is not merely a teacher, but a Savior. Jesus deals with the existential reality of the human. Individuals do not contain God within themselves. Instead, Jesus comes from God to bring healing for estrangement from God. Jesus not only teaches; he also transforms. The truly religious and transformational leap of faith is a leap to Christ in his historical manifestation. This is a non-rational leap that overcomes (partially at least) the alienation of existence. It is ultimately paradoxical because neither the mind, nor nature can prepare one for this reality. Christ's appearance is not a necessity, but is always a surprise.

Kierkegaard's greatness for theology lies in his profound appreciation not only for the sickness of the human soul, a sickness unto death, but also for his sense of the absolute otherness of God. Christ comes from outside the human realm in order to overcome the estrangement of finitude. Humans had to fall in order to be actualized, to live as humans within finitude, but Christ comes to reconcile us so we may overcome the anxiety and guilt of existence. His understanding of God and the human is not very comfortable, and it led Kierkegaard to attack the optimistic, bourgeois church of his day. In many ways Kierkegaard rediscovered Luther's *deus abscondus* (the "hidden God"), and rescued that doctrine from the attempts to comprehend God by human reason.

Chapter 23

Radical Changes: New Sects and Secularism

THE NINETEENTH CENTURY was an age of great religious creativity and experimentation, particularly in America. Thanks in large part to the guarantee of religious freedom in the First Amendment and stimulated by the Second Great Awakening, a variety of new theologies and churches grew out of traditional Protestantism. For many people, the creation of a new nation and rapid social changes pointed to the inbreaking of the long-anticipated millennial kingdom of Christ on earth. People perceived an outpouring of the Holy Spirit that was seen as a fulfillment of Joel's prophecy that the Spirit would come upon men and women in the last days. In the context of such millennial expectation, a variety of native-born religious movements arose in America.

Shakers

In England, Ann Lee (1736-1784) founded one of the most provocative of the new sects, and brought it to America in 1784. Lee was part of a radical branch of the Society of Friends that promoted the idea of the imminent return of Jesus. James and Jane Wardley converted her to this belief, and in an effort to be spiritually perfect, she committed herself to sexual abstinence over the fierce objections of her husband. Lee soon manifested spiritual gifts, such as healing and prophecy, and gathered a following that revered her as a holy woman. Her preaching brought on persecution and arrest in England, so she led her small group to the New World and settled near Albany, New York. Despite violent opposition from their neighbors, Lee continued to gather converts and build religious communities.

Derisively called the Shakers because of the way members shook under the power of the Spirit, Lee's followers embraced a communal, pacifist, and celibate lifestyle. In some ways, the Shakers represent a Protestant form of the ancient Christian impulse for monasticism. Community members shared their property, wore a common style of clothing, ate and worshipped together. Men and women lived in separate dormitories, and women held positions of authority.

Her followers called Lee Mother Ann, and saw her as the feminine representation of Christ on earth. For the Shakers, God is androgynous, being both masculine and feminine. Christ appeared once as the man Jesus, and returned in the last days as the woman Ann Lee. Christ's true followers live as if they are already in heaven. Eventually the Shakers founded nineteen communities, and may have had as many as 30,000 members at their height in the 1830s, but now are nearly extinct.

The Adventists

In large part because of the great efforts of Finney and his followers to perpetuate a continual revival, upstate New York became known as the "burned over district" in the 1820s and 1830s. Wave after wave of revival and religious enthusiasm swept through the district and inspired new forms of Christianity. William Miller (1782-1849) grew up on the Vermont frontier as a radical Jeffersonian with little Christian conviction until he was converted in a revival following the War of 1812. He diligently studied his copy of the Bible, which happened to contain Archbishop Usher's chronology in the marginal notes.

When Miller came to the Book of Daniel, the only apocalypse in the Jewish canon, he pondered deeply the question of when Christ would return and destroy the kingdoms of the world. Like many previous chialistic scholars, Miller determined that the eschaton was near. He calculated that the 2300 mentioned in Daniel 8:14 meant 2300 years, and that the beginning of those years was 457 BC when the decree went out to rebuild the walls of Jerusalem. 2300 years from 457 BC gives a precise date for the Second Coming of Christ—1843. The 1260 days of the woman in Revelation 12:14 should be added to 538 AD when, according to Miller, the pope became the antichrist. That gives the year 1798 when the papacy fell before Napoleon. The last days, therefore, are the forty-five years between 1798 and 1843, conveniently within Miller's own lifetime. Miller had even more proof that Christ would return in 1843, an idea that he began to proclaim publicly in 1831.

This preaching was well-received in the burned over district where the revivals had raised millennialist expectations. By 1833 there were at least eight ordained ministers preaching Miller's doctrines. Adventist conferences were set up, and the coming end of the world became a new theme in revivalist preaching. Joshua Himes (1805-1895), a Boston minister, saw Adventism and reformism going hand in hand. He published Miller's papers and produced a new hymnal, the *Millennial Harp*. Millennialist journals, such as *The Battle Cry* and *The Advent Herald*, also spread the message on a national scale. New calculations revealed that Christ would return on March 21, 1843. The faithful met that day with great expectation, but Jesus did not come back. When the day passed without the anticipated events, some in the movement redid the figures and set the date for October. Again Jesus did not return. This is known as the Great Disappointment, and it brought ridicule on the Millerites; however, the ridicule merely served to solidify the Adventists as a sectarian movement. Contact with Seventh Day Baptists who observed the Jewish Sabbath rather than Sunday led some in the movement to adopt Sabbatarian practices as they continued to pore over the scriptures. Thus they became the Seventh Day Adventists.

In 1844 a teen-age girl transformed the movement. Ellen G. Harmon (1827-1915) was prone to visions, and after her conversion to Adventism she began to generate an enormous body of prophecy and established her leadership of the movement. She combined Adventist and Sabbatarian ideas with new views about health and diet. In 1855 she and her husband, James White, took their followers to Battle Creek, Michigan. One of their most important converts was Dr. John Kellogg, an advocate of vegetarianism. Along with Kellogg, the inventor of Kellogg's Corn Flakes, the Adventists created a whole theology of health and religion without losing their hope for the millennial kingdom. Through vigorous mission efforts, including wide-spread medical missions, the Seventh Day Adventists have spread around the world.

Swedenborgianism

Many other expressions of nineteenth-century America's quest for spiritual wholeness and health produced alternative forms of religiosity. In some ways the great Age of Invention that was such an expression of American ingenuity and practical zeal extended to the area of religion. Not only could Americans build a better mousetrap, they could build a better path to spiritual and physical health. Not all of these movements were millennialist; some were instead connected to Spiritualism, the belief that the living can have contact with the spirits of the dead. Spiritualist religion developed out of the writings of Emanuel Swedenborg (1668-1771), the son of a Swedish theologian and bishop.

Swedenborg was something of a renaissance man who published important works on geology, anatomy, neurology, paleontology, physics and astronomy. Thus he had a well-deserved reputation as a man of science. Late in life, however, he turned his scientific mind to the questions of religion, and his answers surprised his Enlightenment contemporaries. He claimed that God had appeared to him in a vision and ordered him "to explain to men the spiritual sense of the Scripture." His *Arcana Coelestia* (Secrets of Heaven) ran to thirty enormous volumes before his death.

Swedenborg claimed that Jesus had come again, as predicted, but in a spiritual sense. The Second Coming is really Swedenborg's own unlocking of the hidden meaning of scripture. Many Americans, who for various reasons were turned off by the dominant revivalistic Protestantism, were attracted to this quasi-scientific religion that explained how heaven and earth are joined together. Human happiness does not come from an emotional conversion made from a fear of damnation, but a rational understanding of the underlying spiritual purpose of life. Moreover, Swedenborg offered an answer to the period's anxiety over death. Hell was not abolished, but heaven's progression would redeem it. All souls will be saved. Furthermore, the chasm between the living and dead is not a permanent divide. Swedenborg himself related conversations that he had with famous men long dead. His followers could certainly expect to talk to dead wives and husbands; hence the popularity of seances in the late nineteenth century. Swedenborg's ideas gave impetus to a variety of new medical ideas, such as homeopathy and chiropractic.

Christian Science

The most important expositor of what we could call harmonial religion and the religion of healing was Mary Baker Eddy (1821-1910). A clock-maker named Quimby who was acquainted with Swedenborgianism healed the chronically ill Mary Morse Baker (after marriage, Mary Baker Eddy) in 1862. She became a vigorous promoter of Quimby's theories, and eventually developed her own distinctive system of science, religion, and health. She claimed that she had unlocked the true spiritual meaning of the Bible. Disease is merely a state of the mind and soul. Health comes when a person recognizes his or her true spiritual state, and can thus overcome the illusion of illness. In the late nineteenth-century her Church of Christ Scientist was one of the fastest-growing religious movements in the country, peaking at about a quarter of a million active practitioners.

Communal Enterprises

One further religious impulse in ante-bellum America bears mentioning in the context of alternative religions, communalism. America was the land of opportunity in many ways, and European settlers found freedom from a great number of traditional constraints that marked life in Europe. They had an opportunity to take a tract of land and create a new society. The Puritans made an effort to create a new Christian society in the seventeenth century as did the Moravians and the Ephrata community in the eighteenth, but the nineteenth century opened the door to a proliferation of communal experiments. Some of these, such as Robert Owen's community, were based on secular socialism, but some of the most successful were religious communes.

George Rapp (1757-1847), a German Pietist, became convinced that the early church's communalism described in Acts 4 should be the norm for all true Christians. He led his fellow believers out of Germany to western Pennsylvania in 1804. There they established the community of Harmony. Like the Shakers, the Rappites combined communalism with celibacy (after 1807), strict discipline, and hard work. The community prospered in the wilderness through farming, weaving, brewing, and other trades. Pressure from outsiders led them to move and found New Harmony in Indiana in 1815 where they recreated their initial success. As with many such millennialist communities, it proved difficult to keep up the initial vigor as the return of Christ was delayed, and the communal life finally ended in 1916.

John Humphrey Noyes (1811-1886) embodied many of the religious and social movements of the early nineteenth century. He came out of the burned over district of New York, having converted in the great revival of 1831. He went to Andover and Yale to study for the ministry, but the established churches did not accept his form of evangelicalism. Like Finney, he was an abolitionist who preached perfection from sin and held strong millenarian beliefs; however, his view of the millennium and perfection differed from those of the evangelical mainstream.

Using early biblical criticism, Noyes argued that the biblical prophecies of the end time pointed to the destruction of Jerusalem in 70 AD. Since he believed that the prophecies of scripture are true and reliable, then Christ must have actually returned in 70, but in a spiritual sense. The millennial age thus began in 70 AD. For Noyes, the Second Coming of Christ meant that one could achieve perfection in this life. It just took 1800 years to realize the human potential for perfection. As an unlicensed traveling preacher, Noyes soon had a small gathering, and in 1838 he set out to create a model society based on his idea of perfection. True Christian perfection could not be achieved until individuals gave up private property. He showed remarkable skill in rational organization, and his communal enterprise was one of the most successful in American history. After they moved to Oneida, New York they became prosperous manufacturers of flatware.

While the Oneida com-munity today is most famous for its manu-facturing, Noyes became an infamous figure because of the turn his perfectionist views took. Like Rapp and Lee, Noyes believed that marriage was a barrier to perfection, but he did not reject sexuality. He taught that sex is healthy and natural, but marriage creates unhealthy barriers and jealousies between people, just like personal property does. Marriage laws made women chattels. For Noyes, if sexuality could be liberated from marriage, people would find new and better paths to spiritual growth and build social cohesiveness. Noyes instituted a system known as the Complex Marriage, which was not exactly free love. People were ranked according to their spiritual maturity. Only the more spiritual persons could instigate a sexual encounter, and either party could reject advances. An older and more mature person would initiate an adolescent into sex. Children lived with their mothers, but were more or less raised communally.

The system scandalized their neighbors, and in the 1870s the threat of prosecution under state adultery and child molestation laws forced Noyes to flee to Canada. Eventually, however, the residents of Oneida found that monogamy was more attractive than complex marriage. When the community dissolved in the 1880s, most members had already settled on a mate. Oneida should be seen as one of many experiments in the common nineteenth century quest for a new form of Christianity in a new age.

The Latter Day Saints

Historically and sociologically speaking, the single most important religious movement to emerge on American soil is the Church of Jesus Christ of the Latter Day Saints (Mormons). Although many Christian churches do not accept Mormonism as Christian, it clearly comes out of the Christian tradition. The Latter Day Saints, in their own way, portray another type of radical Christian reform, and remain one of the most vibrant and aggressively expansionist churches in the world.

Joseph Smith (1805-1844), the founder of the Mormons, was "Seer, a Translator, a Prophet, an Apostle of Jesus Christ, and Elder of the Church through the will of God the Father, and the grace of your Lord Jesus Christ," according to his official title, but life was not easy for the young Smith. His family were poor farmers in New England who moved frequently to avoid debts and bad harvests. In 1816, they moved to Palmyra, New York, hoping to benefit from the Erie Canal boom. Smith was thus another product of the burned-over district. He heard one revival preacher consign his recently dead brother to hell because he was unconverted. Smith was also well acquainted with the many religious debates that occupied the nation's attention in the early 1800s, and the *Book of Mormon* offered answers to most of them. As Alexander Campbell said, Smith's book claims to be ancient, but it debates "every error and almost every truth discussed in New York for the last ten years."[28]

As a young man, Joseph Smith believed he had the gift of divining, and he hired out his services to treasure seekers. In 1826 he claimed "he had a certain stone, which he had occasionally looked at to determine where hidden treasures in the bowels of the earth were."[29] He later reported that he had received a heavenly messenger named Moroni who brought a mission from God. Moroni told Smith about a book written on golden pages, and gave Smith the exact location of the book. Along with the plates of gold, Smith would find two seer stones, the Urim and Thummim, by which he could translate the ancient testament.

Fearing that his neighbors would steal his new treasure, Smith and his new bride, Emma Hale, moved to Harmony, Pennsylvania to live with his wife's family. Once they settled, Smith began the work of translating the mysterious text written in a form of hieroglyphics. He sat on one side of a curtain and dictated to his wife on the other side.

The Book of Mormon

A well-to-do farmer named Martin Harris, who had known Smith in Palmyra, was convinced of the authenticity of Smith's find, and moved to Harmony to act as his scribe. Harris managed to lose the first 116 pages of the translation, and was disturbed that Smith could not simply retranslate it, but Smith reported that he had been informed by the angel to skip that section in

---

[28] Marty, *Pilgrims in Their Own Land*, 201.

[29] Klaus J. Hansen, *Mormonism and the American Experience* (Chicago: University of Chicago Press, 1981) 3.

favor of a more spiritual section later in the golden book. The translation went slowly until April 1829, when a schoolteacher named Oliver Cowerdy became the new scribe. In 1830, the *Book of Mormon* was completed and ready for publication. Smith allowed some of his close companions, including Harris, to see the mysterious golden plates, and although some of them later left the Mormon movement, none of them ever changed their stories or denied the existence of the golden plates. Once Smith completed the translation he returned to the plates to Moroni.

What is in the *Book of Mormon*? It tells of the origins of the native Americans. They are indeed children of Israel, but not the ten lost tribes of legend. Rather they descend from Lehi, a prophet of Jerusalem who fled the city before the Babylonians captured it. The Lord guided Lehi and his family across the deserts and oceans to America where they established a great culture based on the Law of Moses. After his resurrection, Jesus Christ came to America to preach the gospel to these New World Jews, and the church was born in America. But all was not well. The descendants of Lehi's son Nephi remained true to the old ways of farming, but became wealthy and effete. The descendants of Lehi's son Laman became fierce hunters and nomads who waged constant war on the Nephites. Eventually the Nephites were destroyed and only the Lamanites remained, but they knew nothing of their ancestry. Cursed by God with dark skin, they became the Indians. Mormon was one of the last Nephites, and he who wrote the Book. His son, Moroni, hid it in the hills until the proper time when it was revealed to the seer, Smith.

Following the dictates of the *Book of Mormon*, Smith gathered a small band into a Christian Church, later named the Church of the Latter Day Saints, to prepare the American Zion for the return of Christ. In January of 1831 they began their march west. In Kirkland, Ohio they built a temple and a bank, but the economic crisis of 1837 ruined their plans. In the midst of riots and fires, Smith fled to Missouri, where a growing Mormon colony was already established.

Tensions grew in Missouri as well. A Mormon war broke out when Smith proclaimed he would wreak vengeance on his enemies like a second Muhammad. He wound up in jail and his followers moved on to Illinois where they founded the community of Nauvoo, which began as a great success. Local politicians wanted Mormon votes and granted the city a unique charter that gave the church great authority. Smith developed a disciplined private army and proclaimed himself the King of the Kingdom of God. His revelations continued in the early 1840s, and the Mormons became more clearly distinct from traditional Christianity. Smith secretly instituted the Old Testament practice of polygamy, rumors of which scandalized the country. Although his close companions, John Taylor and Brigham Young (1801-1877) claimed to hate the idea at first, both gave in. By 1846 Young had thirty-five wives, eight of them Smith's widows.

In 1844, Smith announced his candidacy for the US presidency, a pronouncement that frightened non-Mormons. The Illinois militia moved into Nauvoo. On 27 June 1844, the militia lynched Joseph and Hyrum Smith. Brigham Young took charge of the community and led the Saints on a great trek across the desert to Utah where they could live in relative isolation. Their communal structure allowed them to establish several functioning communities in an inhospitable region. In 1849 Young proclaimed the establishment of the State of Deseret in the Salt Lake Basin, and in 1852 he published Smiths' secret prophecy on polygamy. There were moves to make Utah a state, but the federal government refused to allow polygamy. In 1879, the Supreme Court ruled that the freedom of religion did not allow people to use religious beliefs to undermine traditional monogamy upon which "society may be said to be built." By 1890, however, the Mormons were growing less comfortable with polygamy, and a new revelation allowed them to give up this barrier to statehood.

Mormon Doctrine

A look at the beliefs of the Mormons offers a nice window into the religious views and anxieties of Americans before the Civil War. Smith highlighted the early republic's view of America as a land of millennial promise. It was a once and future land; the garden of Eden and the New Jerusalem. The original garden of Eden had been located just a few miles from Independence, Missouri, but the flood brought Noah and his descendants to the Middle East. Thus the new world is part of salvation history. Smith also accepted materialism, which meant for him that God has a body, wives, and sex. Moreover, matter can never be destroyed, and life is a process of evolution and improvement. Every human being is on a process toward becoming a god. The saints will be gods, and unbelievers (gentiles) will suffer a form of purgatory until they receive a share of glory. Moreover, there is no great divide between the living and the dead. In fact, Smith even preached that the dead could serve as missionaries to other dead people. Through prayer and ritual, the living can save their departed ancestors.

With the Mormons, we see perhaps the most extreme attempt to reform Christianity for the modern age. All aspects of the church: theology, ecclesiology, morality, and even the scriptures were reformulated in order to answer the anxieties of nineteenth century America. The Mormons shared in the great evangelical revival and the millennial hopes of their time, and like the revivalists, they took upon themselves the task of creating a better world through conversion and sanctification.

Opponents of Christianity

We have seen a variety of challenges to traditional Christianity, and a variety of ways in which Christian thought responded to such challenges. In the last half of the nineteenth century there emerged other intellectual movements that did not merely challenge orthodox Christianity; they attacked the nature of religion itself. Although Hegel saw his work as a grand vindication of Christian theology, some of his followers took his thought in ways he had not imagined.

Karl Marx (1818-1883) used Hegelian philosophy to forge a new theory of history and human society. Marx accepted Hegel's idea that human history is a progression through conflict, but he rejected the idea of the Spirit in favor of materialism. History is a dialectic of conflicting interests and systems of economics that creates new systems which are then in turn supplanted through conflict. Capitalism replaced feudalism and would in turn be overthrown by the proletariat (working class) seeking to overcome their sense of economic alienation. Marx promoted a millennial goal of a society where the means of production and the benefits of production would be synthesized and workers would overcome their alienation. Religion, which is used by the oppressors to keep the oppressed ignorant and subservient, will be swept away in the course of history. Religion uses flowers to hide the chains of the oppressed. Marx himself offered a secularized version of Judeo-Christian religion in which the apocalypse is replaced by the revolution, and the millennium by the workers' state. The twentieth century theologian Paul Tillich classified Marxism as a form of religion. It certainly offered a powerful alternative to Christianity among the disaffected masses of Europe.

Ludwig Feuerbach (1804-1872) also rejected the claims of religion. For him, history is the gradual emancipation of the human spirit from superstition and false consciousness. The human spirit merely projects "God" on the universe. "It is a universal doctrine in our upside-down world that nature sprang from God, whereas we should say the opposite, namely, that God was abstracted from nature and is merely a concept derived from it."[30]   The human spirit will only be free when it gets rid of this projection and accepts its own divinity.

Sigmund Freud (1859-1939) accepted Feuerbach's idea of projection and also saw the abolition of religion as a necessary step for human health. Freud, like Kierkegaard, studied the human soul or psyche, and he postulated that all humans suffer from existential guilt; that is, guilt by virtue of existing. Guilt is tied up with sexuality, the drive to perpetuate the existence of the species. He theorized that all humans are a bundle of barely repressed sexual drives, that are the seat of much of our creativity and disease. Complexes exist deep in the unconscious of every rational being, but as we mature we must cope with various guilt-complexes. A healthy person is one who has dealt with original guilt in order to love and to work (*leben und arbeiten*). Sick individuals failed to deal with their sense of original guilt. One of the most common forms of mental illness is a misplaced guilt complex, the assuming of guilt improperly. Freud saw religion as a major source of such misplaced and pathological guilt, and he was attacked for his theories, especially his view of sexuality. Talk of sex drives, particularly in children profoundly disturbed Victorians in Europe and America. The irony is that Freud had in some ways rediscovered the doctrine of original sin as an existential reality inherent in all persons.

One of the greatest and most tragic geniuses of the nineteenth century was Frederick Nietzsche (1844-1900) who also rejected the Hegelian synthesis. Like Kierkegaard, he preferred to write in fragments instead of systems. He also looked intensely at the type of humanity being produced in the bourgeois and industrial age (the proletariat, bureaucrats, and capitalists) and did not like what he saw. Rather than evolving, humankind had reached a petty, cynical, and only half-alive state of existence. Nietzsche predicted the emergence of the *übermensch*, the Superior Man, who would combine the great aristocratic ideals of the classical age with the biological superiority of evolution. He would embrace the drive to vital life, the will to power, and be able to establish the morality for the next epoch. The idea of God as Father was dead in the human race, it is the *Götterdämerung* (the twilight of the gods), and now the great individual could be as god. In the decades following his death, such ideas would be twisted into the swastika.

---

[30] Ludwig Feuerbach, *Lectures on the Essence of Religion*, trans. Ralph Manheim (New York: Harper and Row, 1967) 103.

Chapter 24

Missions to the World

EVEN AS CHRISTIANITY appeared to be on the decline in Europe, the church was experiencing one of its greatest periods of growth around the world. The effort to evangelize the world in the nineteenth and twentieth centuries was largely successful, at least as far as numbers go, and in the process Christianity became the world's largest and most-widespread religion. At the end of the twentieth century more than two-thirds of Christians live outside of Europe and the United States. The history of Christian outreach, though, is closely related to the history of European colonialism; therefore it is sometimes difficult to separate conversion and conquest.

Christian missions were closely connected with Eurocentric ideas that white European and American culture was the most developed in the world. From this perspective, non-western peoples needed salvation from their religious error as well as their cultural errors; however, they could never become white. Except in rare instances the mission fields remained dependent on American and European missionaries and mission societies until the 1950s. As Christians brought their faith to Asia, they encountered ancient and sophisticated religions that challenged traditional Christian understandings. Their face-to-face encounter with vibrant world religions caused many Christians in the twentieth century to reconsider their understanding of salvation and truth.

India

The East India Company began work in India in 1600, and in 1690 Calcutta became the capital of British activities. In 1757, Britain gained complete control over India. A small, island nation controlled an entire subcontinent with an ancient and advanced culture. Christian missions proceeded slowly, but steadily. An English shoemaker turned Baptist preacher is credited with beginning the great era of Protestant missions. After the Baptists converted William Carey (1761-1834), he taught himself Latin, Greek, Hebrew, Dutch, and French while pastoring a church and making shoes. At a 1792 clergy meeting, Carey spoke his mind and gave what became the watchword for missions for the next 100 years. "Expect great things from God and attempt great things for God." Following his own advice, Carey founded the Baptist Missionary Society and soon set sail for India. At that time the East India Company banned missionaries from working among the native peoples. The Company feared that the missionaries would cause turmoil among the Indians and reduce trade and profits. Undaunted, Carey sailed to India on Dutch ships. He found that it can be very difficult to attempt great things for God, and he quickly realized the need to learn the local language and customs. He set to work learning Bengali, and in 1809 he published the first translation of the entire Bible in Bengali. By the time he died, he had translated portions of the Bible into thirty-five languages.

Carey's work became the inspiration for an explosion of missions in other areas of the British Empire. Soon, liberals such as the social reformer William Wilberforce (1759-1833), were vigorously endorsing the goal of Christian-izing and civilizing the pagan peoples of the world. Carey and Wilberforce successfully advocated for the abolishment of *suttee*, the practice of burning a widow on her husband's funeral pyre. Like the Roman Catholic missionaries who came to Goa 200 years earlier, Protestants had most success among the lower castes. Missionaries and their converts worked to abolish the caste system and expand education to women. By 1914, over one million Indians had been baptized. In that year over 5000 Protestant missionaries worked in India.

Hindu Reaction

One unintended consequence of such zealous evangelization is that it encouraged educated Hindus and Buddhists to define and defend their religion. National independence and religious identity were joined as a form of defense against Western cultural imperialism. Interestingly, Hindu and Buddhist ideas greatly affected some missionaries and their families. In India, the church encountered something unknown for centuries: an ancient and vibrant religion that shared no affinities to Christianity. Before this time, Christians had only known of so-called primitive or animistic religions of tribal peoples or the other religions of the Book (Judaism and Islam), but in India the missionaries encountered elaborate and sophisticated religious systems and literature. While not many Westerners converted, many did find they had to alter their traditional theology. Much of the West's early knowledge of Hinduism and Buddhism came from these missionaries and their families.

One of the great swamis of the nineteenth century was Vivekananda (1863-1902) whose father wanted him to become a British officer. Instead he led an ascetic life alone in the forest for ten years, after which he emerged as a swami. In 1893, his master sent him to the World's Parliament of Religion in Chicago. This was one of the great events of the century, and was connected with the five-hundredth anniversary of Columbus' voyage. Inspired by New England transcendentalists, like Henry David Thoreau, who found other religions interesting, the Parliament opened September 11, 1893. It was primarily a Christian event, or to be most precise, a liberal Protestant event, but repre-sentatives of most of the major world religions participated. Vivekananda spoke on the universal truth of Hinduism, and gave an impassioned state-ment that Hinduism is the highest religion because it tolerates other religions. In fact, it includes all religions. An exclusive claim of truth and salvation proves immaturity, according to Vivekananda. Some Christians agreed.

China and Japan

In the Far East, European colonizers encountered one of the world's oldest societies, the Celestial Empire. For centuries China and Japan had been closed to Westerners, especially Christian missionaries, but the Opium War of 1839-1842 forced China to open its borders for trade. The war began when the Chinese government tried to stop the British from importing the highly profitable narcotic into China. When the treaties were signed, the British had control of five port cities and the island of Hong Kong. Protestant and Catholic missionaries poured into China for the next half century. By 1914 there were over 2000 Catholic missionaries, 5000 Protestant missionaries, and two million converts. Since the missionaries were clearly connected to British imperialism, they became particular targets for violence in the Boxer Rebellion at the turn of the century.

The most famous of the mission pioneers was Charlotte Digges (Lottie) Moon (1840-1912), a Southern Baptist from Virginia. Moon personified many features of nineteenth century Christianity. She converted at a revival service in 1858, and became a student leader at the Albemarle Female Institute, an evangelical school. She studied biblical languages with Crawford Toy (1836-1919). Twenty years later, Toy would lose his position at Southern Baptist Theological Seminary for teaching biblical criticism. A proposed marriage between Toy and Moon also ran into difficulty because of theological incompatibility. During and following the Civil War, Moon supported herself as a teacher, and in 1873 felt a call to go to China. There she worked to improve the status of women as well as to preach the gospel. Against the advice of her superiors, Moon went alone into the P'ingtu Province where she taught the "Heavenly Book" for fourteen hours a day. She managed to survive the Boxer Rebellion and the subsequent famine, feeding hundreds from her own resources. Her death in 1912 was hastened by malnutrition and overwork, but she refused to leave her home to return to America.

Japan was also opened to Western missionaries by military means when Commodore Perry brought his warships to the island in 1853. The Japanese government quickly adopted Western science, technology, and trade, and in 1905 the Japanese navy defeated Russia in a brief war that shocked the West. Christian missionaries worked with initial success, but nationalist resistance to the Westerners led to a revitalization of native religions before World War II.

American Protectorates

The first concerted efforts of American missionaries were related to the moves America made toward establishing a world empire, namely the American ventures into Hawaii and the Philippines. An independent American Board of Foreign Missions was established to help with such enterprises. In 1820, a party of New England missionaries arrived in Hawaii, and successfully converted a number of prominent tribal leaders. Unfortunately, they also introduced diseases that decimated the population. A century later, due to disease and immigration, only 10 percent of the residents of Hawaii were native. By 1893, when a pro-American party deposed Queen Liluokalani, the nation was already heavily evangelized.

The Spanish American war of 1898 was a major step on the road to an American empire. After its stunning defeat of Spain, America had to decide what do with Cuba, the Philippines, Guam, and other new territories acquired in the war. The natives of the islands had fought with the Americans in a war of independence, but President McKinley moved to annex the new possessions. Before announcing his decision, he met with some of the leading Protestant clergy to ask for their support. He admitted that he had been in doubt over what to do, but then he prayed for guidance, and the answer came. He could not turn the lands back to Spain, France or Germany. Nor could he give them self-rule; the people were too child-like for that. Instead, America should take them over, civilize and Christianize them. The fact that many of the people were already Roman Catholic did not affect his decision, and Protestant leaders saw a great opportunity in the opening up of new territories.

Church officials proclaimed that imperialism brought the gospel and liberation, but some Christian leaders, such as William Jennings Bryan, pointed out the chilling irony that American Protestants were using rhetoric that sounded very similar to that of the conquistadors 500 years earlier. Bryan thundered that the Gospel does not need a Gattling Gun, but few missionaries heard his warning.

Africa and the Middle East

In the last half of the nineteenth century, the European powers competed with one another to carve up Africa and the Middle East into colonies. Christians had lived in the Middle East and northern Africa since the Roman Empire, but sub-Saharan Africa remained largely unevangelized. It was virtually unknown to Europeans and Americans who had exported slaves from these regions for years without concern for the people or cultures that lived there. With colonialism, though, European governments had a vested interest in understanding this vast land.

David Livingstone (1813-1873) stands out as the prime example of the heroic era of Christian missions to Central Africa. A self-educated mill worker from Glasgow, Livingstone studied medicine in the hope of serving in China. War prevented him from traveling there, so the London Missionary Society sent him to South Africa where evangelization was rapidly progressing. Livingstone combined Christian zeal with the restless energy of the explorer, continually seeking out villages that had never heard of Jesus. In the process, he opened up much of Central Africa to Western culture, produced written languages for numerous tribes, and gathered converts. Like most missionaries, Livingstone aggressively opposed the slave trade and brought modern medicine and agriculture to the people to whom he ministered.

Women in Missions

David Livingstone remains for many people the model of the intrepid missionary, but by 1900 nearly 60 percent of the active missionaries in the field were women. Initially women were recruited for mission work in order to evangelize other women in societies where it was improper for a man to speak to a woman in public. Soon missionary women went beyond that role and assumed leadership duties that were denied to them at home. They worked in the medical clinics and schools, supervised the staffs of the various missions, and helped with preaching, teaching, and evangelizing. Women such as Lottie Moon found far more opportunity to exercise authority in China than in the United States where they often could not even address their home congregations during Sunday morning service. Likewise, Roman Catholic missions depended on the sacrificial service of women in various religious orders, such as the Ursulines.

Furthermore, the energetic efforts of women in the United States and England provided much of the financial support for Protestant missions. By 1900, over forty women's missionary societies in the United States provided full financial support for over 1,200 missionaries. Typically the societies were founded in congregations with little or no support from the pastor. Often they were intercongregational and interdenominational. Women were the fundraisers, treasurers, and leaders of their own societies. Invariably, as time passed and the societies grew more successful, the various congregations and denominations put pressure on them to submit to the leadership of the local pastor or a denominational board made up entirely of men. By 1930 virtually none of the societies remained under female leadership.

The Evangelization of the World in this Generation

Much of the mission enterprise resulted from the work of lay persons rather than clergy. When John R. Mott (1865-1955) was the secretary of the YMCA in the 1880s, he dedicated his life to the spread of Christianity. In the 1890s Mott recruited college students through the Student Volunteer Movement for the grand enterprise of global evangelization. Mott welcomed Christians of every denomination in his societies. What shocked his contemporaries was that his welcome specifically included Roman Catholics and the Eastern Orthodox churches. Mott also popularized one of the most confident slogans of modern times: "The Evangelization of the World in This Generation." He did not mean that everyone in the world would become

Christian, but that the youth of that generation would work tirelessly to make sure that the Christian message could be heard in every nation on earth.

As part of his effort, Mott helped organize the World Missionary Conference in Edinburgh, Scotland in 1910. The conference marks the beginning of the modern ecumenical movement since the participants realized that divisions between the Christian churches hurt the mission enterprises. Church divisions made it difficult to use resources effectively and created confusion for converts. Mott urged the delegates at Edinburgh to unite for the spread of the Gospel. Eventually, this union for missions led to the formation of the World Council of Churches.

Nineteenth-century Protestantism was a dynamic movement at home as well as in the mission field. We have already seen how the Second Great Awakening encouraged the formation of social reform societies. By the middle of the century, some of the societies had grown into major crusades to rid society of injustice and poverty. Foremost in this history was the war against slavery.

Abolition

It took decades for abolition to gather strength. Slaveholders justified their practice by a direct appeal to the Bible. Traditional churches, such as the Anglicans, found it particularly hard to reject the authority of the Bible and centuries of church tradition. Moreover, grave concerns existed about overturning social norms, even unjust ones. Thus, it is not surprising that the first voices against slavery came from the Christian fringe, not the center. The Society of Friends taught that the Inner Light should guide the Christian, not the dead word on paper. Believers must act according to what is right today, according to what is good and true, regardless of the social consequences.

When a Quaker named John Woolman (1720-1772) was asked to draw up a bill of sale for a slave woman in New Jersey in 1742, the reality of slavery confronted him. In 1743, he set out to tell other Quakers that slavery contradicted the religion of Jesus, and in 1746, he began writing one of the first anti-slavery tracts, *Some Considerations on the Keeping of Negroes*. Thanks to Woolman's efforts, the Philadelphia Yearly Meeting of the Society of Friends voted in 1758 to expel slave holders. His journal became a source of inspiration for later abolitionists in England and America.

The Second Great Awakening brought renewed attention to the slave issue. It did not take long for a generation of young evangelicals in the mid-

West to question the justice of slavery. Lane Theological Seminary and Oberlin College in Ohio were hotbeds of this new activist evangelicalism. Theodore Dwight Weld (1803-1895) was one of Finney's most ardent converts, and while a student at Lane Theological Seminary, he led a student revolt on the issue of slavery. The new president was Lyman Beecher, who listed slavery as an enemy of the kingdom of God, but Beecher preferred the gradualist approach to abolition. Weld equated Christianity and abolition, arguing that slavery destroyed the souls of both slaves and masters. Southern plantations daily crucified Christ, and the churches played the role of Pontius Pilate. For eighteen nights in October 1834, the students and faculty at Lane debated the issue. When Beecher and the trustees refused to adopt abolition, Weld led his classmates out of the school, leaving only five students enrolled.

Of course the greatest of the white abolitionists was William Lloyd Garrison (1805-1879) who founded the *Liberator* in 1831. Garrison was originally a Baptist, but Lyman Beecher converted him to Presbyterianism. Garrison, like Weld, believed in Beecher's moral call to make America into the Kingdom of God on earth. Garrison believed that the revivalists' call for freedom meant more than freedom from sin, it meant true freedom, and he challenged preachers to prove why their doctrines only applied to white men. He challenged Jacksonian Democrats to prove why their egalitarian rhetoric only applied to white men. Garrison went so far as to publicly burn a copy of the Constitution during a Fourth of July service to protest America's great hypocrisy. One minister immediately proclaimed that Garrison stood in the succession of the prophets, a descendent of John the Baptist, Luther, Wesley, and George Fox.

At least one church dedicated itself from the beginning to complete freedom for all black people. The African Methodist Episcopal Church, Zion (AME Zion) included a number of members who stand in the pantheon of freedom. Frederick Douglass (1817-1895) was a lay preacher who helped convince Lincoln to sign the Emancipation Proclamation. Douglass knew that the Exodus required struggle, and he advised young men "to agitate, agitate, agitate." Harriet Tubman (1820-1913) used the AME Zion church as the foundation for her Underground Railroad system. She knew that the Exodus needed a Moses. In 1832, Maria Stewart spoke before the Afric-American Female Intelligence Society in Boston, setting forth a picture of the avenging God of the Old Testament who would soon unleash violent wrath on sinful America. Abolition may come in violence and bloodshed, but it would come, Stewart proclaimed. She knew that the Exodus called for God's justice.

Even more imposing than Tubman or Stewart was Sojourner Truth (1797-1883), who as a slave in upstate New York was named Isabella Van Wagener. In 1843, she had a vision that changed her life and her name. She became a Sojourner for Truth, for the Truth that God wanted to set his people free. When she heard Frederick Douglass give a speech that ended in despair on the plight of the African Americans, Sojourner challenged him. "Frederick, is God dead?" No, and freedom would come.

Divided Churches

Slavery divided American churches. In 1837, the Presbyterians split between the Old School and a New School of liberal evangelical crusaders. The Old School felt that the abolitionists denied the authority of the Bible. The split largely followed geographic lines. In the 1840s the Baptists divided over the issue of whether slave-holders could become foreign missionaries. In 1845, the southerners organized themselves into the Southern Baptist Convention in order to preserve the Bible and slaves from northern attacks.

The most significant church division occurred among the Methodists. By 1840, the Methodist Church was the largest organization of any kind in America, but that union was crumbling. One hundred forty-five thousand Methodists were of African descent, and yet a number of Methodist clergy owned slaves themselves. The southerners in 1840 published a Southern Book of Concern that defended slavery on biblical grounds and accused the northerners of substituting politics for religion. Sin, not slavery, was the problem. In 1844, the General Conference removed slave-holder James Osgood Andrew from his episcopal post. The Southern Methodists immediately seceded from the national church and formed a separate body. It would take over a century before the Presbyterians and Methodists would heal divisions over slavery and the Bible.

The Women's Movement

The Seneca Falls Convention of 1848 is famous as the beginning of the movement for women's rights, particularly the right to vote, but often overlooked is the connection between the women's movement and Christian social reform. Many of the participants at Seneca Falls actively participated in the abolition movement, and believed that the gospel calls for the liberation of all human beings. Sarah Grimke, (1792-1873) and her sister Angelina (1805-1879) were the children of Episcopalian slave-holders in Charleston, S.C. who were converted to abolition and then women's rights. After reading the Journal of John Woolman, Sarah became a Quaker and moved to Philadelphia in the early 1820s. Angelina followed Sarah's footsteps, and in 1829, she joined her in Philadelphia. Four years later she joined the Philadelphia Anti-Slavery Society, and in 1836, published *An Appeal to the Christian Women of the Southern States*. She urged women to use their influence to convince their husbands to free their slaves. In her hometown she had a prophet's welcome. The entire shipment of her books was burned publicly, and her family was told never to let Angelina come home.

Theodore Weld included Angelina in his training sessions for novice abolitionists, and encouraged her to speak to groups of women interested in abolition. When men began attending her lectures, it created a scandal. Women had been preaching in backwoods revivals for decades, but not in polite society in the cities. When the two sisters took their message to New England in 1837, they found the pulpits closed to them. Catherine Beecher attacked them for having broken the "beneficent and immutable Divine law" that forbade women to address men. The Grimke's defended their right to speak in public and the ensuing controversy made them famous. Over the course of twenty-three weeks the sisters spoke to some 40,000 people, something unheard of for women.

Elizabeth Cady Stanton (1815-1902) helped organize the Seneca Falls Convention, and soon became the leading voice in the Women's Suffrage Movement. Like the Grimke's, Stanton went through a personal spiritual pilgrimage from evangelicalism to abolition to suffrage. She felt frustrated that ministers refused to let her speak in the pulpit and criticized her for addressing men publicly. She finally came to the opinion that Paul's words about women had no more force in the modern world than his words on slavery. As the suffrage movement heated up, Protestant churches closed ranks against women publicly preaching.

Finally, at the end of the century, Stanton published *The Woman's Bible*, one of the hallmarks of biblical criticism in America. It was a commentary that focused on women in the Bible, using the latest findings of German scholarship. All of the scholars who contributed to the commentary were women. Although welcomed by some women, the publication made Stanton an arch-heretic in the eyes of the Christian establishment. Even the evangelicals forgot their earlier history of spirit-filled women preaching in revivals and turned their backs on the women's rights movement. By the turn of the century only a few denominations, mainly the Congregationalists and the Methodists, ordained women. The efforts of Stanton and Lucretia Mott (1793-1880), a Quaker, finally resulted in women gaining the right to a voice in American politics, but their voice in the church continued to be controversial well into the twentieth century.

Temperance

Other than abolition, the most successful and controversial of the holy wars fought by Protestant activists in the nineteenth century was against John Barleycorn. Like so many social reforms, the Temperance Movement began during the Second Great Awakening, but gathered political steam toward the end of the century. Until the 1820s alcohol was not really considered a religious issue. Drunkenness had always been seen as a sin, but alcohol was an accepted part of life. Asbury's circuit riders carried whiskey along with their Bibles. Over the course of the nineteenth century, though, the evangelical establishment began pushing the idea of alcohol as a sin. The roots of the change lie in two different soils.

One was the general desire to reform society according to the new Christian ethos. Alcoholism certainly caused some of the greatest social problems of the time. Liquor sellers aggressively encouraged alcoholism. Saloons were located right across the entrance from factories, mines, or wherever men toiled in meaningless labor. Alcohol literally destroyed families, led people deeper into poverty, and increased the already shocking amount of violence in American society. Therefore social reformers set out to limit or abolish alcohol as a way to preserve the family and society.

The other root of the temperance movement lay in the holiness movement associated with Phoebe Palmer. Alcohol was blamed for keeping people from experiencing sanctification. The preachers of holiness urged Christians to avoid all alcohol, and soon began to ban alcohol in their groups and churches. The evangelical South, where drinking alcohol became the litmus test of a person's Christianity, shows the great success of the temperance movement. Many denominations, particularly of the Methodist variety, required ministers to pledge that they would never drink alcohol. Many Protestant churches quit using wine in communion so as to not tempt their people.

The irony of the evangelical crusade against alcohol is that they found it hard to use the Bible to support the cause. Certainly the Bible condemned drunkenness, but as drinkers often pointed out, Jesus not only drank wine, he made it. Therefore the anti-alcohol crusaders resorted to interpretation to plead their case. Some argued that the New Testament speaks of new wine, which is unfermented. Others argued that wine was suitable in Jesus' time, but he would condemn the use of alcohol in the modern world. Despite difficulties over biblical interpretation, temperance fit in so nicely with concerns for personal holiness and the preservation of the family that soon Protestantism and Prohibition were united.

One of the most effective temperance fighters was Frances Willard (1839-1898), the leader of the Women's Christian Temperance Union. Willard was a Methodist who saw her temperance work as a part of her divine calling as a Methodist and a woman. She did not meddle in politics; she promoted personal holiness and protected the family. She herself was a very public figure who, like Stanton, argued for the right of women to preach even if they were not ordained. She organized groups of women to hold "pray-ins" at local saloons. The women knelt in prayer before the entrance praying in order to prevent patrons from entering.

In 1895, a coalition of Protestants formed the Anti-Saloon League. By this time Prohibition had been joined to concerns about immigration and the apparent loss of Protestant dominance. The Anti-Saloon League proclaimed that decent, Christian, native-born Americans were dry, and that the wets were all Catholics, Jews, heathens, and other foreigners. In 1920 the drys won, and alcohol was outlawed in the United States. The evangelist Billy Sunday held a funeral for John Barleycorn during which he proclaimed that slums, prisons, and jails would be no longer needed as sober Americans became prosperous, hard working Protestants. The final victory of the social reforms of evangelical America was Prohibition, but the victory clearly demonstrated the myopia of addressing social problems as individual sins. Prohibition led directly to the great organized crime syndicates of the twenties, and in the long run may have ruined as many lives as it had hoped to save. Slums and prisons remained.

Industrialization and Christianity

In many ways, alcoholism was more of a symptom than a cause of the great social problems that had beset Europe and America in the nineteenth century. Industrialization and the resulting urbanization of society wreaked havoc on the fabric of Western society, and caused immense suffering among the poorest in the land. Cities grew at an astounding rate, swallowing up the countryside villages. Some German cities had urban parishes with more than 20,000 people in them. Medieval cathedrals had been designed to hold the entire population of a town, but in Berlin there was only room for 25,000 people in all the churches in a city of over 800,000 souls. New inventions, such as steel, railroads, trolleys, and the elevator assisted such growth. Soon skyscrapers dwarfed the old churches and cathedrals, and the modern metropolis was born. By 1900 more people worked in factories than farms, and lived in cities rather than in villages.

Life in the city was different than in the country, as everyone who has read the morality tale about the country mouse and the city mouse knows. The city discourages personal relationships and encourages people to ignore one another. The city offers pleasures and recreations unknown in small towns. One does not have to wait for the big harvest festival or the fair to find dancing, music, shows, games, and of course, sex and alcohol. The industrial metropolis offered those things every day in the midst of hunger, crime, prostitution, disease, and early death.

Charities

The church had never before faced social problems like those of the industrial age. Although Christianity had originally been an urban movement, the church had come to maturity in the parish life of villages where people in the pews knew each other on a day-to-day basis. They worked together and worshipped together. Business ethics was based largely on the conviction that you dealt with people you knew and with whom you lived. Charity also worked on a face-to-face encounter. Churches, individuals, and aid societies distributed necessary commodities to people they knew by name in the community. Most Christians assumed that a shared system of values existed that included piety, patriotism, hard work, and family, but industrialization changed this.

Industrialization produced a large underclass that worked for machines, not people. Workers became human resources to be used and disposed of like any other resource. In an age before robotics, the ideal worker was viewed as a robot, or at least as a cog in a grand industrial machine. With a stroke of a pen, 5000 wage earners could be laid off. Desperate people clinging to survival, lived at the mercy of industrialists. Moreover, the new economy was concentrated in the hands of corporations, groups of people bound together to maximize profits. Faceless, nameless, impersonal corporations made decisions that could reduce working people to poverty. In the new industrial age, poverty had less to do with ones' Protestant work ethic than with fluctuations in the business cycle. Recessions and Depressions cycled with economics booms. A bad year could throw hundreds of thousands of hard working people out on the streets.

Many preachers held to the old view of poverty and morality. The Brooklyn liberal Henry Ward Beecher said that workers should not complain about their lot because poverty results immorality. "No man in this land suffers from poverty unless it be more than his fault - unless it be his sin...it is owing to the want of provident care, and foresight, and industry and frugality."[31]

Not all Christians shared his attitude, however. William Booth (1829-1912) was a Methodist minister who noticed that Christians spent vast sums to bring the gospel and modern medicine to India and Africa while tens of thousands of souls remained lost in the cities of England. He publicized the urban crisis in his book *In Darkest England and the Way Out.* In the 1860s he left the Methodist connection and organized his followers into an army to bring salvation to the urban poor. They reached out to the most neglected, especially alcoholics, and brought the gospel along with physical assistance. His Salvation Army pioneered ways for the poor to help themselves, and in 1880, he brought his Salvation Army to America where his daughter Evangeline led the mission. She soon became one of the greatest religious leaders in America, working tirelessly for the poor in the city slums, bravely going into areas deemed unsafe for women. Evangeline saw her work as a continuation of what Wesley had begun, but she was even more effective than Wesley in reaching those at the bottom of society. Before long, most of the members of the Army were made up of persons who had been rescued. Former drunks became officers who received a uniform and training in how to carry out the battle against sin and poverty.

The English social reformers Elizabeth Fry (1780-1845) and John Gurney (1788-1847) dedicated themselves to a different aspect of the suffering of the poor. The English justice system treated criminals harshly and the poor suffered the most. One could be imprisoned for not paying debts or for begging on the streets. Petty offenses received long prison systems, and the prisons themselves were models of barbarity. Fry, Gurney, Wilberforce, and others argued that a Christian nation must have just and fair laws that treat even criminals humanely.

At the same time, other Christian reformers worked to stamp out prostitution in the cities. Magdalene Societies sheltered and educated prostitutes so they could find another means to live. Eventually, activists succeeded in outlawing prostitution in England and America. Christian

---

[31] Quoted in Ahlstrom, *A Religious History of the American People,* 2 vols. ((New Haven: Yale University Press, 1972) 2:255.

activists also succeeded in passing child labor laws to protect children from economic exploitation. The Young Men's Christian Association (YMCA) founded by George Williams (1821-1905) provided a different approach to the problems of urbanization. The YMCA offered ided Christian fellowship and healthy recreation for young men dislocated by urbanization.

Catholicism and Labor

We have already met Cardinal Gibbons, the great archbishop of Baltimore who helped create an American Catholic Church. One of the greatest challenges Gibbons faced involved organized labor. One reason that anti-immigration forces lost in nineteenth century America was that American industry wanted large numbers of disposable workers. The huge factories, meat-packing plants, steel mills, and other industries that mushroomed in America needed men, women, and children who desperately needed work. People did not have to speak English to work in a factory; they just needed to show up and not complain. If they were injured and died, replacements were at hand. The capitalists welcomed the huge influx of eastern and southern European immigrants whom they exploited as human resources for the industrial revolution. Eventually laws were put into place to protect vulnerable workers, especially women and children, but millions of workers did not wait for the government. They organized themselves into labor unions to demand better conditions.

Protestants, in general, sided with the owners during strikes. They used parables of Jesus to prove that an owner can pay whatever he likes, and the worker should not complain. Moreover, they pointed out that in Europe workers turned to socialism or Marxism in an effort not simply to get better conditions but to radically transform society. Catholics, on the other hand, were caught in a bind. The church in Europe sided completely with the owners against the workers. The *Syllabus of Errors* condemned much of what the labor movement tried to achieve and their means to achieve it. However, most of the Catholics in America were factory workers. If the church hierarchy sided with the owners and capital, then there was a genuine threat that it would lose most of its membership. Moreover, many of the local priests and nuns sympathized with the plight of the workers in their parishes. They knew the conditions people lived and worked in, and they wanted to help.

Gibbons urged the American bishops to go easy on labor organizations. These organizations were often secret societies, such as the Noble and Holy Order of the Knights of Labor, and they could be perceived as unchristian, but

Gibbons urged the bishops to look the other way. Moreover, he personally supported the streetcar drivers in their Baltimore strike of 1886, one of the few church leaders to do so. Gibbons along with some other American archbishops promoted a new Catholic defense of labor as something "natural and just." Workers have a right to safe and fair working conditions.

By 1890, the crisis within the Catholic Church over the labor issue had passed. Pius' successor, Leo XIII (1878-1903), in 1891, issued an official letter title *Rerum novarum*, that openly endorsed Gibbon's views on labor and urged bishops to advocate for better working conditions as part of the call of Christ. Because of Gibbons and Leo, the Catholic Church in America maintained the loyalty of millions of immigrant workers; however, such was not the case in Europe. In part due to a half-a-century of opposition to organized labor and new ideas of social reform, the Catholic Church in Europe was being reduced to a church for villagers, old women, and a few wealthy aristocrats.

Christian Socialism and the Social Gospel

Karl Marx's communism was only one form of socialism being promoted in the nineteenth century. Other intellectuals and activists believed that the teaching of Jesus is the basis for socialism. Churches should join the workers in their struggle to share in the fruits of their labor. The roots of German Christian Socialism were in the Inner Mission begun by Johann Hinrich Wichern (1808-1881) who was profoundly influenced by Schleiermacher's theology. Like William Booth, Wichern believed that the church must focus as much attention on the urban poor as it had on oversees missions. He established a very influential orphanage, the Rauhe Haus and trained workers for his goal of "social rebirth." The church must work with the Holy Spirit to revitalize all areas of life: the state as well as the family and the church. The Inner Mission helped coordinate and inspire a number of charitable organizations similar to those in England. Finally, Bismarck, despite his personal hatred of socialism, agreed to institute a number of social reforms advocated by the Inner Mission as a way to stem the growth of Marxism.

One of the most significant movements to emerge from Liberalism in America was the Social Gospel. The leaders of the Social Gospel took a hard look at the new economic system and saw that it contradicted the biblical idea of the Kingdom of God. No amount of moral persuasion and preaching could help the vast sea of people suffering from the effects of industrialization and urbanization. Something new was needed. The Social Gospelers were open to new ideas from sociology and economics as well as theology. They studied current thought, and sought to influence public policy on behalf of the poor.

Washington Gladden (1836-1918) in Ohio was one of the first liberal ministers interested in the Social Gospel. Gladden had many industrialists in his congregation, but during the violent labor strikes of the 1880s, he shocked his congregation by siding with labor against capital. He urged the owners in his congregation to treat their workers according to Christian principles, using Jesus' dictum to treat others as you want to be treated. A few years earlier he had published a book titled *Working People and Their Employers* in which he argued that Christian ethics should apply in the factory as well as in the church. How can a man share Holy Communion with someone who pays him slave wages and keeps his children in the slums?

Even more influential than Gladden was a German-American named Walter Rauschenbusch (1861-1918) who was a "born-again" Baptist familiar with German liberalism. He had a conversion experience as a young man and never lost his appreciation for such religious experience, but he pressed Christians to have a second conversion to active participation in the world's problems. It was to be a conversion to the task of making the gospel of Christ real for those who suffered in body as well as soul. Humanity needs to be redeemed, not just from sin and death, but from the dehumanizing and diabolical forces of industrialism and poverty.

In 1886 Rauschenbusch became the pastor of a German Baptist church in an area of New York City known as "Hell's Kitchen." It was a cesspool of crime, violence, and despair. During the eleven years that Rauschenbusch walked the streets of Hell's Kitchen, and witnessed the hopelessness and helplessness of those left behind during the Gay Nineties, he realized that the theological education he had received in seminary had little relevance. A new theology, a new conception of what it meant to be a minister and a follower of Jesus Christ was needed. He found it in the Lord's Prayer: "Your Kingdom Come, Your will be done, on earth." His "Kingdom Theology" was a call to make the cities of America into the Kingdom of God.

He burst on the national scene with his book *Christianity and the Social Crisis* in 1907 in which he outlined the depth of the social problems facing America. Marx and his followers had diagnosed the problem, but for Rauschenbusch, Communism did not hold the solution, Christianity did. In 1912 he wrote *Christianizing the Social Order*, a call for Christian America to rise up and force government and industrialists to look at the poor as brothers and sisters.

Conclusion

Christianity in the nineteenth century experienced its greatest changes since patristic days. It may be argued that even the Reformation had less impact on Christianity than the myriad of social and intellectual movements of the nineteenth century. The church lost most, if not all of its political authority, and even control of education and medical care. The Christian message competed with sophisticated and ancient religions around the world and with new, persuasive secular philosophies and ideologies in Europe. Ancient dogmas confronted new scientific facts and theories, and traditional structures confronted a new emphasis on individualism, autonomy, and self-gratification. Christianity responded to the challenges in many ways: from reasserting ecclesiastical authority and orthodox to creating new theologies, institutions, and even new religions; however, the full effect of anti-Christian ideologies and secularism would not be felt until the next century.

The average observer surveying Christendom in 1900 would have been most impressed with the grand sweep of Christianity. The gospel was being preached over much of the globe. Christians labored to relieve the worst effects of industrialization through charity and legislation. Christian ideals of brotherhood, redemption, and hope seemed to be triumphing as education and technology spread to all races and classes. The new century was welcomed as the harbinger of human progress materially, culturally, and spiritually. Little did Westerners, whether Christian or not, suspect that August 1914 would unleash the greatest period of violence, bloodshed, and barbarity Christendom had ever known.

Part 5

The Twentieth Century

As we have seen, the nineteenth century raised very significant intellectual, social, and political challenges for traditional Christianity. The nineteenth century also saw the greatest numerical and geographical expansion of the Christian religion in its history, and Christian leaders responded creatively to the problems and possibilities of the Victorian era. It appeared to many in the church that the twentieth century would be the dawn of the most glorious era of the Christian age when Christian values would infuse and inform all aspects of world society. As has often been the case in the long history of Christianity, though, such confidence was not justified.

Rather than marking the pinnacle of human social progress and the triumph of Christian values, the twentieth century proved to be the bloodiest period of human history with barbarism and cruelty systematically employed on an unimaginable scale in Armenia, Germany, Russia, Cambodia, Rwanda, Burma, China, Uganda, Yugoslavia, and other troubled corners of the globe. Moreover, the personal and social dislocation of rapidly changing technologies and advances in scientific knowledge continued to undermine traditional attitudes, and leave millions searching for meaning in a mechanized and bureaucratized world. The institutional church was shaken, and in some areas of the world virtually destroyed in the process, but it also rediscovered vital aspects of the Christian message and mission.

Chapter 25

Christianity and Two World Wars

The War to End All Wars

THE LIBERALS' CONFIDENCE in the progress of Western culture under Christian influence shattered during the years 1914-1918. Before World War I, it was generally believed that the entire world was becoming more civilized, and that Europe and America were the vanguard of human progress. People acknowledged that conflicts would still exist, of course, but they would remain minor and lead to even more progress. Woodrow Wilson expressed a commonly held hope when he proclaimed that World War I was to be "the war to end all wars." It was to be the Great War to make the world safe for democracy and Christianity. Ironically, those involved in the massive war, the Germans, French, Americans, Italians, English, and Russians all viewed the war in similar ways. The conflict would insure the continual progress of Western civilization. Church leaders on both sides supported the war effort, and proclaimed that fighting for one's country is a Christian duty.

In America, Roman Catholics saw the war as a great opportunity to prove to a skeptical and anti-Catholic nation that Catholics were also patriots. The National Catholic War Council was so successful that one-fourth of the Army and half of the American Navy was Catholic, even though only twelve percent of the U. S. population was Catholic at the time. Protestants were equally energetic in promoting the war. The Federal Council of Churches, the leading body of liberal ministers, actively and effectively raised money and men for the war effort. The FCC was so successful in its organization that its leaders believed that the success during the war would be easily duplicated in transforming America in the post-war years.

Preachers who had studied in German universities and read German theology now preached that Germans were inhuman barbarians bent on destroying Christianity and civilization. The Young Men's Christian Association, which reached out to youth in the growing cities, distributed handbooks on hand-to-hand combat that assured potential soldiers that Jesus himself would use a bayonet to fight the Germans who were "the most deadly enemy of his Father's kingdom in a thousand years." Both Protestant and Catholic sermons portrayed Jesus as the white horseman of the Apocalypse, but this time he wore olive drab and carried a rifle and bayonet.

America was not alone in making the war a religious crusade. Soldiers on both sides in the Great War were assured that God was on their side alone. Only a few Christians of conscience, such as the Mennonites and William Jennings Bryan (1860-1925), Wilson's Secretary of State, spoke out against the militarism of the war. Most Europeans and Americans gleefully watched young men go off carrying their nation's flag and praying to the Father in heaven for victory.

We cannot go into the details of the actual fighting and history of the war, but we should remember that the young men at the front encountered warfare as it had never been fought before. Machine guns and poisonous gases brought unheard destruction. Death and terror became mechanized and depersonalized. The hero of Remarque's *All Quiet on the Western Front* found that he could kill without thinking until he had to kill a man alone, face-to-face, in a fox-hole. At other times, he had killed like a machine, but when he saw that his enemy was a man like himself, it profoundly disturbed him.

For the most part, the war bogged down into a trench warfare in which neither side could gain a decisive advantage; in which wave after wave of soldiers were thrown against the full force of modern technology. "No Man's Land," the stretch of land between the two entrenched armies in France, was virtually destroyed by the constant bombardment and assault. Years later, No Man's Land could be seen stretching across the body of France like an ugly scar that would not heal. It was not the only wound that did not heal. Over 20 million soldiers died in the conflict, many of them of disease. National leaders seemed oblivious to the death toll, but the soldiers and their families understood. Moreover, millions of civilians died during the war, and in the great influenza epidemic that swept Europe following the years of privation.

After the war, it was revealed that much of the war propaganda had been fabricated and that national competition and industrial profits caused the war, not the clash of great ideals. Many in the younger generation realized that human beings were mere cogs in the machinery of the state and industry that depended on warfare. The churches that had so readily preached the cause of the state were discredited in many people's eyes. The dream of continual progress toward the kingdom of God on earth was an illusion blown apart on the fields of France. How could the most Christian countries of the world kill millions of young men and unleash the technological terrors of modernity on women and children? The words of that great liberal hymn "Joyful, joyful, we adore thee" which proclaims, "ever singing, march we onward, Victors in the midst of strife; joyful music leads us sunward in the triumph song of life" seemed blasphemous in the face of the absolute evil unleashed by the Christian kings and emperors of Europe.

Theology of Crisis

One of the first theologians to offer a compelling alternative to classical liberalism in light of the persistence of human evil was Karl Barth (1886-1968), a Swiss pastor in the Reformed Church. In 1919, Barth shook the theological world with his commentary on Romans (*Der Römerbrief*, significantly revised in 1922) in which he argued stridently for a return to a biblical theology. He rejected the methodology of Schleiermacher who sought to integrate Christian faith and Western culture through a theology of religious experience, and instead built on the theology of Luther and Calvin. His analysis of nineteenth-century theology and philosophy was unsparing in its criticism. Philosophies that elevated human autonomy and theologies that made religious truth dependent on human history and human intellect had led the church astray. Liberal theologians had tried to create God in their own image, a God without condemnation of human hubris, a God inseparable from human culture and nature. This God, for Barth, is nothing other than an idol, a religious plaything created by humans so we would not have to face the truth about our sinful natures and ourselves.

Like Luther, Barth stressed the hiddenness of God. Human reason can never know God, or even prove the existence of God because sin and pride have corrupted reason. Humans by nature do not want to know God and obey God, they want to be God, as the story of Adam and Eve indicates. The only way to know God is through God's own revelation. Barth, more so than any previous theologian, condemned the ancient Christian tradition of natural theology, whether in the form of Roman Catholic/Thomist rationalism or romanticism and experiential theology. He remained adamant that only God can break through the impasse and reveal himself and his will to human beings. God's revelation comes in the person of Jesus Christ and in the word of God in scripture. Barth rejects all religions, including much of Christianity, as myth and idolatry. Only the biblical revelation of Christ reveals the true nature and will of God.

For decades, theology and biblical studies had drifted apart. The former was increasingly tied to philosophy and history while the later focused on questions of origin rather than the meaning of biblical texts. Barth advocated a return to biblical study as the study of the Word of God, much as Calvin had attempted in his *Institutes of the Christian Religion*. Christian theology must deal with the entire Bible, not simply the life of Jesus, and in his study of Paul and the Old Testament prophets, Barth saw his own suspicions of human idolatry confirmed. God speaks "No" as well as "Yes" to creatures. God speaks in judgment against efforts to force God to work according to human desires, and at the same time God calls humans to renewed, life-giving obedience. All Christian theology is to be based on the biblical witness, and Barth sought to realize this goal in the many volumes of his monumental *Church Dogmatics*, which appeared from 1932 to 1967. Due in part to the impressive scholarship and the prophetic vigor of the *Church Dogmatics*, Barth's theology dominated Christian thought, especially Protestant thought, in the middle decades of the century.

Barth's insistence on the Bible as the only source of Christian theology should not lead one to assume that he was a fundamentalist. He was a great student of modern philosophy, particularly Kierkegaard whose appreciation for existential paradox inspired Barth's own understanding of dialectic. Moreover, Barth did not reject the discoveries of modern science or biblical scholarship. For him, revelation does not depend on an idea of biblical verbal inerrancy, but on the unique witness of Jesus Christ and the inner truth that runs throughout scripture. Scientific discoveries can add nothing to nor detract from the message of judgment and redemption found in the word of God. A transcendent deity is not subject to scientific inquiry or political propaganda.

Fascism and Nazism

Karl Barth's insistence that Christianity must resist all attempts at deifying the nation or culture provided the foundation for his resistance to the Nazi Party in Germany. The horrifying story of the Third Reich and the evil it unleashed on the peoples of Europe cannot be given justice in these few pages, but a few words are needed. Fascism in Italy and Nazism in Germany both arose during the economic crises of the 1920s and 1930s following the humiliation of Germany and Italy in the First World War.

Benito Mussolini (1883-1945) built Fascism in Italy. Fascism combines state totalitarianism with fervent nationalism and capitalist economics. Unlike Communism, Fascism did not abolish individual property or proclaim a worker's utopia, but it did proclaim the importance of the nation over the rights of the individual. Fascism attempts to maintain law and order by any means necessary, and to channel all of the nation's resources toward a common purpose. Through effective use of paramilitary militias and mob violence, Mussolini took a leading role in the Italian government in 1922. Promising to restore the former glories of the Roman Empire with its militaristic ethic, Mussolini proclaimed himself dictator in 1928.

The following year Pope Pius XI signed an agreement with Mussolini that protected the Catholic Church in Italy and allowed devout Catholics to participate actively in the political life of the nation. The papacy viewed the Fascists as an effective bulwark against Communism and secular liberalism. The concordat gave sovereignty to the Vatican City and provided state money for clergy salaries. In Spain, the Catholic hierarchy also supported the Fascist forces during the bloody Spanish Civil War (1936-1939). The Republicans in Spain were decidedly anti-clerical, and burned a number of churches during the war. When General Francisco Franco (1892-1975) won the war and proclaimed himself dictator, he sought to make Spain solidly Catholic. Not only did he directly support the church and its hierarchy, he censored Protestant publications and closed Protestant churches. While the Catholic Church's collaboration with the Fascists in Italy and Spain insured the institutional survival of the church, it weakened its moral authority in the rest of the Western world.

The situation for the church in Germany was tragic. Scholars continue to debate why the Nazis were able to come to power and carry out the monstrous atrocities of the holocaust and the pacification of Eastern Europe, but it seems clear that nothing would have happened without Adolph Hitler. It is also clear, though, that Hitler could not have carried out his systematic destruction of German Jews without the willing participation of large numbers of ordinary people in Germany, Austria, Poland, Hungary, France, and other occupied nations.

By contrast, in Denmark where people banded together to resist the anti-Jewish laws, most of the Jews survived. Thousands were smuggled to Norway and Sweden. Thousands more were hidden. During the occupation of Denmark the neighbors of Jews who had fled kept their property in order and willingly returned it to those who returned from exile. The entire police force of one Danish town went to a concentration camp for refusing to enforce anti-Jewish laws. However, in other areas of Nazi control diligent officials often exceeded their orders when rounding up Jews and other "undesirables."

Nazism is similar to Fascism, and Hitler was an ally of Mussolini and Franco; however, his program differed in significant ways. The Nazi ideology was based in part on a distorted understanding of the nineteenth century philosopher Friedrich Nietzsche (1844-1900) who argued that religion, particularly Judaism and Christianity, was the enemy of the human race. Christianity, accordingly to Nietzsche, promotes a slave mentality and makes a virtue of weakness. Religion teaches you to turn the other cheek, to love your enemy, to be humble and meek. Thus religion keeps people from exerting their will to power. Intellectuals and especially artists should instead proclaim the will to power, the will to create and assert one's creative self in the world, as the highest goal of human existence rather than worry about ethics and morality. The truly free person, the most human person, lives beyond the social constraints of good and evil. Such a person creates like a god.

The Nazis used Nietzsche to legitimate their complete disregard of human rights and ethics. Moreover, after his death, Nietzsche's philosophy had become attached to racist ideology. Hitler and his comrades exalted white Europeans, especially Germans, as the master race, and blamed all of Germany's social and economic problems on the Jews and other races who weakened the German will. Inferior races that threatened to undermine Germany must be removed, controlled, and enslaved. After Hitler became chancellor of Germany in 1933, he began passing increasingly repressive laws against Jews, Gypsies, and Slavs. Five years later, he instituted a euthanasia program that used lethal injections to rid the nation of the mentally ill and retarded as well as the infirm. Around the same time, his aides created a series of concentration and work camps where they tortured and killed millions. Historians estimate that the Nazis killed more than ten million citizens of the Third Reich, some six million of whom were Jews.

Nazism was not anti-religious in the way Stalinism was in Russia, but neither was it Christian. Nazi propaganda looked to the pre-Christian history of Europe, to the old Germanic myths, to give life to their theories. The German race, history, and language were deified. Nazism was nationalism on a scale never before encountered. The Nazis claimed German blood contained quality that tied the German nation to the great barbarian chieftains, to the great medieval emperors, to the gods of yore. Hitler used mythology, including a pre-Christian religious symbol, the swastika, and rituals, such as carefully organized rallies and parades, to tap into the religious needs of the people, and join them together socially and politically. Hitler created a religion for his state with him as the savior and ruler, *der Führer*, who was representative of the gods of long ago. The operas of Wagner, which glorified Germanic mythology, inspired Hitler's demonic dream. The German nation was the true chosen people, and his Reich would be the millennial kingdom, the Thousand Year Reich, that would establish glory and order for its people. War and struggle were the path for this millennial goal, which would be achieved through force not prayer. Nothing was permitted to oppose the Reich.

How did Christians respond to Nazism? Early in his reign as chancellor, Hitler neutralized Catholic opposition through a special concordat with the papacy. Raised in Catholic Austria, Hitler promised that he would protect Catholic interests throughout the Reich. Catholic parochial schools would be expanded, and Catholic organizations would have protection as long as they remained politically uninvolved. Clergy were exempted from the military draft and the church agreed to include prayers for the German people in the liturgy. As soon as Hitler had secured his power, though, he simply ignored the concordat and proceeded to move against opposition to his policies within the Catholic Church, and introduced Nazi propaganda into Catholic schools. Even so, the papacy was too paralyzed by its fear of Communism and its policy of appeasement to stand effectively against Hitler. A number of priests, monks, and nuns, such as Edith Stein (1891-1943), died in the camps for their efforts on behalf of Jews in occupied lands, but the church hierarchy remained largely silent.

Hitler had even less respect for the Protestant Church than he did for the Catholic Church, but he encouraged the German-Christian movement within the Lutheran Church. Essentially, the German-Christian movement brought Nazi racist ideology into Christian theology, drawing heavily on the long history of Christian anti-Semitism. Some theologians even went so far as to "prove" that Jesus himself was not a Jew. He was an Aryan, and thus Christianity must be "cleansed" of its Jewish corruption. When Hitler swept into political power, the German-Christian took over many of the regional churches. Even Protestants who did not accept the radical anti-Semitism of Hitler and the German-Christians found much in Hitler's program that agreed with the dominant theology of "culture-Protestantism" and the dream of creating the millennial kingdom through religious education. Moreover, the German church was so used to supporting the state that many did not publicly oppose the new *Führer*.

Some church leaders and theologians perceived the great threat that Nazism posed for Christianity and the world. One of these was Karl Barth who saw that biblical faith, the faith revealed in Jesus Christ, is fundamentally and irreconcilably opposed to totalitarian ideologies in general and Nazism in particular. In 1934, Barth and a number of German pastors broke away from the state church, which German-Christians under Ludwig Müller controlled, and formed the Confessing Church, an informal confederation of anti-Nazi congregations. The Barmen Declaration of May 1934 expressed the Confessing Church's conviction that the church was bound to the revelation of God in Jesus Christ, not to any revelation in history or culture or nature or the state. The declaration clearly separated Christianity from the mythology of the Nazis and all other attempts to deify the nation or the state. Barth was exiled for his efforts, but as war approached, Hitler allowed some toleration of the Confessing Church as long as its pastors remained politically inactive.

The most famous pastor of the Confessing Church was the theologian Dietrich Bonhoeffer (1906-1945). Bonhoeffer signed the Barmen Declaration and taught in the Confessing Church's theological seminary at Finkenwalde until the Nazi government removed him from his position and banned him from Berlin in 1936. In 1939, he was safely teaching at Union Theological Seminary in New York City, but when the Second World War broke out he felt that as a pastor he had a duty to return to Germany. He believed that Christ would be in Germany, and he must follow Christ. During the war, Bonhoeffer had a role in the resistance movement against Hitler, and even participated in the plot to assassinate Hitler in 1943. He was arrested and sent Buchenwald where he continued his writing and his pastoral work among Christian and Jewish prisoners. He was hanged at Flossenburg less than a month before the Allies liberated his prison camp.

Few people have grasped the dilemma of modern humanity more clearly than Bonhoeffer. In his theological works, Bonhoeffer addressed the issue of "God of the gaps." For centuries people have used God to fill in gaps in knowledge or strength. As science and technology have advanced, the role of God in the world diminished. Each generation points to a mystery in the natural world and says it is the work of God. At one time it was the force of gravity, at another the bonding of atoms. Wherever uncertainty or ambiguity arises, God has been pressed into service. Some apologists have seemed pleased at gaps in human knowledge because they allow them to insert the "God hypothesis."

Moreover, in personal life, modern people push God away from the centers of existence (the world of commerce, love, and intellect), and encounter God only on the fringes, in dark areas of the soul, particularly in the fear of death. As the ability of humanity to remove sources of anxiety increases, so does the need for a god decrease. In this sense, the world is coming of age. Unlike the typical theologian or apologist, however, Bonhoeffer embraced the coming of age for the world. It is wrong to resist the maturing of the human race as autonomous, rational beings, but it is also wrong to reduce God to the role of mortar filling in the gaps of the human edifice. Using God to fill in the gaps places God at the periphery of life, and at the same time keeps humans immature. Bonhoeffer contrasted the religious person and the mature person. The former is basically immature and unwilling to accept responsibility for the world. "God" becomes a solution to his or her problems without any concern for moral or intellectual integrity. The mature person, on the other hand, is freed from childish anxieties and is autonomous. He or she is then able to truly reach out in moral responsibility for others. As the years advanced, Bonhoeffer found that "a Christian instinct frequently draws me more to the religionless than to the religious, by which I mean not with any intention of evangelizing them, but rather, I might almost say, in 'brotherhood.'"

More radically than Barth, Bonhoeffer rejects religion without rejecting God, and he denied that true Christianity is religious. Although it may have been corrupted and turned into a religion, the faith of Jesus and the Bible is not religious. He personally participated in the rituals of Christianity, including the daily reading of scripture, but he saw it as the discipline of the Christian community, not part of a religion. Part of his theological task, as he saw it, was to restore a religionless Christianity to the Western world. This would create a mature faith that would be lived in the midst of secular life. It is a faith that is at the center, not the boundaries, of life.

Bonhoeffer believed firmly that his own actions were a consequence of his faith in the God of Jesus, and that his faith gave him strength to resist evil in Germany. Faith assists strength; it does not prey on vulnerabilities. Jesus does not offer a magical release from the difficulties of life, he shares them, and in sharing he prepares the faithful person for a transformation to maturity. Jesus is transcendent because he was and remains the "man for others." It is responsible faith and participation with Christ in the world that gives freedom and joy to life. The Christian, the disciple of Christ, must take moral responsibility for his or her actions while demonstrating compassion and full solidarity with all of the oppressed of the world. The cost of discipleship is intense because "when Jesus calls a man, he bids him to come and die." Those who hide in sanctuaries praying for their own salvation, or those who separate their religious life from their secular life turn their backs on Christ and on faith, according to this theologian and martyr.

Communism

Another great totalitarian force emerged after the First World War when the 1917 Russian Revolution created the first communist nation in history. It was a government based in part on the political and economic theories of Karl Marx, but the Soviet Union was unquestionably the creation of Vladimir Illych Lenin (1870-1924) and Josef Stalin (1879-1953). For many people in Europe, the war and subsequent depression made clear what some intellectuals had been claiming since the middle of the nineteenth century; namely that struggle and conflict govern history, not God's providence and beneficence. All war is economically motivated, according to Marx. The followers of Marx, especially the Bolsheviks in Russia, pointed to World War I as proof that industrialists were willing to sacrifice human beings on the altar of wealth. Moreover, by actively recruiting soldiers for the war, the church had proven that it was merely an arm of the ruling elite. "God" is an illusion that keeps people enslaved to the masters who willfully send them off to die in their wars.

Communism is an ideology of great power and persuasion, even among those who rejected the practices of Lenin and Stalin. Communism offered an explanation of both the natural and the political world, and it also offered a secular view of salvation in its dream of the worker's state. Moreover, it gave an official cult based on a dominant ruler such as Stalin. The revolutionary leaders in Russia and China were presented as infallible savior figures—messiahs ruling for the benefit of all. In short, Communism became a new type of godless religion in the twentieth century, particularly in Asia where heresy against communist ideology was persecuted with a severity that Torquemada would have appreciated.

Lenin was the leading spokesman for the Communist cause in Imperial Russia. Unlike Marx, Lenin believed that the people should revolt and set up the worker's state even before the nation became fully industrialized. Lenin had been exiled from Russia because of his revolutionary views, but during the war the German government secretly smuggled him back into Russia in order to undermine the Russian war effort. He was successful beyond their worst nightmares, leading a revolution in 1917 and creating the militant

Soviet Union. As soon as Lenin was in power, he recalled Russian troops from fighting Germans and set up a totalitarian state where religion itself was abolished.

Religion was rejected as anti-revolutionary and dangerous because it would keep society from progressing materially and intellectually. Traditional religious institutions and theologies must be swept away or at least repressed. Particularly under the ruthless Josef Stalin, the state tried to control all aspects of life from employment to education to publication of ideas. It was a state built on a materialist ideology that could tolerate no other view of reality.

The Soviets moved quickly against the Russian Orthodox Church in 1918. Most church lands became the property of the state, but the state refused to pay the salaries of the clergy. Education was taken out of the church's hands, and the state legally recognized only civil marriages. Many church leaders responded by supporting the anti-revolutionaries and tsarists. Thousands of priests and monks perished in the civil war and subsequent repression. In 1929, Stalin instituted harsher measures against religion. The state strictly controlled the publication of religious books, including the Bible.

Confirmed Christians could not teach in schools or join the Communist party. The erection of new church buildings was forbidden and many former church buildings were desecrated or used to promote anti-Christian propaganda. For slightly more than a decade, the week officially contained only six days because the Christian Sabbath had been simply removed. It should be noted that the Stalinist campaign against religion was directed against Jews and Muslims as well, particularly in the southern Soviet republics. As many as ninety percent of the churches, mosques, and synagogues that had been in existence in 1917 had been forcibly closed, converted, or destroyed by 1940.

Following the victory of the Allies in 1945, the Soviet Union exerted hegemony over Eastern Europe, including East Germany. In a few years, all of the countries of Eastern Europe had communist governments in alliance with the Soviet Union. Each country was technically independent, but attempts by the Hungarians in 1956 and the Czechs in 1968 to moderate their authoritarian governments and distance themselves from the Soviet Union led to brutal repression. The southern nations (Bulgaria, Yugoslavia, and Romania) had large Orthodox populations, and the Orthodox Church functioned under Soviet rule much as it had under Ottoman rule. It adapted as much as possible to restrictive measures and maintained the traditional liturgy of the church.

Hungary had originally granted recognition to the Catholic Church through an agreement with the Vatican, but in 1949 the primate of the church of Hungary was sentenced to life imprisonment on the charge of treason. The following year, fifty-nine religious orders were made illegal. The state confiscated their property, and more than 10,000 nuns and monks were left homeless. The state also took over most of the church schools.

The repression was less severe in Czechoslovakia where the communists simply made the Catholic clergy state employees at minimal wages. By this time, church adherence was already minimal in Czechoslovakia. In contrast, Poland was heavily Roman Catholic and the church in Poland effectively resisted the government's efforts to eradicate religion. The Catholic Church became a focal point for Polish nationalism and anti-communism.

In communist China, the persecution of Christianity was the most severe and most effective. Before World War II, Christianity grew rapidly in China. There were some two million Chinese Christians in 1914, and one of the most revered leaders of the age, the first president of the Chinese Republic, Sun Yat-sen (1866-1925) was a Protestant educated in Christian schools in China and Hawaii. In 1926, the pope consecrated the first Chinese bishops of the Roman Catholic Church, and twenty years later China had its own hierarchy and cardinal. By the time of the brutal Japanese occupation of China in the 1930s there were approximately three million Catholics and over half-a-million Protestants in China. However, Chinese nationalists contin-ued to view Christianity as a Western incursion into China, and the growing communist movement shared the anti-religious attitudes of Stalin.

Mao Zedong (1893-1976), the son of a Confucian father and Buddhist mother, successfully took control of the nation during a civil war following the defeat of Japan. Mao combined Chinese nationalism with communist theory, and over time he established nearly complete control over the vast and diverse nation. He expelled or imprisoned foreign missionaries, and he forced the churches to cooperate with communist officials or be closed down. Con-vinced that the Party's leaders were losing touch with communist ideals, Mao reached out to the Chinese youth to revitalize communism in a program called the Cultural Revolution. The revolution peaked in the 1960s and left millions dead or in prison, and the Chinese economy in shambles. Christ-ianity was nearly eradicated yet again in China.

Christian Realism

Lenin and Mao adapted Marxist theory to create communist empires in Asia, but Marxist ideas also inspired one of the most creative and effective approaches to Christian ethics in the West in the first half of the twentieth century. Like Karl Barth in Europe, an American pastor in the 1920s and 1930s also attacked the groundless optimism of liberalism in light of the war and subsequent depression. Unlike Barth, Reinhold Niebuhr (1892-1971) was primarily an ethicist rather than a biblical scholar. He had been educated in the liberal theology of Adolph von Harnack, but as pastor of the Bethel Evangelical church in Detroit from 1915 to 1928 he witnessed first hand both disillusionment of the war and the disturbing social realities of industrial capitalism. Throughout his career he retained the Social Gospel's insistence that Christianity is essentially social in nature rather than a matter of personal morality; however, he rejected the naive optimism of the first generation of Social Gospelers like Rauschenbush. The response of the churches to World War I and their support of Henry Ford's industrial methods demonstrated that there was truth in Marx's claim that religion gives an aura of sanctity to institutions of oppression, and encourages the victims of injustice to accept the status quo without complaint.

Niebuhr drew on the thought of Barth and other "theologians of crisis" in formulating a new perspective on church and society. Marx was right about how religion is co-opted by political and economic powers, but Barth described such religion as idolatry not Christianity. Christianity in its essence is prophetic and critical of unjust institutions, both social and ecclesiastical. "Prophetic religion" rejects the platitudes and sentimentality that characterized late Victorian Christianity, and insists on a disillusioning assessment of the human condition. Niebuhr encouraged pastors to use secular sources, Marx in sociology and Freud in psychology, to explore the reality of human evil and self-deception. They reveal what prophetic religion has taught for three thousand years; namely the reality of human depravity. In this respect, Niebuhr reaffirmed the ancient doctrine of original sin as a social rather than a personal doctrine.

Perhaps his most important contribution to human understanding is his book *Moral Man and Immoral Society* in which he shows that even apparently moral individuals willingly participate in the immoral actions of society. His analysis of the immorality of American society, particularly in regards to race and class, allowed him to see that institutions themselves tend toward evil even when populated by "decent" people. Niebuhr thus anticipated the shocking realization that many honest, family-oriented, and patriotic Germans obeyed orders to ruthlessly exterminate the Jewish race in Germany.

Prophetic religion also offers a vision of what human society should be, not a utopian dream or sentimental ideal, but the real goal of human endeavor. All social and ecclesiastical structures must be criticized for failing to move toward that goal. For Niebuhr, true Christianity insists on the rights of every human being to life and dignity, even at the cost of economic productivity. Niebuhr had no illusions that Christianity would be the dominant force in modern society. He even expressed doubts whether genuine and prophetic Christianity dedicated to the execution of divine justice would even be a dominate force in the church, but he did believe that the prophetic witness could act as a catalyst for change. He called his approach "Christian Realism" because it combined the ethical goals of Jesus with an honest assessment of contemporary reality. It is not sufficient to use moral persuasion to transform society; Christians must actively participate in the rough and tumble world of politics and protest. Under his influence, the Federal Council of Churches reorganized in the 1940s as the National Council of Churches, and became heavily involved in the Civil Rights movement of the 1950s and 1960s. Despite his use of socialist criticism in his theology, Niebuhr was a vocal opponent of Soviet-style Marxism.

Within the Catholic Church, devout priests and lay persons also combined Marxism with the social implications of the New Testament. In France, which had a secular government after 1905, many priests reached out to the pro-Communist working class by working alongside them in factories. However, when a number of the "worker priests" became leaders in the labor movement in the 1950s, Pope Puis XII reassigned them. In America, Dorothy Day (1897-1980), a socialist writer who converted to Catholicism in 1927, founded the Catholic Worker newspaper. It focused on America's social problems during the Great Depression. She continued her work after the Second World War seeing to the needs of the homeless and hungry in New York.

Chapter 26

Modernism, Ecumenism, and Fundamentalism

IT IS GENERALLY acknowledged that the modern world is characterized by rapid change and social dislocation. Modern art visualized the disruption of modern life with paintings and sculptures that are intentionally disorienting. Pablo Picasso was famous for his portraits where the facial features are in disarray while Paul Klee reduced the world to geometric forms. Modern music rejected harmony and rhythm while experimenting with bizarre combinations of tones. Technology contributed to the modern sense of insecurity. A 100 year-old person in 1990 would have seen the rapid demise of the horse as a primary means of transportation, the electrification of homes accompanied by television and refrigeration; the creation of the sky scraper; the development of the airplane from a simple glider to a supersonic jet; the conquest of space; the creation of the personal computer, and massive social movements including the gradual liberation of women. Technological changes helped change social mores and morality as birth control made pre-marital sex less dangerous and the automobile made dating more private. Absolute truths fell to scientific advances and the increasing awareness of other cultures past and present.

Within Protestantism, there have been two major responses to the shifting sands of modern culture: modernism and fundamentalism. Both represent the extreme poles, however. Most Christians tend to be in the middle, leaning toward one pole or the other with some oscillation. The modernist response has been to embrace the ambiguities and relativity of modern culture and seek to respond to its currents. The fundamentalist response has been to declare war on social change and enforce an earlier view of morality as an absolute truth. One of the ironies of history is that fundamentalism, though claiming to protect traditional Christianity, is a thoroughly modern movement inconceivable before the invention of the printing press and mass media.

Modern Theologies

In the United States, the dean of the divinity school of the University of Chicago, Shailer Matthews (1863-1941) pushed for a new theology in his 1924 book, *The Faith of Modernism*. Matthews criticized Christians who hung on to obsolete doctrines and indefensible views of the Bible: "The world needs new control of nature and society and is told that the Bible is verbally inerrant. It needs a means of composing class strife, and is told to believe in the substitutionary atonement...It needs faith in the divine presence in human affairs and is told it must accept the virgin birth of Jesus Christ."[32] For Matthews and his supporters, America and Christianity remained the last best hope for the world, but only if the church embraced modern scholarship and science.

The premier theologian of modernism was the biblical scholar Rudolf Bultmann (1884-1976). From 1921-1951 Bultmann was professor of New Testament studies at Marburg, and in that position he wrote some of the most controversial and influential biblical commentaries of the twentieth century. Fundamental to Bultmann's thought is the realization that the world-view of the Bible is fundamentally at odds with the modern scientific perspective. The Bible presupposes a three-storied universe: Heaven, Earth, and Hell. Demons possessed persons and caused illness, but prayers and divine agents could bring healing or prevent natural disasters. Bultmann, like many scholars of antiquity and religion, calls this pre-scientific perspective a mythological view of the world. Where no natural cause could be found, mythology projected supra-human agents to effect a cause. Thus a devastating tornado or volcanic eruption must be a sign of divine wrath on individuals. Such a view of nature is fundamentally opposed to the scientific world view that sees the universe as a coherent whole operating by knowable and consistent laws of cause and effect.

Bultmann argued that modern people must reject mythology at all levels. He claimed it is simply wrong and destructive to live in the scientific world during the day, but retreat to a mythological world in one's religious activities. Believers in the enchanted world of the Bible are self-deceptive,

---

32 Shailer Matthews, *The Faith of Modernism* (New York: MacMillan, 1924) 10, 83.

since they enjoy all the benefits of the modern scientific, objectified world; use technology based on science, not on prayer; depend on weather reports based on meteorological observations; use telephones and televisions to communicate, not prayer; and when sick they visit a doctor, not an exorcist. However, when Bultmann urges people to give up mythology, he does not see this as abandoning religion. The mythological perspective itself is a barrier to true faith. For Bultmann, the message Bible must be "demythologized' not only to make it acceptable to modern people but also to allow it to become an authentic expression of faith. Mythology is not merely opposed to science, it is opposed to God.

In proposing that the meaning of the Bible can be found by demythologizing, Bultmann points to New Testament itself. Originally, Jesus' proclamation (*Kerygma*) of the Kingdom of God was connected to a mythological belief in the imminent destruction of the world. The expected end did not come, and yet the proclamation continued to have an impact. The announcement that the Kingdom of God is among you is a call to a radical change of life and attitude, a call to authentic living in the face of existential anxiety. In a real sense, we all live in the shadow of the eschaton since we all live in the shadow of death. Thus, although the world-view of the Bible is completely unacceptable to modern persons, mortals will continue to be challenged by the call to faith in Christ the crucified.

Bultmann, like Barth—with whom he bickered for years—was influenced by the existentialist philosophers Kierkegaard and Heideggar. He used the German word *Angst* to describe the real-life condition of human beings. Angst can be translated by fear, anxiety, or dread, but it is a non-specific dread that lies in the very nature of existence itself. One of the primary causes for angst is our historicity. Every day is filled with a multitude of independent decisions, each of which affects a person profoundly. It is the awareness of the responsibility of human choice that causes existential anxiety. People make millions of choices, any one of which could be absolutely crucial for their futures or their selves, but at the time of decision it is not clear which choice is going to be significant. Furthermore, every decision is limited by prior decisions, many of which were made by strangers. Language, culture, education, income, physical qualities all limit our range of choices. Herein lies the angst, the tension between what one chooses and the limits placed upon that choice. Ultimately, no matter what choices humans make, each person will die one day.

According to Bultmann, and other existentialists, this drives all people to try to overcome angst in a number of inauthentic ways that minimize the number of significant decisions we have to make. Humans give authority for their lives over to the government, to business, or to the church. People use technology to hold back nature and try to create predictability and conformity at all levels, participating in their own dehumanization. The *Kerygma* of Jesus can free individuals to lives of courage and true humanity. Biblical faith is not about avoiding existential angst, but confronting it. Biblical faith removes all grounds for self-sufficiency that would avoid angst. Faith stands in contrast to security. Security says to stay here and not risk. Faith says, "Go from your country and your kindred and your father's house to the land that I will show you." (Gen. 12:1) In the New Testament, Jesus and Paul abolish all false hope in the security of the law and pseudo-religion. However, the Bible does not cast humans adrift on the sea of existence without hope or strength. Faith is the moment of decision for or against self-understanding, for or against embracing an ambiguous future. The message of Christianity is in truth an existential, not a mythological, *Kerygma* in the sense that it reveals the angst of life and calls the hearer to embrace life and step into an uncertain future. The new life in Christ, the true resurrection, is when an individual embraces the insecurity of life and chooses to live in the uncertain world as an active and authentic being.

Among the theologians of the twentieth century, two had a significant impact on the intellectual world outside of the church. One was Reinhold Niebuhr. The other was Paul Tillich (1886-1965) whose sermons, such as the famous "Courage to Be," inspired even atheists with courage and hope in the possibility of a better world. Tillich's strengths lay both in his great command of the history of philosophy and in his engagement with virtually all of the intellectual currents of the twentieth century. Tillich was a product of the best German universities and well-versed in nineteenth-century theology and philosophy. He was frequently at odds with Karl Barth who accused him of being a pantheist. Tillich preferred the term "panentheist" meaning that God is in all things without being simply identified with all things.

Like Bultmann, Tillich was influenced by existentialism and he grounded Christian theology in the decision of faith, which he defined as "ultimate concern." Faith is that which gives each individual's life meaning, purpose, and integration. As such, almost anything can be the object of faith, and Tillich was able to describe ideological movements, such as Nazism, as religious movements. People had indeed placed their ultimate concern in the Nazi or Communist states. In America, he realized, many people likewise placed their ultimate concern in the capitalist/consumerist culture. Wherever the object of one's' ultimate concern is not truly ultimate, however, it becomes demonic and destructive to human life. The world-wide devastation of the Second World War was the result of a demonic faith.

In contrast to Barth and Bonhoeffer, Tillich freely accepted Christianity as a religion that must be expressed in coherent and historically conditioned symbols. A symbol for Tillich is a sign that participates in that to which it points. Symbols give meaning to human existence and are essential to human life unless they replace that which they symbolize. For instance, the Bible is one of the central Christian symbols, but the Bible points to God. If it becomes the object of ultimate concern itself, then it ceases to serve as a symbol and becomes an idol. Tillich was sympathetic to Bonhoeffer's call for a Christianity divorced from an inauthentic religiosity, but rejected the idea that Christianity could ever exist without religious and cultural symbols. The key to maintaining the authenticity of Christianity was not to absolutize what was relative. Tillich's positive, yet critical, appraisal of the relativity of symbolic forms allowed him to take a more positive perspective toward other religions than most Christian theologians. Without rejecting the truth of Christianity, Tillich took seriously the truth claims and symbols of other religions as conveyors of revelation. If God is indeed the creator, or in Tillich's phrase, "the ground of Being itself," then it is safe to assume that all people would have some access to God through symbolic forms. For Tillich, there should be a way for people of faith to learn from all religions by using diverse symbols rather than fighting over them. Absolutizing symbols leads to intolerance and repression, but focusing on the meaning to which symbols point leads to better understanding, and, perhaps, reconciliation.

The Ecumenical Movement

Liberal Protestantism and the evangelical mission to redeem the world together spawned an international effort to restore the unity of Christianity. Known as the Ecumenical Movement, this was an ambitious effort to bring together Christians of many different denominations into cooperative projects and even create union churches. The Ecumenical Movement has its roots in nineteenth century revivalism and the holiness movement which had encouraged ministers to focus on the salvation of souls without worrying about divisive theological points. The social crusades in the nineteenth century, especially the Temperance Movement, encouraged Christians of different churches to join spiritual forces to battle a common enemy. Non-sectarian or inter-church agencies, such as the YMCA, were active in Europe and America, and it was only a matter of time before clergy and laity began to make serious strides toward ending fundamental divisions.

Prompted in part by the economic success of corporations around the turn of the century, Josiah Strong (1847-1916), organized the Evangelical Alliance in the 1880s and 1890s to bring together the resources of various Protestant bodies. In 1885 he published a clarion call for Protestant union in America, *Our Country: Its Possible Future and Its Present Crisis,* in which he tried to frighten readers with the possibility of a Catholic overthrow of America followed by complete moral disintegration. For Strong, only a cooperative effort of the Anglo-Saxon Protestant churches could save America from the corrosive influx of Catholic immigrants. He worked tirelessly to bring that union into existence, laying the groundwork for the Federal Council of Churches, founded in 1908. In 1950, the Federal Council was transformed into the National Council of Churches of Christ, a much larger agency representing not only traditional Protestant denominations, but also some Eastern Orthodox churches in America. Strongly influenced by the theology of Reinhold Niebuhr, the National Council played a role in the Civil Rights movement and in the campaign to use public policy to eradicate poverty in the 1960s.

The National Council also sponsored the most thorough retranslation of the Bible in English since the King James Bible in the sixteenth century. The Revised Standard Version tried to stay in the tradition of the King James and American Standard Versions, but it made use of the best available manuscripts and biblical scholarship to produce the most accurate translation of the Old and New Testaments in English up to that time. However, many people were shocked at some of the translation choices and perceived a commitment to liberalism on the part of the translators. The 1950s and 60s witnessed a battle of the Bibles as conservative agencies, such as the Gideons International, aggressively promoted the King James Bible as the only legitimate Bible. More than one copy of the RSV was publicly burned by angry preachers. Eventually a team of theologically conservative scholars produced the very accurate and highly readable New International Version in the 1970s that has virtually replaced the KJV in evangelical churches. Conservative Protestant churches, primarily evangelical and holiness, formed a separate federation of churches, the National Evangelical Association, in 1943. The NEA has actively promoted Christian radio and television ministries and helped organize large evangelical crusades.

The ecumenical movement was an international effort throughout the twentieth century. John R. Mott, the founder of the Student Volunteer

Movement, was a tireless campaigner for Christian union as well as the evangelization of the world. When he received the Nobel Peace Prize immediately after World War II, he summed up his career "as an earnest and undiscourageable effort to weave together all nations, all races, and all religious communications in friendliness, in fellowship, and in cooperation."[33] Unlike most of his contemporaries, Mott believed that ecumenism should fully include the Roman Catholic and Eastern Orthodox churches. In fact, he offered his assistance to the beleaguered Coptic and Nestorian churches in the Middle East without concern for ancient divisions. Mott was convinced that divisions in Christianity were seriously hampering the mission of evangelizing the world. How could Africans or Asians decide for Christ if they were hearing conflicting views of the gospel from Anglican, Baptist, or Methodist missionaries? Why should churches waste limited resources in competition instead of joining those resources for the common cause of spreading the gospel and alleviating the suffering of millions?

Mott's prodding led directly to the 1910 World Missionary Conference in Edinburgh that marks the genesis of the World Council of Churches. Four years in the planning, the Edinburgh conference brought together more than a thousand delegates from 160 of the major Protestant churches to discuss how to unite their efforts. One concrete result of the conference was the formation of the International Missionary Council which joined the World Council of Churches in 1961.

The success of the Edinburgh Conference encouraged the establishment of the Universal Christian Conference on Life and Work in 1925 and the World Conference on Faith and Order at Lausanne in 1927. The former, like the Federal Council of Churches, focused primarily on how to mobilize cooperative Christian action to improve social and economic conditions. The latter addressed the sensitive issue of building a theological consensus for further Christian ecclesiastical reconciliation. Although these movements were dominated by liberal Protestantism, they were actively encouraged by the Ecumenical Patriarch of Constantinople who wrote an encyclical calling for "all churches of Christ" to work towards better cooperation. This gave permission for the various Orthodox bodies to participate in the discussions of the councils, despite misgivings about appearing to compromise the traditional faith.

Following World War II, the Life and Work and Faith and Order conferences united to form the World Council of Churches in 1948. Churches

---

33 Marty, *Pilgrims in Their Own Land*, 342.

from former mission fields in Asia and African became active participants in the work of the Council, and in 1961, the World Missionary Conference merged with the Council. Also in that year the Vatican began sending official representatives of the Roman Catholic Church to participate fully in the Council's discussions. At its inauguration, the World Council represented 144 churches; forty years later the number had doubled. Seven years later, the Catholic Church joined the Faith and Order Commission and has contributed greatly to the development of ecumenical theology. One of the major achievements of the Faith and Order Commission was the production of the Lima Document, *Baptism, Eucharist, and Ministry* in 1983. This represented the fruit of half-a-century of serious doctrinal discussion on three areas that have divided Christians for centuries. While some areas were noted as still disputed (such as infant baptism) the document demonstrated a wide area of theological convergence acceptable to most branches of Christianity.

The ecumenical movement also contributed to a number of church unions during its heyday in the second half of the twentieth century. In Canada, Methodists and Presbyterians joined to create the United Church of Canada in 1924, and in India, the Church of South India was created through a union of Anglicans, Presbyterian, Congregationalist, and Methodists. Even more diverse traditions were united in the Church of North India which included the Church of the Brethren and the Baptists. In the United States, various Methodist churches formed the United Methodist Church in 1968 after a number of preliminary mergers. In 1957 four Reformed churches created the United Church of Christ, and in 1983 the Presbyterians healed old divisions. Various Lutheran bodies formed the Evangelical Lutheran Church in America in 1988. Each of these union efforts also created opposition that led to the formation of new denominations, such as the Presbyterian Church in America.

One of the most ambitious ecumenical undertaking has been the Consultation on Church Union (COCU) which has brought together Metho-dists, Episcopalians, Presbyterians, and Disciples of Christ in productive conversations. Several denominations have also conducted bilateral ecumenical dialogues that in the 1990s led to a number of agreements to enter into "full communion" with one another although not merger.

Fundamentalism

A major force in Protestantism in the twentieth century, Fundamentalism was another interdenominational movement with a different perspective than the ecumenical movement. While evangelicals in general would have agreed with Bultmann that Christianity is a matter of personal decision, they strongly disagreed about the nature of that decision. For evangelicals, every individual must decide to accept Jesus as "personal Lord and Savior" in order to go to heaven after dying. Included in this acceptance of Jesus must be an affirmation of his divinity and the reality of both heaven and hell, propositions under attack in modern theology. Moreover, evangelicals responded in different ways to modern culture. Some embraced new technologies and social changes as a way to bring the gospel to each new generation. This is seen in the masterful use of television and popular music by evangelists Jimmy Swaggert, Pat Robertson, and Jim Bakker to attract millions of followers. Others were critical of innovations and tried to offer an alternative to popular culture and entertainment. In general, evangelicals agree on the need for a divine Savior to rescue souls from everlasting damnation. Although Fundamentalism was a minority movement within twentieth century Christianity, but it had a strong influence on American evangelicalism and politics.

Fundamentalism represented a particular type of evangelicalism that took a stand against modern cultural changes, biological and physical sciences, and biblical criticism, focusing their proclamation on the imminent return of Christ. Rather than demythologize the Bible as Bultmann proposed or viewing the Bible metaphorically as the liberals proposed, fundamentalists based their theology on the literal, historical nature of biblical prophecy, particularly on the physical return of Christ and the final destruction of Satan. Millennialism has a long history in Western religion, and it was the impetus for a number of new sects and religions in America. In the nineteenth century, a new type of millennialist thought came to America from England. John Nelson Darby (1800-1882), a former Anglican priest and founder of the Plymouth Brethren in 1828, promoted the idea that human history is defined in terms of "dispensations" or ages of the Holy Spirit. The Bible describes in detail each dispensation, and the final dispensation will be the millennial kingdom. Biblical prophecy gives the key to understanding the last dispensation. According to Darby, any prophecy that has not been fulfilled historically will be fulfilled before the coming of Christ. He inspired a prophecy movement that examined the apocalyptic books of the Bible as a way to understand modern history.

The great American evangelist Dwight L. Moody accepted much of this dispensationalist teaching and by the end of the century he made it a part of his own revivalism. In 1878 and 1886 Prophecy Conferences were held in

New York and Chicago. Interested persons also participated in the annual Niagara Bible Conference that popularized the idea that the biblical prophets were writing about events to be fulfilled in the twentieth century. In 1909, Cyrus Ingerson Scofield (1843-1921) published his enormously popular Reference Bible. It was a monumental work of biblical research, with extensive notes and graphs, all of which presented a dispensationalist theology. Scofield used the chronology developed by Archbishop Ussher in the seventeenth century to buttress his argument for the fulfillment of ancient prophecies.

Dispensationalism is based on a view that the Bible in all of its details is factual. Adam, Eve, and Noah must be historical figures because they represent God's early dispensations. As such, dispensationalists opposed biblical scholars who viewed the first eleven chapters of Genesis as Israelite folklore similar to other folklore in the ancient world. They also held to an understanding that the Holy Spirit personally composed the entire Bible without error, rejecting the research of scholars into the origins of the scriptures. A popular pamphlet series designed to defend the Bible from biblical critics, *The Fundamentals: A Testimony to the Truth*, appeared between 1910 and 1915. Included were nearly 100 articles that sought to defend traditional faith from new theories and interpretations, particularly biblical criticism and liberal theology. The authors of the *Fundamentals* were not all dispensationalists, but they put theological differences aside to proclaim what they considered essential Christian truths, especially the deity of Christ, the virgin birth, the historical resurrection, the inerrancy of scripture as the word of God, and the reality of sin and Satan.

World War I put the fundamentalist controversy on hold as Christians of all kinds joined in the war effort, but by 1920, fundamentalists fought to preserve their churches from heresy. The fight was most bitter among the Baptists. Many of the leading liberals and advocates of the Social Gospel, such as Fosdick, Rauschenbusch, and Matthews, were Baptists. A hallmark of Baptist theology in America had long been the right of individuals to interpret scripture without the imposition of ecclesiastical hierarchies and creeds, but the Baptist revivalistic tradition had also long endorsed anti-intellectualism and a personal conversion experience as the true mark of religion. For many Baptists, northern as well as southern, intellectuals were threatening to undermine faith by questioning the reality of hell and the atoning death of Christ. One of the key events in the controversy was Harry Emerson Fosdick's well-publicized 1922 sermon, "Shall the Fundamentalists Win?" Fosdick argued that the church in the twentieth century must be inclusive and embrace difference rather than be intolerant and backward looking. He lost his church because of the sermon, but John D. Rockefeller built him the magnificent Riverside Church in New York and launched Fosdick's successful radio ministry.

John Roach Straton of New York led the fundamentalist movement in the northern Baptist church. In 1924 he engaged the Unitarian minister Charles Francis Potter in a radio broadcast debate on a number of controversial points. Listeners voted for the winner each night. Straton won on the divinity of Jesus, but lost on all of the other points, including inerrancy of the scriptures. It was a humiliating defeat that confirmed Straton's fears that America was losing its soul to modernists and Catholics.

Straton and other fundamentalist Baptists like the Texan Frank Norris formed separate fundamentalist denominations. One of the most important institutions to emerge from the fundamentalist movement was the Bible College which trained men and women for evangelistic service and Christian education. The first such school was founded by the Christian and Missionary Alliance at Nyack, N.Y. in 1882, but the most influential school was the Moody Bible Institute in Chicago founded in 1889. R. A. Torrey (1865-1928), the first head of the Moody Institute, also established the Bible Institute of Los Angeles in 1907 to help evangelize the growing West Coast. Within half-a-century, the number of Bible Colleges swelled to nearly 200 in the United States, half of them granting degrees, all them dedicated to conservative evangelical theology.

Princeton Theological Seminary, once a center of conservative Presbyterian theology was the scene of another battle over the Bible. J. Gresham Madchen (1881-1937), a brilliant Greek scholar who had studied theology in Germany, was appalled at what his professors were teaching about the Bible and church history. He decided that liberal theology had drifted so far from traditional Calvinist doctrine that it was actually a new religion, or at least a great heresy. He pushed the cause of the inerrancy of scripture at Princeton and aggressively opposed the liberal theologies of his colleagues. The battle grew so bitter that in 1929 Princeton Seminary was reorganized. Madchen left to form rival Westminster Seminary in Philadelphia.

The most famous event in the fundamentalist conflict was the "Scopes Monkey Trial" of 1925. The controversy began in March of that year when the Tennessee state legislature forbade the teaching of evolution in the public schools. Darwin's theory of evolution had become the archenemy for fundamentalists and other conservative Christians for a number of reasons. They believed that evolution contradicted the literal reading of the book of

Genesis, thus undermining confidence in the verbal inerrancy of the Bible and the idea of dispensations. Likewise, evolution was viewed as immoral because it reduced humans to the level of animals instead of being created in the image of God. Similarly, evolution seemed to offer a competing view of nature, one that did not require God. For the fundamentalists, evolution became the symbol of all that was wrong with modernism. If evolution was allowed to be taught, then American society would crumble.

John T. Scopes, a high school teacher, intentionally violated the law and taught Darwin's theory. In July he went on trial. William Jennings Bryan agreed to prosecute the case. For him, it was not Scopes on trial; it was America's future as a Christian nation. The celebrated jurist Clarence Darrow was hired by the American Civil Liberties Union to defend Scopes as a man with the right to teach what science teaches without interference from preachers and legislators. Although Scopes was convicted, the trial did not go well for the fundamentalists. At one point Darrow put Bryan on the stand and showed him to be both scientifically and biblically ignorant. It was a low point for the fundamentalists as they were held up for ridicule in the popular media.

For the most part, the fundamentalists lost the first round of their war against modernity, but they did not give up the fight. According to premillennialist theory, the world will increasingly fall under the influence of the antichrist and true believers will become a persecuted minority. Eventually there will be a period of seven years in which the full force of evil will be unleashed on the world, culminating in a world-wide conflagration called the battle of Armageddon. The faithful remnant, however, will be miraculously taken up into heaven, "raptured," and spared from the turmoil and suffering of the years of tribulation. Eventually the armies of darkness will be defeated, and the antichrist will be killed. Satan will be imprisoned when Christ returns in wrath and glory to rule from the throne of David in Jerusalem. Then the raptured and the resurrected will enjoy a thousand year reign of harmony and true religion. In the meantime, the faithful should be vigilant, observing the signs of the coming eschaton and spread the word of warning throughout the world. News of wars, natural disasters, and social decay is evidence that prophecy is being fulfilled and that the righteous must be prepared. They must avoid all compromises with the Antichrist who will work to take over the church and pervert it before the end. The popular appeal of this idea was demonstrated in the phenomenal sales of Hal Lindsay's *Late Great Planet Earth* in the 1970s.

Neo-evangelicalism

After the debacle of the Scopes Trial, Fundamentalism retreated from the national scene, but developed a well-organized sub-culture. The victory of Darwinism in the public schools and universities was merely proof that the antichrist was in power and the end was near. Central to the life of Fundamentalism was the creation of Bible Colleges where future pastors and Sunday School teachers could be educated in biblical literalism and dispensationalist theology without interference from modern scientific or religious theories. Fundamentalist activist Carl McIntyre created the American Council of Churches in opposition to the National Council in 1941. The following year the National Evangelical Association was created to bring together many different conservative denominations to promote conservative Protestation causes nationwide without engaging in the strident politics advocated by McIntyre. Prior to World War II, the term neo-evangelical was coined to describe those conservative Protestants who were influenced by fundamentalist ideas but who did not completely reject the secular world. Neo-evangelicals set out to redeem the world through evangelism and the proclamation of traditional values.

Fuller Theological Seminary in southern California, named for the radio evangelist Charles Fuller, emerged as the intellectual center of neo-evangelicalism. Neo-evangelicals also developed a number of non-denominational, "parachurch" organizations such as Campus Crusade and Intervarsity to work on school and university campuses across the United States. Their purpose was to lead students to conversion and protect them from the corrosive influence of secular education. The American Francis Shaeffer (1912-1984) brought neo-evangelicalism to Europe through his L'Abri Fellowship in England and Switzerland. In the 1960s and 1970s Shaeffer established himself as one of the leading conservative theologians and apologists with a number of works on Christian rationalism. Fundamentalists and neo-evangelicals also embraced mass media, establishing independent presses, magazines, and radio stations. In the 1970s, conservative evangelicals made effective use of cable television to broadcast their message on an international scale. Inspired by the activities of the evangelical sociologist Tony Campola, many evangelicals in the 1980s recaptured the holiness movement's earlier committment to social justice for the poor.

Initially conservative evangelicals, like many Protestants since the sixteenth century, identified the antichrist with the papacy; however, in the twentieth century new candidates for the archenemy of Christianity emerged.

Most prominent was the Soviet Union and communism in general. Evangelicals generally opposed the United States' alliance with the Soviet Union during World War II and welcomed the Cold War state of hostility. Billy Graham (1918-), the greatest of the modern revivalists, began his public career with crusades for Jesus and against communism in the 1950s. Throughout the 1960s Graham supported conservative politicians while expanding his evangelical activities on a world-wide scale. In the late 1970s and 80s, however, he distanced himself from fundamentalists and many evangelical leaders when he reached out to the people of the Soviet Union. He also openly criticized the stockpiling of nuclear weapons, warning that Armageddon should not be hastened by any human means.

Pentecostalism

Pentecostalism was another conservative Protestant movement developed out of nineteenth-century evangelicalism, but it brought a different point of view to bear on the issues of the twentieth century than did fundamentalism. Pentecostalism held to a literal reading of the Bible and the reliability of biblical prophecy, but instead of focusing on doctrinal purity and the second-coming of Christ, pentecostals proclaimed that miracles did not stop working after the age of the apostles. In a response to the growing interest in health movements like Christian Science, homeopathy, and Adventism, holiness preachers in the 1880s and 90s gave increasing attention to the subject of divine healing. The biblical accounts of Jesus' healing ministry were taken as the paradigm for the work of God in all ages. Prayer and faith could work miracles in the modern world just as they had in the first century. A. J. Gordon's popular 1882 work, *The Ministry of Healing: Miracles of Cure in All Ages* connected healing to the baptism of the Holy Spirit and brought this idea of faith healing to a broad audience.

The fascination with a recovery of apostolic spiritual gifts gained ground in the holiness movement and in Bible Colleges, such as the one led Charles F. Parham (1873-1929) in Topeka, Kansas. Parham reported that he and some students were studying the second chapter of Acts that records the gift of tongues of fire at the first Christian Pentecost. A few days later, one of the students experienced the gift of speaking in an unknown tongue.

There were other places in America where believers were searching for such apostolic gifts, but speaking in tongues (*glossalalia*) burst onto the national scene in 1906 when an African American holiness preacher named William Seymour (1870-1922) established the Apostolic Faith Gospel Mission on Azuza Street in Los Angeles. Seymour was initially a fairly typical revivalistic preacher, but soon he began preaching that the gifts of the Holy Spirit, such as healing, prophecy, and speaking in unknown tongues could be experienced in the modern age by those baptized in the spirit. Seymour, drawing on a long holiness tradition, argued that biblical literalism demands that Christians accept the contemporary reality of spiritual gifts. The second baptism of sanctification was a direct experience of the Holy Spirit that would be accompanied by signs and power, most particularly speaking in tongues. The Pentecost that the apostles experienced could be experienced by any believer today. Seymour's preaching led to a spectacular revival that was reported in newspapers across the country. Soon thousands were flocking to Azuza Street for prayer, preaching, healing, and the gift of the Spirit. Many of the participants, including a large number of women, became preachers and missionaries around the United States and Europe.

Following this out-pouring of the Spirit, a number of new denominations sprang up, the most notable of which was the Assemblies of God in 1914. Amid great growth and success, Pentecostal churches have divided over a number of sectarian issues, such as whether baptism should be in the name of the Trinity, or only of Jesus. They also divided over whether tongues are a required sign of second baptism and necessary for salvation or are merely a special grace. Such divisions have been easy because pentecostal and holiness groups have had little concern for church structure. Virtually anyone with a spiritual gift can gather a following and form a church. Unlike early fundamentalism which took a hard stand against women's rights in the church and society, the early pentecostal movement featured many female preachers and ministers, largely because it was a movement based on the authority of personal spiritual experience. A woman with the spiritual gifts had more authority than a man without them. Over time, as pentecostals developed closer ties with fundamentalists and other evangelicals, the forces of patriarchalism and biblicism eroded female leadership in most pentecostal churches.

One of the most prominent early pentecostal preachers was Aimee Semple McPherson (1890-1944). Despite two divorces, three marriages, and a national scandal, McPherson's status as a celebrity in the 1920s and 30s rivaled that of the movie stars of the era. Sister Aimee was an attractive and vivacious woman who traveled the country bringing "the story of hope, the words of joy, of comfort, of salvation" to cities nationwide. Her revivals lacked the hellfire and damnation of other revivalists, such as Billy Sunday. Rather, she eased people into heaven and promised that conversion would bring happiness. She was one of the earliest evangelists to use radio to spread the word of salvation, and her services were broadcast across the country. In 1922 she established a permanent base in Los Angeles where she built the Angelus Temple, a 1.5 million dollar edifice. In 1927, she formed the Foursquare Gospel Church, making her one of the few women in history to establish a religious denomination. Her church now numbers some 200,000 members. The "foursquare" refers to the fundamental doctrines of pentecostalism: salvation, baptism by the Spirit, physical healing, and the second coming of Christ.

The pentecostal message of the on-going work of the Holy Spirit in the daily lives of believers spread beyond its roots in holiness churches in the twentieth century. Pentecostal churches sent out thousands of charismatic preachers around the world who held countless revivals, often in very poor countries. Pentecostal denominations were among the fastest growing churches in the past century, in part because of the ease with which the movement could adapt local popular culture in worship and prayer. Pentecostals also made effective use of popular media, particularly television, making figures like Oral Roberts and Jim Bakker household names. Moreover, the Pentecostal movement inspired a charismatic revival in Roman Catholic and mainstream Protestant congregations world-wide. Informal and flexible in style, charismatic worship offered the hope of healing and wholeness to millions who felt alienated from traditional Christianity.

Religion and Politics

Fundamentalism and pentecostalism, in different ways, spoke to the anxieties of the modern age with a message that God is still active in the world and that the Bible remains both historically accurate and relevant for the twentieth century. They strongly opposed many of the social changes of the period, such as the women's movement, and asserted the "family values" and mores of nineteenth-century America. Children should obey their parents, women should be submissive to their husbands and not work outside of the home, and schools should teach discipline and respect for authority. Biblical authority was to be the bulwark to hold back the corruption of modern thought. During the social turmoil of the 1960s in America, and with the aid of television, conservative evangelicalism began a comeback that gained momentum in the 1970s and 1980s.

Jimmy Carter, elected in 1976, was the first American president to profess that he was a "born again" Christian. As such, he was an evangelical, and his presidency brought national media attention to the resurgence of evangeli-calism. However, it was the political ascendancy of Ronald Reagan that demonstrated the new power of fundamentalism. Jerry Falwell (1934-), a fundamentalist pastor in Virginia founded the Moral Majority, a grass roots political organization that helped insure the election of Reagan. In the late 1980s, Pat Robertson (1930-), the millionaire founder of the Christian Broadcasting Network and the Family Channel, created the Christian Coalition, a powerful grass-roots conservative political lobby. The conserva-tive movement represented by Falwell and Robertson, unlike earlier funda-mentalism, did not focus on old doctrinal debates over the virgin birth or the substitutionary atonement. Instead it directed its effort to opposing abortion, feminism, homosexuality, and the welfare state as symptoms and causes of American moral decay. Through political means as well as prayer and evangelism, conservative evangelicals hoped to reform Western society. In the process, some fundamentalist leaders even established relations with conservative Catholics fighting for similar issues.

The Feminist Controversy

As noted in an earlier chapter, the Women's Movement in nineteenth-century America was closely connected to evangelical Christianity and abolition. In the twentieth century, many liberal Protestant churches promoted the rights of women and several denominations officially allowed the ordination of women in the 1950s. Churches allied with the National Evangelical Association generally rejected women's ordination as un-biblical (even though some of the Pentecostal and Holiness churches had women ministers in their early years), and the more hierarchically organized churches (Catholic, Orthodox, Anglican) rejected women's ordination as contrary to church tradition. In 1978, the Episcopal Church joined the ranks of those who ordain women and put pressure on the world-wide Anglican fellowship to follow suit.

The Women's Liberation movement in America in the 1960s and 1970s brought with it a strong critique of all Christian churches as oppressive to women. Feminist biblical scholars and historians, such as Elisabeth Schlüssler Fiorenza and Phyllis Tribble, demonstrated not only how the biblical text is shaped by ancient notions of the divine right of patriarchy, but also how women were often liberated by Jesus and held leadership positions in the early church. Feminist theologians, such as Rosemary Radford Ruether, made the issue of women's liberation central to their theology, critiquing the history of

Christianity. Feminists pointed to the church's frequent repression and support for the abuse of women as evidence for the danger of patriarchal theology while also recovering the voice of previous generations of women who contributed much to the development of and the ministry within the church.

The key question for Christian feminist thinkers was whether sexism can be removed from Christianity in the way that racism was removed in the previous century. Those who believed this possible worked to uncover the almost hidden presence of women among Jesus' disciples and Paul's coworkers. Feminist scholars raised awareness of the sexism in liturgical language and the dominance of male imagery for God in worship despite the church's teaching that God is not human and is thus neither male nor female. Feminist critique led many denominations to revise their hymns and liturgies to more accurately reflect the presence of women in the believing community and to use biblical feminine metaphors for God.

This revision of cherished hymns and prayers generated great controversy in most churches, and "inclusive language" was even rejected by some feminists as still too dependent on the male imagery of Father and Son. Some scholars, like Mary Daly, decided that Christianity is hopelessly patriarchal, rejected the church entirely and proposed a new sisterhood dedicated to the worship of the goddess, much to the ire of conservative Christians and some liberal ones. As an alternative to what they see as neo-pagan feminism, many evangelical churches created a wide variety of women's ministries in the 1980s and 1990s. One of the most popular was Women Aglow which sought to empower women in their traditional roles as wives, mothers, and spiritual friends without threatening the patriarchal hierarchy.

African American Christianity

Perhaps the most significant Christian endeavor in the United States in the twentieth century was the movement for civil rights for African Americans. In a previous chapter, we looked at the abolition movement and the rise of the Black Church. Christianity, which had been used for the oppression of the slaves by white masters, also provided the spiritual and institutional strength for the descendants of slaves to demand full liberation in the twentieth century. The ancient narrative of a God who looked down on his suffering people and brought them out of Egypt with signs and wonders gave courage to another people wandering in the wilderness of the Reconstruction South.

Reconstruction had begun with great promise for blacks; however, the old plantations were not broken up as promised. The people who had worked the land and purchased it by labor did not receive ownership. Instead, they were reduced to being share-croppers, a new form of economic slavery in the South. Moreover, many southerners had responded to the disaster of the war by endowing the old Confederacy with a mythic aura that directly linked segregation and Christian virtue. The Ku Klux Klan, a white terrorist organization, was blessed by a Baptist minister at its founding in 1866 in Polaski, Tennessee. It adopted a fiery cross as its symbol. In the 1890s, lynchings of black men became commonplace and racist ideology generally acceptable. "Jim Crow" laws made it illegal for blacks and whites to eat together in public places or even use the same rest rooms. Rigid segregation was enforced in the South and legitimated by the U.S. Supreme Court in its Plessy vs. Fergussen decision in 1896. President Woodrow Wilson segregated the civil service and military. Nearly every door for advancement and security was closed to persons of African descent in the United States, but there was one arena where African Americans could assemble with little fear and openly discuss their tribulations, the Christian church.

For over 100 years, the black church was a sanctuary that offered hope for a better day in this life as well as the next. In 1866, the Colored Primitive Baptists organized a convention. The same year saw the creation of the first state convention of regular Black Baptists in North Carolina. In 1866, the Southern Methodist Church let its black members separate and form the Colored Methodist Episcopal Church, now called the Christian MEC. The rush of activity in organizing separate congregations and denominations points to the importance of independent institutions for the recently-freed slaves. During Reconstruction, the church emerged as the most stable and safe form of association for African Americans. Educated Blacks quickly rose to prominence within their churches and labored to increase the educational level of their parishioners. These churches produced the first African American periodicals, economic opportunities, and educational institutions. The church became a school for democracy, even if it was a racially biased democracy. When W. E. B. Du Bois (1868-1963) founded the National Association for the Advancement of Colored Persons in 1905, he naturally turned to the clergy for leadership.

After World War I, there was a massive black exodus from the rural South to the urban North. It is estimated from census data that from 1920 to 1960 over two and a half million African Americans gave up on Jim Crow and sharecropping and moved to the northern cities. Whereas in 1900 seventy percent of the African American population lived in rural areas, in 1965 seventy-five percent lived in cities, most of them in the North. This dislocation and urbanization was a more difficult adjustment for blacks than it had been for whites in the 1880s and 1890s. They found that racial hatred crossed state lines. Northerners were little less contemptuous of blacks than southerners. While there was less naked and organized violence in the North, the Klan had more members in Ohio than in North Carolina in the 1920s. Moreover, rural, uneducated blacks were easy targets for economic exploitation in the cities. So, by choice and necessity African Americans began living in urban ghettoes such as Harlem in New York City. In many ways the move north repeated the immigrant experience of many groups, but because most of the traditional paths out of the ghetto were closed to blacks. The pentecostal movement took hold in the black urban areas. Thousands of small, storefront pentecostal holiness churches sprang up after World War I. By 1933, seventy-two percent of the black churches in Chicago were storefront churches. These churches valued Spirit-filled, charismatic leadership over education and status, thus they attracted a number of creative local preachers, many of whom were women. Some of these charismatic leaders became very powerful and created large denominations such as the Church of God in Christ.

In a world of change, the church remained a force of stability, but the black community experienced a process of secularization in the city similar to other groups. The city offered excitement and entertainment outside of the church, and the ghettoes provided gathering places free from white control other than church. One aspect of secularization is seen in music. The old spirituals became the new blues and jazz. Church dancing became street dancing. The great musician W. C. Handy once said, "The dove descended on my head just as it descended on the heads of those who got happy at camp meeting. The only difference was that instead of singing about the New Jerusalem my dove began to moan about high-brown women and the men they tied to their apron strings."[34] For many preachers that difference was significant and disturbing. In an effort to maintain a hold on the youth who were being seduced by the charms of jazz and other entertainment, many urban churches encouraged showmanship in the pulpit and popular music in worship. In the 1960s some of the great pop singers, such as Aretha Franklin and James Brown moved easily between the sanctuary and recording studio.

---

34 Quoted in Ahlstrom, *A Religious History of the American People*, 2 vols. (New Haven: Yale University Press, 1972) 2:574.

Black Theology

With the segregation of the churches and the fight for rights for African Americans, there emerged distinctive black theologies. One common feature was a belief that African Americans would be the redeemers of the nation or of the world. In this view, expressed so movingly in the hymn "Lift Every Voice and Sing," the suffering of African Americans was equated to that of Christ. As his suffering was redemptive for the human race, so would be the suffering of blacks. More radically, Theophilus Steward used history and scripture to show that in the great sweep of salvation history, America was being replaced. Steward argued that whites were bent on self-destruction and were the most inhuman and warlike race in history. Africans would have to lead the way into the future. Related to this theology of redemptive suffering was a millennial vision. There were three dispensations: The Semites were the Jews of the Old Testament, who were supplanted by the Jephthites, the white evangelicals. The final dispensation was that of the Hamites who would issue in the millennial age. This theology completely overturned the old argument about the curse of Ham, which the whites had used to justify oppression of African peoples. The Nation of Islam, a radical sectarian movement led by Elijah Muhammad (1897-1975) incorporated this theology. According to Elijah's prophecies, soon after the year 2000, the Black Nation will again be the rulers on earth and the White Nation and its Christian religion will end.

Black Power

One of the greatest leaders in the early days of the Nation of Islam was Malcolm X (1925-1965), born Malcolm Little, who was murdered in 1965 under suspicious circumstances. Malcolm became an energetic and devoted apostle of the movement, and brought the cause of black unity and black pride to the attention of the larger world during the Civil Rights movement. Malcolm went to Mecca and encountered the larger Muslim world, and this seems to have disillusioned him to the Nation itself. In 1964 he left the Nation and founded the Muslim Mosque, Inc. Shortly after that he founded a non-religious Organization of Afro-American Unity. Malcolm X's call for Black Power during the early 1960s found a Christian response in the theology of James Cone (1938-) who applied the theologies of Bonhoeffer and Niebuhr to the African American situation. Cone defined Black Power as a cry for the recognition of full black humanity, including full power for political and economic self-determination. Christ, according to Cone, is always found in the midst of the struggle for justice. "We must therefore be reminded that

Christ was not crucified on an altar between two candles, but on a cross between two thieves. He is not in our peaceful, quiet, comfortable suburban churches, but in the ghetto fighting the racism of churchly white people."[35] He presented the Christian doctrine of the end-time quite different from traditional Christianity. Eschatology is the historical liberation of the oppressed. The promise of heaven is realized on earth, but only if people make the kind of trouble necessary to bring about justice. Cone rejected white denominations, asserting that they are not truly churches because they do not manifest the New Testament call to liberation. They were not communities where the dividing wall of hostility has been broken down. In fact, the white denominations have so distorted the meaning of Christianity that they can be considered the antichrist, according to Cone.

The Civil Rights Movement

The leading figure of the Civil Rights movement was one of the greatest religious figures of the twentieth century. Martin Luther King, Jr. (1929-1968) was a product of the black church who advocated a quite different theology than that of Cone or the Nation of Islam. He found the way to build a more just human society in the non-violent ethical teachings of Jesus. King urged the oppressed to seize justice through the transforming power of Christ-like love for their enemies. When Rosa Parks refused to give up her seat on a bus in Montgomery, Alabama in 1955, defying the city's segregation laws, King, a young pastor, organized a successful city-wide bus boycott. King was influenced by the works and example of Mohandas Gandhi who used non-violent civil disobedience to secure India's independence from Great Britain. Adopting similar strategies, King used the ancient biblical story of liberation to inspire a generation of Christian activists to demand their human rights while displaying love for their enemies. King urged his followers not to give into hatred, but to break through with a redemptive love that would transform all social injustices.

As president of the Southern Christian Leadership Conference, King organized voter registration drives and major rallies throughout the South. He was arrested more than a dozen times for violating segregation laws in various cities. In his famous *Letter From a Birmingham Jail* in 1963, King responded to criticism of his law-breaking. Drawing upon the biblical example of Shadrach, Meshach, and Abednego, King stated "that an individual who breaks a law that conscience tells him is unjust, and who

---

[35] James Cone, *Black Theology and Black Power* (New York: Seabury Press, 1969) 66.

willingly accepts the penalty of imprisonment in order to arouse the conscience of the community over its injustice, is in reality expressing the highest respect for law."[36] He went on to express his disappointment with the church in general for having become so comfortable with the status quo that it could no longer express outrage or make real the radical hope of the gospel.

King organized the massive, bi-racial march on Washington, D.C., which brought a quarter of a million people to the steps of the Capitol in 1963. His speech "I Have a Dream" combined the Christian hope of redemption with the American dream of equality and justice. The following year he received the Nobel Peace Prize, and his efforts were rewarded with the passage of the Civil Rights Act of 1964. He continued agitating for social and economic justice until he was assassinated in 1968, the day after telling his followers that he was like Moses looking into the promised land. King was one of the great leaders of the Civil Rights movement, but we must not overlook the thousands of individuals who stepped out in front of police dogs and hostile crowds with words of forgiveness, nor those who were murdered for their activities. Symbolic of the whole Civil Rights movement and the power of the black church was a school girl named Ruby Bridges (1954-) who personally desegregated the New Orleans school system in 1960 simply by having the courage to walk past mobs of angry white parents shouting threats. For most of the year, she sat alone in a classroom all day until the school was finally forced to integrate. The psychiatrist Robert Coles once asked Ruby what she did as she endured the hatred of the mob and other children. She replied that she prayed for them.

---

[36] Martin Luther King, Jr., "Letter from a Birmingham Jail."

Chapter 27

Vatican II and the Modern Catholic Church

New Catholic Theologies

THE CATHOLIC CHURCH in the nineteenth century sought to reign in theological speculation and prevent the corrosive influence of modern ideas and science. However, not all Catholic intellectuals were content with repeating the dogmas of the past while science was opening new vistas on the future.

Jesuit priest Pierre Teilhard de Chardin (1881-1955), the most creative and controversial of Catholic intellectuals, embraced Darwinism and attempted to bridge the theory of evolution in line with Christian theology. Teilhard was a paleontologist well respected in the scientific community, especially for his work on pre-human bones (Sinanthropus) discovered in China. Ironically Teilhard had been sent to China by the Jesuit order in the 1920s as a way to prevent him from publicizing his theological ruminations on the significance of evolution. Part of what disturbed the Jesuits, and eventually the Vatican, was Teilhard's complete acceptance of evolution as a scientific fact. For him, it was as pointless for the church to argue against evolution as it had been to argue against the rotation of the earth in the seventeenth century. By the end of the twentieth century, the Vatican reconciled Catholic teaching and biological evolution, but it did not endorse Teilhard's rethinking of Christian doctrine in light of evolution. In essence, Teilhard argued that evolution is not the *descent* of man, as Darwin had phrased it, but the *ascent*. Evolution is the process of the development of consciousness. In the modern period the human race is poised for a new stage of development. The resurrected Christ, the cosmic Christ, marks the Omega point or goal of this human, spiritual evolution.

Teilhard was forbidden to publish his thoughts during his life, so his friends published his papers after his death. Teilhard's papers caused a sensation, but few readers were able to digest his difficult writings. In the 1940s and 1950s, the less esoteric, but controversial work of two French

Catholic theologians, Yves Congar and Henri de Lubac, proposed ways in which Catholicism could learn from Protestant theologians and biblical scholars. For Congar, the Catholic Church should acknowledge those parts of the sixteenth-century reformers' critique that were accurate, such as the church depending too much on monarchical authority and tradition. Although traditionally orthodox in regards to the basic doctrines of the church, such as the Trinity and the sacraments, Congar found some of his writings censured by the Vatican. More than any other theologian Congar prepared the soil for the Second Vatican Council.

The most controversial and influential Catholic theologian of the twentieth century was the Jesuit Karl Rahner (1904-1984), who played a strong role in Vatican II. Rahner was a Thomist, but he attempted to revise Thomas' thought in answer to the anti-metaphysical criticism of Immanuel Kant. In doing so, Rahner made extensive use of the existentialism of the German philosophers Martin Heidegger and Martin Buber. Rahner shifted the starting point of theology away from God's revelation, focusing instead on human person and history. According to Rahner, the human spirit, or personhood, is transcendent because it is dependent on God. The ground of our self-awareness and awareness of the world lies in our relationship to the ultimate person, God. The church's "means of grace" and the Bible are effective symbols that deepen our self-awareness in relationship to the source of meaning. For Rahner, the self-communication of the ultimate subject (God) to the transcendent human subject involves the "divinization of the world through the Spirit of God." Within the strictures of the church's dogma, Rahner opened avenues for creative engagement with modern philosophy and science. Through his work in editing a ten-volume lexicon of Catholic theology and ecclesiology as well as the encyclopedia *Sacramentum Mundi*, Rahner exerted a strong influence on European theologians.

Hans Küng (1928-) and Edward Schillebeeckx (1914-) answered the challenge of Rahner to create a Catholic theology that is faithful to the historical doctrine of the church and to the reality of the modern world. Küng took up the old task of Christian apologetics, and tried to demonstrate how his choice to be a believing Christian remains a rational choice even in the world of post-modern European intellectuals. He encouraged the Catholic Church to continue down the path of serious engagement with modern thought and to reject doctrines, such as papal infallibility that he considered detrimental to the development of Christianity. Schillebeeckx was willing to directly challenge papal authority in intellectual matters, and developed Rahner's idea of a multi-disciplinary theology that incorporates the insights of science, phenomenology, politics, and psychology. For Schillebeeckx, context is vital to the theology, and he tried to shift from an exclusive focus on theory to one of praxis. It is the experience of the faith community trying to live authentically in the world that is the focal point for all true theology.

Hans von Balthasar (1905-) was the most articulate opponent of this shift from the revelation of God to the human subject or the acting community. Von Balthasar, like the Protestant Karl Barth, argues that theology must have its own point of reference unique from the claims of science or philosophy. His mastery of patristic and medieval theology allowed him to demonstrate what has been consistent in the history of Catholic doctrine and to argue that theology is properly the work of saints and martyrs, those who live the reality they study. Theology is a contemplative activity that is especially needed in the confusion of modern living. Most important for Balthasar is the scandal of the cross. True theology begins with a meditation on this scandal that disrupts all accepted forms of understanding is disrupted. The cross is the revelation of a God whose identification with lost humanity is so great that in Christ, God experienced the godlessness of the lost. Unlike most theologians, Protestant and Catholic, von Balthasar made Holy Saturday, the symbol of Christ's descent to the grave and hell, a central idea. However, for von Balthasar, theology is more than just getting the story of Christian doctrine right, it is a process by which the believer's mind is shaped by the revelation of God. The symbols of revelation, including the sacraments of the church, help shape the mind to understand God's redemptive actions and motivate the believer to doxology and obedience.

Vatican II

The most significant event of modern Catholic history was no doubt the meeting of the Second Vatican Council (1962-1965) called by Pope John XXIII (1881-1963) just months after his election in 1958. Angelo Guiseppe Roncalli was an old man when he was elected pope, and it appears that many cardinals viewed him as an interim whose pontificate would give the church time to adjust after reign of Pius XII. However, by choosing the name John, unused since the Council of Constance, Roncalli indicated that he was not going to maintain the status quo. In fact, he once said that a person's proper mission in life is not "to be a museum keeper, but to cultivate a flourishing garden of life and to prepare a glorious future."

Prior to becoming pope, Roncalli had a distinguished career as a church administrator, especially in Bulgaria and Turkey, and established working relations with the Orthodox Church hierarchy during World War II. As pontiff, he established the Secretariat for Promoting Christian Unity and sent representatives to the 1961 meeting of the World Council of Churches. He researched the life and activities of the sixteenth-century Catholic reformer Charles Borromeo who was instrumental in making the Council of Trent an effective agent for church renewal. He intended to do something similar in his day by "letting some fresh air" into the Catholic Church through a process of "up-dating" which he called *aggiornamento*. Thus he decided to assemble the largest ecumenical council in the history of Christianity.

Over two thousand bishops assembled for the four sessions of the Second Vatican Council. Hundreds of representatives from Africa, Asia, and Latin America made this the most global council in church history and kept the proceedings from being dominated by European concerns. Moreover, at John's insistence, at least eighty representatives from Protestant and Orthodox churches observed the proceedings, marking a radical change of perspective from the First Vatican Council. John insisted that this council would be pastoral rather than dogmatic. The Second Vatican Council did not contradict the doctrinal statements of its predecessor, but it did make a number of far-reaching doctrinal refinements. For John, this was a matter of bringing out the true meaning of old doctrines in a new age rather than the creation of new doctrines; past misunderstandings were to be removed.

Some of the legislation of the council had an immediate impact on the average worshiper. The laity, in what some saw as a concession to Protestants, were allowed to drink from the cup during the Eucharist. True to the emphasis of the liturgical reform movement, the Eucharist was also highlighted as the central act of the Christian community. All Catholics were encouraged to participate fully and often in communion. To aid this participation, the use of the vernacular was allowed in the liturgy. Initially Latin was retained for the institution of the Mass itself, but shortly after the council the practice died out throughout the world. Catholic liturgy books were rewritten in the language of the people and new songs were added to the worship. While affirming the importance of tradition in interpreting scripture and defining orthodox belief, the council strongly encouraged Catholics to read the Bible for themselves and allowed scholars to employ the modern tools of biblical and historical criticism in their research. The council reaffirmed clerical celibacy, but provision was made for the ordaining of married men to the diaconal ministry. Deacons were given authority to perform weddings, funerals, baptisms, and other clerical duties except for the consecration of the Eucharist. As part of the process of rapprochement with the eastern Orthodox churches, the council affirmed the validity of the priesthood of married priests in the Orthodox church.

John XXIII died in 1963 and was succeeded by Paul VI (1897-1978) who continued the council and implemented its reforms. Much of this involved making effective the council's understanding that the church is "the people of God," rather than an institutional hierarchy. It was acknowledged that the "people of God" may also include some who are not in full communion with the Catholic Church. Catholic theologians since the Vatican II have contributed greatly to the ecumenical movement. Anti-Semitism was condemned by the council, and the Vatican's Secretariat for Non-Christian Religions engaged in productive dialogue with Jewish scholars on Jewish-Christian issues. Last, and most important, the Second Vatican Council and recent popes strongly promoted the cause of human rights around the world. These rights include freedom of religion (including the freedom to err in religion), freedom from oppression, and the right to life. The indiscriminate slaughter of civilians in the War and threatened by the age of nuclear weapons was condemned. The identification of human rights as a central component in the message of Christ helped inspire one of the most influential theological movements of the modern era: liberation theology.

Liberation Theology

For centuries, devout Catholics have looked to Mary the mother of Jesus for support and guidance. Her image adorns churches and homes around the globe and the papacy has placed the Catholic Church under her special care. Little is known about her, but in the Magnficat, recorded in the Gospel of Luke, Mary says of God: "He has brought down the powerful from their thrones, and lifted up the lowly; he has filled the hungry with good things, and sent the rich away empty." (Luke 1:52) These words, often set to beautiful compositions, have been sung by the faithful through the ages, but for millions of impoverished Catholics in Latin America, the Magnicat held a special relevance. According to an energetic group of radical Catholic priests and theologians in the 1960s and 1970s, God clearly has a preference for the poor. The rich are sent away empty while the poor are blessed.

The movement that made these ideas the heart of Christian theology is known as Liberation Theology, and for over twenty years it was a dynamic, revolutionary force in the Catholic Church. From the beginning of the Iberian conquest of the New World, the Catholic hierarchy was in close alliance with political and economic power in Latin America. Through the bewildering shifts of power and rise and fall of dictatorships, the church focused on the spiritual needs of its flock without challenging the political and economic status quo. In nearly every country in Latin America, most of the church's members lived in grinding poverty and were denied basic human rights. In some instances, bishops directly cooperated with regimes that oppressed their own flock. However, Pope John XXIII, during his brief reign, issued a declaration that the church was the church of the poor. All bishops and priests were urged to reach out to those who were suffering in body as well as in soul.

Dom Helder Camara (1909-), the Archbishop of Ollinda in Brazil took up the challenge that John XXIII and the Vatican Council had given to the church. Camara had previously supported the ruling authorities in Brazil, but in the 1960s he began to focus his attention on the poorest of the poor in his diocese. His efforts went beyond typical Christian charity to embrace a new theological perspective. Who is Christ? "The man who needs justice, who has a right to justice, who deserves justice."[37] Dom Helder made the ancient idea of the image of God central to his theology. The suffering inflicted upon the poorest peoples of the earth so dehumanizes them that it threatens the very image of God. According to Camara, the church cannot save souls without at the same time preserving and fighting for the human rights of God's own children. Humans are obligated by God to work to improve the conditions of all people, but particularly the poor who are enslaved and dehumanized by poverty.

This theology of liberation found its most articulate spokespersons in Gustavo Gutiérrez (1928-) and Leonardo Boff. For them, the Bible is essentially the story of God's effort to liberate his people from economic and political oppression. The story of Israel began when God heard the suffering of his enslaved people and intervened to bring them into liberation. Prophets, especially Amos, preached about God's righteousness in terms of economic justice. Hebrew law in the book of Deuteronomy shows a preference for the poor, the fatherless, the widow, and even the sojourner with no fixed home. Liberation theologians refused to spiritualize the work of Christ. Instead, they stressed that when Christ was born, he was born to an unmarried peasant girl and placed in a cattle trough. Shepherds came to visit him. Christ lived among the poor of the world and offered them liberation. For the liberation theologians, the suffering Christ was the "worker Christ." However, speaking

---

[37] Dom Helder Camara, *The Church and Colonialism*, trans. William McSweeney (Denville NJ: Dimension Books, 1969) 12.

on behalf of the poor could be dangerous, even for bishops. Christ was crucified by the Romans for defending the rights of the poor, and likewise, in 1980, a death squad murdered one of the most visible advocates for the poor, Archbishop Oscar Romero (1917-1980), the primate of El Salvador, while he was celebrating the Mass.

Much of what liberation theologians and priests said came directly from the Christian tradition, including papal documents, but they also made extensive use of Marxist economic theory to critically analyze the situation in the Third World. Poverty in Latin America, Asia, and Africa is in part a result of European and American colonialism as well as the political oppression of military dictatorships. A small, powerful elite, descendants of the European invaders owned most of the land. Most of the labor was supplied by exceedingly poor farmers entirely at the mercy of the landlords. Liberation theologians focused their efforts on education, particularly demystification, to show the poor the reality of the plight and the reasons why. Basic Christian Communities taught reading, scripture, political organization, and economics, to help give the poor a voice in their own fate. Basic to this idea of "theology from below," that is from the eyes of the poor, is that the divinity of Christ and his sacrifice for sin were de-emphasized in favor of the message of Christ's solidarity with the suffering and oppressed. Inspired by liberation theology and the example of bishops like Romero, scores of priests and nuns actively promoted political reform movements, educated and organized peasants, and even supported revolutionary movements. Two Roman Catholic priests were active participants in the Sandinista government in Nicaragua that took power in the 1980s. Because of this involvement in revolutionary politics, many in the Catholic Church objected to liberation theology as a rejection of Christian doctrine and an unholy alliance with Marxism and revolution.

Other Reactions to the Council

It is hard to underestimate the impact of the Second Vatican Council on the Catholic Church around the world. It led to a reinvigoration of Catholic activity in Europe and spawned vigorous movements in Latin America. In the United States, it gave Catholics permission to live in the mainstream of American society and led to an increase in popular devotion. The mystical writings of Thomas Merton (1915-1968), an American Cistercian monk and anti-war demonstrator, resonated with both Catholics and Protestants who were seeking a deeper spirituality. At the same time, however, the rapid changes of the council caused a great deal of concern. At the parish level, the laity had to deal with a new style and even a new language for worship. The observance of the Friday fast, once a hallmark of popular Catholic identity. was no longer obligatory, and one of the most popular saints, Christopher, was officially removed from the list of saints because he never actually lived. Thousands of nuns gave up the habit and adopted secular dress. A penitent person could confess face-to-face to a priest. On certain occasions, Catholics could worship in Protestant churches. What was exciting and liberating to some was confusing and alienating to others. It seemed the Catholic Church was losing its identity, perhaps even its claim to being orthodox.

Following the council there were repeated calls to return to traditional Catholic devotional practices. Some of these calls reputedly came from the Virgin Mary herself. The twentieth century saw a dramatic rise in the number of reports of apparitions of the Virgin. The most famous was the appearance at Fatima in the waning years of the First World War, but popular devotion to Marian apparitions increased notably after the Second Vatican Council. Visitations were reported in Japan in the 1970s, Venezuela (1967-1984), Ireland (1985), and Spain in the 1980s. The most celebrated of the modern visitations began in 1981 at Medjugorje in Yugoslavia. Even during the carnage of the Bosnian War, millions of pilgrims flocked to Medjugorje hoping for a sign, a message, or a miracle. The common message of these visitations was a warning of impending world disaster and a call to increase individual Catholic piety, especially through the sacraments of penance and the Eucharist, as well as faithfully praying the rosary. In 1999, Pope John Paul II made his final world tour which included an emotional visit to the shrine of Our Lady of Guadalope in Mexico, the most popular Marian shrine in the Americas. The pontif called the Catholic faithful to increased devotion to Mary as the millennium came to a close.

The most controversial issues to emerge following the Second Vatican Council concerned human sexuality. As secular governments in the industrialized world removed a number of legal and economic barriers to divorce, the number of divorces went up dramatically in the 1960s and 1970s. In some countries, such as the United States, the divorce rate reached fifty percent. Although decrying the decline of the family, Protestant churches adjusted to the new reality of divorce relatively easily since marriage is not a sacrament in the Protestant Church. For the Catholic Church, though, divorce and remarriage became an item of bitter contention since remarried persons are forbidden to partake of the sacrament without an official annulment. Along with an increase in divorce there was an identifiable increase in premarital sex and cohabitation among both Protestants and Catholics in Europe and America during this period. By the end of the century, even staunchly Catholic countries like Ireland, Ecuador, and Spain were liberalizing their birth control and divorce laws.

Pope Paul VI's encyclical *Humanae vitae* in 1968 addressed a relatively new issue in sexual ethics: artificial birth control. Artificial contraception had become widely available in the industrialized world by this time, and many public policy advocates saw great hope in family planning as a way to ease poverty in the Third World, but the Vatican saw a threat to fundamental Catholic morality. *Humanae vitae* decreed that although procreation is not the only legitimate use of sexuality in a marriage, a couple ought not use artificial means "to render procreation impossible." The declining birth rate among American Catholics combined with the research of social scientists indicate that this has been a papal pronouncement largely ignored by the laity. The encyclical did have one effect. It was a sign of increasing conservatism in the Vatican following the sweeping changes of the Second Vatican Council.

Humanae vitae also strongly reiterated the church's opposition to abortion, and on this issue it resonated with the sentiments of the laity. Following the 1972 Supreme Court decision in the case *Roe v Wade* which made it illegal to outlaw abortion in the United States, Catholic bishops have led the opposition to abortion around the world. The Catholic Church has officially declared that human life begins at conception and those who participate in abortion are excommunicated by their actions. The bitter battle over abortion in the United States in the 1980s brought together conservative Catholics and Protestants despite their deep theological divisions. Since then anti-abortion has been a centerpiece of the Vatican's international diplomacy.

John Paul II

The person who has done the most to define and guide the post-Vatican II Catholic Church is also the first non-Italian to become pope since the sixteenth century. Karol Wojtyla (1920-) was born in Poland during that nation's brief period of independence following the collapse of the Russian and German empires in World War I. Wojtyla, unlike most of his predecessors in the Vatican, came from the rural working class, and he never lost his ability to communicate with the poor and laboring around the world. He was profoundly shaped by having lived under two totalitarian regimes and known people who died in Auschwitz and the Soviet gulags. In Poland, more than any other country, the Catholic Church was a source of popular resistance to foreign invaders, and as the archbishop of Krakow, Wojtyla repeatedly drew upon the ancient heritage of the Catholic Church in promoting Polish national identity and pride.

When Pope John Paul I died in 1978 after only thirty-three days in office, the conclave of cardinals selected the athletic Wojtyla who had distinguished himself in asserting the rights of the church in Poland without politicizing the Gospel. He appeared to be the one who could hold together the traditionalists who wanted to overturn Vatican II and those who saw Vatican II as the start of a new era of reformation. A devotee of the mystics John the Cross and Teresa of Avila, and sincere in his devotion to Mary, Wojtyla has long been noted as a mystic and pastor rather than an administrator and bureaucrat. He is also attached to orthodox theology and assisted in drafting *Humanae vitae*. As a young man, Wojtyla had been an actor; as pope he would use mass media more effectively than any world leader since World War II. John Paul II asserted his authority over the curia immediately after his election and began his practice of reaching out to the crowds. In the 1980s he traveled more widely than any pope in history, beginning with an historic visit to Mexico where he quickly became a celebrity. That same celebrity followed him wherever he traveled in the early years of his pontificate.

Philosophically and personally, John Paul was opposed to Marxism which he saw as a fundamental denial of the full humanity of the individual. Unlike some of his predecessors in the Vatican, John Paul was convinced that the idea of human rights is essential to the message of Christ, and as pope he vigorously advocated for freedom of worship and conscience along the lines of Vatican II. His first encyclical, *Redemptor Hominis*, defended all religions in the face of materialistic economic and political systems, whether communist or capitalist. His 1981 trip to his homeland contributed directly to the rise of the Solidarity labor movement led by Lech Walesa. Millions of Poles came to see him celebrate Mass, at times defying governmental interference. He is credited with helping to bring democracy to Poland in 1988. It may have been his effective agitation against communism in Europe that led to the May 13, 1981 assassination attempt by a Turkish terrorist. John Paul attributed his survival to the direct intervention of the Virgin Mary and had the bullet placed in the shrine of Our Lady of the Rosary at Fatima in Portugal.

John Paul was disappointed that the end of communism in Poland and elsewhere did not lead to a period of spiritual rebirth in Europe. Instead, he saw an increase in immorality and apathy, especially in the industrialized nations. He blamed liberal theologians and bishops for encouraging a climate of freedom without restraint. Among the prominent Catholic theologians who were either condemned, silenced, or otherwise disciplined by the Vatican were Hans Küng and Edward Schillebeeckx who questioned papal infallibility. Charles Curran in the United States lost his teaching position for questioning the papal ban on artificial conception. Liberation theology in particular came under papal censure because of its use of Marxist theory. The Brazilian theologian Leonardo Boff was silenced in 1984 and subsequently left the priesthood. John Paul also used his authority to appoint archbishops and cardinals to place his conservative stamp on the next generation of Catholic leaders. Central to John Paul's agenda is an uncompromising attitude toward birth control, abortion, and church authority. He made it clear that the ordination of women to the sacramental ministry is out of the question, even raising the possibility that this is an infallible papal decree.

Despite such efforts at crushing dissent, controversy continues in the Catholic Church over how to proceed in the reforms of Vatican II. In the United State and Europe there is a severe shortage of priests and nuns, and where the church has been shaken by revelations of pedophile priests. As a result calls for extending ordination to women and married persons have become more persistent. Despite areas of real conflict and contention, the Catholic Church at the end of the twentieth century is strong, vibrant, and once again playing a major role in international politics and social reform, due in large measure to the personal charisma and dynamism of John Paul.

Mother Teresa

Another leading twentieth century Catholic figure was already being proclaimed a saint by popular acclamation during her lifetime. Agnes Gonxa Bejaxhiu (1910-1997), a diminutive woman from Albania, took the name Teresa when she joined the Sisters of Our Lady of Loreto at the age of eighteen. She was sent to Calcutta, India where she taught in the convent school until receiving a calling to help the poorest of the poor in one of the poorest cities on earth. Her mission was to help those dying on the streets to die with comfort and dignity regardless of their religion or status. In 1950, her new religious order, the Missionaries of Charity received official blessing from the Vatican. It soon grew to over three thousand members laboring on five continents. Teresa's approach to the poor was as profound as it was simple. In her words, she "saw the eyes of Christ in the eyes of the poor" regardless of their religion. She never deviated from official Catholic doctrine, including the teaching on birth control, nor did she directly challenge corrupt governments, but she did present herself and her sisters as servants for all in need. A recipient of the Noble Prize for Peace, Teresa was honored with a state funeral in India where Christianity remains a minority faith. For many around the world, Christian and non-Christian alike, she represented the height of Christian virtue and compassion without the conflict that Christianity often brings.

Conclusion

A New World Order?

THE LAST DECADE of the twentieth century brought profound changes and challenges to the Christian world, and the year 1989 marked a watershed in European history. Like dominoes, the communist governments of Eastern Europe fell in bloodless popular rebellions in which Catholic and Protestant churches played a key role. In part because the Soviet Union was involved in a military quagmire in Afghanistan and because a new generation of Soviet leaders led by Mikhail Gorbachev sought to reform Marxist society through more openness, Russian tanks did not put down those rebellions as they had done in 1956 and 1968. In Leipzig, tens of thousands of people staged candlelight processions to demand democratic reforms. Eventually the government opened the borders to travel, and in November 1989, the most dramatic symbol of the Cold War, the Berlin Wall, was torn down. Thousands of Germans, including soldiers that once guarded the gateway to the West, joined in dismantling the wall. Two years later, after a failed coup by Soviet hard liners, Boris Yeltsin took power in Russia. Statues of Lenin were toppled and freedom was proclaimed. Quickly, the Soviet Empire crumbled as nation states like the Ukraine asserted independence.

Christians were again free to worship and evangelize in Eastern Europe, and many looked forward to the creation of a new Christian society. Throughout Latin America, democratic governments slowly emerged from the chaos and hardship of civil wars and dictatorships. Again the churches played an important role in promoting a free society and reconciling former enemies. In Ireland, after decades of Protestant and Catholic violence, partisans on both sides reached a peace agreement in 1998. Christianity expanded rapidly in Africa and Asia in the 1990s and those churches have increasingly asserted their own voice in Christian discussions. At the end of its second millennium, Christianity has more adherents in the Southern Hemisphere than in the North. At the 1998 Lambeth Conference of Anglican bishops, it was the African bishops who defeated efforts to extend the right of ordination to homosexuals. The often-used phrase "post-Christian world" has some relevance for Europe and America, but hardly describes the Southern Hemisphere where Christianity is one of the most dynamic forces shaping society.

The End of Apartheid

It was in South Africa that Christianity may have had the most profound impact on a political system. For much of the twentieth century, the white majority ruled South Africa under a system of apartheid, or racial segregation and black subordination. The secret police and the army were used to control the black population through terror. Beyers Naudé, a white Protestant pastor, and Archbishop Desmond Tutu (1931-), the first black to be the primate of the Anglican Church in South Africa, led the Christian opposition to apartheid. Through their efforts, apartheid was acknowledged as a heresy in many Christian churches. Christians around the world joined in putting pressure on the South African government to end the system. In 1990, the white prime minister of South Africa, F. W. de Klerk began the process of dismantling apartheid and preparing for a democratic South Africa. He released the anti-apartheid activist Nelson Mandela who was subsequently elected president of the nation in the first non-racial election held in 1994. Mandela was concerned that his revolution not escalate the cycle of violence as other revolutions have done. He appointed Tutu to establish a Truth and Reconciliation Commission that was empowered to grant amnesty for those who publicly confessed their atrocities. This idea of using confession and forgiveness in order to bring about lasting peace may be the most profound application of Christian ethics in the political arena since the abolition of slavery.

Conflicts and Challenges

Many Christians in the early 1990s took comfort in the words of the American president George Bush who pointed to the birth of "a new world order" as evidence of the triumph of the cross; others saw in this an ominous threat of the antichrist who would institute an evil world government. Many Protestant churches have been embroiled in divisive battles over feminist theology and homosexual rights. For some, the message of Christ is a message of inclusiveness and compassionate love for all people, especially those whose rights have traditionally been denied. For others, the suggestion that women can be ordained and that homosexuals should be accepted in the fellowship of believers is itself an offense to God and a rejection of Christian morality. The Bulgarian Orthodox Church called for the Orthodox churches to leave the World Council of Churches in 1998 over the issue of homosexuality.

The 1990s, which began with such promise for a more humane world also saw some of the worst religious and ethnic warfare since the seventeenth century. Yugoslavia disintegrated into a number of smaller warring states. Catholic Croatia, Orthodox Serbia, and Muslim Bosnia were the setting for brutality not seen since the days of Hitler and Stalin. Serbian leaders in particular instituted a policy of "ethnic cleansing" by which tens of thousands of Muslims were driven from their homes and thousands more executed. The world watched in horror as Sarajevo was reduced to rubble by militia armies in the name of creating a Christian nation. In Rwanda, ethnic hatred between Tutus and Hutus led to the massacre of more than a million people. Many of the murderers as well as their victims were Christians. Throughout Africa and the Middle East, Christians became the target of Islamic fundamentalist groups after the victory of the allies against Sadam Hussein in the Gulf War in 1991. In Sierra Leone, the Sudan, Pakistan, Egypt, and elsewhere, Christians, particularly nuns, were targets of terrorist violence. The late twentieth century became a new age of martyrdom, even more random and cruel than the days of the Roman Empire.

At the end of the twentieth century, much of the previous hostility between theologians and scientists had broken down, particularly in the area of physics. New discoveries point to the probability of a grand design after all. At the same time, dramatic technological advances emerged that raise profound ethical issues. New fertilization techniques made "surrogate motherhood" and artificial insemination routine, further confusing the definition of family in modern society. Geneticists mapped the human genome that will make genetic engineering a regular part of medical science. Scottish scientists successfully cloned a large mammal for the first time, and human cloning became a real possibility. This raises questions about the traditional Christian doctrine of the soul. Is the soul itself subject to genetic engineering? Is a clone really human? For some, genetics represents the next stage in human progress, but for others it raises the grim specter of Aldous Huxley's *Brave New World* and the eventual dehumanization of the race itself. Neurologists also provided evidence that religious belief is centered in a particular portion of the brain, raising new questions about the nature of faith. On a global scale, cloning pales in comparison to the controversy over the eventual self-destruction of human kind. Although the threat of nuclear war diminished after the end of the Cold War, there is increasing evidence that the Northern hemisphere's industry and consumption has already begun to affect the global climate. Many Christians see the increasing destruction of nature as a grave sin against God who commanded humans to be stewards of creation.

Clearly the challenges that will face Christianity in the next century will be great. As these words were being written, many Christians were eagerly anticipating the return of Jesus and the ending of this present age. They search for signs of the rise of the antichrist and the final battle against evil. It is widely believed that the millennial year (AD 2000) would bring this about. In other words, for many believers, this effort in writing a history of Christianity has been in vain because the end will come before it is even published. Other Christians are celebrating a year of Jubilee, and have called upon secular governments to make the jubilee real by releasing Third World countries from their crippling debt.

Having seen so many false predictions of the imminent end of the world over the past 700 years of Christian history, I believe that history will continue and that the church will survive. We have seen how Christianity has faced many severe challenges, and how the Christian message has continued to thrive in radically different social contexts. Throughout the centuries the church has constantly reformed and reformulated itself, sometimes in the midst of violent conflict. There have always been those who have cynically manipulated the faith of believers to enhance their own wealth and power. This is true in the present age, but we have seen that there have always been those Christians who have courageously brought a message of hope to a troubled world. At the end of the second millennium, in the midst of continual change and reformation, Christianity continues to produce apostles, prophets, and martyrs ministering to a broken world.

Suggestions for Further Reading

General Works

Ahlstrom, Sydney E. *A Religious History of the American People.* 2 vols. New Have: Yale University Press, 1972.

Armstrong, Karen. *A History of God: The 4,000-year Quest of Judaism, Christianity and Islam.* New York: Ballantine Books, 1993.

Bokenkotter, Thomas S. *Concise History of the Catholic Church* , rev. New York: Image Books, 1990.

Clark, Elizabeth, and Herbert Richardson. *Women and Religion: A Feminist Sourcebook of Christian Thought.* New York: Harper & Row, 1977.

Gaustad, Edwin Scott. *A Religious History of America.* Revised ed. San Francisco: Harper, 1990.

González, Justo L. *Church History: An Essential Guide.* Nashville: Abingdon, 1996.

González, Justo L. *The Story of Christianity*, vol. 2: *The Reformation to the Present Day.* San Francisco: HarperSanFrancisco, 1984.

Greeley, Andrew. *The American Catholic.* New York: Basic Books, 1977.

Latourette, Kenneth Scott Latourette. *A History of Christianity*, vol. 2: 1500-1975. San Francisco: HarperSanFrancisco, 1953, 1975.

Mac Haffie, Barbara. *Her Story.* Philadelphia: Fortress, 1986.

Meyendorff, John. *The Orthodox Church: Its Past and Its Role in the World Today.* Tuckahoe, N.Y.: St. Vladimir's Press, 1981.

Noll, Mark A. *A History of Christianity in the United States and Canada.* Grand Rapids, Mich.: Eerdmans, 1992.

Tillich, Paul. *A History of Christian Thought: From Its Judaic and Hellenistic Origins to Existentialism.* Ed. by Carl E. Braaten. New York: Simon and Schuster, 1972.

Walker, Williston, and others. *A History of the Christian Church*, 4th ed. New York: Scribner's, 1985.

Ware, Kallistos T. *The Orthodox Way* . Tuckahoe, N.Y.: St. Vladimir's Press, 1995.

Part 1: Renaissance and Reform

Bloch, Marc Leopold Benjamin. *Feudal society*. Tr. by L. A. Manyon. Chicago: University of Chicago Press, 1961.

Bowie, Fiona, ed. *Beguine spirituality : mystical writings of Mechthild of Magdeburg, Beatrice of Nazareth, and Hadewijch of Brabant*. Tr. by Oliver Davies. New York : Crossroad, 1990.

Cohn, Norman. *The Pursuit of the Millennium: Revolutionary Millanararians and Mystical Anarchists of the Middle Ages*, 2nd ed. New York: Oxford, 1970.

Davis, Natalie Zemen. *Society and Çulture in Early Modern France*. Stanford University Press, 1975.

Dolan, John P., ed. and tr. *The Essential Erasmus*. New York: Meridian Books, 1964.

Erasmus. *Collected Works of Erasmus*. Toronto, Buffalo, London: University of Toronto Press, 1984

Gilmore, Myron P. *The World of Humanism 1453-1517*. New York: Harper & Row, 1952.

Huizinga, J. *The Waning of the Middle Ages*. Garden City, NY: Doubleday, 1954.

Jones, Cheslyn, Georffrey Wainwright and Edward Yarnold. *The Study of Liturgy*. New York: Oxford, 1978.

Knowles, David and Dimitri Obolensky. *The Middle Ages*, vol. 2 of *The Christian Centuries*. Darton: Paulist Press, 1983, c. 1969.

Knowles, David. *The Evolution of Medieval Thought*. New York: Random House, 1962.

Kristeller, Paul Oskar. *Renaissance Concepts of Man*. New York, 1972.

Lossky, Vladimir. *The mystical theology of the Eastern Church*. Tr. by members of the Fellowship of St. Alban and St. Sergius. Crestwood, New York: St. Vladimir's Seminary Press, 1976.

Oakley, Francis. *The Western Church in the Later Middle Ages*. Ithaca: University of Cornell Press, 1979.

Oberman, Heiko. *The Harvest of Medieval Theology*. Cambridge, Mass.: Harvard University Press, 1963.

Pelikan, Jaroslav. *The Growth of Medieval Theology (600-1300)*, vol. 3 of *The Christian Tradition: A History of the Development of Doctrine*. Chicago: University of Chicago Press, 1978.

Pelikan, Jaroslav. *The Spirit of Eastern Christendom*, vol. 2 of *The Christian Tradition: A History of the Development of Doctrine*. Chicago: University of Chicago Press, 1978.

Southern, R. W. *Western Society and the Church in the Middle Age,.* vol. 2 of *The Pelican History of the Church*. Penguin Books, 1970.

Spinka, Matthew. *John Hus: A Biography*. Princeton, N.J.: Princeton University Press, 1968.

Sumption, Jonathan. *Pilgrimage: An Image of Medieval Religion*. Totowa, N.J., 1975.

Thomas, Keith. *Religion and the Decline of Magic*. London, 1971.

Volz, Carl A. *The Medieval Church: From the Dawn of the Middle Ages to the Eve of the Reformation*. Nashville: Abingdon, 1997.

Wilson, Katharina M. *Women Writers of the Renaissance and Reformation*. Athens, Ga.: University of Georgia Press, 1987.

Part 2: The Protestant Reformation

Bainton, Roland H. The Reformation of the Sixteenth Century. Boston: Beacon Press, 1985.

Bainton, Roland. *Here I Stand! A Life of Martin Luther*. Nashville: Abingdon, 1970.

Bouwsma, John. *John Calvin: A Sixteenth-Century Portrait.* Oxford, New York: Oxford University Press, 1988.

Breen, Quirinus. *John Calvin; a study in French humanism*. With a foreword by John T. McNeill. 2nd. ed. Hamden, Conn.: Archon Books, 1968.

Bromiley, G. W., ed. *Zwingli and Bullinger*. Library of Christian Classics: Ichthus Edition. Phil.: Westminster, 1953.

Calvin, John. *Institutes of the Christian Religion*, vol. 1, ed. John McNeill, tr. Ford Lewis Battles, vol. 20 of *The Library of Christian Classics*. Philadelphia: Westminster Press, 1960.

Cameron, Euan. *The European Reformation*. New York: Oxford, 1991.

Caraman, Philip. *The Lost Paradise: An Account of the Jesuits in Paraguay, 1607-1768*. London: Sidgwick & Jackson, 1975.

Chadwick, Owen. *The Reformation*, vol. 3 of *The Pelican History of the Church*. Grand Rapids, MI: Eerdmans, 1964.

Dillenberger, John, ed. *Martin Luther: Selections from his Writings*. New York: Anchor Books, 1961.

Douglass, Jane Dempsey. *Women, freedom, and Calvin*. Philadelphia: Westminster Press, 1985.

Elliott, J. H. *Europe Divided 1559-1598*. Ithaca, N.Y.: Cornell University Press, 1968.

Elton, G. R. *Reform and Reformation: England 1509-1558*. London, 1977.

Gerrish, Brian, ed. *Reformers in Profile*. Philadelphia: Fortress Press, 1967.

Ginzburg, Carlo. *The Cheese and the Worms: The Cosmos of a Sixteenth Century Miller*. Tr. by John and Anne Tedeschi. Baltimore: Johns Hopkins University Press, 1980.

Heal, F. and R. O'Day, *Church and Society in England, Henry VIII to James I*. London, 1977.

Hill, Charles. *Intellectual Origins of the English Revolution*. Oxford University Press, 1965.

Hillerbrand, Hans, ed. *The Protestant Reformation*. New York: Harper & Row, 1968.

Krahn, Cornelius: *Dutch Anabaptism: Origin, Spread, Life, and Thought, 1450-1600*. The Hague, 1964.

Lindberg, Carter. *The European Reformations*. Oxford: Blackwell, 1996.

Macek, Josef. *The Hussite Movement in Bohemia*. Prague: Orbis Books, 1958.

McGrath, Alister. *The Intellectual Origins of the European Reformation*. Oxford and New York: Basil Blackwell, 1987.

Moeller, Bernd. *Imperial Cities and the Reformation*. Tr. by H. C. Erik Midelfort and Mark U. Edwards, Jr. Philadelphia, 1972.

Mullett, Michael. *The Catholic Reformation*. New York: Routledge, 1999.

O'Malley, John. *Praise and Blame in Renaissance Rome*. Durham, N.C.: Duke University Press, 1979.

O'Malley, John. *The First Jesuits*. Cambridge: Harvard University Press, 1993.

Oberman, Heiko. *Luther: Man Between God and the Devil*. New Haven: Yale University Press, 1989.

Ozment, Steven. *Reformation Europe: A Guide to Research*. St. Louis: Center for Reformation Research, 1982.

Ozment, Steven. *Protestants: The Birth of a Revolution*. New York: Doubleday, 1992.

Pelikan, Jaroslav. *Reformation of Church and Dogma (1300-1700)*, vol. 4 of *The Christian Tradition: A History of the Development of Doctrine*. Chicago: University of Chicago Press, 1984.

Scribner, Robert W. *Popular Culture And Popular Movements In Reformation Germany*. London and Ronceverte, WV: Hambledon Press, 1987.

Trevor-Roper, H.R. *Religion, the Reformation and Social Change, and other essays*. 2nd ed. London and New York: MacMillan, 1972.

Webster, Charles. *From Paracelsus to Newton: Magic and the Making of Modern Science*. Cambridge University Press, 1982.

Williams, George. *The Radical Reformation*. Philadelphia, 1962.

Yates, F.A. *The Rosicrucian Enlightenment*. Boston: Routledge & Kegan, 1972.

Part 3: Religion of the Heart in the Age of Reason

Becker, Carl. *The Heavenly City of the Eighteenth-Century Philosophers*. New Haven: Yale University Press, 1932.

Bonomi, Patricia. *Under the Cope of Heaven*. NY: Oxford University 1986.

Brown, Dale. *Understanding Pietism*. Grand Rapids, Mich.: Wm. B. Eerdmans, 1978.

Butler, Jon. *Awash in a Sea of Faith: Christianizing the American People*. Cambridge: Harvard University Press, 1990.

Campbell, Ted. *Religion of the Heart: A Study of European Religious Life in the Seventeenth and Eighteenth Centuries*. Columbia, S.C.: University of South Carolina Press, 1991

Cragg, Gerald. *The Church in the Age of Reason 1648-1789*. Pelican History of the Church, vol. 4. New York: Viking Penguin Books, 1970.

Gaustad, Edwin Scott. *The Great Awakening in New England*. New York: Harper and Brothers, 1957.

Gay, Peter. *The Enlightenment: An Interpretation*. 2 vols. New York: Norton, 1969.

Gay, Peter. *The Enlightenment: An Interpretation*. 2 vols. *The Rise of Modern Paganism. The Science of Freedom*. New York: W. W. Norton & Co., 1966, 1969.

Girard, René. *Violence and the Sacred*. Translated by Patrick Gregory. Baltimore: Johns Hopkins University Press, 1972.

Goen, C. C. *Revivalism and Separatism in New England 1740-1800*. New Haven: Yale University Press, 1962.

Hazard, Paul. *The European Mind: 1680-1715*. Translated by J. Lewis May. Cleveland: Meridian Books, 1963.

Heimert, Alan. *Religion and the American Mind: From the Great Awakening to the Revolution*. Cambridge, Mass.: Harvard University Press, 1968.

Lovejoy, David S. *Religious Enthusiasm in the New World*. Cambridge, MA: Harvard University Press, 1985.

Mandler, Ira. *Religion, Society, and Utopia in Nineteenth-Century America*. Amherst, Mass: University of Massachusetts Press, 1984.

May, Henry F. *The Enlightenment in America*. New York: Oxford University Press, 1976.

Pelikan, Jaroslav. *Christian Doctrine and Modern Culture (since 1700)*, vol. 5 of *The Christian Tradition: A History of the Development of Doctrine*. Chicago: University of Chicago Press, 1989.

Redwood, John. *Reason, Ridicule and Religion: The Age of the Enlightenment in England 1600-1750*. London: Thames and Hudson, 1976.

Rood, Wilhelmus. *Comenius and the Low Countries: Some Aspects of Life and Work of a Czech Exile in the Seventeenth Century*. New York: Abner Schram, 1970.

Sandberg, Karl C., tr. and ed. *The Great Contest of Faith and Reason: Selections from the Writings of Pierre Bayle*. New York: Frederick Unger, 1963.

Sedgwick, Alexander. *Jansenism in Seventeenth-Century France: Voices in the Wilderness*. Charlottesville, VA: University of Virginia Press, 1977.

Stoeffler, F. Ernest. *German Pietism During the Eighteenth Century*. Studies in the History of Religions, vol. 24. Leiden: E. J. Brill, 1973.

Trevor-Roper, Hugh. *Catholics, Anglicans and Puritans: Seventeenth Century Essays*. Chicago: University of Chicago Press, 1988.

Walzer, Michael. *The Revolution of the Saints: A Study in the Origins of Radical Politics*. New York: Athenium, 1968.

Part 4: The Nineteenth Century

Bays, Daniel H., ed. *Christianity in China: From the Eighteenth Century to the Present*. Palo Alto, Ca.: Stanford University Press, 1996.

Doan, Ruth A. *The Miller Heresy, Millennialism and American Culture*. Philadelphia: Temple University Press, 1987.

Eddy, Mary Baker. *Science and Health with Key to the Scriptures*. Reprint. Boston: Christian Science Board of Directors, 1980.

Gerrish, B. A. *A Prince of the Church: Schleiermacher and the Beginnings of Modern Theology*. Philadelphia: Fortress, 1984.

Hansen, Klaus J. *Mormonism and the American Experience.* Chicago: University of Chicago Press, 1981.

Hatch, Nathan O. *The Democratization of American Christianity.* New Haven: Yale University Press, 1989.

Misner, Paul. *Social Catholicism in Europe: From the Onset of Industrialization to the First World War.* New York: Crossroad, 1991.

Neill, Stephen. *A History of Christian Missions.* New York: Penguin Books, 1964.

Raboteau, Albert. *Slave Religion: The 'Invisible Institution' in the Antebellum South.* New York: Oxford University Press, 1978.

Reuther, Rosemary Radford and Sosemary Skinner Keller, eds. *Women and Religion in America.* 3 vols. San Francisco: Harper & Row, 1981.

Schleiermacher, Friedrich. *On Religion: Speeches to its Cultured Despisers.* Tr. Richard Couter. New York: Cambridge University Press, 1988.

Shipps, Jan. *Mormonism: The Story of a New Religious Tradition.* Urbana: University of Illinois Press, 1985.

Smith, Timothy. *Revivalism and Social Reform.* Baltimore: Johns Hopkins, 1980.

Troeltsch, Ernst. *Religion in History.* Ed. and tr. by James Luther Adams and Walter F. Bense. Philadelphia: Fortress, 1991.

Welch, Claude. *Protestant Thought in the Nineteenth Century.* 2 vols. New Haven: Yale University Press, 1972 and 1985.

Part 5: The Twentieth Century

Balmer, Randal. *Mine Eyes Have Seen the Glory: A Journey into the Evangelical Subculture of America.* New York: Oxford University Press, 1989.

Dana, Robert L. *American Women in Mission: A Social History of Mission Thought and Practice.* Macon, Ga.: Mercer University Press, 1997.

Dayton, Donald W. and Rober K. Jonston, eds. *The Variety of American Evangelicalism.* Knoxville: University of Tennessee Press, 1991.

Dussel, Enrique, ed. *The Church in Latin America, 1492-1992.* Maryknoll, NY: Orbis Books, 1992.

Helmreich, Ernst Christian. *The German Churches Under Hitler: Background, Struggle, and Epilogue.* Detroit: Wayne State Press, 1979.

Hutchinson, William R. *The Modernist Impulse in American Protestantism.* Cambridge: Harvard University Press, 1976.

Isichei, Elizabeth. *A History of Christianity in Africa*. Grand Rapids: Eerdmans, 1995.

Marsden, George. *Fundamentalism and American Culture*. NY: Oxford, 1980.

Martin, David. *Tongues of Fire: The Explosion of Protestantism in Latin America*. Oxford: Blackwell, 1990.

Marty, Martin E. *Modern American Religion*. 2 vols. Chicago: University of Chicago Press, 1991.

Miller, Glenn T. *The Modern Church: From the Dawn of the Refomation to the Eve of the Third Millennium*. Nashville: Abingdon, 1997.

Moore, R. Laurence. *Religious Outsideers and the Making of America*. New York: Oxford University Press, 1986.

Moore, R. Laurence. *Selling God: American Religion in the Marketplace of Culture*. New York: Oxford University Press, 1994.

Niebuhr, Reinhold. *Leaves from the Notebook of a Tamed Cynic*. Louisville: Westminster/John Knox, 1980.

Synan, Vinson. *The Holiness-Pentecostal Movement in the United States*. Grand Rapids, Mich.: Eerdmans, 1972.

Thurian, Max and Geoffrey Wainwright. *Baptism and Eucharist: Ecumenical Convergence in Celebration*. Grand Rapids: Eerdmans, 1983.

Tillich, Paul. *Dynamics of Faith*. New York: Harper Torchbooks, 1957.

Wilson, Bryan. *The Social Dimensions of Sectarianism*. Oxford: Clarendon Press, 1990.

Wuthnow, Robert. *The Restructuring of American religion: Society and Faith Since World War II*. Princeton, N.J.: Princeton University Press, 1988.

Index

a'Kempis, Thomas, 41, 147, 198
a'Becket, Thomas, 45
Abolition, 286-288, 290, 351
Abortion, 331, 346
Act of Supremacy, 73, 138, 126, 134, 138
Act of Uniformity, 134, 138, 187
Adventists, 270-271
Africa, 57, 230, 250, 252, 253, 284, 321, 341, 351, 353
African Methodist Episcopal Church, 252-253
Agricola, Rudolf, 71
Alba, Duke of, 118
Albigensian, 114
Aldersgate, 217
Alexander I (Tsar), 240
Alexander V (Pope), 24
Alexander VI (Pope), 55
Allen, Richard, 252
American Council of Churches, 327
American Revolution, 190, 243
American Tract Society, 248
Ames, William, 137
Amsterdam, 119
Anabaptist, 104-111, 117, 136, 146, 153
Anagni Palace, 23
Anglican Church, 124, 127,134, 187, 188, 190, 216, 217, 218, 219, 225, 286
Anne of Cleaves, 127
Antichrist, 43, 44, 48, 51, 52, 86, 91, 137, 167, 240, 270, 326, 327, 328, 336, 353,

Anticlericalism, 34, 45, 47, 48, 233, 238
Antwerp, 34, 119
Apartheid, 351
Apocalypic, 44, 91, 107, 108, 230, 239, 324
Apostles' Creed, 70
Aquinas, Thomas, 14, 27, 28, 66, 68, 178, 235, 255
Arabic, 56, 65
Archbishop of Canterbury, 47, 131, 133, 134
Aristotle, 27, 29, 30, 70, 177, 178
Armageddon,326, 328
Armenian, 76, 297
Arminianism, 120, 139, 216, 244
Arminius, Jacob, 119-120
Arnauld, Antoine, 202-203
Arnauld, Mother Angelique, 202
Arndt, Johann, 198, 205
Arnold, Gottfried, 209-210
Asbury, Francis, 244-245, 290
Assemblies of God, 329
Astronomy, 30, 177-180
Atheism, 187, 194, 227, 229, 230, 247, 258
Augsburg Confession, 96, 97, 153, 154, 204, 214
Augsburg Interim, 97, 153
Augsburg, Peace of, 92
Augustine, 5, 29, 31, 32, 68, 102, 104, 202, 203, 229
Augustinian, 27, 31, 40, 203
Austin, Ann, 172
Avignon, 19-22, 113

Azuza Street Revival, 329

Bach, Johann Sebastian, 162
Backus, Isaac, 255
Bacon, Francis, 139, 179
Bacon, Roger, 30, 43
Balthasar, Hans von, 341
Baptism, 12, 49, 105, 106, 111, 247, 322
Baptist, 138, 187, 208, 225, 242, 245-246, 282, 287, 324, 333
Barmen Declaration, 308
Baroque, 161
Barth, Karl, 303-304, 308, 313, 318-319, 341
Basic Christian Communities, 344
Basle, 25, 94, 98, 119
Basle, Council of, 25-26, 53
Baur, F. C., 262
Bayle, Pierre, 186-187, 194
Beecher, Catherine, 289
Beecher, Henry Ward, 265-266, 292
Beguines, 34, 35, 36, 40
Benedict XI (Pope), 19
Benedictine, 23, 40
Benevolence Societies, 248
Bengel, Albrecht, 211
Beza, Theodore, 113, 115-116, 136
Bible (see Scripture), 28, 46, 50, 53, 65, 71, 93, 105, 110, 121, 122, 125, 128, 137, 138, 141, 168, 178, 204, 205, 208, 230, 247, 252, 286, 289, 290, 309, 316, 320, 328, 329, 330, 339, 341
Bible College, 327
Biblical Criticism, 211, 230, 261-266, 289, 304, 323, 341
Biel, Gregory, 83
Bishops/Archbishops, 8, 10, 11, 14, 18, 42, 45, 46, 47, 52, 58, 66, 84, 90, 98, 103, 122, 1321, 135, 137, 139, 145, 149, 168, 233, 234, 343
Black Church, 333-335
Black Virgin of Czestochowa, 163
Blaurock, George, 105-106

Bockelson, Jan, 108
Boff, Leonardo, 343, 348
Bohemia, 1, 48, 50, 51, 154, 155
Böhme, Jakob, 197-198, 205
Boleyn, Anne, 125-126, 127, 130
Bologna, 25, 148
Bonaparte, Napoleon, 196, 226, 231-232, 263,
Bonhoeffer, Dietrich, 308-309, 319
Boniface VIII (Pope), 17-19, 232
Book of Common Prayer, 129-130, 136, 141, 187
Book of Concord, 154, 155, 204
Book of Discipline, 126
Book of Martyrs, 133, 135, 139
Book of Mormon, 275-276
Book of Sports, 138
Booth, William, 293
Booth, Evangeline, 293
Bora, Katherine von, 88
Borromeo, Charles, 150-151, 341
Boston, 168, 172, 190, 223, 233, 264
Bourbons, 115-116
Boxer Rebellion, 283
Bradwardine, Thomas, 31
Brahe, Tycho, 176
Brazil, 166
Brebeuf, Jean de, 165
Briçonnet, Guillaume, 74
Bridges, Ruby, 337
Bridget of Sweden, St., 21
Brothers and Sisters of the Common Life, 40-41, 75
Browne, Robert, 136
Bryan, William Jennings, 284, 302, 326
Buber, Martin, 339
Bucer, Martin, 94, 96, 98, 101, 154
Buddhism, 281
Bulgaria, 58, 59
Bullinger, Johann, 101
Bultmann, Rudolf, 316-318, 323
Burned Over District, 270
Bushnell, Horace, 265
Byzantine Empire, 1, 58, 69, 238

Calendar, 11, 195
Calvin, John, 97, 99-103, 104, 113,
    147, 169, 202, 207, 221
Calvinism (see also Reformed), 93,
    103, 118, 141, 153, 154, 181, 216
Camara, Dom Helder, 343
Campbell, Alexander, 247-248
Campbell, Thomas, 247
Campola, Tony, 328
Campus Crusade, 327
Cane Ridge, 248-249
Canon Law, 10, 46, 50, 70, 86, 99, 125
Canada, 107
Canterbury, 9, 47
Capitalism, 79, 103, 114, 169, 313,
    319
Capuchins, 146
Caraffa, Giovanni (see Paul IV)
Carey, Lott, 253
Cardinals, 17, 19, 22, 23, 224, 83, 145,
    150
Carey, William, 231
Carlstadt, 89-90, 95
Carter, Jimmy, 331
Cartwright, Thomas, 135-136
Castellio, Sebastian, 101
Castille, 63-65
Categorical Imperative, 256
Catherine of Aragon, 125-126
Catherine of Siena, St., 21, 38
Catherine the Great (Russia), 193
Catholic League, 95
Celestine V (Pope), 17, 18, 44
Celibacy, 7, 10, 72, 86, 994, 210, 270,
    341
Chalcedon, 51
Channing, William Elery, 264
Chardin, Teilhard de, 338
Charles I (England), 138, 139, 140, 167
Charles II (England), 173
Charles IV (Emperor), 48
Charles V (Emperor), 80, 86, 117, 125,
    126, 132, 148, 165
Charles VIII (France), 55
Chaucer, Geoffrey, 9

Chauncy, Charles, 190, 225
Chelcicky. Peter, 53-54
Cherbury, Herbert of, 184-185
China, 56, 163, 164, 282, 285, 310,
    312
Christian Church (see Disciples of
    Christ)
Christian Science, 272
Christian Socialism, 295-296
Church Dogmatics, 304
Church of Christ Scientist. See
    Christian Science
Church of England (see Anglican
    Church)
Church of God in Christ, 334
Church of North India, 322
Circuit Rider, 244
Cistercian, 40, 43
Civil Constitution of the Clergy, 195
Civil Rights Movement, 335, 336-337
Clarendon Code, 187
Clarke, John, 172
Clement V (Pope), 19-20
Clement VII (Pope), 23, 95
Clement XIV (Pope), 161
Clergy (see also Priesthood, see also
    Bishops), 10, 46, 103, 150, 238, 322,
    331
Clericis Laicos, 18
Cloning, 353
Cloud of Unknowing, 37
Coke, Thomas, 245
Colet, John, 72-74, 75
Coligny, Gaspard de, 116
Colored Methodist Episcopal Church,
    334
Columbus, Christopher, 63, 66-67,
    238
Comenius, John Amos, 180-181
Communalism, 52, 107
Communism, 310-312, 318, 348
Complutensian Polyglot, 65
Conciliarism, 25-26, 50
Concordat of Bologna, 113
Cone, James, 336

Confessing Church, 308
Confession, 12, 13, 48, 81
Confirmation, 13
Congar, Yves, 338
Congregationalism/Congregationalist
  Church, 225, 245, 265, 289, 322
Congress of Vienna, 231
Consensus of Sandomier, 162
Conservatism, 232-234
Consistory, 100-101, 122
Constance, Council of, 24-225, 26, 50,
  86, 94
Constantine (Emperor), 53, 209
Constantinople, 26, 56, 57, 58, 59, 60,
  69, 80
Contarini, Gasparo, 144-145, 149
Conventicles, 205-206, 216
Conventuals, 43
Copernicus, Nicholas, 154, 176
Coptic Church, 57, 321
Covenant, 28, 141, 168
Coverdale Bible, 129
Cranmer, Thomas, 126-130, 132
Cromwell, Oliver, 141-142
Cromwell, Thomas, 126-128, 132
Crusades, 59, 63
Cultural Revolution, 312
Cusa, Nicholas of, 70-71
Cutler, Timothy, 190, 225

d'Ailley, Pierre, 23, 51
Daly, Mary, 332
Danse Macabre, 37
Dante Alighieri, 14, 68
Darby, John Nelson, 323
Darwin, Charles, 258-259
Darwinism, 326-327, 338
Davenport, James, 224-225
Day, Dorothy, 314
Death, 13, 14, 37
Deism, 14-186, 189, 212, 227
Denck, John, 110, 205
Denmark, 306
Dentiere, Marie, 98
De Sales, Francis, 152

Descartes, Rene, 178, 181-182
Deventer, 39, 75
Devotio Moderna, 39-41, 206
Diderot, Denis, 194
Diocese, 20, 65, 118, 144, 149
Dippel, Johann Konrad, 209
Disciples of Christ, 248
Disestablishment, 229, 233
Dispensation, 23
Dispensationalism, 323, 324, 326
Divorce, 13, 126, 345
Dominican, 11, 36, 38, 64, 177, 200
Donation of Constantine, 69-70
Dort, Synod of, 120-121
Dostoyevsky, Fyodor, 241
Douglass, Frederick, 287
Dow, Lorenzo, 243
Du Bois, W. E. B., 334
Duns Scotus, 27-28, 30, 43, 83
Dunster, Henry, 173
Dutch Reformed Church, 119-120
Dyer, Mary, 172

Eck, John, 85-86
Eckhart, Meister, 36, 197
Ecumenical Movement, 319
Eddy, Mary Baker, 272
Edict of Nantes, 117, 202
Edict of Toleration, 116
Edward III (England), 17-18, 45
Edward VI (England), 127, 130-131
Edwards, Jonathan, 220-221, 248
Elizabeth I (England), 130, 133-136
Elizabethan Settlement, 133-135
Emerson, Ralph Waldo, 264
England, 17, 23, 30, 43-47, 54, 64, 72,
  124-142, 175, 188, 199, 236, 293
Enlightenment, 68, 159, 175-185, 191-
  194, 208, 216, 235, 254, 256, 272
Erasmus, Desiderius, 74-77, 87, 93,
  109, 128, 129
Etaples, Jacques Lefevre, 73-74
Ethiopia, 57-58
Eucharist, 9, 12, 29, 49, 51, 89, 94, 95,
  100, 102, 111, 116, 128, 130, 131,

134, 149, 210, 222, 235, 249, 264, 296, 322, 341, 345

Evangelical Party, 219, 236

Evangelicalism, 215, 242, 250, 251-252, 289, 320, 323, 331

Existentialism, 241, 266-268, 317

Extreme Unction, 12, 13

Falwell, Jerry, 331

Farel, Guillaume, 98-99

Fascism, 304-305

Federal Council of Churches, 301-302, 314

Feminism, 288, 331, 332

Fénelon, 201

Ferrara, Council of, 26

Fetter Lane Society, 217

Feuerbach, Ludwig, 278

Ficino, Marsilio, 70-71, 73

Filioque Clause, 26

Finney, Charles, 248, 270

Fiorenza, Elisabeth, 382

Flacius, Matthias, 153

Florence, 54, 72, 95

Florence, Council of, 26, 60

Fosdick, Harry Emerson, 325

Four Articles of Prague, 52-53

Foursquare Gospel, 330

Fourth Lateran Council, 12, 149

Fox, George, 110, 199

Foxe, John, 133-135, 139

France, 17, 19, 21, 23, 54, 64, 73, 74, 99, 113-117, 156, 175, 200, 201-203, 232

Francis I (France), 113

Francis II (France), 115, 121

Franciscans, 11, 40, 42, 43, 53, 67, 146, 147

Franck, Sebastian, 110

Francke, August Hermann, 206-208, 209

Franco, Francisco, 305

Franklin, Benjamin, 189-190, 224

Fraticelli, 44

Frederick III (Palatinate), 154

Frederick IV (Palatinate), 155

Frederick the Great (Prussia), 191, 193, 208

French Revolution, 160, 194-196, 231, 236

Frequens, 25

Freud, Sigmund, 279, 313

Fry, Elizabeth, 293

Fuller Theological Seminary, 327

Fundamentalism, 304, 323, 327, 330, 331

Fundamentals, The, 324

Galilei, Galileo, 176, 178-180

Gallicanism, 202

Garrison, William Lloyd, 287

Geneva, 97-101, 113, 119, 122, 131

Genevan Academy, 102

Germany, 23, 71, 85, 86-91, 92, 97, 127, 153, 197, 198, 232, 295, 302, 305-309

Gerson, Jean, 23,24, 31, 51

Ghandi, Mohandis, 336

Ghent, 119

Gibbons, Cardinal, 234, 294-295

Giles of Rome, 27

Gladden, Washington, 296

Glossalial, see Tongues

Gomarus, Franciscus, 120

Gordon, A. J., 328

Grace, 12, 31, 36, 72, 73, 102, 120, 121, 202, 204, 217, 222, 339

Graham, Billy, 328

Granvelle, Cardinal, 118

Great Awakenings (First and Second), 242-244, 246-247, 269, 268, 290

Great Bible, 129

Great Schism, 23-25, 46, 48, 49

Grebel, Conrad, 105-106

Greece, 59, 60, 238-240

Greek, 65, 69, 72, 75, 87, 93, 222, 281

Greek New Testament, 65, 76, 93, 128, 211

Gregory of Rimini, 31

Gregory VII (Pope), 18

Gregory XI (Pope), 22, 46
Gregory XIII (Pope), 117, 146
Gregory XVI (Pope), 237
Grimke, Angelina, 288-289
Grimke, Sarah, 288
Groote, Gerard, 39
Grotius, Hugo, 120
Guise, 114-115, 121
Gurney, John, 293
Gutenberg, Johann, 71
Gutièrrez, Gustavo, 343
Guyon, Madame, 200-201

Hadewijch of Antwerp, 34-35
Hagia Sophia, 60
Half-way Covenant, 169
Halle, 206-208, 211, 213, 214
Handel, George Fridrich, 162
Hapsburgs, 156, 191, 231-232
Harmony Commune, 273
Harnack, Adolf von, 208, 263, 313
Harvard College (University), 173,
    223
Hawaii, 283
Haydn, Joseph, 162
Hebrew, 70-72, 87, 93, 262
Hegel, Georg Wilhelm, 199, 212, 256-
    257, 266
Heidegger, Martin, 317, 339
Helvetius, Claude Adrien, 194
Henry II (France), 114-115
Henry IV (England), 47
Henry IV (France), 116-117
Henry of Navarre (see Henry IV)
Henry VIII (England), 62, 73, 125-
    131, 202
Herder, Johann Gottfried, 235
Heresy/Heretic, 8, 19, 25, 35-36, 40,
    42-44, 47, 49, 50, 55, 63, 86, 112,
    114, 125, 132, 145, 210
Herrnhut, 211, 213
Hesychast, 59, 61
Hinduism, 281-282
Hitler, Adolph, 305-308
Hodge, Charles, 259

Hofmann, Melchior, 108
Holiness Movement, 219, 249-251,
    290, 319, 328
Holocaust, 311
Holy Communion. See Eucharist
Holy Days, 11, 93, 135
Holy Spirit, 12, 43, 89, 101, 120, 171,
    204, 214, 247, 249, 269, 328-330
Homosexuality, 331, 351, 352
Hong Kong, 282
Hooker, Richard, 136
Howard, Catherine, 128
Hubmaier, Balthasar, 105
Huguenot, 113-117, 202
Humanism, 69, 72, 73, 79, 92, 93, 110
Hume, David, 186, 254-255
Hundred Years War, 23
Hungary, 107, 154, 155, 312
Hus, John, 48-52, 85-86, 102
Hussite, 25, 79
Hutchinson, Anne, 171-172
Hutter, Jacob, 107

Iconoclasm, 8, 14, 89, 94, 99, 118, 130,
    240
Iconography, 61, 238
Iconostasis, 9
Index of Forbidden Books, 179, 233
India, 163, 230, 280, 281, 348
Indians, 165-166
Indulgences, 83-85, 89, 93
Industrialism, 215, 229, 291-296
Inertia, 30, 177
Inner Mission, 295
Innocent III (Pope), 16, 127
Innocent IV (Pope), 16
Innocent VI (Pope), 21
Inquisition, 8, 34, 44, 63, 64, 76, 98,
    101, 114, 145, 147, 178, 209
Institutes of the Christian Religion,
    102
InterVarsity, 327
Ireland, 140, 141, 222, 351
Isabella (Spain), 63-66

Islam, 2, 56, 62, 63, 71, 147, 187, 238-240, 282, 311
Italian Revolution, 232
Italy, 5, 23, 38, 54-55, 69, 70, 75, 145, 146, 177, 232, 305
Ivan III (Russia), 60, 192

Jakoubek of Stribo, 51
James I (England), 138, 137, 168
James II (England), 187
Jansen, Cornelius, 202
Jansenism, 202-203
Japan, 163, 282, 282, 283, 312
Jarratt, Deveraux, 225
Jefferson, Thomas, 175, 189-190, 191
Jerusalem, 108, 213, 277
Jesuits. See Society of Jesus
Jews/Judaism, 19, 61, 63-64, 71, 181, 192, 211, 262, 271, 282, 305, 311, 341
Joachim of Fiore, 17, 43
John of the Cross, 151
John Paul I (Pope), 347
John Paul II (Pope), 345, 346-348
John VIII (Byzantium), 25
John XXII (Pope), 20, 42, 43, 44
John XXIII (Pope), 24, 341-342
John XXIII (antipope), 24, 49, 50
Jones, Absalom, 252
Joseph II (Austria), 192
Jubilee, 5, 353
Julian of Norwich, 37-38
Jussie, Jeanne de, 98
Justification, 82, 145, 153, 221

Kabbala, 70, 71, 211
Kant, Immanuel, 254-256
Kappel, Battle of, 96
Kepler, Johannes, 176-178, 258
Khomiakov, A. S., 239
Kierkegaard, Soren, 266-268, 304, 317
King James Bible, 132, 137, 320
King, Martin Luther, Jr., 336-337
Knights Templar, 78, 19
Knox, John, 121-123, 131, 136

Ku Klux Klan, 333
Kulturkampf, 233
Küng, Hans, 339, 348

L'Hopital, Michel de, 115
Labor Unions, 294, 347
Laity (see also Priesthood of all Believers), 10, 141, 245, 346
las Casas, Bartolome de, 67, 165-166
Laski, Jan, 130, 162
Latitudinarianism, 186-187, 189, 226
Latter Day Saints, 247, 274
Laud, William, 139-140
Lee, Ann, 269-270
Leibnitz, Gottfried Wilhelm von, 164, 183-184, 194, 211, 256
Leipzig, 85, 350
Lenin, Vladimir Illych, 310-311, 313
Leo X (Pope), 86, 93, 125
Leo XIII (Pope), 295
Lessing, Gotthold, 227
Liberalism, 189, 190, 230, 254-266, 301, 303, 313, 319
Liberation Theology, 342-344, 348
Lima Document, 322
Lindsay, Hal, 327
Livingstone, David, 284
Loci Communes, 87, 153
Locke, John, 175, 184, 186, 221
Lollards, 47
Long Parliament, 140
Lord's Supper. See Eucharist
Louis of Nassau, 118
Louis the Bavarian (Emperor), 21, 44
Louis XIV (France), 201-202, 203
Louis XVI (France), 195
Loyola, Ignatius, St., 64, 146-148
Luther, Martin, 31, 37, 49, 77, 80-91, 92, 95-97, 104, 128, 143, 154, 202, 205, 217, 303
Lutheran Churches, 92, 96, 108, 125, 128, 134, 153-154, 156, 162, 198, 207, 210, 263, 307, 322
Lutheran League, 95

Madchen, J. Gresham, 325
Madison, James, 186, 191
Malcolm X, 335
Mandela, Nelson, 351
Manz, Felix, 105
Marburg Colloquy, 95
Marian Exiles, 132
Marriage, 12, 13, 46, 49, 87, 88, 97, 130, 250, 270, 274, 315, 345
Marsilius of Padua, 21, 29, 127
Martin V (Pope), 25
Martyr, 42, 51-52, 105, 123, 127, 133, 353
Marx, Karl, 279, 295, 310, 313, 314
Marxism, 294, 347
Mary Stuart (Queen of Scots), 121-123
Mass (see Eucharist)
Massachusetts Bay, 138
Matthew Bible, 129
Matthew of Janov, 48
Matthews, Shailer, 316
Mattys, Jan, 108
McGready, James, 247
McPherson, Aimee, 330
Meaux, 74, 98, 100, 114
Mechthild of Magdeburg, 34
Medici, 54-55, 70, 150
Medici, Catherine d', 114, 115-116
Medjugorje, 345
Melanchthon, Philip, 85, 87, 96, 104, 145, 153
Mennonites, 109, 188
Merici, Angela, 145
Merton, Thomas, 344
Metaphysics, 27, 30, 255, 260, 263
Methodists, 215-220, 242, 244-245, 252-253, 288, 289, 290, 293, 322, 333
Michael of Cesena, 44
Michael Paleologus (Byzantium), 58
Milic of Kromeriz, 48
Millennium, 179, 269, 270, 273, 278, 335, 353
Miller, William, 270-271

Missions /Missionaries, 163+166, 208, 213, 237-238, 277, 280-286, 323
Modernism, 234
Molinos, Miguel de, 200
Monasteries /Monasticism, 7, 10, 32, 34, 39, 40, 43, 59, 81, 94, 127, 151, 193, 263, 270, 345
Monophysite, 57+58
Moody Bible Institute, 325
Moody, Dwight L., 324
Moon, Charlotte Digges (Lottie), 282-283, 285
Moravians (see also Unitas Fratrum), 213-214, 217, 218
More, Thomas, 72-75, 87, 126-128
Mormon. See Latter Day Saints
Moroni, 275
Mother Teresa, 348-349
Motherhood of God, 38, 214
Mott, John R., 285, 321
Mott, Lucretia, 289
Mozart, Wolfgang Amadeus, 185
Muhammad, Elijah, 335
Muhlenberg, Henry, 214
Münster, 107-109, 171
Müntzer, Thomas, 91-92, 104-105
Music, 49, 51, 88, 209, 219
Mussolini, Benito, 305
Mysticism, 32-39, 69, 71, 108, 111, 151-152, 197-198, 226, 235, 239, 240

Nation of Islam, 335
National Association for the Advancement of Colored Persons (NAACP), 334
National Catholic War Council, 301
National Council of Churches of Christ, 314
National Evangelical Association (NEA), 320
Naudè, Beyers, 351
Nazism, 279, 304-308, 318
Nestorian, 56

Netherlands, 34-35, 39-41, 74, 108, 109, 117, 138, 156
New International Version (NIV), 320
New Light, 223-225
New Testament, 43, 65, 70, 74, 103, 104, 105, 106, 135, 168, 203, 262, 314, 316-318
New York City, 296, 324
Newman, John Henry, 236
Newton, Isaac, 182-184, 193, 198
Newton, John, 219
Nicene Creed, 26
Niebuhr, Reinhold, 313-314, 320
Nietzsche, Frederick, 279, 306
Nikon, Patriarch, 192
Ninety-Five Theses, 85, 111
Noailles, Cardinal Louis Antoine de, 203-204
Nominalism, 29
Noyes, John Humphrey, 273-274

Observants, 43-44, 65
Ochino, Bernardino, 146
Oetinger, Friedrich Chrisoph, 211-212
Old Believers, 192
Old Lights, 223-225
Old Testament, 43, 71, 103, 105, 106, 108, 141, 168, 261, 262, 276, 313
Oneida, 274
Oratorians, 144, 162
Oresme, Nicholas d', 30
Orthodox Church, Greek, 1, 26, 57-60, 192, 238, 311, 321
Orthodox Church, Russian, 60, 163, 192-193, 239, 311
Osiander, Andrea, 154
Oxford Movement, 236

Pagan/Paganism, 7, 8, 68, 69, 75, 175, 332
Palatinate, 92, 154
Palmer, Phobe Worrall, 249, 290
Pantheism, 198, 232
Papacy/Papal, 16, 18-26, 42, 43, 46, 55, 57, 64, 79, 83, 84, 94, 122, 126, 129, 130, 134, 145, 164, 179, 201, 232, 270, 328
Papal States, 21, 232
Papal Supremacy, 16-22, 63, 71, 126, 199, 201-202, 232, 339
Paracelsus, 110
Parham, Charles F., 328
Parker, Matthew, 134
Parks, Rosa, 336
Parliament, 72, 132, 135, 138-140, 187
Parr, Catherine, 128, 130
Pascal, Blaise, 203
Paul, St., 72, 73, 75, 76, 82
Paul III (Pope), 148
Paul IV (Pope), 144-145, 149
Paul VI (Pope), 346
Paulist Fathers, 236
Peasants' Revolt (England), 47, 50
Peasants' War (Germany), 90-91, 105
Penance, 10, 83, 84, 149
Penn, William, 188
Pennsylvania, 111, 188,213
Pentecostalism, 328-330, 334
Peter the Great (Russia), 192
Petrarch, 21, 68
Philadelphia, 189-190, 223, 233, 286
Philip II (Spain), 117, 132, 134
Philip of Hesse, 93, 95, 97
Philip the Fair (France), 17, 62
Pia Desideria, 205
Pietism, 111, 197, 204-214, 217, 221, 259, 263
Pilgrimage, 5, 9, 39, 82
Pisa, Council of, 23-24
Pius IX (Pope), 232-233
Pius XI (Pope), 305
Plato/Platonism, 27, 29, 33, 36, 55, 70, 73, 177
Plymouth Brethren, 223
Podiedonostev, C.P., 240
Poissy, Colloquy of, 115-116
Poland, 154, 162, 163, 346, 347
Pole, Reginald, 180, 181, 198, 199, 205
Polygamy, 97, 108, 274, 276

Pope (see Papacy)
Pope, Alexander, 183
Porete, Marguerite, 35
Port Royal, 202-203
Prague, 48-51, 52, 155
Predestination, 30, 46, 102, 120, 139,
    141, 202, 216
Presbyterian, 103, 123, 135-136, 140,
    187, 203, 222, 246, 287
Priesthood, 10, 12-14, 18, 57, 83, 89,
    130, 141, 144-146, 172, 187, 195,
    341
Princeton Theological Seminary, 325
Princeton University, 222
Prophetic Religion, 313, 343
Protestantism, 2, 79, 95, 96, 98, 113,
    124, 143, 145, 148, 157, 208
Puritans, 137-142, 166-174, 175, 179,
    187, 216, 220
Purgatory, 14, 84
Pusey, Edward, 236
Pym, John, 140

Quakers. See Society of Friends
Quesnel, Pasquier, 203
Quietism, 200-201, 206, 209

Radewijns, Florentinus, 39
Rahner, Karl, 339
Rapp, George, 273
Rauschenbusch, Walter, 296-297, 313
Reagan, Ronald, 331
Reformed Churches, 92, 93, 96-99,
    113, 121, 134, 135, 141, 153, 154,
    162, 207
Relics, 2, 8, 9, 14, 39, 50
Renaissance, 5, 20, 69, 72, 83
Reuchlin, Johannes, 70-71
Revised Standard Version, 320
Revivals, 220, 225, 248, 319
Ricci, Matteo, 164
Ritschl, Albrecht, 208, 263
Robertson, Pat, 323, 331
Robinson, John, 137
Rolle, Richard, 37

Romanticism, 235
Rome, 5, 9, 18, 20, 22-23, 60, 82, 97,
    192, 232
Romero, Oscar, 344
Rosary, 345
Rudolf II (Emperor), 155, 176
Russia, 58, 213, 239, 310-311

Sacraments, 12-14, 31, 38, 46, 49, 70,
    75, 83, 89, 110, 134, 149, 153, 199,
    218, 263, 345
Sacred Heart of Jesus, 235
Sacrosanct, 24
Sadoleto, Cardinal, 100, 145
Saints/Sainthood, 8, 9, 15, 39, 81, 84,
    99, 135, 169, 201, 277, 345, 353
Salvation Army, 293
Samhain, 7
Savonarola, Girolamo, 54-55, 86
Schillebeeckx, Edward, 339-340, 348
Schleiermacher, Daniel Ernst, 208,
    259-261, 265, 303
Schmalkaldic League, 96
Scholasticism, 69
Schwenkfeld, Caspar, 110-111, 205
Scofield, Cyrus Ingerson, 324
Scopes Trial, 326, 327
Scotland, 9, 23, 27, 121-123, 137
Scripture (see also Bible), 30, 46, 48,
    50, 51, 73, 86, 89, 102, 123, 263
Sea Beggars, 118
Secretariat for Non-Christian
    Religions, 342
Secularization, 68, 195, 229-230
Seneca Falls Convention, 288
Separatists, 138, 167
Serbia, 58-59, 238
Servetus, Michael, 101
Seymour, Jane, 127, 130
Seymour, William, 329
Shaeffer, Francis, 327
Shakers, 269-270
Sigismund (Emperor), 24, 50, 53
Simon, Richard, 261
Simony, 49, 93

Sin, 10, 12, 13, 31, 33, 81, 82, 219, 221, 235, 244, 248, 260, 273, 279, 287, 303, 313, 324
Sixtus IV (Pope), 64
Slavery, 199, 219, 250-252, 284, 286-288
Slavophiles, 239
Smith, Amanda Berry, 253
Smith, Joseph, 274-277
Smyth, John, 138
Sobornost, 239
Social Gospel, 295-297, 313, 324
Society of Friends (Quakers), 172-173, 188, 199-200, 269, 286, 288
Society of Jesus, 147-148, 155, 161-162, 163, 163, 166, 203, 238
Sojourner Truth, 287-288
Solidarity Labor Movement, 347
Soloviev, Vladimir S., 239
Sorsky, Nilus, 61
South Africa, 284, 351
Soviet Union, 310, 328, 350
Sozzini, Fausto, 162
Spain, 54, 62-67, 117, 131, 143, 146, 151, 163, 165, 236-237, 305
Spanish American War, 283
Spener, Philip Jacob, 205-206, 207, 216
Speyer, Diet of, 92, 107
Spinoza,Baruch, 181-182, 198
Spiritualism, 271
Spiritualist, 108
St. Bartholomewís Day Massacre, 116-117
Stalin, Joseph, 310-311
Stanton, Elizabeth Cady, 289-290
Stein, Edith, 307
Stigmata, 39
Stone, Barton, 247-249
Strasbourg, 36, 94, 98, 100, 108, 131
Straton, John Roach, 325
Strauss, David F., 262
Strong, Josiah, 230
Suleiman the Magnificent, 60
Sunday School, 249

Suso, Henry, 36-37
Suttee, 281
Sweden, 25, 26, 206
Swedenborg, Emanuel, 271
Switzerland, 74, 92-103, 105, 107, 135, 156
Syllabus of Errors, 232-233
Symbol/Symbolism, 14, 36, 71, 95, 110, 319, 339

Taborites, 52-53, 89, 108
Tauler, Johannes, 36, 197, 200
Taylor, Nathaniel William, 248
Temperance Movement, 290, 319
Tennent, Gilbert, 223-225
Tennent, William, 222
Teresa of Avila, St., 64, 151-152, 347
Tersteegen, Gerhard, 209
Tetrapolitan Confession, 94, 96
Tetzel, 84
Theatines, 144-145
Thirty Years War, 54, 107, 138, 155-156, 159, 197, 226
Thomasius, Christian, 208
Tillich, Paul, 279, 318-319
Tillotson, John, 186-187
Tindal, Matthew, 185
Toland, John, 185
Toledo, 65
Toleration Act, 199
Tolstoi, Leon, 240
Tongues, Speaking in, 329
Torquemada, Thomas de, 64, 310
Torrey, R. A., 325
Toy, Crawford, 283
Transcendentalism, 264
Transubstantiation, 12, 149
Trent, Council of, 148-152, 157
Trible, Phyllis, 332
Trinity, 29, 101, 257, 329
Troeltsch, Ernst, 4, 111-112
Tubman, Harriet, 287
Tudor, Mary, 130, 131-133
Turks, 57-59, 80, 238-239
Tutu, Desmond, 351

Tyndale, William, 125, 128-129

Unam Sanctum, 18
Uniates, 57
Unitarian, 101, 162, 183, 190, 226,
    247, 264
Unitas Fratrum, 54, 104, 154, 162,
    180, 213
United Church of Canada, 322
United States, 188, 190-191, 226, 280
Unity of the Brethren (see Unitas
    Fratrum)
University of Alcal· de Henares, 65,
    147
University of Cambridge, 76, 126, 135
University of Chicago, 375, 429
University of Florence, 96
University of Leipzig, 206
University of Leyden, 119
University of Oxford, 27, 30, 45, 72-
    73, 215
University of Paris, 24, 27, 31, 36, 39,
    98, 99, 147
University of Prague, 48-49
University of Salamanca, 65, 147
University of Tübingen, 211
University of Wittenberg, 85, 89
Urban V (Pope), 21
Urban VI (Pope), 21
Ursulines, 145, 233, 285
Utopia, 73
Utraquists, 51-53, 54, 154

Valla, Lorenzo, 69-70
Vatican, 22, 144, 178, 195, 201, 232,
    305, 338
Vatican Council, First, 233
Vatican Council, Second 149, 341-
    345, 346
Venice, 144
Vestments, 14, 89, 131, 135, 136
Via Antiqua, 28, 45
Via Moderna, 28-31, 83
Virgin Mary, 147, 235, 342, 345, 347
Vivekananda, 282

Voltaire, 193-194, 257
Voluntarism, 28
Vulgate (Latin Bible), 46, 71-72, 74,
    76, 128, 149

Waldensians, 46, 53, 209
Washington, George, 186
Watts, Isaac, 215
Weber, Max, 103, 169
Weigel, Valentin, 198
Weld, Theodore Dwight, 287-289
Wellhausen, Julius, 261-262
Wesley, Charles, 216-219
Wesley, John, 206, 216-219, 224
Wesley, Suzanna, 216
Westminster Confession, 140, 222,
    223
Westphalia, Treaty of, 156, 159, 206
White, Ellen Harmon, 271
White Mountain, Battle of, 155, 180
Whitefield, George, 216-217, 218, 223,
    224-225
Whitgift, John, 136
Wichern, Johann Hinrich, 295
Wilberforce, William, 219-220, 281
Willard, Frances, 291
William of Occam, 21, 29-30, 43
William of Orange, 118-119, 187
Williams, Roger, 170-171, 172, 188
Wilson, Woodrow, 301
Windesheim, 40
Winthrop, John, 138,168, 169
Wishart, George, 121
Wojtyla, Karol (see John Paul II)
Wolsey, Cardinal Thomas, 125-126
Woman's Bible, The, 289
Women's Christian Temperance
    Union, 291
Women's Movement (see Feminism)
Woolman, John, 286, 288
World Council of Churches, 286, 321-
    322, 341, 352
World Missionary Conference, 286,
    321

World War I, 230, 301-303, 310, 324, 334

World War II, 308, 319, 322, 327, 328, 346

World's Parliament of Religion, 282

Worms, Diet of, 86

Wyclif, John, 45-47, 48, 54, 86, 102, 127, 128

Xavier, Francis, 147, 163

Ximenes de Cisneros, 64-66

Yale University, 223, 225

Yat-sen, Sun, 312

YMCA (Young Men's Christian Association), 285, 293, 302, 320

Young, Brigham, 276-277

Zedong, Mao, 312-313

Zelivsky, 51

Zell, Katherina, 94

Zinzendorf, Nikolas Ludwig Graf von, 212-214, 217, 218

Zizka, Jan, 51-52

Zurich, 93-97, 105, 146

Zwikau, 89

Zwingli, Ulrich, 93-97, 102, 104, 105, 106, 131, 134